The Transcendentalists

The Transcendentalists

———

BARBARA L. PACKER

The University of Georgia Press   *Athens & London*

Published in 2007 by The University of Georgia Press
Athens, Georgia 30602
by arrangement with Cambridge University Press
© Cambridge University Press 1995
Reprinted with permission
2007 Addendum to the Bibliography
© 2007 by the University of Georgia Press
All rights reserved
Printed and bound by Thomson-Shore, Inc.
The paper in this book meets the guidelines for permanence
and durability of the Committee on Production Guidelines
for Book Longevity of the Council on Library Resources.

Printed in the United States of America
11   10   09   08   07   C   5   4   3   2   1
11   10   09   08   07   P   5   4   3   2   1

Library of Congress Cataloging-in-Publication Data

Packer, Barbara L.
The transcendentalists / Barbara L. Packer.
p.   cm.
Originally published as: The Cambridge history of
American literature, volume 2, Prose Writing 1820–1865,
chapter 2. Cambridge [England] : Cambridge
University Press, 1994–<2004>
Includes bibliographical references and index.
ISBN-13: 978-0-8203-2958-1 (pbk. : alk. paper)
ISBN-10: 0-8203-2958-4 (pbk. : alk. paper)
ISBN-13: 978-0-8203-2957-4 (hardcover : alk. paper)
ISBN-10: 0-8203-2957-6 (hardcover : alk. paper)
1. American literature — 19th century — History and
criticism. 2. Transcendentalism (New England) I. Title.
PS217.T7P33 2007
810.9'13 — dc22   2006039278

British Library Cataloging-in-Publication Data available

The Transcendentalists originally appeared as a chapter in
The Cambridge History of American Literature, vol. 2, Prose
Writing 1820–1865, edited by Sacvan Bercovitch (New York:
Cambridge University Press, 1995).

CONTENTS

Acknowledgments   *vii*

1 Unitarian Beginnings   *1*

2 The Assault on Locke   *20*

3 Carlyle and the Beginnings
of American Transcendentalism   *32*

4 *"Annus Mirabilis"*   *46*

5 The Establishment and the Movement   *62*

6 Letters and Social Aims   *94*

7 The Hope of Reform   *129*

8 Diaspora   *165*

9 The Antislavery Years   *218*

Selected Bibliography   *275*

Index   *289*

ACKNOWLEDGMENTS

I should like to thank the Committee on Research of the UCLA Academic Senate for grants supporting this project. A fellowship year at the Center for Advanced Study in the Behavioral Sciences at Stanford gave me time to begin the work, and sabbatical leave from the University of California, Los Angeles, enabled me to complete it. I am grateful to Dean Grodzins, Gary Hall, and Robert Perrin for allowing me to read their unpublished studies of Theodore Parker, Emerson, and Daniel Webster. Michael Colacurcio and Dean Grodzins read parts of the manuscript and offered valuable advice. Several talented research assistants—Sybil Brabner, Deanne Lundin, and Mary Flory—helped me at different times during the writing of the chapter. Three debts are especially great. My husband, Paul Sheats, gave me encouragement and intellectual companionship throughout the long process of writing; my colleague Daniel Calder gave me invaluable assistance in getting the project off the ground; and my patient editor at Cambridge University Press, T. Susan Change, gave a kind of support few editors are called upon to give. Finally, I thank Sacvan Bercovitch for inviting me to participate in this collective project and for offering wise advice at every stage of composition, and Cyrus Patell, who offered fellowship as well as assistance with communications and bibliographies.

For this stand-alone edition, I am grateful to Cambridge University Press for granting permission to reprint "The Transcendentalists," to Joel Myerson for encouraging me to reprint it, and to Nancy Grayson, Jon Davies, and Walton Harris of the University of Georgia Press for bringing the project to fruition.

The Transcendentalists

UNITARIAN BEGINNINGS

WHEN RALPH WALDO EMERSON, in an introduction to a lecture series entitled "The Present Age" (1839–40), tried to explain the origins of the movement everyone was calling "transcendentalism," he found himself describing a cluster of discontents. The young people who form "the party of the Future" are, he admitted, "stiff, heady, and rebellious" and united only by the ferocity of their rejections: "They hate tolls, taxes, turnpikes, banks, hierarchies, governors, yea, almost laws. They have a neck of unspeakable tenderness; it winces at a hair." The belief that obsesses and propels them – *that the individual is the world* – "is such a sword as was never drawn before. It divides and detaches bone and marrow, soul and body, yea, almost the man from himself." Even the groups these young people join are devoted to the enlargement of the individual: "The association of the time is accidental and momentary; the detachment is intrinsic and progressive."

How had such insistence on the centrality of the individual arisen, and what were its effects? New Englanders had always been remarkable for the chilliness of their temperament, yet the New England Protestantism of an earlier age still vested its hopes in forms that were practically or imaginatively social: the family, the town meeting, the heavenly host, the City of God. And the young people Emerson spoke of yearn for love as much as they demand independence. In his 1841 lecture "The Transcendentalist," he describes them with sympathy: "These persons are not by nature melancholy, sour, and unsocial . . . ; they have even more than others a great wish to be loved. Like the young Mozart, they are ready to cry ten times a day, 'But are you sure you love me?'"

Yet somehow their impulse to repel outweighs their impulse to associate. "They are lonely; the spirit of their writing and conversation is lonely; they repel influences; they shun general society; they incline to shut themselves in their chamber in the house, to live in the country rather than in town, and to find their tasks and amusements in solitude." Even so, Emerson refuses to dismiss his small brigade of self-tormentors as useless or pitiful. The very extravagance of the demand they make on human nature will yet lead their unthinking countrymen out of the wilderness of skepticism and greed in which all wander. "Their heart is the ark in which the fire is concealed, which shall burn in a broader and universal flame."

The contrast between this ardency and the amiable quiet of Bostonians thirty years earlier was striking. When Emerson looked over the writings left by his father, William Emerson (1769–1811), he found nothing beyond "candour & taste." His father's generation now seemed provincial and self-effacing in its literary ambitions. The literary society William Emerson had helped organize in 1805, the Anthology Club, was formed to publish a journal of American belles lettres. The *Monthly Anthology and Boston Review* contained a useful monthly catalogue of books published in America, and its reviews were vigorous. But the editors had difficulty finding enough original prose or poetry to fill the magazine or enough subscribers to keep it alive. It ceased publication a few months after William Emerson died in 1811.

As for his father's religion, the liberal wing of New England Congregationalism eventually known as Unitarianism, Emerson's dissatisfaction with it was slower to crystallize. During his boyhood, the men who led the revolt against the Calvinist doctrine of total depravity seemed brave to him. A Christ who ennobled through his example rather than atoned through his bloody sacrifice and a God who encouraged human striving after perfection rather than a humiliating dependence upon his inscrutable will were advances in the history of spirituality that marked Christianity's emergence from superstition. Unitarianism held out the promise of a Christianity enlightened enough to be tolerant and otherworldly enough to inspire and console. Even the civility of Unitarian discourse, which the younger generation eventually came to find wearying, had an ideological function in its own day, marking as it did a deliberate refusal to participate in the theological disputes that had split Congregationalism in the early decades of the century. The editors of the *Monthly Anthology* were firm in their warning to potential contributors: "No Religious controversy."

Visitors to Boston were bemused and at times exasperated by this parade of tolerance. A Presbyterian named Ashbel Green attended a meeting of the Boston Association of Ministers in 1791 and found a perfect jumble of theological opinions: He counted Calvinists, Arians, Arminians, and at least one Socinian. Partly because of this diversity very little religious discussion actually took place at the meeting, and Green thought it would be much healthier if the different parties were to go their separate ways. Yet he knew that his belief that the association ought to separate along doctrinal lines "would be esteemed by them as the effect of bigotry and narrowness of mind, and so they will meet and shake hands, and talk of politics and science, and laugh, and eat raisins and apples, and drink wine and tea, and go about their business."

Ten years later, the situation had hardly changed. Another visiting Presbyterian, Dr. Archibald Alexander, noted that "at that time all controversy was proscribed by the liberal party." Despite the variety of opinions and the growing gap between the most liberal and the most orthodox, there was as yet "no public line of demarcation among the clergy. One might learn with ease what each man believed, or rather did not believe, for few positive opinions were expressed by the liberal party." Alexander's comment suggests that the liberals were already distinguished more by what they denied than by what they believed — at least in the eyes of their opponents.

Alexander thought that he detected policy in this refusal to debate doctrinal differences. Under the banner of "tolerance" the liberals were gradually taking over the important offices of Harvard College, where "all the young men of talents" were liberal in sentiment and read with avidity the tracts and books that prominent liberal patrons presented to the library. This quiet liberal infiltration would soon be replaced by open war. When the Reverend David Tappan, a moderate Calvinist who occupied the important position of professor of divinity at Harvard, died in the fall of 1803, liberals saw an opportunity to confirm their growing domination of the college. President Joseph Willard, unable to find an orthodox candidate of sufficient stature to fill the position and unwilling to appoint the liberal candidate, Dr. Henry Ware, stalled for a year. Then Willard too suddenly died. Now the Fellows of the Harvard Corporation were faced with the task of choosing both a new president and a new Hollis Professor.

The six-member board was split more or less evenly between liberals and orthodox, but the stalemate that resulted was not entirely ideological. As in most academic disputes about appointments, vanity, resentment, and personal ambition also played a part in the forging of alliances. The Corporation met several times during the closing months of 1804 but was unable to agree on a candidate or accept a compromise. Finally, in February 1805, one of the orthodox Fellows switched his vote, and Henry Ware, the liberal candidate, was appointed. But Harvard's Board of Overseers still had to concur in the appointment. In the weeks between the Corporation meeting and the meeting of the Overseers one of the defeated orthodox Corporation Fellows, Eliphalet Pearson, prepared a highly colored account of the controversy in a last-ditch attempt to defeat Ware's appointment. Pearson's diatribe was never published — the meeting of the Overseers took place sooner than he expected, and they voted in favor of Ware — but the language of his account suggests the political terms in which the theological debate was conducted.

Harvard's theological liberals, like their orthodox opponents, were staunch Federalists, still smarting from their defeat at the hands of Jefferson's Democrats. But Pearson insinuated that the liberals, those "warmly attached to what they call *rational* Christianity, and flattering themselves that this part of the country was nearly ripe for a revolution in religion," were really Jeffersonian sympathizers in disguise, Jacobins in sheep's clothing. "Much is said about *liberality* & *charity*. Charming words, syren sounds, like *liberty* & *equality* on other tongues. God in mercy grant that they may not prove equally *delusive* & *fatal*." Pearson excoriated the liberals for engaging in just those political tactics that they had long professed to abhor. Even the liberals must agree that these tactics, when used in the recent federal elections, had "subverted the federal government." "Can Federalists then adopt a policy and make use of weapons in the cause of *religion*, which they so justly brand with infamy in the cause of politics? *O tempora! O mores!*"

It is doubtful that Pearson could have succeeded in getting his opponents to see themselves as Jacobins even if he had published his account before they voted. If anything, the theological liberals tended to be both wealthier and more conservative politically than the orthodox. Whereas few would have gone as far as the Harvard student Andrews Norton (1786–1853), who wrote his father that he would like to replace the assertion "All men are created equal" in the Declaration of Independence with "Most men are fit for nothing but to be governed," those Boston merchants and professionals who patronized the liberal clergy were in little danger of political radicalism. Indeed, when a similar dispute split the congregation in nearby Charlestown into old (orthodox) and new (liberal) churches, the members of "respectability, culture, and weight of influence in the town" were the ones who left the old church for the new. A candidate for the pulpit of the new church noted with satisfaction that his prospective congregation was "respectable in numbers and constantly increasing and in wealth is undoubtedly the first in the town." Indeed, at the recent Thanksgiving Day contribution for relief of the poor they had contributed one hundred and five dollars, whereas the orthodox had managed to collect only eighty-eight dollars.

This association between wealth and religious liberalism naturally invited the taunts of the orthodox and would later invite the scorn of the Transcendentalists. But the liberals could reply, and did reply, that their prosperity came from the same strenuous effort at self-culture that formed so large a part of their ethical system. To worship, as the orthodox did, a God who had predestined the greater part of the human race to eternal damnation by a decree promulgated before the foundation of the earth and to hope to be rescued from that damnation only by an influx of grace as unmerited as it was irresistible were beliefs seen by the liberals to be pernicious to the character and dangerous to the Republic. The great liberal preacher William Ellery Channing (1780–1842) argued that Calvinist doctrines of predestination all tend "strongly to pervert the moral faculty, to form a gloomy, forbidding, and servile religion, and lead men to substitute censoriousness, bitterness, and persecution, for a tender and impartial charity" ("Unitarian Christianity," 1819). In an 1820 essay entitled "The Moral Argument Against Calvinism," he was even blunter: "Calvinism owes its perpetuity to the influence of fear in palsying the moral nature."

The conflict between liberals and conservatives within New England Congregationalism, growing sharper throughout the eighteenth century, broke out into open warfare after the controversy at Harvard over Ware's appointment. The friendly custom Congregational ministers had of exchanging pulpits with one another (it relieved them of the duty of writing two sermons every Sunday and gave their parishioners a chance to hear a variety of opinions) began to break down as orthodox ministers refused to exchange with liberal ones. Parishioners naturally resented being deprived of something they regarded as their right, and in some cases they even went to court to force their ministers either to comply with the old custom or else to resign their parishes. Churches split, families quarreled, and one disgruntled member of Harvard's Board of Overseers became convinced that it was necessary to found an orthodox seminary (the Andover Theological Seminary) to serve as counterweight to the now hopelessly liberal Harvard. Things got so bad, Channing complained, that orthodox ministers denounced liberal Christianity as "the last and most perfect invention of Satan, the consummation of his blasphemies, the most cunning weapon ever forged in the fires of hell" ("Unitarian Christianity Most Favorable to Piety," 1826).

For a time the liberals tried to resist the term of opprobrium the orthodox fastened upon them – "Unitarian" – partly because they disliked doctrinal controversy and partly out of a hope that a final rupture within New England Congregationalism could be prevented and peace restored. As a French traveler to Boston in 1791 admiringly noted: "The ministers rarely speak dogmas: universal tolerance, the child of American independence, has banished the preaching of dogmas, which always leads to discussions and quarrels. . . . The ministers of different sects live in such harmony that they supply each other's places when any one is detained from his pulpit." But the orthodox were intransigent, and the liberals finally adopted "Unitarian," using the term with defiance and pride. Channing included the word in a whole series of sermon titles and magazine essays during the second decade of the nineteenth century. And in his famous sermon "Unitarian Christianity" (celebrating the ordination of Jared Sparks in Baltimore in 1819) Channing proclaimed Unitarianism the only form of Christianity adapted to the progressive improvement of mankind:

Our earnest prayer to God is, that he will overturn, and overturn, and overturn the strong-holds of spiritual usurpation, until HE shall come, whose right it is to rule the minds of men; that the conspiracy of ages against the liberty of Christians may be brought to an end; that the servile assent, so long yielded to human creeds, may give place to honest and devout inquiry into the Scriptures; and that Christianity, thus purified from error, may put forth its almighty energy, and prove itself, by its ennobling influence on the mind, to be indeed "the power of God unto salvation."

Channing's sermon so exhilarated Andrews Norton that he was inspired to write in his diary a threat as militant as anything that might be thundered by the Calvinists: "Orthodoxy must be broken down. *Babylon est delenda.*" Norton was admittedly the most pugnacious of the Unitarians, and it would be difficult to match his ferocious tone elsewhere in the liberal camp. Still, his exultation is an important clue to the spirit of the Unitarian movement. The Unitarians of Channing's generation saw themselves as heirs to the reforming zeal that had inspired the earliest Protestants; the "Babylon" they sought to destroy was the Calvinism that even as it decayed still tried to direct worship toward a God who tortured his own Son in order to ransom from punishment a tiny fraction of the souls he had created. In place of this "servile" religion, the Unitarians offered a "manly" reverence toward a Father who loved and a Son who came to save sinners from *sin* rather than from *punishment.* This benevolent deity offered men and women the chance to achieve salvation through a rigorous and continuous effort of self-culture. So pronounced was the Unitarian distrust of sudden conversion experiences that Channing declared himself unable to believe that the English poet John Milton had meant what he had said when he argued that the Holy Spirit gives us "immediate illumination" to read the Scriptures. Such hope for immediate insight "disparages and discourages our faculties, and produces inaction of mind," leading us to think we will receive in a "sudden flash from Heaven" the truths we should seek by the right use of our own powers ("Remarks on the Character and Writings of John Milton," 1826).

For preaching their faith the Unitarians had heard themselves vilified and had emerged triumphant, at least in their own eyes. If Unitarianism lacked the wide popular appeal of the evangelical movements, its influence during the 1820s seemed to be growing in the cities among the powerful and well-educated; congregations were formed in New York, Philadelphia, and Baltimore. Unitarians could feel proud that they had achieved their gains without appealing to either superstition or ignorant fears. In 1882 Joseph Henry Allen, a lecturer in ecclesiastical history at the Harvard Divinity School, reminded his Harvard audience that the two points most strongly marked in the history of the Unitarian movement were "first, that it was a movement of

Reason in sympathy
w/ Science = imperialism

Reason in sympathy with the scientific spirit; and second, that it was a
movement of Right, in sympathy with the revolutionary spirit." Whether
the Unitarians were really so friendly to either the scientific or the revolutionary spirit may perhaps be doubted, but they saw themselves in this way — as
a vanguard, as a band bravely advancing on chaos and the dark.

Revolution and science, however, make uncomfortable bedfellows for a
religion that wished to remain grounded in biblical revelation and, at the
same time, loyal to an empiricism hostile to violations of natural law. How
difficult it could be to keep revelation and reason together is suggested by a
delicious remark Allen attributes to Channing: "He said we did not know
enough about the nature of matter to criticise the story of the Ascension."

Channing's puzzlement about how the Ascension fit into a Newtonian
universe and his willingness to suspend judgment in the face of scriptural
authority resemble the modesty of the philosopher and biblical critic he
revered, John Locke (1632–1704). In the *Essay Concerning Human Understand-* #
ing (1690) Locke carefully marks the limits of human knowledge. We can
know intuitively only those truths that belong to deductive logic — the
axioms of geometry, say, or the principle of noncontradiction in logic. All
other propositions are based on information received through the senses, that
is, from experience. Our assurance that iron will not float on water is essentially a form of probabilistic reasoning, which can produce only "confidence,"
not absolute certainty. Because we have never seen iron float in the past, we
are justified in assuming that it will not float in the future.

When propositions concern things beyond the reach of the senses — the   Revelati...
existence of angels, the resurrection of the dead — we can learn of them only
through *revelation*. But we must not accept as divine revelation every testament promulgated by a visionary, "else we shall expose ourselves to all the
extravagancy of enthusiasm, and the error of wrong principles" (*Essay* 4,
16.14). "To know that any revelation is from God, it is necessary to know
that the messenger that delivers it is sent from God, and that cannot be
known but by some credential given by God himself" (*A Discourse of Miracles*,
1702). The miracles of the Old and New Testaments constitute such credentials. They are events perceivable by the senses and hence verifiable by
witnesses; at the same time, they are violations of the normal laws of nature
and hence testify to a power superior to nature. Locke points out that it is no
sign of skepticism to demand miraculous proofs. "Gideon was sent by an
angel to deliver Israel from the Midianites, and yet he desired a sign to
convince him that his commission was from God" (*Essay* 4, 19.15). Gideon is
in fact Locke's exemplary reasoner. There is something patient and Newtonian about Gideon's experiments with the fleece in the sixth chapter of

Locke — don't accept Revelation unless
Credentialed by God — Miracles

Miracles violate Laws of Nature — Resurrect/Ascension — must Be God's work!

Judges, where he asks God to give him a sign first by drenching with dew a fleece laid on the threshing floor while keeping the floor itself dry, and then, the next night, asks for a dry fleece and a wet floor.

Both in the *Essay* and in the later *Discourse of Miracles* Locke remains determined to deny the claims of religious "enthusiasts" who think they can perceive truth directly. He dismisses them contemptuously as partisans "of illumination without search, of certainty without proof." He argues that "light, true light, is or can be nothing but the evidence of the truth of any proposition; and if it be not a self-evident proposition, all the light it has, or can have, is from the clearness and validity of those proofs upon which it is received" (*Essay* 4, 19.13). He does not flinch from the obvious consequences of his opinions and goes out of his way in the *Discourse of Miracles* to consider a case in which violations of natural law were produced by sorcery:

> The producing of serpents, blood, and frogs, by the Egyptian sorcerer and by Moses, could not to the spectators but appear equally miraculous, which of the pretenders then had their mission from God; and the truth on their side could not have been determined if the matter had rested there. But when Moses' serpent ate up theirs, when he produced lice which they could not, the decision was easy.

An empiricism so robust was difficult for most people to sustain without flinching, and many of Locke's contemporaries objected to the way he had in effect substituted an act of reasoning upon probabilities for true religious faith and limited our knowledge to the Jesus of history rather than the Jesus of faith. But Locke's experience of the bitter sectarian warfare that divided England during his lifetime had left him distrustful of anyone's claim to possess a truth not verifiable by the normal operations of intellect. To the fourth edition of the *Essay Concerning Human Understanding* (1700) he added a new chapter called "Enthusiasm." In this chapter he pauses to consider the "third ground of assent," which for some people takes the place of faith — "*enthusiasm:* which, laying by reason, would set up revelation without it."

Enthusiasm is a kind of shortcut by which people seek to avoid the laborious processes of reasoning or of judging the credibility of testimony.

> In all ages, men in whom melancholy has mixed with devotion, or whose conceit of themselves has raised them into an opinion or a greater familiarity with God, and a nearer admittance to his favor than is afforded to others, have often flattered themselves with a persuasion of an immediate intercourse with the Deity, and frequent communications from the Divine Spirit. (*Essay* 4, 19.5)

These "conceits of a warmed or overweening brain," once indulged, are almost impossible to dislodge.

> Reason is lost upon them, they are above it: they see the light infused into their understandings, and cannot be mistaken; it is clear and visible there, like the light of

*Enthusiasm = Religious Exuberance —
Short-cuts Reason — feel hand of God within
know they are Right because
of strength of
emotion*

UNITARIAN BEGINNINGS

bright evidence: they feel the hand of God moving them within, and the impulses of
the Spirit, and cannot be mistaken in what they feel. (*Essay* 4, 19.8)

This is the way of talking of these men; they are sure, because they are sure; and their
persuasions are right, because they are strong in them. (*Essay* 4, 19.9)

To make the strength of one's persuasion the test of whether or not a
revelation can claim to be divine leaves us reasoning in circles. Enthusiasts
say, "*It is a revelation, because they firmly believe it; and they believe it, because it is a
revelation.*" But if a firm persuasion of the truth of a doctrine guarantees its
truth, "How come . . . the intractable zealots in different and opposite
parties?" A lifetime of anger against the bigotry of enthusiasts is condensed
into Locke's reminder that "St. Paul himself believed he did right well, and
that he had a call to it, when he persecuted the Christians, whom he confidently thought in the wrong: but yet it was he, and not they, who were
mistaken" (*Essay* 4, 19.11–12). Miracles provide us with an escape from the
blindness of enthusiasm, for they mark with sensible proofs those few and
simple doctrines God has deemed necessary for salvation.

The connection Locke establishes between empiricism, belief in biblical
miracles, and freedom from religious fanaticism made his philosophy powerfully appealing to the liberal theologians of New England. They thought
they could detect the dangerous spirit of "enthusiasm" in every crisis of New
England's history, from the Antinomian Crisis of 1636–8 through the Great
Awakening of the 1740s to the evangelical revivals of their own day. As an
antidote to such excesses they offered the tolerant, rational patience of Locke,
whose works formed a central part of the Harvard curriculum. In 1808 the
precocious student Edward Everett (1794–1865) found that the easiest way
for him to get through the required weekly recitations on Locke's *Essay* was
to commit the whole text to memory.

I recollect particularly on one occasion of the review on Thursday afternoon that I was
called upon to recite early and I went on repeating word for word, and paragraph after
paragraph, and finally, not being stopped by our pleased tutor, page after page, till I
finally went through in that way the greater part of the eleven recitations of the week.

Yet in the century since Locke's death his particular synthesis had come
under attack from several directions, and the version of his philosophy that
still dominated Harvard in the early nineteenth century bore the scars of the
battles that had been waged to defend it. The most powerful challenge came
from David Hume (1711–76). Whereas Locke argues that miraculous events
testify to the truth of the doctrine they accompany, Hume points out that one
cannot accept miracles as "credentials" before deciding whether the reports of
the miracles are themselves credible. True, we must accept many facts on

*Locke · denounces Religious Enthusiasm (emotionalism)
Condones Miracles That are Tested by Reason
(empirical Testing)*

Miracles — is The Report itself True?
Testifiers = Gullible — superstitious —
or venal

Hume "Of Miracles"
Enquiry concernin'
Human understand-
1748

10   THE TRANSCENDENTALISTS

testimony, but our belief in testimony alters with our sense of the inherent probability of the events it relates. In the famous tenth section of his *Enquiry Concerning Human Understanding* (1748), entitled "Of Miracles," Hume subjects the very idea of belief upon testimony to withering scrutiny. "The reason why we place any credit in witnesses and historians, is not derived from any connexion, which we perceive *a priori,* between testimony and reality, but because we are accustomed to find a conformity between them." When the fact testified to is "such a one as has seldom fallen under our observation" what results is not conviction but mental strife:

The very same principle of experience, which give us a certain degree of assurance in the testimony of witnesses, gives us also, in this case, another degree of assurance against the fact, which they endeavor to establish; from which contradiction there necessarily arises a counterpoize, and mutual destruction of belief and authority.

Hume points out that we do not call an event "miraculous" unless it is "a violation of the laws of nature." But the laws of nature are drawn from uniform experience, which in itself constitutes "a direct and full *proof,* from the nature of the fact, against the existence of any miracle." This proof from uniform experience could only be destroyed by "an opposite proof, which is superior." But believers in miracles can offer only the testimony of witnesses against the strong proof of natural law, and testimony is a weak form of proof. The claim that a miraculous event has been witnessed must always be weighed against our suspicions that the testifiers are gullible, superstitious, or venal.

When anyone tells me, that he saw a dead man restored to life, I immediately consider with myself, whether it be more probable, that this man should either deceive or be deceived, or that the fact, which he relates, should really have happened. . . . If the falsehood of his testimony would be more miraculous, than the event which he relates; then, and not till then, can he pretend to command my belief or opinion.

The theologians who shaped New England Unitarianism argued against such skepticism in various ways (though Emerson was later to suspect that the repeated attempts to confute Hume proved only that Hume had never been confuted). Some, like Andrews Norton, devoted themselves to tipping the scales of probability in favor of testimony rather than experience, attempting to gather historical evidence that the Gospels were genuine in hopes of proving that the events narrated in them really happened as described. Others, like Channing, attacked Hume's dismissal of all miracle stories by arguing that the strikingly original character of Jesus and of the religion he preached testifies to the existence of the very supernatural order whose existence Hume was taken to have denied. "That a religion, carrying in itself such marks of divinity, and so inexplicable on human principles, should receive outward confirmations from Omnipotence, is not surprising. The extraordinary character of the religion accords with and seems to demand extraordinary interpositions in its behalf" ("The Evidences of Revealed Religion," 1821). An opponent might point out that Channing has slipped back into the circularity that Locke condemned in the enthusiasts: We recognize in Jesus' sayings a divinity that convinces us that the miracles ascribed to him could have happened.

How do we recognize the teachings of Jesus as divine in origin? Locke had refused to allow the fragmentation of reason into any subsidiary faculties; we must judge the truths of religion with the same faculty we use to sift any other kind of evidence, and all evidence is ultimately from the senses. But Locke's philosophy was not the only explanation available of the mechanisms of understanding. Two traditions in British philosophy, one older than Locke, one younger, had attempted to reestablish the objectivity of moral distinctions in a material universe that seemed to have no room for them. One group of seventeenth-century English theologians known as the Cambridge Platonists urged a return to an ontology that treated moral truths as objectively real. Ralph Cudworth (1617–88), a philosopher much admired by the New England Unitarians for his mixture of spiritual generosity and metaphysical intensity, argued that the principles by which we organize sense experience and recognize moral truths are innate, and that the laws they perceive in the moral and physical universes are immutable. God himself cannot violate the moral law, which is as much a part of the nature of things as is the law of gravitation. The study of nature penetrated through appearances to natural law, which was moral because the universe itself was moral throughout its structure.

Emerson

Interest in the Cambridge Platonists was part of a general reassessment of seventeenth-century English culture taking place in Britain and America during the early decades of the nineteenth century. In his influential 1826 essay on the genius and character of Milton, Channing praised the stimulating difficulty of Milton's periodic prose; he dismissed Joseph Addison as "easy reading" in the same passage – a significant revolution in taste, because Addison's writing had always been admired in America as a model of perspicuity and grace. Samuel Taylor Coleridge's philosophical handbook *Aids to Reflection* (1825), which helped to spark the Transcendentalist movement when it was published in an American edition in 1829, included copious quotations from the "elder divines" of the English church, who were held up to admiration for both the spiritual intensity they express and the undisciplined richness of their prose.

The moral realism of the Cambridge Platonists was still wedded to an

Aids To Reflection /1825

idealistic ontology that was difficult to sustain before the methodological revolution effected by Locke, a revolution as important to the Unitarians as was belief in the existence of moral absolutes. The problem was hardly trivial, for Unitarianism insisted that it was morally superior to the Calvinism it superseded. If all ideas are derived from sensation and reflection, it is difficult on the face to explain where we get our ideas of moral good and moral evil. Were such ideas (as skeptics like Thomas Hobbes and Bernard de Mandeville had argued) merely projections onto the sensible universe of our own fears and desires?

The philosopher Francis Hutcheson (1694–1746) attempted to find some way of grounding moral principles in human nature itself. His *Inquiry into the Original of Our Ideas of Beauty and Virtue* (1725) takes as its target Mandeville's attempt in *The Fable of the Bees* (1705) to unmask all moral virtues as hypocritical disguises for self-preservation or self-interest. Hutcheson's argument against such cynicism is that we all readily understand the difference between actions prompted by self-interest and those prompted by virtue. A "moral sense" must be therefore as much a part of our human equipment as the physical senses of sight and hearing.

Hutcheson points out that all imaginative literature implies the existence of a moral sense in the observers because self-interest could hardly prompt sympathy with a character known to be fictive. "If there is no moral Sense, which makes rational Actions appear Beautiful, or Deform'd; if all Approbation be from the Interest of the Approver, *What's* HECUBA *to us, or we to* HECUBA?" Even if we are made aware of this moral sense chiefly through the sentiments of approbation or distaste it provokes in us, the moral sense is more than an emotion. Its ultimate function is cognitive and, like the bodily senses, it operates more swiftly and surely to apprehend the moral qualities of actions than the reasoning process can. The same deity who has endowed us with bodily senses acute enough to preserve our lives has also instilled in us a moral sense whose operation – necessary for our survival – is as ineluctable as gravity, as trustworthy as the axioms of geometry.

Hutcheson's postulation of an innate moral *sense* differs from the Cambridge Platonists' belief in objective moral *law* by locating moral absolutes entirely within human nature; he never suggests that the law of gravitation is the same as purity of heart, or that the human spirit is one with the Divine Intelligence that informs the universe. Yet his humbler and more naturalistic explanation seemed to offer a way to retain belief in moral absolutes during an age of empiricism. For that reason it exercised a powerful attraction throughout the eighteenth century. Belief in the existence of a "moral sense" functioning intuitively to judge right and wrong offers us protection against the radical individualism of Hobbes and Mandeville, but it does more than *[handwritten margin notes: "Hutcheson Moral sense (Right from wrong) makes us social beings vs. Empirical question of Senses"]*

that. It reinstalls within the self the social world that empirical philosophy
threatens to obliterate. The swift reflexes of the moral sense, manifesting
themselves in our consciousness as sentiments of approbation or disapproba-
tion, link us in feeling to those other selves whose very existence empirical
philosophy often has difficulty proving.

Another stay against radical skepticism came from a group of Scottish
philosophers of the late eighteenth century. Refusing to accept Hume's skeptical deductions from Locke's principles, philosophers like Thomas Reid
(1710–96) insisted that there were some things in the mind that were not
before in the senses. These "intuitions," or "immediate beliefs," are "part of
our constitution, and all the discoveries of reason are grounded upon them.
They make up what is called *the common sense of mankind*." Another Scottish
philosopher, Dugald Stewart (1753–1828), gives examples of some commonsense propositions – "I exist, I am the same person to-day as I was yesterday;
the material world has an existence independent of my mind; the general
laws of nature will continue in future to operate uniformly as in time past" –
and compares them to the *Elements* of Euclid, barren in themselves but
necessary for reasoning about everything else.

[handwritten margin notes: "Reid: Intuition or Immediate beliefs Common Sense"]

This limited reaffirmation of the old doctrine of innate ideas was influential at Harvard during the early nineteenth century, where it was seen as a
friendly corrective to Locke's radical empiricism. "Commonsense" propositions had to do with epistemology rather than ethics, but the conviction that
there were intuitive principles in the mind that could be relied upon made
the doctrine of the moral sense seem more plausible. Indeed, Stewart, whose
Elements of the Philosophy of the Human Mind (Vol. 1, 1792) was an assigned
text at Harvard, argued that the moral sense ought to be classed among the
original and universal principles of the human mind, because its judgments
appear in children in the very infancy of their reason, long before they are
capable of forming abstract conceptions of right and wrong.

[handwritten margin note: "Dugald Stewart"]

Stewart's arguments concerning the moral sense seemed persuasive to at
least one reader who was not convinced that the Scottish school had succeeded
in refuting the epistemological and religious skepticism of Hume. When
Ralph Waldo Emerson (1803–82) submitted an essay, "The Present State of
Ethical Philosophy," for the Bowdoin Prize at Harvard during his junior year
in 1820, he admitted that Stewart's school had not quite managed to remove
the "terror which attached to the name of Hume," but he expressed complete
confidence in its postulation of a "moral faculty" which is an "original
principle of our nature."

Humean skepticism was not, however, the only danger that Unitarian
beliefs faced. Challenges from both natural science and biblical criticism
were shaking the foundations upon which Christian faith had rested, and to

these challenges the moral sense could supply no immediate answer. The science of geology was particularly unsettling. When geologists offered evidence that the earth was very much older than the Mosaic account of Creation suggested, orthodox ministers could simply denounce them. But Unitarians had always prided themselves on being hospitable to scientific inquiry and secure in their faith that no contradiction could exist between God's revealed Word and the truths inscribed in the Book of Nature. They were therefore faced with tasks of recuperative hermeneutics that grew more formidible all the time.

Even if the Mosiac chronology were quietly sacrificed to scientific enlightenment – something the Unitarians could more easily do because they believed in *progressive* illumination and were willing to regard Genesis as a fable suited to the childhood rather than to the maturity of the race – there remained the problem of the documents upon which Christianity itself was based. Unitarians firmly believed in the historical accuracy of the New Testament; they believed that Jesus of Nazareth lived, preached, performed miracles, died, and rose again and that the documents collected in the New Testament gave a faithful account of these events. Indeed, liberals were if anything more firmly wedded to the "historical Jesus" than their orthodox counterparts. Enthusiasts might need no more to confirm their faith than a firm persuasion of the spirit, but liberal Christians wanted to prove the divine origin of their religion by tracing it back to the moments when Divine Omnipotence could be proved to have altered the course of empirical events; they needed history to establish faith.

The growth of historical criticism in Germany during the last quarter of the eighteenth century seemed at first to promise to aid scholars seeking to make contact with distant historical reality. The philologians of Göttingen and Halle sought to understand ancient documents through more rigorous methods of textual criticism than had ever before been attempted, but they also insisted that the ancient documents could be deciphered only by placing them against the background of the culture from which they grew, a culture whose shape must be painstakingly reconstructed from surviving archaeological, literary, religious, and art-historical evidence. American scholars, eager to acquire this exciting new approach to classical and biblical authors, began to make pilgrimages to Germany to study with the great scholars of the day and to bring back their texts and methods to America.

Edward Everett and George Ticknor (1791–1871) both hastened upon their arrival in Germany in 1815 to study the most revolutionary of all philological manifestos, the *Prolegomena ad Homerum* (1795) of Friedrich August Wolf (1759–1824). Everett spent eighteen hours a day working through the Latin text by the scholar Ticknor called the "Ishmael of criticism," and when George Bancroft (1800–91) joined them a few years later he too became an initiate. "In Philology, Wolf & yet Wolf & yet Wolf," he grumbled in a letter to Andrews Norton (December 14, 1818). Wolf's hostility toward and contempt for all previous Homeric critics accounts in part for the nickname Ticknor gave him, but his monumental self-confidence also extended to the text of Homer itself, a text that it was the avowed aim of the *Prolegomena* to correct and restore. Wolf's method, as one modern scholar explains it, involved the location of discrepancies and anachronisms within the received text and the ruthless elimination of all explanations and rationalizations for them, as well as the substitution of new explanations supported by his extensive knowledge of Greek grammar and history.

Emerson would remember with some amusement Everett's attempt to graft the sophisticated techniques of German philology onto the rudimentary Harvard curriculum during Everett's tenure there as professor of Greek, which coincided with Emerson's own undergraduate days. But Emerson also remembered how exciting the discoveries seemed to the students. "It was all new learning, that wonderfully took and stimulated the young men," he wrote. And, Emerson continued:

Though nothing could be conceived beforehand less attractive or indeed less fit for green boys from Connecticut, New Hampshire, and Massachusetts, with their unripe Latin and Greek reading, than exegetical discourses in the style of Voss and Wolff and Ruhnken, on the Orphic and Ante-Homeric remains, – yet this learning instantly took the highest place to our imagination in our unoccupied American Parnassus.

Emerson once remarked that Wolf's thesis – that the written text of Homer was produced by a redactor who combined chants originally composed by an illiterate bard – inaugurated a new epoch in criticism. In the *Prolegomena* Wolf had asserted that we must give up the hope "that the original form of the Homeric Poems could ever be laid out save in our minds, and even there only in rough outlines." The scholar, laboring to dissolve and then recreate the text by rejecting all that is interpolated or corrupt, gives the great original poem of Western culture the only true shape it can have and effects on the textual level that transfer of the world into the mind that Emerson saw as the peculiar achievement of his age.

Yet Wolf himself confessed his indebtedness to an older tradition of textual scholarship. The great advances made by German biblical scholars during the eighteenth century in the understanding of ancient Near Eastern languages and the collation and correction of biblical texts had provided Wolf with a model for his own enterprise. His book was explicitly modeled on one of the most controversial works of biblical criticism, Johann Gottfried Eichhorn's

Einleitung in das Alte Testament (1780–3). Wolf's modern editors point out that Eichhorn (1752–1827) had ventured to treat the text of the Old Testament "as a historical and an anthropological document, the much-altered remnant of an early stage in the development of human culture."

More was at stake here than the reconstruction of the text itself: Eichhorn was proposing an entirely different way of *reading* the Old Testament, and the apologetic possibilities it offered were vast. Biblical scholars in England and America quickly saw in works like Eichhorn's a way of saving the Old Testament from on the one hand the ridicule of Deists and on the other the blind veneration of the believers in literal inspiration. The brilliant young Unitarian minister Joseph Stevens Buckminster (1784–1812) made sure he acquired Eichhorn's *Einleitung* during his tour of Europe. On that trip Buckminster spent a recent inheritance, amassing a library of three thousand volumes, including Johann Jakob Griesbach's Greek text of the New Testament (1796–1806) and many works of biblical criticism.

When Buckminster returned to New England in 1807 he began writing in the *Monthly Anthology* and its successor, the *General Repository and Review,* about Griesbach's achievement. In these pieces he explained the methods of the new textual criticism and urged the adoption of Griesbach's text, a one-volume edition of which Harvard had published in 1809 and adopted for use in its own classrooms. Although conservatives were shocked to hear someone assert that the received text of the Bible contained "corruptions," liberals were delighted to have Buckminster cast doubt upon the authenticity of scriptural texts that Trinitarians cited in support of their own theological position.

Buckminster was appointed to Harvard's newly created chair of biblical criticism, but he died at the early age of twenty-eight before he could assume the post. An auction held after his death offered the theological works he had amassed in Europe to bidders who were as eager to acquire the new books of criticism as he had been himself. A bidding war over the Eichhorn volumes erupted between Moses Stuart (1780–1852), the head of the recently founded Andover Theological Seminary, and Edward Everett. Shortly after the auction, Stuart (who had won the bidding war) invited Everett to Andover for an overnight visit during which he tried to interest Everett in translating another influential work of German biblical criticism, Johann Gottfried von Herder's *Vom geist der ebräischen poesie* (1782–3). Everett declined the translation task but borrowed the Eichhorn volumes and began immersing himself in them.

The friendship that sprang up between the liberal Everett and the orthodox Stuart is significant, for it suggests that the interest in the new methods of biblical criticism at this point transcended doctrinal divisions. Stuart even asked Everett to consider founding an "oriental club" at Cambridge where scholars could meet to discuss the new developments in the study of the scriptures. The club never materialized, but something of the ecumenical spirit that prompted the suggestion surfaced again when James Marsh (1794–1842), who had studied with Stuart at Andover, finally published a translation of Herder in 1833. The *Christian Examiner,* Boston's Unitarian quarterly, contained a series of essays devoted to Herder in 1834 and 1835, essays that would have a profound effect upon the way the young men and women who were beginning to be called Transcendentalists would interpret both Scripture and nature.

When Harvard appointed Everett professor of Greek in 1814 it took the unusual step of offering him a chance to study in Germany before he took up his duties at home; it even advanced him the money to pay for the enterprise. Everett had already begun to translate Eichhorn, and a five-hundred-page book he published in 1814 showed him becoming proficient enough in the new techniques of biblical interpretation to suggest innovations of his own. A disgruntled former minister had published a book examining the "grounds" of the Christian religion and finding them wanting. He argued that the writers of the Gospels had grotesquely twisted the meaning of Old Testament prophecies upon which they based their claims that Christ was the Messiah. Everett's *Defence of Christianity* replied that the Gospel writers were not misusing prophecies but rather employing them in a manner familiar to Jewish culture – employing them, in fact, just as the rabbis had in the Mishnah. Everett's book seemed promising. It suggested that the historical methods of German scholarship might support and defend Unitarian theology. His Harvard colleagues sent him to Germany hoping that he would bring home all that was most advanced in both the classical and biblical scholarship of the day.

Everett did become a brilliant student at Göttingen; in 1817 he became the first American to be awarded the Ph.D. But though he studied sacred criticism with Eichhorn himself he never taught the subject when he returned to Harvard. A few references in letters to doubts and anxieties that perplexed him shed some light on his refusal to teach at Harvard what he had learned in Germany. The letters suggest that Everett may have abandoned sacred criticism because he had begun to have fears that Eichhorn's latest conclusions were irreconcilable with even the most liberal interpretations of Scripture accepted by the Unitarian church.

Eichhorn by this time had turned his attention from the Old to the New Testament, and under his gaze the three synoptic Gospels dissolved into a set of redactions of a still more primitive gospel whose skeletal remains are visible beneath the concealing and elaborating flourishes of the canonical texts. In a rather truculent letter, Everett wrote to his brother Alexander that he planned to "trouble nobody's faith or peace" when he returned so long as he was left alone but that if he were not left alone he would "exhibit the subject of Christianity, which the modern historical and critical enquiries fully establish" (Everett to Alexander Everett, September 3, 1815). This way of putting matters makes German criticism sound much more like a threat than a promise. Several months later the whole enterprise seemed to weary him. Why should scholars waste such time and energy in their quest for the historical Jesus? Everett, who succeeded Buckminster for a brief but memorable pastorate in the pulpit of the Brattle Square Church before resigning to take up the Harvard professorship, confessed to his brother that he still felt a "strong attachment to the act of preaching." But he wished something could be done "to separate the public worship of God and the public teaching of duty, from all connection with arbitrary facts, supposed to have happened in distant nations and ages" (Everett to Alexander Everett, January 5, 1816). Everett's brusque dismissal of the crucifixion and resurrection of Jesus as "arbitrary facts" is probably, as has been suggested, a rephrasing of Gotthold Ephraim Lessing's assertion that accidental historical truths can never prove the necessary truths of reason. But it also hints at a restlessness always implicit in Unitarianism's exaltation of the moral sense. If the sense of duty is the inner divinity of which Jesus was only the most perfect exemplar, why do we need Jesus at all, let alone the miracles that prove his mission divine?

Whatever Everett's doubts, he did keep them to himself when he returned home, and the new scholarship from Germany continued to be discussed and studied by Unitarians. A steady stream of American students found its way to German universities; the latest books of sacred criticism were sent home from Europe and reviewed in American periodicals. Some English translations of prominent works of German scholarship – Bishop Herbert Marsh's 1802 translation of J. D. Michaelis's *Introduction to the New Testament* and Bishop Connop Thirlwall's 1825 translation of F. D. E. Schleiermacher's *Critical Essay upon the Gospel of St. Luke* – contained long historical essays by the translators surveying the development of biblical criticism and explaining the details of famous controversies. These accounts of progressive intellectual discovery in a subject so long characterized by bitter sectarian disputes suggested that theology too might finally begin to join the "progress" of intellect instead of merely opposing it.

True, the alleged impiety of the German critics and the skepticism inherent in every kind of textual criticism made some fear that (as Thirlwall put it) the new biblical criticism might "tend to destroy the reverence with which Christians are accustomed to regard these works as Holy Writ and containing the words of God." The trustees of the Andover Theological Seminary became worried enough in 1825 to warn that "the unrestrained cultivation of German studies has evidently tended to chill the ardor of piety," and at Harvard, Andrews Norton eventually became so convinced of the destabilizing effects of German criticism that he refused to let his son study the German language. To braver spirits, however, such anxieties only testified to the power of the new criticism. Watching the textual obscurities of centuries melt before the blast of the new historical criticism gave the young scholars of the era a confidence that, like the mysteries of nature, the mysteries of Scripture were soluble.

This sense of an imminent clarification, of a final destination for the progress of ethical philosophy and religious understanding, is Unitarianism's enduring legacy to the men and women who came to maturity in the first three decades of the nineteenth century. When the author and biographer Edward Everett Hale (1822–1909) looked back from the 1890s on the climate in Divinity Hall at Harvard in the late 1820s, he wished above all to communicate to his readers the sense of

a certain enthusiastic expectation which at the time quickened the lives of all young people in New England who had been trained in the freer schools of religion. The group of leaders who surrounded Dr. Channing had, with him, broken forever from the fetters of Calvinistic theology. These young people were trained to know that human nature is not totally depraved. They were taught that there is nothing of which it is not capable. From Dr. Channing down, every writer and preacher believed in the infinite power of education. In England the popular wave for the diffusion of useful knowledge had set in; and what was called the "March of Intellect" had begun. The great German authors swayed the minds of our young students with all their new power, and with the special seduction which accompanies a discovery, the study of German being wholly new. For students who did not read German, Coleridge was opening up the larger philosophy.

Hale mentions other signs of the times – the belief in the power of association and the organization of philanthropic societies:

For such reasons, and many more, the young New Englanders of liberal training rushed into life, certain that the next half century was to see a complete moral revolution in the world. . . . And no one rightly writes or reads the life of one of these young men or women, unless he fully appreciates the force of this enthusiastic hope.

THE ASSAULT ON LOCKE

TOWARD THE END of the 1820s the philosophical synthesis that had supported Unitarianism throughout its period of expansion began to show signs of strain. Unresolved contradictions within it – the tension between sensationalism and idealism in its epistemology, the mingled attitude of desire and fear that marked its dealings with German biblical criticism – began to trouble new generations of students. Writings of the English and German Romantics kept arriving on American shores and finding enthusiasts among the young, despite their elders' contempt for the bathos of Wordsworth, the licentiousness of Goethe, the obscurity of Kant and of Coleridge. Reformers were beginning to demand that the churches leave their careful doctrine of individual self-culture and do something about the scandal of urban poverty or the greater scandal of slavery. By the end of the 1820s the discontents among the younger Unitarians had begun to find public expression.

The first sign of the trouble that would later be labeled "Transcendentalism" came with an attack on two fronts: on the philosophy of John Locke and on the educational system at Harvard. The two things were naturally allied in the minds of the young men who had been subjected to them simultaneously, and the connection was reinforced by the fact that Harvard's heavy reliance on drill seemed perfectly tailored to Locke's view of the mind's structure. If the mind is an empty tablet and if all ideas come from sensation and reflection, then memorization ought to be the foundation of all learning and recitation the proper medium for its display. Edward Everett's learning *An Essay Concerning Human Understanding* by heart and reciting it day after day to his pleased tutor symbolizes perfectly what the old system valued.

Classes at Harvard (as at most American colleges) were "recitations" at which students were called upon to display their knowledge of the assigned materials. The students received an immediate score for their performance, and these scores were then used to determine rank in class and share of honors and privileges. How deadly, how infuriating, this system seemed to the young students (who often entered college when they were fifteen) can be seen in the anger that still animates the pages of the autobiography James

Freeman Clarke (1810–88) began a few months before his death. Clarke, a Unitarian minister and a Transcendentalist, recalled his dismay at finding that the Harvard system seemed designed to frustrate curiosity.

No attempt was made to interest us in our studies. We were expected to wade through Homer as though the Iliad were a bog, and it was our duty to get along at such a rate *per diem*. Nothing was said of the glory and grandeur, the tenderness and charm of this immortal epic. The melody of the hexameters was never suggested to us. Dr. Popkin, our Greek professor, would look over his spectacles at us, and, with pencil in hand, mark our recitation as good or bad, but never a word to help us over a difficulty, or to explain anything obscure, still less to excite our enthusiasm for the greatest poem of antiquity.

What intellectual excitement there was on campus was provided by the student-run literary societies. Campus literary societies had been fixtures of American college life since the eighteenth century – sponsoring debates, discussions, and oratorical displays; assembling libraries for the use of their members; encouraging original composition in verse and prose. They provided what one historian has called an "alternative curriculum" to the official one, an arena in which the students could find an outlet for the curiosity and love of literature that the classroom refused to acknowledge. The contrast between the grim, competitive atmosphere of the classroom and the freedom of the literary society only helped fuel undergraduate dissatisfaction with the college authorities. "When I recall what my classmates were interested in doing," Clarke remembered,

I find it was not college work, which might have given them rank, but pursuits outside of the curriculum. . . . We unearthed old tomes in the college library, and while our English professors were teaching us out of Blair's "Rhetoric," we were forming our taste by making copious extracts from Sir Thomas Browne, or Ben Jonson. Our real professors of rhetoric were Charles Lamb and Coleridge, Walter *Romantics* Scott and Wordsworth.

The appetite for Romantic literature Clarke and his classmates had developed in the "unofficial" Harvard curriculum received a powerful stimulus from another source of information about new developments in European thought, Madame de Staël's celebrated survey of German life and thought, *De l'Allemagne*. Anne-Louise-Germaine Necker, Baroness de Staël (1766–1817), exiled from France by the anger of Napoleon, had published an account of her travels through Germany in London in 1813. (An earlier, Paris edition had been confiscated and pulped on Napoleon's orders.) Her hostility to the French emperor, her admiration for British constitutional liberties, and her praise for the Scottish Common Sense philosophers all combined to win her the admiration not only of the British public but also of readers in New England.

Madame de Staël. De L'Allemagne (Emerson)

De Staël's account of the development of European philosophy from Locke through the post-Kantians constitutes a sustained critique of the philosophical tradition that Harvard students had been taught to revere. De Staël excoriates the mocking, corrosive, godless skepticism of French Enlightenment culture and traces its lineage back not to Hume or Voltaire but to Locke himself. In de Staël's narrative of European intellectual history, Locke is the innocent originator of a mistake whose full implications were left to others to work out. De Staël argues that Locke's English piety and devotion to liberty prevented him from seeing that his sensationalist philosophy led inevitably to the tyrant worship of Thomas Hobbes and the skepticism of David Hume. The French followers of Locke had no such inherited defenses, and so they embraced without restraint a system that de Staël sums up as "materialism built upon sensation, and ethics founded upon interest."

Against the "scoffing skepticism" she sees as the product of a philosophy that derives ideas from sensations, de Staël opposes the inwardness and spirituality of the German tradition, beginning with Gottfried Wilhelm Leibniz (1646–1716) and culminating gloriously in Immanuel Kant (1724–1804). Leibniz had added to Locke's assertion that there is nothing in the intellect that was not previously in the senses this "sublime restriction" – *except the intellect itself.* Kant had then set himself the task of determining the laws that govern the intellect; he had asked himself, "What are the laws and sentiments which constitute the essence of the human soul, independently of all experience?"

Nothing less than absolute certainty would content Kant. He found this certainty in those "necessary notions," those laws of understanding, that determine the ways in which we can conceive of the world of the senses. He demonstrated that these notions – such as space, time, cause and effect, unity, plurality, possibility, and reality – are within us, and not the objects we contemplate; "in this respect, it is our understanding which gives laws to external nature, instead of receiving them from it."

Kant, according to de Staël, did not reject the world of experience; indeed, "nothing is more luminous than the line of demarcation which he traces between what comes to us by sensation and what belongs to the spontaneous action of our souls." He never attempted to move into the pure idealism of his successor, Johann Gottlieb Fichte, who, with "scientific strictness," made the whole universe "consist of the activity of mind." But in making our minds the active shapers of sense impressions instead of the passive recipients of them, Kant restored to the mind its centrality and dignity. This same dignity also informs Kant's ethical system, which makes conscience the "innate principle" of our moral existence: "The feeling of right and wrong is, according to his ideas, the primitive law of the heart, as space and time are of the understanding." Our inner assurance of moral liberty is the proof that we

[handwritten margin note at top: Conscience: primivitive Law of heart — innate principle of Moral Existence > felt]

possess it, for neither moral liberty nor conscience can be the result of experience. Both are _felt_ instead in that "power of reaction against circumstances, which springs from the bottom of the soul."

De Staël's great work of popularization made the young Bostonians aware of the massive changes that had taken place in Continental philosophy. Her vivid, epigrammatic style was a refreshing change from the dryness of metaphysical treatises, and the value she placed upon the dignity of the individual and upon moral liberty made her appealing to anyone raised in the tradition of Unitarian humanism. Emerson clearly loved de Staël; beginning in the early 1820s he fills his journals with maxims and anecdotes copied from _De l'Allemagne,_ maxims to which he accorded an important place in his first book, _Nature_ (1836). If he did not learn from de Staël any details of Kant's terminology (she disapproved of it), he did get the sense that answers to his pressing spiritual questions were likely to come from Germany or at least from those others who derived their ideas from that fertile source.

[handwritten margin note: de Staël — De l'Allemagne & Emerson]

Samuel Taylor Coleridge was the most famous of these cultural mediators after de Staël, and the American publication of two of his prose works by James Marsh, the president of the University of Vermont, helped fan the fires of interest in German philosophy. Marsh was not a Unitarian. He had been a student of Moses Stuart's at Andover, but already during his years at the seminary he had become dissatisfied with both the prevailing methods of instruction at American institutions of higher learning and the philosophical system taught in them. He became convinced that Lockean empiricism and the Scottish Common Sense philosophy that came after it had entangled theology in a "metaphysical net" from which it could never break free. The fruitless doctrinal disputes among orthodox theologians led many faithful Christians either to abandon their faith altogether or to take refuge in unreflecting fideism. After Marsh left the seminary he began to search for something that would satisfy not only the intellect but also the emotions, not only the head but also "the heart in the head."

When Marsh stumbled across the works of Coleridge – first the _Biographia Literaria_ (1817) and then _Aids to Reflection_ (1825) – he became convinced that Coleridge's adaptation of Kant offered a way to rescue American theology from its marriage to a sensationalist philosophy inherently hostile to piety. He decided to publish an American edition of Coleridge's _Aids to Reflection._ This edition appeared in 1829, and Marsh prefaced it with a long "Preliminary Essay" in which he argued for the relevance of Coleridge's beliefs to the state of American theology. Marsh realized that his planned publication might be obnoxious to orthodox theologians; he also knew that he might have trouble getting the book reviewed in a country where literary magazines scrupulously avoided theological discussions and theological magazines were firmly committed to the doctrines of particular sects. He sent copies of his edition to prominent theologians at Andover and Princeton, hoping to enlist their support, only to find that they strongly objected to Coleridge's explanation of the Atonement as something that causes "subjective change" in us rather than as something that satisfies the legal demands of divine justice.

Meanwhile, Marsh's attack upon the prevailing system of metaphysics — "I mean the system, of which in modern times Locke is the reputed author" — was winning him converts among the very Unitarians he had made no effort to attract. The young Boston liberals had little interest in Marsh's attempt to place the doctrines of the Trinity or the Atonement upon firm metaphysical grounds. But they loved his attack upon the philosophical system they detested. Marsh described empirical philosophy as a system that by insisting that all knowledge is ultimately derived from sensation "tends inevitably to undermine our belief in the reality of any thing spiritual in the only proper sense of that word" and then "coldly and ambiguously" refers us for the support of our faith to "the *authority* of revelation."

In *Aids to Reflection* Coleridge makes a strong distinction between what is spiritual and what is natural and in so doing eliminates the need to reduce the one to the other. He argues that the faculties by which we perceive these different spheres of reality are as different as the spheres themselves, although these faculties somehow reside in a single human mind. The *Reason* is the supersensuous, intuitive power, at once the source of morality and of the highest kind of intellection; the *Understanding* is the humbler servant who works by combining and comparing ideas derived from sensation, who helps us reflect and generalize — the faculty Locke had mistaken for the whole of the mind, in other words.

The distinction between the Reason and the Understanding helps Coleridge dispose handily of a century's worth of Deist attacks upon the "unintelligible" doctrines of Christianity. *Of course* religious concepts like the Trinity, the Atonement, and Original Sin appear contradictory to the Understanding; they are spiritual doctrines rather than natural ones and must of necessity appear absurd to the faculty devoted to judging the natural world. The truths of Reason, in fact, can be expressed to the Understanding only as a paradox: "Before Abraham was, I am," or "God is a circle whose center is everywhere and his circumference nowhere." Locke's patient attempt to arrive at truth by comparing and analyzing sensory impressions can never succeed because the truth he was looking for resides elsewhere. "In Wonder all philosophy began; in Wonder it ends: and Admiration fills up the interspace."

Coleridge's distinction between the Reason and the Understanding seemed to offer Unitarians a way out of their spiritual dilemma — a way for them to satisfy the hunger for contact with the transcendent without abandoning the values of tolerance and rational enquiry. Clarke remembered how his discovery during his senior year at Harvard in 1829 of Coleridge's philosophy helped turn him toward the ministry: "Coleridge the poet I had known and loved. Coleridge the philosopher confirmed my longing for a higher philosophy than that of John Locke and David Hartley, the metaphysicians most in vogue with the earlier Unitarians down to the time of Channing." Like most of his friends Clarke had grown up among the ideas of sensationalist philosophy; he tells us that one of his earliest philosophical lessons had been Locke's polemic against innate ideas:

But something within me revolted at all such attempts to explain soul out of sense, deducing mind from matter, or tracing the origin of ideas to nerves, vibrations, and vibratiuncles. So I gave it up, until Coleridge showed me from Kant that though knowledge begins *with* experience it does not come *from* experience. Then I discovered that I was born a transcendentalist; and smiled when I afterwards read, in one of Jacobi's works, that he had gone through exactly the same experience.

As many people have noticed, Coleridge's terminology, though translated from Kant (*Vernunft* and *Verstand*), differs in significant ways from its source. For Kant, the Reason consists of all the categories of mental activity that make perception possible but cannot themselves be derived from it, the things Madame de Staël had called "necessary notions": space and time, causality, proportionality, relation, and so on. Kant's Reason is neither a repository of particular truths nor the faculty of intuitively apprehending them. But few of Coleridge's American readers knew *The Critique of Pure Reason* (1781), and most were happy to use Coleridge's terms as if they were Kant's.

"There is no delight like a new classification," Emerson would later observe. In the years following Marsh's edition of Coleridge, people rushed to apply the distinction between the Reason and the Understanding to every knotty problem that had perplexed them. Clarke noted how it had helped him when he came to the study of theology. It taught him to regard doctrinal differences as insignificant, as the product of the Understanding's attempt to formulate discursively the truths perceived immediately and intuitively by the Reason. Clarke thought that even the split between Unitarian and Trinitarian, apparently so wide, might simply be a different way of *expressing* the belief that Christ is "a visible manifestation of the invisible and eternal."

Emerson was quick to adopt the new classification too. Writing to his brother Edward in 1834 he asks whether Edward draws "the distinction of Milton Coleridge & the Germans between Reason & Understanding," a distinction he himself now regards as "a philosophy itself." "The manifold applications of the distinction to Literature to the Church to Life will show how good a key it is," he announces, and explains the difference to Edward in the shape of a little allegory. "Reason is the highest faculty of the soul – what we mean often by the soul itself; it never *reasons,* never proves, it simply perceives; it is vision. The Understanding toils all the time, compares, contrives, adds, argues, near sighted but strong-sighted, dwelling in the present the expedient the customary." So far the Understanding is merely the myopic servant of a visionary, but a little farther on the allegory darkens.

The thoughts of youth, & "first thoughts," are the revelations of Reason. . . . But understanding that wrinkled calculator the steward of our house to whom is committed to support of our animal life contradicts evermore these affirmations of Reason & points at Custom & Interest & persuades one man that the declarations of Reason are false & another that they are at least impracticable. Yet by & by after having denied our Master we come back to see at the end of years or of life that he was the Truth. (Emerson to Edward Emerson, May 31, 1834)

The Understanding now becomes a voice of wordly prudence, and the individual who listens to its promptings instead of to the Reason's is, like Peter in Gethsemane, denying the true Christ he will someday acknowledge again in tears and repentance. When Emerson heard an orthodox preacher say that "the carnal mind hates God continually," he could sit through the sermon without impatience because he could translate the preacher's words into his own new tongue: "I say, 'It is the instinct of the Understanding to contradict the Reason.' "

The hostility between the Reason and the Understanding explained a primal split in consciousness as well as the oscillations between uplift and collapse, nobility and timorousness, that plagued the aspiring. Even more, it offered to a class of people for whom the biblical history of the Fall and the redemption was losing intellectual authority the chance to interpret their inner life with the vividness of the faith once delivered to the Saints. The young Cambridge student of divinity who read his life as perpetual warfare between the holy promptings of the Reason and the worldly prudence of the Understanding had an inner life as complicated, as full of disheartening falls and miraculous recoveries, as any spiritual autobiographer of the seventeenth century.

How were the Reason and the Understanding related in the life history of the individual? Were they twin born, or siblings sometimes cooperative, sometimes bitterly hostile? The answer came this time not from philosophy, but from poetry, particularly from the poetry of Coleridge and William Wordsworth. Neither man had been very popular in the United States in the early decades of the century, when Lord Byron and the Irish poet Tom Moore were all the rage. Joseph Dennie (1768–1812) had reviewed some of Words-

worth's earlier lyrics with favor in his Philadelphia *Port Folio,* but Dennie had
few imitators. Boston's *Monthly Anthology,* when it noticed Wordsworth at
all, found his experiments politically dangerous and poetically ludicrous.

Suddenly, in the late 1820s, converts to Coleridge discovered that the
verse they had once derided contained spiritual truths as profound as Kant's
and equally as useful in the fight against sensationalism. Sampson Reed, a
young Harvard graduate who had converted to Swedenborgianism in 1820,
published in 1826 a small book entitled *The Growth of the Mind.* In it Reed
argues against the reigning Lockean view of the mind's structure and suggests instead a model of mental development illustrated by the poetry of
Wordsworth and other English Romantics. The mind, in this view, is not a
passive receiver of stimuli, but a germ that grows and expands by assimilat-
ing things from its environment. In 1831 James Marsh issued the second of
his Coleridgean publications, an American edition of Coleridge's periodical
The Friend (1809–10), which contained extracts from Wordsworth's unpublished
autobiographical poem later titled *The Prelude.*

The young men and women around Cambridge who read these works
delighted in a portrait of the individual mind and its relationship to nature
that made ordinary perception seem revelatory and ordinary maturation
Odyssean. It bothered no one that the Romanticism intoxicating Cambridge
was decades old, and the Kantianism even older, or that the ideas being
hailed as revolutionary were a jumble of bits and pieces torn from their
contexts and served up by a haphazard collection of editors, translators, and
book reviewers. If anything, this blurring of historical distinctions contributed to the sense of excitement. The fruits of a half-century of European
progress in literature, philosophy, natural science, and sacred criticism all
arrived on American shores more or less at once – Swedenborg and
Schleiemacher, Herder and Strauss, Kant and Schelling, Goethe and Wordsworth, de Staël and Coleridge. Such opulence could hardly fail to suggest
that the world was on the verge of a remarkable synthesis. The opening pages
of Reed's *Growth of the Mind* (1826) give an idea of the mood:

The world is deriving vigor, not from that which is gone by, but from that which is
coming; not from the unhealthy moisture of the evening, but from the nameless
influences of the morning. . . . Both mankind, and the laws and principles by which they
are governed, seem about to be redeemed from slavery. . . . We appear to be approaching
an age which will be the silent pause of merely physical force before the powers of the
mind; the timid, subdued, awed condition of the brute, gazing on the erect and godlike
form of man.

It seems curious to us that among the strong contributors to this sense of
imminent apotheosis were the great British quarterly reviews, the *Edinburgh
Review,* founded in 1802, and its Tory rival, the *Quarterly,* founded in 1808.

The lengthy review essays in these and similar periodicals were expected to do far more than offer opinions (though the opinions in the always anonymous reviews were famous for their frankness and malice). Reviews frequently offered surveys of entire fields. For instance, the December 1826 number of the *Edinburgh* contained a review of seven books and articles dealing with the work of Jean-François Champollion (decipherer of the Rosetta stone); it included an engraved fold-out chart giving a selection of phonetic hieroglyphics and their equivalents in demotic and Greek characters. Furthermore, a review of James Fenimore Cooper's *Notions of the Americans* and of a book by a British traveler in North America contained a survey of recent British–American political relations and a concise history of American literature going back as far as Jonathan Edwards.

This impression of intellectual mastery combined with vigorous expression of opinion gave the reviews an air of authority that could make each essay seem like an education in itself, a quality particularly valuable in the United States, where foreign books were difficult to obtain. The high caliber of the reviewers and their practice of quoting copiously from the books they reviewed gave readers a sense of contact with an intellectual world they might never otherwise approach. It may be true, as Sydney Smith, the editor of the *Edinburgh,* suggested, that every reader took up a review hoping to get wise at a cheap rate; but few periodicals ever made that hope seem capable of fulfillment as easily as his own.

Bostonians who read the British reviews quickly learned that their local idols were not always treated with reverence elsewhere. The *Edinburgh* reviewer of William Ellery Channing's essays on Fenelon, Milton, and Napoleon wrote in 1829: "We do not like to see a writer constantly trying to steal a march upon opinion without having his retreat cut off – full of pretensions, and void of offense." Channing

is always in advance of the line, in an amiable and imposing attitude, but never far from succour. He is an Unitarian; but then he disclaims all connexions with Dr. Priestley, as a materialist; he denounces Calvinism and the Church of England, but to show that this proceeds from no want of liberality, makes the *amende honorable* to Popery and Popish divines; – is an American Republican and a French Bourbonist; – ... likes wit, provided it is serious – and is zealous for the propagation of the Gospel and the honour of religion, but thinks it should form a coalition with reason, and be surrounded with a halo of modern lights.

The writer of the review (who was in fact William Hazlitt) even suspected that Channing's want of moral daring may have been the product of that very democratic system of government whose "establishment of civil and religious liberty" was supposed to free opinion completely. But American democracy did not free opinion; it established a tyranny more onerous than ever. In a mixed government a dissident may appeal from one party to another, but when there is only one "body of opinion" in a country it is invincible. "There can be no reaction against it, and to remonstrate or resist, is not only a public outrage, but sounds like a personal insult to every individual in the community. It is differing from the company; you become a *black sheep in the flock.*" Hazlitt attributed to this subtle pressure "the too frequent cowardice, jesuitism, and sterility, produced by this republican discipline and drilling." So far from fostering individuality, republican government squelches it. "Whoever outstrips, or takes a separate path to himself, is considered as usurping an unnatural superiority over the whole. He is treated not with respect or indulgence, but with indignity." The criticism of Channing was particularly stinging because it could not be ascribed to programmatic anti-Americanism. The *Edinburgh,* though it loved ridiculing the faults of American literature as much as it loved ridiculing everything else, remained friendlier to the United States than did many other foreign periodicals. As another reviewer indulgently wrote: "Though the hussy ran away and married to disoblige us, she is a chip of the old block."

The style of the *Edinburgh* was infectious. Anyone who reads Frederic Henry Hedge's celebrated review of Coleridge's works for the *Christian Examiner* in 1833 can see just where Hedge is affecting the witty nonchalance of *Edinburgh*'s "invisible invincibles" in his study of Coleridge's career. Hedge (1805–90) was probably better qualified than anyone else in America to pull off such an imitation. Born in Boston and sent by his father, Levi Hedge (professor of logic at Harvard), to Germany when he was only thirteen, Hedge spent four years in German preparatory schools, an experience that made him fluent not only in academic German but also in German schoolboy slang. He remained in Germany until 1822, when he returned to Harvard to get his B.A. He entered the Divinity School in 1825 and upon his graduation in 1828 was ordained pastor of the West Cambridge Church. Hedge had read Kant's *Critiques;* he was also well-read in the various post-Kantian idealists who had influenced Coleridge. Already in Divinity School he had earned the reputation for intellectual fearlessness that led one eulogist to remark after his death, "He was not appalled by any result to which his thought might lead." He once mocked the kind of Christian who could be frightened by German biblical criticism. "What a sequel and summing up of the history of Christianity would that be, to say that 'God sent his Son into the World,' 'that the world through him might be saved,' but the Tübingen School and British 'Essays and Reviews' defeated that purpose and it had to be abandoned?"

When James Marsh's edition of *The Friend* appeared in 1831, Hedge seized the opportunity to review a good part of Coleridge's career: the *Poetical Works,* the *Biographia Literaria, Aids to Reflection,* and *The Friend.* Hedge praises the

James Marsh
Frederic H. Hedge

poetry, predicts that the *Biographia* will remain popular when the other prose works have faded, and commends the "depth of thought, clearness of judgment, sound reasoning, and forcible expression" to be found in *The Friend*. He thanks Marsh for the usefulness of his "Preliminary Essay" and ventures to hope that the talent for original philosophy that the "Essay" suggests will find fuller expression later. But distributing compliments is not really Hedge's main purpose in the review. The review's central portions tackle the thickly layered history of transcendental philosophy: first Kant himself, then the post-Kantian Idealists, then Coleridge, and finally Marsh's interpretation of Coleridge.

Hedge begins by warning his readers that unless they are willing to make the strenuous effort demanded by German metaphysicians they will never understand the sense of excitement the new methods create in their adherents. "The effect of such writing upon the uninitiated, is like being in the company of one who has inhaled an exhilarating gas. We witness the inspiration, and are astounded at the effects, but we can form no conception of the feeling until we ourselves have experienced it." The kind of philosopher who "contrives a theory of spirit, by nicknaming matter" and hopes to explain every phenomenon of consciousness by "reducing all things to impressions, ideas, and sensations" will never share in this mysterious exhilaration. Kant and his disciples "wrote for minds of quite another stamp," minds that seek with faith and hope a solution to questions that empirical philosophy declares are impossible to answer – "questions which relate to spirit and form, substance and life, free will and fate, God and eternity."

Hedge thinks that a preoccupation with such questions recurs periodically:

There are certain periods in the history of society, when, passing from a state of spontaneous production to a state of reflection, mankind are particularly disposed to inquire concerning themselves and their destination, the nature of their being, the evidence of their knowledge, and the grounds of their faith. Such a tendency is one of the characteristics of the present age, and the German philosophy is the strongest expression of that tendency; it is a striving after information on subjects which have been usually considered as beyond the reach of human intelligence, an attempt to penetrate into the most hidden mysteries of our being.

The transcendental system is, to be sure, not a *ratio essendi* but a *ratio cognoscendi:* "It seeks not to explain the existence of God and creation, objectively considered, but to explain our knowledge of their existence." In the strongest possible terms Hedge rejects the charge that the transcendental system is a skeptical philosophy: "It seeks not to overthrow, but to build up; it wars not with the common opinions and general experience of mankind, but aims to place these on a scientific basis, and to verify them by specific demonstrations."

Only toward the end of the review does Hedge turn his attention to *Aids to Reflection*. The Coleridgean distinction that had meant so much to his friends – between the Reason and the Understanding – Hedge mentions only in passing; he knows that the way Coleridge used the terms was un-Kantian. Indeed, the final pages of Hedge's review display contempt for Coleridge's pretensions as a religious thinker. "In this work he appears as a zealous Trinitarian, and a warm defender of the English church. We have no doubt of his sincerity; but unless we err greatly, he has either misunderstood his own views, or grossly misinterpreted the doctrines of his church." Coleridge's Trinity might pass equally well for the Godhead worshipped by a Unitarian. Nor do other traditional doctrines fare much better at Coleridge's hands. "His opinion of the atonement is far from Orthodox; the idea of vicarious suffering he rejects with disdain. The strong expressions of St. Paul in reference to this subject, he tells us are not intended to designate the *act* of redemption but are only figurative expressions descriptive of its effects." Any Christian doctrine Coleridge thinks unpalatable he simply pronounces to be a *mystery*. His project of recuperating traditional Christian doctrines through transcendental philosophy turns out to be an affair of language rather than of thought. "Every thing is first mystified into a sort of imposing indistinctness, and then pronounced to be genuine Orthodoxy."

Nevertheless, Hedge welcomes Coleridge's unconscious heterodoxy. He sees Coleridge as a valuable importer and disseminator of ideas that are quite easily separable from the husk of Anglican piety in which they are contained. He ends his review by quoting with approval Coleridge's own defense from the tenth chapter of the *Biographia Literaria:*

Would that the criterion of the scholar's utility were the number and moral value of the truths which he has been the means of throwing into the general circulation, or the number and value of the minds whom by his conversation or letters he has excited into activity, and supplied with the germs of their after-growth.

Judged by such standards, Coleridge's contribution to American intellectual life had been as great as he could have wished.

3

CARLYLE AND THE BEGINNINGS OF
AMERICAN TRANSCENDENTALISM

B Y THE TIME Frederic Henry Hedge had published his review of
Coleridge's career in the *Christian Examiner* another writer had already
begun to take Coleridge's place as supplier of excitations to the New
World, a writer who was less interested in metaphysics than he was in the
conduct of life. In the 1820s a remarkable series of review essays about German
literature began to appear in the British quarterlies and attract the attention of
the young Boston liberals. The style of these reviews – passionate, urgent, full
of humor and outrage – marked them off immediately from the urbane acidi-
ties surrounding them. The reviews were written by Thomas Carlyle (1795–
1881), who had been translating German literary works and writing essays
about German literature in the 1820s and early 1830s. Carlyle's essay on the
German writer known as Jean Paul (Jean Paul Friedrich Richter, 1763–1825)
appeared in the *Edinburgh Review* in 1827, followed in the same year by an essay
on "The State of German Literature." In 1828 Carlyle published two essays in
the *Foreign Review:* an analysis of the "Helena" episode from the second part of
Goethe's *Faust* and a later essay on Goethe's whole career. In 1828 and 1829 the
Edinburgh Review published Carlyle's long biographical essays on the German
classical scholar Christian Gottlob Heyne (1729–1812) and on the German
poet and novelist Novalis (1772–1801). A London magazine, *Fraser's,* published Carlyle's review of the correspondence of Goethe and Schiller in 1831.
In December 1831, Carlyle published in the *Edinburgh Review* his long and
important essay "Characteristics," occasioned by the posthumous publication
of Friedrich von Schlegel's *Philosophische Vorlesungen.*

A mere list of titles and subjects can scarcely explain why Carlyle's influence became so potent in America that (as O. B. Frothingham would later
remember) "the dregs of his ink-bottle were welcomed as the precious sediment of the fountain of inspiration." Americans probably had fewer prejudices against German literature than the British readers whom Carlyle had
tried to hector into admiration, but Americans were equally ignorant. Harvard University did not offer instruction in German until the mid-1820s, and
even then the instructor had difficulty attracting students, because the
courses were counted as electives. Furthermore, few German books were

available in New England bookstores. Why should a group of essays giving biographies and critical accounts of German authors become the rage of intellectual Boston? By 1833 the mania for all things German had become so strong that James Freeman Clarke was almost ashamed to confess to his friend Margaret Fuller that he did not enjoy Goethe's poetry. "Those little *Lieder,* proverbs, etc., are darkness visible to me," he complains. "I really wish you would tell me why and how you like his poetry. Somehow I cannot rightly *auffassen* it" (Clarke to Fuller, September 9, 1833).

The appeal of Carlyle's essays came partly from their willingness to *auffassen,* or apprehend, everything from Goethe's lyrics to the various forms of transcendental philosophy whose ideas were agitating New England theology. In his review of Novalis's writings, Carlyle explains the necessity of giving some account of Fichte's *Wissenschaftlehre,* from which Novalis derived his own philosophical ideas; his summary of the wars between Idealists and empiricists takes the reader all the way from Pyrrho through Kant and the post-Kantian Idealists. Carlyle announces that under the new dispensation inaugurated by Kant — in which time and space are revealed not as external but as internal entities, as forms of the spirit — God's eternity and omnipresence are no longer mysteries. "Nay to the Transcendentalist, clearly enough, the whole question of the origin and existence of Nature must be greatly simplified: the old hostility of Matter is at an end, for matter is itself annihilated; and the black Spectre, Atheism, 'with all its sickly dews,' melts into nothingness forever."

Unlike Coleridge or James Marsh, who looked to German philosophy to solve theological problems, Carlyle gloried in the energy he discovered in German philosophy for its own sake. His essays resonate with contempt for established ideas and practices, and most of all for the complacent shallowness of the fashionable world. Carlyle dwells lovingly on Richter's simplicity, on Fichte's "cold, colossal, adamantine spirit," on Heyne's struggles to educate himself in the face of desperate poverty, and on Schlegel's lifelong efforts to forge a spiritual religion in the midst of denial and unbelief. In "The State of German Literature" (1827) Carlyle introduces his readers to Fichte's lofty conception of the role of the literary man.

According to Fichte, there is a 'Divine Idea' pervading the visible Universe; which visible Universe is indeed but its symbol and sensible manifestation, having in itself no meaning, or even true existence independent of it. To the mass of men this Divine Idea of the world lies hidden: yet to discern it, to seize it, and live wholly in it, is the condition of all genuine virtue, knowlege, freedom; and the end therefore of all spiritual effort in every age. Literary Men are the appointed interpreters of this Divine Idea; a perpetual priesthood, we might say, standing forth generation after generation, as the dispensers and living types of God's everlasting wisdom.

Nor can the literary man shun his obligations to his contemporaries. "For each age, by the law of its nature, is different from every other age, and demands a different representation of this Divine Idea, the essence of which is the same in all; so that the Literary Man of one century is only by mediation and re-interpretation applicable to the wants of another."

To New Englanders, who had scarcely outgrown their Federalist assumptions that a literary man was either a member of the clergy or a lawyer who dabbled in poetry and aimed to win converts to virtue by fictions in which virtue is pleasingly arrayed, such ideas were electrifying. Carlyle was proposing an alternative vocation, a vocation new to America. The literary man need adopt no particular profession; he need produce no poems or plays or essays. The literary life, if sincerely lived, would serve as well as literary works themselves to shadow forth the Divine Idea to the residents of this time and place.

And this time and place need such shadowing forth, for the present (as Carlyle reminds us in "Signs of the Times") is an age of mechanism, an age of soullessness, that believes only in "cause and effect" and no sooner hears of an example of nobility of spirit than it sets about "accounting for it." But if the present appears squalid, we must remember that "The poorest day that passes over us is the conflux of Two Eternities!" If we now "see nothing by direct vision; but only by reflection, and in anatomical dismemberment," we can heal our vision and reintegrate its objects. "Nay, after all, our spiritual maladies are but of Opinion; we are fettered by chains of our own forging, and which ourselves can rend asunder." The events convulsing the political world in recent history are not the signs of an approaching end but the birth pangs of a new world order. "There is a deep-lying struggle in the whole fabric of society; a boundless, grinding collision of the New with the old. The French Revolution, as is now visible enough, was not the parent of this mighty movement but its offspring."

Much that was comforting about the Old World necessarily perishes in this collision of new with old. In "Characteristics" (1831) Carlyle freely admits that the modern Age of Negation appears to offer only despair to the young man whose "whole nature cries aloud for Action" but who can find "nothing sacred under whose banner he can act." The task facing such seekers is as noble as it is daunting. "They have to realise a Worship for themselves, or live unworshipping. The Godlike has vanished from the world; and they, by the strong cry of their soul's agony, like true wonder-workers, must again evoke its presence." Still, though the present is bleak, Carlyle refuses to admit that it is hopeless. "Out of Evil comes Good; and no Good that is possible but shall one day be real," he says. "Nay, already as we look round, streaks of a dayspring are in the east: it is dawning; when the time shall be fulfilled, it will be day."

If Carlyle was right, the bewildering changes taking place in American society might simply be the grinding collision of the new with the old, the darkness that precedes the dawn. (Carlyle's 1829 article "Signs of the Times," after all, begins with a gently mocking rebuke of several British writers who feared that Catholic Emancipation presaged the end of the world. Could Andrew Jackson be worse than Catholic Emancipation?) And if young people were worrying about the disappearance of traditional avenues to power in a rapidly changing society, Carlyle suggested an intoxicating alternative: that their own spiritual struggle might itself *be* action of the most significant kind. They could render the greatest service to their communities simply by recording faithfully what they thought and felt. Such a call to action (O. B. Frothingham said) "kindled all honest hearts." Coleridge had offered philosophy, but what Carlyle offered was "better than philosophy. It was philosophy made vital with sentiment and purpose." Carlyle's new philosophy was the easier to assimilate because it resembled so closely the central Unitarian idea that spiritual life consisted in "self-culture," in the constant striving toward perfection that was every Christian's duty in this life of probation.

Nearly every one of the first-generation Transcendentalists confessed a debt to Carlyle, but Emerson, whose struggles with the problem of vocation were acute, was particularly moved by his words. Emerson's father William had been a theological liberal with an interest in *belles lettres* and had served on the editorial board of the *Monthly Anthology*. His death in 1811 left his widow, Ruth Haskins Emerson, obliged to run a boardinghouse to support her family of five surviving boys. The deprivations they faced, particularly during the difficult years of the War of 1812, left Emerson with a stinging memory of what poverty does to the spirit. But there were nourishing influences as well: the Boston Latin School, the intoxicating oratory of Edward Everett, the possibility of scholarships to Harvard.

Perhaps more important than any of these other influences was the mentorship of Mary Moody Emerson, William Emerson's sister, who lived with the family at various times during Waldo's youth and who kept up a vigorous correspondence with Waldo throughout her long life. Mary (1774–1863) was old enough to remember the earlier generations of family ministers, all of them believers in the doctrines advanced by Jonathan Edwards, convinced of the necessity of conversions and submission to the will of God. Her experience of the intensity of Puritan piety made her ridicule what her nephew later called the "poor, low, thin, unprofitable, unpoetical Humanitarians" of Boston's liberal religion. She kept a spiritual diary that spanned fifty years and ran to a thousand pages. While she lived with the Emerson family she supervised the education of the boys and wrote the family long prayers, which long after her death still echoed in Waldo's memory "with their prophetic and apocalyptic ejaculations." She was a voracious reader not only of theologians and philosophers (Plato, Plotinus, Spinoza, Cudworth, Butler, Clarke, Jonathan Edwards) but also of poets and prose writers (Akenside, Young, Byron, Wordsworth, de Staël). Even when she was not living with the Emerson family she superintended the boys' reading by letter and debated with them the meaning of what they had read. When Waldo entered Harvard in 1817 and made the unsettling acquaintance of the "Scotch Goliath," David Hume, he peppered her with letters containing Humean arguments in hopes that she might refute them. He often recorded her sayings in his journals and tended to adopt her oracular prose style whenever he strove after effects of elevation or spiritual intensity in his own writing.

Mary naturally wished to see the ministerial tradition of the family continued. At first the task fell to the eldest of the Emerson brothers, William (his father's namesake). After a period of schoolkeeping following his Harvard graduation in 1818 William had finally saved enough to pay for a trip to Göttingen to study theology – a course of study that was by now becoming familiar for Americans. He set sail for Europe in December 1823. At first William's letters home were enthusiastic. But gradually he found himself undergoing a crisis of faith similar to the one that seems to have afflicted Edward Everett ten years earlier. Unable to believe any longer in the historical veracity of everything in the Bible, and unable to reject the conclusions of the biblical criticism that had undermined his faith, William made a pilgrimage to Weimar to ask advice of Goethe, who had received earlier American students kindly. Goethe urged him not to abandon the ministry because he could not share all of his parishioners' beliefs. Even if William thought seriously of complying with this advice, he changed his mind during a rough voyage home, when a severe storm made him confront his conscience directly. He decided to give up the idea of becoming a minister, turning instead to the law.

Mary naturally was involved in the uproar that William's decision provoked in the family; to her, the whole episode testified to the "strange apathy of the skeptics of this period" who could bear to live without the presence of divinity. But William was not the only son in the family. Waldo, whose studies at Harvard's Divinity School were interrupted by bouts of ill health, received "approbation" to preach from the Middlesex Association of Unitarian Ministers on October 10, 1826. He preached in churches around New England until Boston's Second Church invited him to serve as its junior pastor. He was ordained on

March 11, 1829. When Henry Ware, Jr., the Second Church's senior pastor resigned to become Professor of Pulpit Eloquence at Harvard, Waldo was promoted to senior pastor in his place.

The doubts that had bedeviled Emerson throughout the 1820s — stemming from Hume's arguments against miracles and the German critics' attack on the factuality of biblical narratives — had begun to fade before the new light of transcendental philosophy as filtered through de Staël, Coleridge, and Carlyle. If the Reason *is* God, then God is interior to the self, and the self has a principle of illumination no empiricism can menace. All the searches after "evidences," the quests for the historical Jesus or the historical Moses, are fruitless attempts to use the mechanics of the Understanding to discover a truth perceptible to the Reason; they are rendered superfluous by the discovery that the divine is present here and now, in individual human beings, and that it requires of individuals only that they not deny those truths they inwardly perceive. Indeed, submission to the kind of external authority that founds theological schools represents the only apostasy Emerson dreaded — the denial of what one believes to be true in the face of pressure to acquiesce in the beliefs of others.

Such rigorous fidelity to inner conviction would sooner or later cause friction in the life of any practicing minister, even in a denomination as indulgent as the Unitarian. Emerson loved the act of preaching. In the distinctive style of his sermons (over two hundred are still extant) the reader can see many intimations of the style and content of his later orations and essays. His pastoral duties, on the other hand, became increasingly irksome. But the issue on which he finally chose to resign his pulpit had to do with a ritual he had grown to hate celebrating, the Lord's Supper.

Admission to the communion table in Puritan congregations had been restricted to those full church members who could testify to an experience of conversion. It was both a privilege and a badge of spiritual distinction. But with the growth of liberal religion, the monthly communion rite had come to seem to many Unitarians to be at best the relic of an outmoded metaphysical system, at worst an activity slightly ghoulish. An article in the *Christian Examiner* for December 1832 suggests that Emerson was not alone in feeling uncomfortable with the Lord's Supper. According to the writer of this article, many sincere Christians try to live by the precepts of Jesus but cannot bring themselves to take communion because the *elements* of communion service — the bread and the wine — "bear an aspect of strangeness and mystery" that fills the minds of those who would approach them with "dreadful and discouraging impressions."

The writer of the article sees in this attitude the remnants of the superstition Protestantism has only partially expunged:

The peculiar awe, by which this ordinance is separated from every other ordinance of God's appointment; the habit of singling it out, and exalting it above every other mode of worship and means of grace; the singular dread, in the minds of many, of contracting some heinous and mysterious guilt by a wrong participation of it; . . . the very aspect, too, of many communicants, of constraint and almost of distress; the evident feeling which many of them have, that the *elements* are the solemn things in this commemoration, and that it becomes them to have a very special impression of their minds, at the moment when they take into their hands these elements, − all these things, are to our apprehension, proofs, that there is still on this subject a great deal of superstition among us.

The rite the Puritans had celebrated as a confirmation of membership in the society of the Saints had now become an occasion for guilty introspection and feelings of inadequacy or at least a sad reminder of the fervency that has disappeared. The minister, too, was implicated in this unhappiness, because the invitations he issued to attend the Lord's Supper were received by his congregation as occasions for dismay.

   Some ministers nevertheless managed to overcome these scruples and revive enthusiasm for the rite in their congregations. Henry Ware, Jr., Emerson's predecessor at the Second Church, had given monthly lectures on the Lord's Supper that attracted large crowds of communicants. Ware's successful revival of the rite only made Emerson more acutely aware of his own discomfort when called on to celebrate it. "I cannot go habitually to an institution which they esteem holiest with indifference & dislike," he wrote. He proposed to the governing board of his church some revisions in the ceremony, including the removal of bread and wine; he wrote a letter to his parishioners explaining his feelings. And, on September 9, 1832, he preached a sermon, "The Lord's Supper," giving in fuller detail his reasons for believing that Jesus had not intended to institute a permanent ritual when he celebrated the Passover with his disciples and that, therefore, Christians are under no obligation to celebrate the Lord's Supper in any particular way.

   Parts of Emerson's sermon recall Locke's reasonable arguments in the commentaries on the Epistles of St. Paul, as when Emerson points out that Jesus' injunction to "Do this in memory of me" applies as much to the washing of the feet as it does to the consumption of bread and wine, yet no New England church seriously proposes to have its members wash one another's feet. Other parts are clearly influenced by the historical criticism of the Bible as practiced in Germany (Emerson had asked his brother William for help in marshalling arguments against the authority of the rite). The example of the Quakers, who rejected the communion rite along with all other rituals of the established church, may have lent support to Emerson's decision; he was an admirer of George Fox and had recently read William Sewall's history of the Quakers.

The deciding argument for Emerson, however, was more personal than any of these. "This mode of commemorating Christ is not suitable to me. That is reason enough why I should abandon it." Even if Christ *had* intended to enjoin a permanent commemoration upon all Christians, "and yet on trial it was disagreeable to my own feelings, I should not adopt it. I should choose other ways which he would approve more." Such calm insistence upon the primacy of individual judgment is the end point of Protestant Christianity, the point at which even the historical Jesus can be discarded as an impediment to the spirit of the religion he founded. "Forms are as essential as bodies. It would be foolish to declaim against them, but to adhere to one form a moment after it is outgrown is foolish. That form only is good and Christian which answers its end." What Emerson reveres in Christianity is "its reality, its boundless charity, its deep interior life, the rest it gives to mind, the echo it returns to my thoughts." Any form or rite that attempts to attract permanent devotion to itself should be rejected by the church, whose institutions "should be as flexible as the wants of men. That form out of which the life and suitableness have departed should be as worthless in its eyes as the dead leaves that are falling around us." Two main themes of Emerson's mature work are already stated clearly in this sermon: the primacy of the individual and the superiority of the creating spirit to any forms it has generated.

Emerson's young wife, Ellen Tucker Emerson, had died of tuberculosis in 1831; his own health had been poor, and the strain of the crisis in his ministry had worsened it. Many of his parishioners were reluctant to part with Emerson and might have been willing to allow him to celebrate the Lord's Supper as a commemorative rite without bread and wine, but the proprietors of pews finally voted 30 to 24 to accept his resignation. He decided to travel to Europe in hopes of regaining his health and strength. On Christmas Day 1832 he set sail from Boston in the trading ship *Jasper,* arriving in Malta in February 1833. Like most American tourists in that distant age when American tourists were a curiosity, Emerson sought out his literary heroes wherever he could and was received by them. Many of these meetings were disappointing, sometimes comically so. Wordsworth almost made him laugh by suddenly offering to repeat some newly written sonnets for him, striking a pose in the garden walk like a schoolboy reciting. The anti-Unitarian harangue Coleridge delivered when his guest identified himself as a Bostonian sounded suspiciously as if it had been memorized. Only Thomas Carlyle gave Emerson the kind of expansive, exuberant conversation he had come to the Old World for, and the visit began a friendship and a correspondence that was to last (with some notable ruptures) for as long as both men lived.

Before he left for Europe Emerson had managed to find out the identity of the author of the *Edinburgh* articles that had excited him. He was determined to track Carlyle down — no easy task, because Carlyle and his wife Jane were then living in an isolated farmhouse at Craigenputtock in the countryside southwest of Glasgow. To get there Emerson had to hire a gig in the nearest town and travel sixteen miles through the hills. But his reception by the Carlyles was as warm as he could have wished. When he departed a day later after a torrent of talk he left behind an affection almost as great as the one he himself felt. *Sartor Resartus* was about to start appearing serially in *Fraser's*, and Carlyle promised to send Emerson a copy of the whole when publication was complete. *Fraser's* had printed copies of the episodes and stitched the pages together for Carlyle to distribute privately; he sent Emerson one copy for his own use and a few others for distribution to sympathetic friends.

For his part, Emerson elected to become Carlyle's unpaid literary agent in America. Because the United States had no copyright agreement with Great Britain publishers were free to pirate British works without paying royalties to the authors. By negotiating with publishers in the United States on behalf of Carlyle for rights to first American publication of his works, Emerson was able to ensure that his friend received royalties from the American editions of his books. He forwarded all profits from these editions to Carlyle. The bank drafts he sent to Carlyle over the course of their long relationship eventually added up to more than seven hundred pounds. (Carlyle, pleased but embarrassed by this generosity, did what he could to reciprocate by arranging the London publication of Emerson's *Essays* in 1841.)

Emerson's fascination with Carlyle was widely shared among the young Boston liberals. His cousin George Ripley (1802–80), a Unitarian minister in Boston, was so overwhelmed by reading one of the stitched-together copies of *Sartor* that he immediately drafted an effusive four-page letter to Carlyle proclaiming himself Carlyle's grateful disciple. But devotion to Carlyle involved more than feelings of exhilaration, as Ripley and others well understood. The closing paragraphs of "Characteristics" invoke Ecclesiastes: "Whatsoever thy hand findeth to do, do it with all thy might." The necessity of action is made even more explicit in *Sartor Resartus*. If Carlyle preached a new gospel, how were his American disciples to put it into practice?

Because most of Carlyle's Boston admirers were members of the clergy or theological students they naturally thought first of church reform when they sought occasions for principled action. If the Unitarians who had initially broken with orthodoxy at the turn of the century had carried the standard of liberal religion as far as they could, their successors would seize it and carry it the rest of the way – to a religion both enlightened and truly "spiritual." At the same time the reforming spirit began to bear fruit among those who were outside the ministerial class altogether. This wider participation was what gave more than one observer the feeling that some great transformation was about to take place in New England society.

The expansion of the literary universe was perhaps the first evidence of the transformation. Carlyle's essays on German authors moved many of the young people to try to learn what seemed an alien and menacing tongue. Harvard professors like George Ticknor and Edward Everett had brought back from Germany a high regard for the achievements of German scholarship and of German humanism generally; when the young German émigré Charles Follen joined the Harvard faculty in 1825, he too helped to bring German authors into notice. But the most aggressive study seems to have begun outside the academy.

Margaret Fuller (1810–50) was the brilliant and precocious daughter of a strong-willed New England congressman who chose to give his first-born child the kind of education usually reserved for boys. Timothy Fuller, who had graduated from Harvard in 1801 and who served in the United States House of Representatives from 1817 to 1825, appointed himself tutor to his daughter and supervised her reading carefully even when he was away in Washington. When she was eight years old she was already studying Latin and arithmetic and reading accounts of the warrior kings Charles XIII of Sweden and Phillip II of Spain in Valpy's *Chronology of Ancient and English History;* the next year she was reading and memorizing passages of Griesbach's Greek New Testament (the text used by Harvard undergraduates). When she was fifteen she passed on to chemistry, philosophy, and Lord Kames's *Elements of Criticism.* That same year (1825) she addressed a letter to General Lafayette, who had been the recipient of universal adulation when he visited Boston the previous year. She tells him of the "ardent sentiment of affection and enthusiastic admiration" that pervades her soul whenever she thinks of him and of the "noble ambition" the contemplation of his character arouses in her. An odd sentence follows. "Should we both live, and it is possible to a female, to whom the avenues of glory are seldom accessible, I will recal[l] my name to your recollection." What seems missing from the sentence is the hope too intense to be named: *if it is nevertheless possible for me to achieve glory.*

Such ambition seems to lurk behind Fuller's later approach to intellectual life. She treated new areas of study as if they were territories to occupy and did so with a speed that astonished her contemporaries. Her social life in Boston in the late 1820s brought her into contact with the Unitarian literati; she heard Emerson preach and struck up an intense friendship with James Freeman Clarke, then a student at the Harvard Divinity School. Fired with enthusiasm for German literature by Carlyle's essays, she began to study German with Clarke in 1832. He later remembered: "Within a year she had read Goethe's Faust, Tasso, Iphigenie, Hermann and Dorothea, Elective Affinities, and Memoirs; Tieck's William Lovell, Prince Zerbino, and other works; Körner, Novalis, and something of Richter; all of Schiller's principal dramas, and his lyric poetry." When Clarke listened to her talk confidently about German intellectual life he had a "very decided feeling of mental inferiority," as he confided to his journal in 1832. "I felt how she traced ideas through minds & works, how questions rose before her, how she carried the initiative idea everywhere. In other words how comprehensive & understanding is her intellect." In contrast, his own mind seemed "a sheet of white paper on which any one might write."

Yet self-culture was not the only area of interest to the emerging group of Transcendentalists. If the German philosophers were right about the mind's structure and relation to the world, then the prevailing system of education was hopelessly and radically wrong. Rote learning, drill, and coercion were all cruel and wasteful ways to teach children. True education should be a coaxing out or an unfolding of the mind's intuitions, not a cramming session in which unrelated facts are stuffed into empty and recalcitrant heads. In the late 1820s James Marsh had introduced a curriculum at the University of Vermont designed to replace recitation with lectures and discussions and to replace the haphazard curriculum of most American colleges with one in which the various subjects would be arranged to exhibit "a development and a growth" so that studying it "should be a growing and enlarging process to the mind of the student." In 1834 a largely self-taught educator named Amos Bronson Alcott (1799–1888) established a school in Boston where he could put into practice his conviction that children possessed an intuitive knowledge of truth and hence required rather to be "drawn out" than indoctrinated.

After a hardscrabble rural childhood in Connecticut and a series of unprofitable *wanderjahre* as a feckless Yankee peddler in the South, Alcott had turned to teaching in the common schools of Connecticut. Disliking the harsh methods and stultifying practices of the usual schools of the period, he replaced the backless wooden benches of the standard country classroom with comfortable desks and chairs he himself built. He decorated the walls with pictures and cypress boughs and left a bare space in the center of the classroom for pleasant activities like dancing, in hopes that the students would come to associate the classroom with pleasure and not with pain. He tried to engage the students' interest with teaching materials designed to awaken their curiosity and draw upon their own experiences. Although he was by no means a slack disciplinarian he insisted that students themselves judge infractions of rules in a student court; malefactors were not beaten but were instead required to make a public apology to the school.

While he taught he was also trying to work out a theory of education and child development, reading contemporary reformers like the Swiss educator Pestalozzi and studying philosophers from Plato through Kant. On the face of it, education seemed to be a Lockean enterprise, an inscribing on the blank tablet of the mind. Clearly, no child came to school knowing Latin or plane geometry. But if the Platonic, Neoplatonic, and Kantian Idealists Alcott had been reading or reading about were correct, the child's mind already contained within it the principles the teacher was trying to instill. How could one reconcile the contradiction? The problem was solved for Alcott when he read Marsh's edition of Coleridge's *Aids to Reflection*. This work became for Alcott, as it did for so many of his generation, a way of embracing the delights of Idealism without having to give up the solid good of the material world. Alcott now decided that the goal of education was *both* to draw out the spirit of the child and to store in the child's mind useful knowledge. And this goal was achievable because the world itself had been created by God and bore evidence of its divine origin. The world and the mind were hence reciprocal influences, "appulsive and impulsive," which a true pedagogy could unite. "The analogy between the mind and the outward world is the parent of thought," Alcott asserted.

His methods won Alcott the affection of the students, but parents accustomed to measuring their child's progress by the amount of material memorized were impatient with him and unwilling to pay the higher fees he asked or purchase the books and supplies he demanded for his classroom. Although his school in Connecticut received praise from visiting educational reformers, he lost pupils and had to close it. For the next seven years Alcott wandered from place to place — to Boston, then to Germantown, Pennsylvania, then to Philadelphia, and finally back to Boston again — opening and closing schools, experimenting with educational techniques, and reading voraciously in philosophy, theology, and the literature of reform. When his wife, Abba, gave birth to daughters, he determined to observe their behavior closely, convinced that an account of the mind's development from earliest infancy would give better insight into human nature than any explanation the philosophers could provide. A sentence from the manuscript of observations he made about his second child, Louisa May Alcott (born November 29, 1832), suggests how vast his view of his own profession had become. "Education, when duly regarded, is the preservation of the relations of the human being to the universe."

Unfortunately, Alcott's skill at preserving a child's relations to the universe rarely helped him to preserve his own family from want. He was so dedicated an idealist that he reminded his friends of the ancient sages and so impractical a provider that he repeatedly plunged his family into destitution. Irrepressibly hopeful, opinionated, the strictest of vegetarians, he reminded more than one observer of Don Quixote. When his Philadelphia school was on the verge of collapse, one of Alcott's friends alerted William Ellery Channing, who had been among Alcott's earlier Boston patrons, and Channing promised his assistance in securing patrons for Alcott in Boston. In this project he was aided by the enthusiasm of Channing's admirer and secretary, Elizabeth Peabody (1804–94).

Peabody had been so impressed by the journals written by Alcott's young scholars and by Alcott's conversation when she met him ("He stayed and talked like an embodiment of intellect," she wrote) that she helped engage students for him. She also found a suitable room for the school in Boston's Masonic Temple and donated some of her own furniture to furnish the room. Most importantly, she agreed to serve Alcott as an assistant to teach those academic subjects – Latin, arithmetic, and geography – he lacked the formal education to provide.

Peabody's response, like those of Fuller and Alcott, shows how people not part of the traditional Boston–Cambridge educational system could be swept up in the excitement of the new movements and contribute to their development. Born in Billerica, Massachusetts, in 1804, she received a thorough education from her parents in history, rhetoric, and Latin before she began teaching school. Hopeful of earning more money to help educate her brothers by teaching school in either Boston or Cambridge she emigrated to the area in the early 1820s. Peabody was immediately dazzled by the "brilliancy" of Cambridge society. She heard Channing preach; she took Greek lessons from Ralph Waldo Emerson and became friendly with James Freeman Clarke. She wrote several history texts for schools (including studies of the Hebrews and the Greeks) and held evening "conversations" on history for women who would pay her ten dollars for a course of meetings on such subjects as "Some articles on the Poetry &c of the Heroic ages from several sources; Herodotus' History; – Schlegel on Dramatic literature as far as it is applicable to Greece & the time of Socrates." Another course she planned would include "Herder's exquisite book on the 'Spirit of Hebrew Poetry' – Parts of Michaelis upon the Jewish law – The Old Testament history." Ability to converse upon such subjects was a necessary accomplishment in a society where (as she had written in one of her first letters home) "You seem to be moving all the time for every thing about you is an a state of progressive improvement and if you stand still – bye and bye they will forget you were ever 'one of them.' "

In 1833 Johann Gottfried van Herder's *Spirit of Hebrew Poetry* had just been published by James Marsh. The book by now was fifty years old; Moses Stuart had tried to interest Edward Everett in translating it as long ago as 1818, but the task remained unattempted until Marsh began publishing parts of his translation serially in the *Biblical Repertory* in 1826. Many changes had taken place in biblical criticism since Herder's book had originally appeared in 1782, and scholars in New England were already using the work of later and technically more accomplished scholars like Schleiermacher. Nevertheless, when Marsh completed his translation of *The Spirit of Hebrew Poetry* in 1833 and issued it from the same University of Vermont press that had published *Aids to Reflection* in 1829 and *The Friend* in 1831, it provoked considerable interest among the general reading public. Elizabeth Peabody wrote a series of articles prompted by Marsh's translation, for the *Christian Examiner* in 1833 and 1834 (until Andrews Norton, disturbed by the articles, stopped their publication). Herder's approach to the study of texts from "primitive" societies shaped Peabody's understanding of ancient cultures for the rest of her life.

Herder had become persuaded that (as one modern biblical scholar says) "poetry is in its origins no mere deliberate artifact, and language no mere signpost representing sense data and the substances for which they stand." Among primitive peoples poetry is a "spontaneous and natural expression" of feeling and perception: they speak in figures, and their narrative naturally assumes the shape of myth. "In the poetical vein of our native tongue," Peabody wrote, "we must find the key of interpretation to the language of the Old Testament, which is entirely primitive." God speaks to each generation in the language appropriate to it, and the truths about the outward Creation he gave to the ancient Hebrews "were conveyed, not with the logical precision in which they are now stated, but embodied in a narrative, brilliant, bold, glowing, full of imagery, calculated to take hold of the imagination and be amalgamated with the soul."

Obviously, Herder's *Spirit of Hebrew Poetry* offered weapons to anyone eager to attack the prevailing notion of biblical miracles as historical accounts of empirically verifiable violations of the natural order. But even more important, for the moment, was the secret stimulus given to creativity by Herder's glowing evocation of primitive poetry. If the Hebrews were not passive instruments of divine inspiration but rather were poets who perceived vividly and spoke faithfully of what they saw and heard, might not a similar adjustment in vision and a similar determination to be forthright produce a *modern* scripture? And might not a style "brilliant, bold, glowing, full of imagery" reawaken the piety that had animated those early men?

4

"ANNUS MIRABILIS"

I N THE SPRING OF 1836, the year that Perry Miller would call the
"*Annus Mirabilis*" of the Transcendentalist movement, the American Unitarian Association issued a small pamphlet entitled *Christianity as a
Purely Internal Principle*. Its author was a forty-year-old minister named Convers Francis (1795–1863), a genial man whom O. B. Frothingham called "a
liberal scholar, in the best sense of the phrase; learned without pedantry;
open to the light from every quarter; an enormous reader of books; a great
student of German philosophy and divinity, as few at that time were."
Francis had occupied the pulpit at Watertown, Massachusetts, since 1819,
preaching a liberal Christianity that emphasized the human element in the
Bible and publishing reviews in the *Christian Examiner* in which he affirmed
his belief that the human soul was "a particle of the divine mind." In
Christianity as a Purely Internal Principle Francis argues that Christianity's distinction lies in its having been "the first and only system, which professed to build its
kingdom wholly within the soul of man." All attempts to derive religious feeling
from something outward – whether the rituals of the Catholic church or the
emotional conversion experiences of the evangelicals – are false to the spirit of
Christianity's founder, who asked "for no province but the affections, principles,
and motives of man, – for no throne but his heart."

Through
Heart

Francis's pamphlet, an eloquent expression of Unitarian piety, contained
nothing radical, though its emphasis on Christianity as an inward principle
of spiritual enlargement made it dear to the younger people whom he served
as friend and mentor. Francis's slight reputation for daring came from his
willingness to entertain ideas bolder than his own. But even that much
openness was a welcome change from the cautious tone that marked the
regularly scheduled meetings for Unitarian clergy. These gatherings were
increasingly irksome to the younger clergy, who were reluctant to raise
subjects their seniors disapproved of yet who felt frustrated at not being able
to discuss freely the moral and theological issues that concerned them.

These younger clergy decided to form a club of their own. Frederic Henry
Hedge, from his post in Bangor, Maine, had suggested the meeting in a
letter to Emerson during the summer. "The plan is this, to have a meeting,

46

annual or oftener if possible, of certain likeminded persons of our acquaintance for the free discussion of theological & moral subjects," Hedge wrote.
Why was such an association necessary? Because the "lamentable want of
courage" shown at regular conventions of Unitarian ministers and the diffi-
dence of younger ministers in the presence of their "elders & betters" made
candid discussion of theological issues impossible. Membership in this new
society, which was to be by invitation, would be limited to Unitarian ministers like themselves (though Emerson insisted on being allowed to invite
Bronson Alcott). The sole rule the members agreed to was that no one whose
presence might prevent discussion of any particular subject could be invited
to meetings. This club, which was to meet some thirty times in the next four
years, was first called by Emerson "The Symposium"; he later called it by the
less pretentious title "Hedge's Club," because it usually met when Hedge
visited from Bangor. Most people simply called it the Transcendental Club,
using the nickname they were beginning to apply to all members of the
movement.

Hedge, Emerson, George Ripley, and Emerson's cousin George Putnam
met in Cambridge on September 8, 1836, to plan the new club, which
would hold its first official meeting at Ripley's house in Boston eleven days
later. On September 9, 1836, a small book entitled Nature was published in
Boston by James Monroe and Company. The author of the ninety-five-page
book was anonymous, though area residents soon guessed that the author was
Emerson. The book's title page bore an epigraph from Plotinus that spoke of
nature as "but an image or imitation of wisdom, the last thing of the soul."
Later in the book Emerson would say that this absolute Idealism can at one
stroke transfer nature into the mind, leaving matter behind like an outcast
corpse. In its calm assertiveness and refusal to descend into argument, this
brief quotation from the third-century Egyptian philosopher reminds us of a
time when poetry and philosophy were still (to use one of Emerson's favorite
words in Nature) "coincident."

Yet the first words of Nature's "Introduction" come from a different stylistic universe altogether, one full of satire and scorn. "Our age is retrospective.
It builds the sepulchres of the fathers." In two sentences Emerson seems to
dismiss his own era as one in which piety to the dead has taken the place of
fresh creation, and reverence is indistinguishable from morbidity. But then
he proceeds to hold out hope, using the burly Saxon idiom Carlyle favored in
his more encouraging moments. Why, after all, should we pay homage only
to the dead? The whole lesson of nature is regeneration. "The sun shines to-
day also. There is more wool and flax in the fields. There are new lands, new
men, new thoughts. Let us demand our own works and laws and worship."

These two events – the publication of Emerson's Nature and the formation of the Transcendental Club — both suggest something important about Transcendentalism. We often think of the movement as an affair of isolated selves writing in lonely integrity, like Thoreau at Walden Pond. But Transcendentalism was also very much a coterie affair, and the strong emotions it evoked from its participants show how much fire lay beneath the native frost of the New England character. In 1836 few of the darker passions that might be generated by such elevated hopes and intense communing were yet visible. The Transcendentalists then felt confident that they were the conduits for a stream of revolutionary ideas from Europe intended to break up the last ice floes of provincial culture, that they were the renewers of spiritual life. Nowhere is the excitement more infectious than in Emerson's little book, which begins by inquiring "to what end is nature?" and (after carefully ascending a ladder of nature's "uses" to humanity) ends by offering a fable of apocalypse in which fallen man recognizes in the "great apparition" of external nature merely the form of the divine body he has alienated.

Unitarianism had always exalted the study of nature as a way of learning to admire God's infinitely wise design, and Emerson had from an early age filled his journals with facts gleaned from his scientific reading, convinced that "the axioms of physics translate the laws of ethics" (a maxim he borrowed from Madame de Staël's *De l'Allemagne*). His sermons were made vivid by his free use of these natural analogies. As he became increasingly dissatisfied with Christianity as a historical religion he longed to find its ethical truths inscribed elsewhere. Natural science provided one way of transforming the vast text of nature into legible truths; the Swedenborgian doctrine of "correspondence" seemed to offer another.

Emerson was strongly attracted to the system of beliefs that American admirers of the Swedish visionary Emanuel Swedenborg (1688–1772) were expounding in their periodical the *New Jerusalem Magazine*. The doctrine of "correspondence," or the belief that each object in the sensible world corresponds to some truth in the moral world, offered hope that nature itself might be a storehouse of meanings more coherent and more universally accessible than Scripture. Although Emerson rejected the rigid sectarianism of the Swedenborgians, he found the idea of correspondence intoxicating.

A simple translation of natural objects into meanings is one kind of "correspondence," but Emerson often uses the word to refer to a different kind of tallying, one that suggested itself to him when he visited the Jardin des Plantes in Paris during his European tour of 1833. As he stood before the specimens in the cabinet of natural history, he believed that he could see "the upheaving principle of life" suggested by the rows and rows of related specimens. "Not a form so grotesque, so savage, nor so beautiful but is an expression of some property in man the observer, — an occult relation be-

Correspondential World

VAST Allegorical universe

NATURE AS SACRED TEXT — NOT Bible

tween the very scorpions and man." This revelation caused him to announce, "I am moved by strange sympathies, I say continually, 'I will be a naturalist.'" Here the human being is at the center of the correspondential universe, and the natural world radiates out from him like a vast Unconscious; the task of the naturalist is to reverse the process (whatever it was) that alienated these human properties into the foreign shapes that constitute the vast allegory we behold as the universe.

Emerson's desire to explore these two kinds of "correspondence" received an unexpected stimulus from the new lyceum movement just gaining strength in the United States. When he returned home from Europe, Emerson discovered that this adult education movement (loosely modeled on the *Lyceum* workingmen's colleges in England) and its appetite for trained lecturers gave him a handy pulpit from which to preach on any topic that appealed to him. Throughout the winter of 1833–4 Emerson delivered a number of lectures on natural history to different groups in Boston. Writing a course of lectures for a lyceum audience was very much like writing sermons, except that in Emerson's lectures nature had now become the sacred text to be expounded instead of merely the source from which illustrative metaphors could be drawn. "A fact is an epiphany of God."

Still, isolated facts, no matter how radiant with spiritual meaning, could never compose themselves into a new scripture without *theory,* an ordering principle emanating from the mind that arranges phenomena in such a way that they suggest the presence of an underlying *law* – as the phenomena of electricity suggest the more general law of *polarity* operating throughout nature. These terms are taken from Coleridge, whose "Essays on Method" in *The Friend* Emerson studied while he was working on *Nature.* By March 1836 Emerson had hit on a scheme that would allow him to arrange and classify the hundreds of observations about nature he had been collecting in his journals for years. Nature strives upward. It ministers to human needs, satisfies the love of beauty, furnishes us with language by providing sensible images for abstract thoughts. "Finally; Nature is a discipline, & points to the pupil & exists for the pupil. Her being is subordinate, his is superior. Man underlies ideas. Nature receives them as her god." But Idealism, though it seems at first like the goal toward which nature is tending, is quickly swallowed up in even vaster schemes for human glorification. As Emerson complains in "Spirit," the chapter that follows "Idealism," a theory of nature that only denies the existence of matter cannot "satisfy the demands of the spirit. It leaves God out of me."

Emerson means that final sentence quite literally. No religion or philosophical system that places God outside the self seems credible to him; it denies that primary experience of divinity that is exhilaration's gift to the

NATURE PROVIDES Sensible images for ABSTRACT Ideas

God outside the self is unbelievable denies experience of divine within —

influx of Power

spiritual intuition

soul. However impotent human beings seem when they compare themselves to the vast forces of the natural world, they still have sensations of omnipotence in those isolated moments when the "axis of vision" becomes coincident with the "axis of things." Records of such influxes of power are sprinkled throughout *Nature,* most notoriously in the "transparent eyeball" passage from its first chapter: "Standing on the bare ground, – my head bathed by the blithe air, and uplifted into infinite space, – all mean egotism vanishes. I become a transparent eye-ball; I am nothing; I see all; the currents of the Universal Being circulate through me; I am part or particle of God."

The *conviction* that nature is phenomenal and the *feeling* that we are divine combine to provide at last an answer to those venerable questions, "What is matter? Whence is it? and Whereto?" If we carefully attend to the truths that arise to us out of the recesses of consciousness we will learn that

✱✱

spirit does not act upon us from without, that is, in space and time, but spiritually, or through ourselves. Therefore, that spirit, that is, the Supreme Being, does not build up nature around us, but puts it forth through us, as the life of the tree puts forth new branches and leaves through the pores of the old.

The model for this curious extrusion theory of creation might have come from Fichte, whose ideas Emerson had found summarized in Carlyle's essay on Novalis, or from Alcott, who had cobbled together his own mythology from the Platonic and Neoplatonic philosophers he had read in Thomas Taylor's translations. Emerson had met Alcott when he visited the Temple School; the two had immediately become attracted to one another, and Alcott had visited Emerson in Concord and involved him in voluminous and gratifying conversation. But however Emerson came by his extrusion theory of creation, he finally dismisses it as inadequate. Though it reassures us that "the world proceeds from the same spirit as the body of man," it does not tell us how to make that world subject to our *will.* In the sexually charged language that dominates the closing chapters of *Nature,* Emerson complains, that "its serene order is inviolable by us."

"Prospects," the final chapter in *Nature,* does not offer advice about violating the serene order of nature, but it does explain how nature came to frustrate our desires in the first place. Emerson explains this not in discursive prose but in a fable, like the small fables embedded in Platonic dialogues or the *Märchen* contained in the German texts described by Carlyle. The fable in *Nature* describes man as a divine being who, fallen into division, is now the "dwarf of himself," timidly adoring a universe that is his forgotten emanation. The only divine power yet remaining in this dwarf is "instinct," a power not inferior but superior to man's will. Instinct is to the will what the Reason is to the intellect, and when we learn to work upon nature with all

Man once was divine now fallen – a dwarf
• instinct is to will
• what Reason is to intellect

[handwritten top margin: Emerson Subordinates - Visible + outward To inward + invisible / falleness illusion, Resulting from weakness of will]

our might we will find that the "fallenness" of nature was an illusion created by the weakness of our wills. "The problem of restoring to the world original and eternal beauty, is solved by the redemption of the soul." When that restored world will come we cannot say, for it is, like the kingdom of heaven in the Bible, something that "cometh not with observation." But it will be beyond our present "dream of God."

Alcott was delighted with Emerson's little book, describing it in his journal as "the production of a spiritualist, subordinating the visible and outward to the inward and invisible." He was pleased to discover in it allusions to the vast manuscript on childhood development, entitled "Psyche," he had left with Emerson the summer before. From England, Carlyle praised *Nature* as the "foundation and Ground-plan" on which he was sure Emerson would build his future achievement. In Boston a reform-minded Unitarian minister named Orestes Brownson (1803–76) reviewed *Nature* in the weekly paper he edited, the *Boston Reformer;* he hailed it as "an index to the spirit which is silently at work among us, as a proof that the mind is about to receive a new and more glorious manifestation." But Brownson's praise was tempered by dismay at Emerson's philosophical Idealism. To doubt the existence of the phenomenal world as Berkeley and Fichte had done seemed to Brownson to begin a process of questioning that would end by undermining the questioner. "He who denies the testimony of his senses, seems to have no ground for believing the apperceptions of consciousness; and to deny those is to set oneself afloat upon the ocean of universal scepticism."

Brownson differed in significant ways from most of his clerical colleagues. Orestes Brownson was born in 1803, the son of a poor Vermont farmer who died leaving his widow with six young children. She tried to keep the family together, but eventually she had to place Orestes and his twin sister, Daphne, with an elderly couple to raise. Strict Congregationalists, they gave him an appetite for religion that had him reading volumes of theology and arguing predestination while he was still a child. He early determined to become a minister, though his formal schooling had been limited to a brief stint in an academy in upstate New York, where his reunited family had moved when he was fourteen.

Brownson's spiritual life was restless, driven by a need for solace and a hunger for doctrinal consistency that sent him on a pilgrimage through various denominations. Moved by a Presbyterian sermon when he was about nineteen he joined the Presbyterian church, but he found himself repelled by its Calvinist theology. When he was subsequently stricken with a serious illness he had time to study the Universalist tracts a proselytizing aunt urged upon him and decided to join the Universalists. He liked the Universalist opposition to Calvinist preoccupation with sin and damnation as well as its

[handwritten bottom margin: Outward + Visible subordinated To inward + invisible]

reassurance that all men would be saved. When he had recovered from his illness he began a career as a Universalist minister.

His demands for logical consistency, however, soon made havoc of Brownson's second faith. He distressed his new colleagues by airing his doubts in the *Gospel Advocate and Universal Investigator,* a Universalist journal of which he had become editor. Perplexed by the problem of social evil here on earth, he went to hear the British radical Frances Wright lecture when she came to Utica, New York, and struck up a friendship with her. She led him to read the writings of the British social reformer Robert Owen, whose suggestions for solving the problems of poverty and degradation intrigued him, if they did not entirely convince him. He joined the Workingmen's party and briefly edited one of their newspapers, the New York *Free Enquirer.* By 1830, however, both his faith in the party and his faith in God were beginning to crumble. Labor seemed to him too weak ever to compete politically in the United States with capital; and the "natural theology" of moral philosophers like William Paley (1743–1805) seemed so unconvincing that reading them precipitated Brownson headlong into the skepticism of Hume.

After a few months of lingering in the bleak world to which his reason seemed to condemn him, his heart, that "witness within" whose testimony he found corroborated by the whole of external nature, recalled Brownson to faith. A friend read to him Channing's sermon "Likeness to God," and it so impressed him that he began to consider Channing his "spiritual father" and to think of himself as a Unitarian. He persuaded a Unitarian congregation in New Hampshire to offer him a position as its minister.

Gradually Brownson's vigorous preaching and lyceum lecturing attracted notice in Boston, where he often traveled. George Ripley befriended him and urged him to accept pulpits closer to Boston. He served for two years in Canton, Massachusetts, whose working-class population reawakened in him an interest in social issues which his contemporary reading in the works of Saint-Simon (1760–1825) helped to crystallize into a philosophy of reform. Brownson decided that Christianity was to be a social gospel: The "church of the future" he imagined would employ moral reform to make war against the personal selfishness that underlies systems of social inequality. Ripley had high hopes that Brownson's preaching might attract hearers among the working classes where Unitarianism's appeal was marginal and so help revitalize a denomination whose decorousness threatened to extinguish its life.

By the time Brownson had moved to Chelsea and started holding independent services in Boston during the early months of 1836 he had begun to speak out frankly against social inequality. On the last Sunday of May he preached a discourse, "The Wants of the Times," that warned of the conflict breaking out all over the world "between the many and the few, the privileged and the underprivileged." He urged the formation of a Society for Christian Union and Progress that would put into effect the principles of Jesus, "the prophet of the workingmen."

Doubtless at Ripley's urging, Brownson was invited to the first full meeting of the Transcendental Club on September 19, 1836. He proved to be a difficult companion – a brilliant talker fond of argument and impatient with woolly reasoning, who chewed tobacco and pounded on the table when he was angry. By the summer of 1837 the club's members appear to have decided that Brownson had (as Hedge later put it) become unbearable, for his name no longer appears on any lists of the members who attended meetings. But in 1836 he still was publicly identified with the Transcendentalists, and the book that he published on November 29 of that year was interpreted as one of their manifestos.

New Views of Christianity, Society and the Church drew heavily on Brownson's reading in French and German authors, particularly Victor Cousin, whose philosophy of eclecticism was naturally appealing to a self-taught man. In *New Views* Brownson unfolds a theory of history that portrays civilization as a continual struggle between spiritualism and materialism. Jesus, as the God-man, unites both spirit and matter (this is what is meant by "the atonement"); the "church of the future" must do so too. So far Brownson's doctrine sounds innocuous enough, yet the historical interpretations he generates with it are surprising. The "spiritual principle" is represented in history by Asia, Egypt, Judea, and the Catholic church; the material principle, by Greece, Rome, and Protestantism.

Protestantism (which was necessary to rescue the human race from the excesses of the spiritual principle) as a material religion is friendly to civil and political liberty and to industry; its exploits in recent history have been nothing short of miraculous. It imagines for man "a new paradise . . . inaccessible to the serpent, more delightful than that which Adam lost" and tries to realize that paradise on earth. Protestantism reaches its ultimate development in the American and French revolutions, particularly in the latter. "God was converted into a symbol of the human reason, and man into the Man-Machine; Spiritualism fell, and the Revolution marked the complete triumph of Materialism."

But the revolution failed, and men once again took "refuge in heaven." The English discovered the mysticism of the East in the Hindu scriptures, and the influence of the spiritual world is once again visible in European literature, in Byron, Wordsworth, and the Schlegels. A new synthesis is now possible. Unitarianism, as the "last word of Protestantism," clearly belongs to the material order: "It vindicates the rights of the mind, accepts and uses the reason, contends for civil freedom and is social, charitable, and humane."

Like all Protestant sects it lacks true spirituality; such piety as it has is merely a reminiscence of the beliefs of the medieval church. "It saves the Son of man, but sometimes loses the Son of God." Its contribution to progress up to now has been largely negative, "a work of destruction," clearing away the rubbish of the old church to make way for the future.

Unitarianism is the only sect that has "the requisite union of piety and mental freedom"; it alone can create a philosophy "which explains Humanity, determines its wants and the means of supplying them." Out of Unitarianism therefore shall come the "church of the future" and the salvation of the human race. Traditional Unitarians must have felt that such left-handed compliments to Unitarianism were almost worse than the abuse of the Calvinists; the more far-seeing among them might even have been able to predict that Brownson would end his spiritual quest in 1844 by converting to Roman Catholicism. But the radical theses he was propounding were largely overlooked amid the outbreak of hostilities in another controversy involving Brownson's friend George Ripley.

In March 1836 Ripley had published a long article entitled "Schleiermacher as a Theologian" in the *Christian Examiner.* In it he spoke favorably of Schleiermacher's attempt to formulate a "religion of the heart" based on intuition and a sense of communion with God. Later in the year Ripley reviewed the British Unitarian James Martineau's *Rationale of Religious Inquiry* (1836), which had attempted to apply inductive logic to questions of religious certainty and had placed great stress upon the miracles of Jesus as authenticating events. Ripley did not deny that the miracles had occurred and were important, but he argued that Jesus' moral teachings were self-evidently true and did not need to be confirmed by miraculous displays of power.

When Andrews Norton read Ripley's review he was furious enough to consider severing all connection with the *Christian Examiner,* of which he was an official "sponsor." Norton had retired from Harvard in 1830 to devote himself full time to his scholarship, but he had become increasingly distressed by the drift toward political and theological radicalism among the faculty and students of the Divinity School as well as by the refusal of the *Christian Examiner* to close its pages to writers Norton considered irresponsible. He had earlier tried and failed to convince the *Examiner*'s editor that the magazine was the "sole work in the world" in which intelligent Christians could express "correct views of religion"; allowing it to be polluted by the "crude thoughts" of undisciplined speculators was a betrayal of public trust (Norton to James Walker, December 7, 1835).

Norton finally decided to remain a sponsor of the *Examiner;* but he published a letter in the Boston *Daily Advertiser* on November 5, 1836, attacking Ripley

Miracles are proof of divine origin of Christianity [handwritten annotation]

and warning of the danger of doctrines that tend to destroy the only evidence upon which belief in the divine origin of Christianity can rest. Ripley replied in a dignified letter four days later that though he remembered with gratitude the instruction he had received from his former teacher, surely Norton of all people was scarcely in a position to brand doctrines as heretical or try to suppress their publication. Interest in the controversy was sufficiently great for the weekly *Christian Register* to print the exchange of letters in its November 12 issue; later correspondents continued the controversy.

Late November offered more material from the Transcendentalists to distress conservative Unitarians. On November 14 Emerson's childhood friend William Henry Furness (1802–96), now a Unitarian minister in Philadelphia, published his *Remarks on the Four Gospels.* In *Remarks* Furness attempts to replace the standard Unitarian interpretation of miracles as an interruption of the laws of nature (given by Channing in his famous Dudleian lecture, "The Evidences of Revealed Religion") with one that would see miracles as the "demonstrations of a supreme spiritual force, existing in the nature of things" and acting in harmony with the other agencies we witness every day. At about the same time, Ripley published a pamphlet, provocatively entitled *Discourses on the Philosophy of Religion Addressed to Doubters Who Wish to Believe,* which attempts to turn the tables on attackers like Norton by arguing that people who are afraid of free discussion are the real religious doubters – fearful that open inquiry will expose some rottenness at the core of their faith.

Ripley announces that he has no wish to discredit the Christian miracles; he says he believes in them and finds them holy and precious. But he refuses to believe that "human nature is so shackled and hemmed in, even in its present imperfect state, as to be confined to the objects made known by the eye of sense." Only the things which are unseen possess independent reality: "The material universe is the expression of an Invisible Wisdom and Power." To focus our attention exclusively upon that universe – the "dry husk and shell of matter" – in an attempt to verify faith is to "lose sight of the Infinite and Divine energy" from which matter draws its being. How much more pious it is to trust to the voice of the Reason within us, that Reason which is an "emanation from the mind of God" and a "partaker of the divine nature."

These opening squalls in the controversy over biblical miracles that would occupy so much of the next ten years were soon swallowed up by a much larger storm of public outrage. In the last week of December 1836, Bronson Alcott published the first volume of his *Conversations with Children on the Gospels,* a record of the conversations he had had with children in his Temple School. That school had opened its doors on September 22, 1834, with about thirty pupils, many of them from influential Boston families. For a time all seemed to be going well. Alcott's assistant, Elizabeth Peabody, had pub-

lished her one-volume *Record of a School* in 1835; it explained Alcott's methods and philosophy and had attracted favorable notices, though it did not
lead to the rush of new enrollments Alcott had hoped for. Educational
reformers from as far away as Germany began to visit the school and seek
Alcott's advice.

There were, however, also rumblings of discontent. Alcott's insistence on
relating every subject to the spirit began to alarm some of the parents.
Apparently, someone must have told Alcott that his teaching methods were
looked on with disfavor, for one day he asked the children if they would like
him to stop talking about conscience and spirit and begin teaching exclusively about rocks and trees and engines. In a letter Peabody described how
the children responded to Alcott's question: "One boy got up. – Oh *he is so
lazy* he cannot even play – said ever so many." Several more stalwarts braved
community disfavor and stood up to cast their votes for the material world,
but when Alcott warned them he could no longer read to them out of
Pilgrim's Progress or from Spenser (because these works involved the conscience), their opposition collapsed. "Well, said Mr. A. who had rather the
school would be as it is full of thoughts & feelings about conscience, God, the
mind, the soul – with all my punishments & all my disagreeable fault finding & the necessity of self-control & selfknowledge &c &c &c – They all rose
with acclamation" (Peabody to Elizabeth Davis Bliss, 1835).

Presumably Peabody meant only to suggest the children's love for Alcott
by this brief sketch, but his considerable talent for moral coercion emerges
from it as well. Her growing discomfort with this aspect of Alcott's pedagogy was one of the things that led her to resign from the school in the spring
of 1836. But by that time she had already completed a second book about the
school, recording a series of conversations about the gospels that Alcott had
begun in the school on Saturday, October 10, 1835. These "conversations"
were meant both to illustrate Alcott's teaching methods and to serve as
empirical proofs of the truths of Christianity. As Peabody pointed out in her
introduction to the two-volume record, "Mr. Alcott felt that what the children should freely say, would prove to be a new order of Christian Evidences,
by showing the affinity of their natures with that of Jesus." The spirit
incarnate will recognize the spirit inscribed, and the "juvenile commentary"
thus produced would serve, Alcott hoped, as "a revelation of Divinity in the
soul of childhood." With such living evidences in the souls of little children,
the elaborate structures of Unitarian historical scholarship – trying to trace
testimony back to the original witnessers of miracles – would be shown to be
unnecessary.

To provide the texts around which his conversations would be organized
Alcott selected and arranged passages from the Gospels in the manner of an

old gospel harmony to form a chronological account of the life of Jesus. He began with the opening chapters of John, then moved on to Luke for the Annunciation and Nativity stories, and continued until he reached the fiftieth conversation at the end of the second volume, which carried the children only as far as the twelfth chapter of Matthew and the third chapter of Mark. Alcott would read a biblical passage aloud to the children (who ranged in age from six to twelve) and then ask them what they liked or remembered about it. Sometimes he asked them to visualize the scene, oftener to speculate or comment upon matters discussed in the text. At the end of most conversations he asked them if they understood what the subject of the conversation had been.

Such methods sound innocent enough in themselves, but in Alcott's hands they had results that led Andrews Norton to judge the published book "one-third . . . absurd, one-third blasphemous, and one-third obscene." Alcott's serene conviction that the souls of the children already contained the loftiest philosophical truths led him to try to coax abstract principles out of them by the Socratic method. The resulting dialogue (as the children adopted his terminology and tried with increasing desperation to guess what he was driving at) often sounds as if it had been written by a particularly relentless dramatist of the absurd.

Bostonians might have forgiven Alcott his unorthodox teaching methods, but they could not agree with him that such subjects as conception, childbirth, and circumcision should be discussed with the children as openly as angels, miracles, or the sayings of Jesus. The conversations that deal with these subjects are often sweet and funny (as when a chivalrous little boy suggests that the pain of childbirth ought to be given to men "since they are so much stronger"), and they seem so innocent to a modern reader that it takes an effort of historical imagination to understand how anyone could have thought them obscene. But Elizabeth Peabody had become worried enough about possible scandal by the summer of 1836 to beg Alcott by letter to excise certain things from her written transcription of the conversations before the book was published. She did not wish it known that she had even participated in the conversation about the Circumcision, and she thought that certain remarks – such as little Josiah Quincy's inspired guess that the infant's body was formed "out of the naughtiness of other people" – should be eliminated entirely. Alcott complied with her first request, but printed all the remarks she had marked out as possibly dangerous or offensive in footnotes with the heading "Restored by the Editor" – where, naturally, they caught the eye of critics more easily.

Alcott also adopted the book as his own, though in fact only an editor's preface and an introduction were written by him. The rest of the book is as much Peabody's as was *Record of a School*. The two title pages of the printed *Conversations* suggest as much. The first one reads "CONVERSATIONS / WITH / CHILDREN / ON / THE GOSPELS; / CONDUCTED AND EDITED / BY A. BRONSON ALCOTT." But beneath this page is another, similar in format: "RECORD / OF / CONVERSATIONS ON THE GOSPELS / HELD IN / MR. ALCOTT'S SCHOOL; / UNFOLDING / THE DOCTRINE AND DISCIPLINE / OF / HUMAN CULTURE."

This first volume of *Conversations* begins with a "Recorder's Preface" (by Peabody), an "Editor's Preface" (by Alcott) and an "Introduction" – "The Doctrine and Discipline of Human Culture," which Alcott had written and published separately as a pamphlet in the summer of 1836 and which he now reprinted as the clearest statement of his educational philosophy. The remainder of the long work is a fascinating case study in educational single-mindedness and the fluctuating strategies of the children who have to cope with it. They are sometimes charmed, frequently perplexed, and occasionally stoutly resistant to the things their peculiar teacher is trying to get them to say.

Peabody takes down the conversations but also participates in them (she appears in the text as Recorder); she becomes more and more willing to argue openly with Alcott as the book progresses, even taking him aside at some points to object strenuously to what he is doing. As the book proceeds we gradually become aware of her artistry. She arranges the conversations with an unerring sense of what makes them at once touching and funny. For Peabody is a keen ironist, as anyone who has read her letters can testify, and in presenting a series of the conversations between an innocent reformer and a roomful of children encouraged to be perfectly candid she finds rich possibilities for humor.

The children are all empiricists, as sturdy as Locke and as skeptical as Hume, and for the most part they stubbornly resist Alcott's attempt to tow them into the Unconditioned. Moreover, they are Bostonians, the children of the city's merchant and professional elite, and their view of the world reflects the values of their parents. One boy imagines the angel visiting Joseph in a "splendid" room. Peabody asks him how a poor carpenter in Nazareth could have a splendid room. The boy replies, "An angel would not come into a poor looking room. It would not be appropriate." After this Peabody adds a parenthetical note: "After some conversation, Edward seemed to think that such outward splendors were not particularly appropriate to angels, at least, upholstery." When Alcott asks if there are any students who worship money, two boys boldly stand up, prompting another to jeer and point out that one of them had wanted to know what became of the money when Jesus overturned the tables of the moneychangers in the Temple. When Alcott asks a boy about his mission in life the boy replies promptly, "I shall use my Soul in selling oil."

The conflict of wills grows stronger in those more important conversations dealing with matters such as miracles and the relationship of human nature to divinity. These were the conversations (even more than the ones about birth and circumcision) that provoked the real outrage against Alcott in the public press early in 1837, outrage that led to the vilification of Alcott and the collapse of the school. Ministers were furious at Alcott for trespassing on their territory; they were also horrified by what seemed like a caricature of certain tendencies that were always latent in Unitarianism – the belief in human perfectibility, for instance – but that Alcott insisted in carrying far beyond what Unitarians sanctioned.

The scandalized ministers and parents ought to have been cheered by what they read in the book when it treats of these subjects, for in fact the children are as resistant to attacks on miracles as they are to the idea of their own divinity. When Alcott asks whether the changing of water to wine at Cana was a miracle worked in the minds of the guests or upon the water, a boy named Augustine replies, "There must have been real wine made, for the governor of the feast tasted it." Alcott tries to nudge them into seeing the miracle as "emblematic," but when he asks them how many "think Jesus turned water into wine, literally and actually," all rise. When he asks them if they would have considered this a very great feat if Jesus had never performed another miracle, a boy named Welles candidly admits, "If he had not done any other miracle, I should have thought that Jesus brought the wine himself." So, too, when Alcott asks "Do any of you think, that if your bodies were taken away, you should be God?," he can get a girl named Emma to concede only that she might be "a part of God." Peabody takes him aside at this point and asks him angrily what he is driving at; he replies serenely that he is "ascertaining their views of the difference between the absolute and the derived, of God in man, and the idea of Absolute being typified in the Derivative." He returns to his questioning, but the children still refuse to be budged from the idea that they are *not* as good as or as powerful as God or Jesus, with or without their bodies.

Reading through the volumes of *Conversations with Children on the Gospels* one has the giddy feeling that the whole controversy that Emerson would touch off with his Divinity School Address the next summer is being previewed in Alcott's schoolroom, with Alcott playing Emerson and the children miniature versions of Emerson's conservative Unitarian critics. In the very last conversation of the second volume, a boy named Charles complains at always being forced to think of God as spirit and spirit as within. "I wish," he says, "that you would let me say that God is up in the sky; for I like to think of God up there, though I know he is in my thought and inspires it. For I like to have such a place; and that is so pure, so blue, and handsome, with such beautiful stars!" Alcott: "But there is a danger of mistaking the forms for the thoughts themselves." Charles: "Oh, I don't think I should ever go as far as that."

As a way of collecting a new set of Christian evidences, Alcott's pedagogy would seem to fail miserably, because the children can never be persuaded to adopt his beliefs and indeed argue back to him more and more as the conversations progress (as does the Recorder, Peabody, who ended her job as amanuensis by quitting the school). Yet Alcott seems as pleased with their resistance as with their concurrence. On the first page of the book itself is an illustration showing Alcott's classroom – Alcott at a desk, and the children ranged rather stiffly around in a semicircle at some distance from him. At the end of both volumes is another illustration, this time of the boy Jesus teaching the elders in the Temple. Between these two emblems occurs the education in self-reliance that finally comes to seem the real message of the book and gives it its power and its innocence.

Such subtleties were lost upon Alcott's reviewers. He had published the first volume of *Conversations with Children on the Gospels* in the last week of December 1836 and had sent review copies of the book to all the newspapers. They began to savage him as soon as the new year arrived. Alcott's good friend and brother-in-law, the minister Samuel May, had written to warn him that the Unitarian establishment would dislike the book because it expressed too plainly the end to which their doctrines led. May was right. Parents began to withdraw children from the school. By the summer of 1837 there were only eleven pupils left.

Margaret Fuller had taken over Elizabeth Peabody's job as assistant in the fall of 1836 (she taught French and Latin and took down the "conversations" that Alcott at that time planned to publish as a third volume in the series). She now found herself obliged to take up Alcott's defense. When her friend the British reformer Harriet Martineau sent her an inscribed copy of *Society in America* that summer – the book contained a violent attack on Alcott's school, which Martineau had never visited but had heard about from its detractors – Fuller rebuked her for her "intemperate tirade" and defended Alcott as a "true and noble man, a philanthropist, whom a true and noble woman, also a philanthropist, should have delighted to honor" (Fuller to Martineau, c. November 1837).

Nevertheless, the emotional support of his Transcendentalist friends could not save Alcott's school. It limped on for another year with five or six students. When it finally closed, Alcott accepted the offer of a job teaching poor children in Boston's South End. That school too collapsed when, with his characteristic fidelity to principle, Alcott refused to dismiss the only black student in the school despite protests by parents of the other children. Transcendentalism had generated several scriptures in 1836; in Alcott it had also managed to create a martyr. It was ready to mount an offensive.

5

THE ESTABLISHMENT AND THE
MOVEMENT

IN THE EARLY MONTHS OF 1837 the Transcendentalists began to
think of themselves as something more than a group of young clergy
eager to escape the circumspection of traditional Unitarian associations
for regions of freer speech. The manifestos of 1836 had given the writers a
collective visibility. Now, as conservatives began writing angry reviews and
warning against the errors of the "new school" of philosophy and religion, the
members of Hedge's Club suddenly found themselves elevated to the dignity
of rebels.

Bronson Alcott was the most savagely assaulted, but by the end of January
Emerson too found himself the target of conservative scorn. In the January
1837 issue of the *Christian Examiner* a young Harvard tutor named Francis
Bowen made a review of *Nature* the occasion for an attack upon the arrogance
and obscurantism of the whole Transcendentalist school. As a reviewer of
Nature itself Bowen was perceptive; he noticed that Emerson's love of Saxon-
isms and deliberate bathos were a kind of protest against "forced dignity and
unnatural elevation," and he declared himself bewildered by the sudden
change of direction in the second half of the book, when Emerson suddenly
aims a "back blow" at the universe he was teaching us to admire and love.

Yet Bowen's praise for the "beautiful writing and sound philosophy" he
found in the book quickly changed to blame when he considered a doctrine in
Nature that he found dangerous: its worship of intuition as the sole trustworthy guide in matters of the spirit. Bowen agrees that mathematical axioms
must be grasped intuitively, but he cannot leap with Emerson to the conclusion that intuition can grasp "the most abstruse and elevated propositions
respecting the being and destiny of man." The distinction is an important
one. Splitting the mind into two faculties incapable of communicating with
one another destroys the hope of a rational Christianity and leaves society
open to all the horrors of religious bigotry. Unless we are willing to agree that
"the argument for the existence of a God, or the immateriality of the soul, is
tested by the same power of mind that discovered and proved any proposition
in Euclid," we have no defense against dogmatism and intolerance. In fact,

Bowen says, the Transcendentalists already speak with the arrogance of religious sectaries:

From the heights of mystical speculation, they look down with a ludicrous self-complacency and pity on the mass of mankind, on the ignorant and the educated, the learners and the teachers, and should any question the grounds on which such feelings rest, they are forthwith branded with the most opprobrious epithets, which the English or the Transcendental language can supply.

Emerson's reply to this kind of criticism was a fierce reaffirmation of his original principles. In the tenth lecture of the "Philosophy of History" series he was then giving at the Masonic Temple in Boston, entitled "Ethics" (February 16, 1837), he reminded his audience that the self-trust he has been recommending to them as the fountainhead of all virtue is "not a faith in man's own whim or conceit, as if he were quite severed from all other beings and acted on his own private account, but a perception that the mind common to the Universe is disclosed to the individual through his own nature."

The very conditions under which Emerson now spoke seemed an allegory of the connectedness he believed in. Ever since his return from Europe in 1833 Emerson had been a popular lyceum speaker, delivering lectures to audiences who had paid a subscription fee to a local lyceum for a season ticket to a course of evening lectures on a variety of topics: natural history, biography, literature, history, travel. By 1836 the fees he received from lyceum lecturing almost equaled the income he received from "supply" preaching in Unitarian churches.

Emerson found lecturing exhilarating. He could speak on any topic that appealed to him and he could assume that his audiences (unlike church congregations) were brought there by desire rather than impelled by duty or custom. But a lyceum lecturer still had to await invitation from lyceum committees to speak and negotiate with the committees about fees and topics. An independent entrepreneur, on the other hand, might offer a course of lectures on his own – hire the hall, print and sell the tickets, write and deliver the lectures – and keep profits greater than the modest fees the lyceums offered. Such was the appetite for lectures in improvement-minded, amusement-starved Massachusetts that (as one historian of the lyceum movement puts it) "everyone from respectable Harvard professors to phrenologists or outright quacks could hire a hall, sell tickets, and hope to clear a profit." In the fall of 1836 Emerson had decided to try his hand at such independent lecturing. He announced a twelve-lecture series to begin in December entitled "The Philosophy of History," hired a room in the Masonic Temple, wrote

his own advertising, and sold tickets (two dollars for the series) through a
bookstore.

On the average, three hundred and fifty people attended each of Emerson's
twelve lectures at the Masonic Temple during the winter of 1836–7. After
paying his expenses he had three hundred and fifty dollars left – proof that
the truths of the Reason he had been patiently depositing in his "savings
bank" (as he called his journals) could be made to yield handsome dividends
in the realm of the Understanding. Moreover, the lecture course, originally
written for the Boston market, could be repeated in other cities or sold to
lyceums in the smaller towns.

The lecturing was important to Emerson in more than financial ways.
When he was twenty-one he had expressed his ambition to thrive in "eloquence," but up until now that eloquence had been mediated through
institutions – the church, the lyceum, or the speaker's platform at some
ceremonial occasion. In the Masonic Temple, Emerson for the first time
found himself speaking to an audience whose only reason for coming was to
hear *him* and whose only reason for staying was that they were interested in
what they heard. It was a strangely thrilling experience for both speaker and
listeners, as surviving accounts from the members of those early audiences
make clear. And it offered empirical proof of a doctrine Emerson had held all
his life: A speaker uttering private thoughts with perfect candor will speak
universal truth.

Emerson was not the only member of the Transcendental Club to experience a surge of self-confidence at about this time. In the middle of January
1837, George Ripley wrote to Convers Francis that he had been thinking for
some time of an ambitious plan to translate modern works of French and
German philosophy, history, and theology. So long as Americans remained
dependent upon British thinkers they could hardly escape from empiricism
in philosophy and probabilistic reasoning in biblical interpretation. Making
translations of important foreign books available in the United States would
show that a world of thought existed outside of the Anglo-American tradition. The title Ripley chose for this vast project, which would eventually run
to fourteen volumes, was *Specimens of Foreign Standard Literature* – "standard,"
because he wanted to drive home the point that what seemed outlandish to
Americans was elsewhere solidly canonical.

But the mood of the country was about to shift. The United States had
been enjoying a period of rapid expansion and financial growth, but the
boom was about to end. President Andrew Jackson, alarmed at the way
unchecked financial speculation was leading to a wild rise in the price of
land, had announced the summer before that the government would accept

only specie in payment for public lands. Speculators suddenly tried to exchange their paper money for specie, and the rapid deflation that followed
triggered a financial panic. By the time Jackson's successor, Martin Van
Buren, took office in March 1837, banks and businesses had begun to collapse.
In May the New York banks suspended payments in specie; many of the
banks failed. Businesses and factories shut down. Wage laborers in the city
faced starvation as the price of necessities doubled while their wages were cut
nearly in half. Subsistence farmers or factory workers who had farms to return
to could ride out the hard times by living on food they raised themselves, but
wage laborers in the bigger cities suffered acutely.

The sight of this misery began to have profound effects on the two Transcendentalists whose ministries brought them into direct contact with the urban
poor, Ripley and Orestes Brownson. Ripley's disenchantment with the current
economic system would eventually lead him to resign his ministry and found
Brook Farm, a community designed as an alternative to the self-destructive
exploitation of unchecked capitalism. Brownson made the business collapse
the occasion for a jeremiad. In May 1837 he preached to his congregation a
sermon on the text "Babylon is falling, and the merchants of the earth shall
weep and mourn over her; for no man buyeth their merchandise any more."
Babylon he identified as the "spirit of gain" that drives the current system; its
downfall is predicted in the current collapse. Capitalism, Brownson argues,
produces nothing; it only robs others of what they have produced. The old
Unitarian answer to the problems of the poor – encouraging them to "rise" in
the world through education and industry – merely turns them from ex-
ploited to exploiters. As the wealth of the exploiting class increases, the misery
of the poor grows; warfare between the classes is inevitable. "One party or the
other must be exterminated before the war will end." But God has promised
victory to the poor and dispossessed, and when the "system of universal fraud
and injustice" is overthrown the *"people"* will see to it that justice reigns.

Emerson's response to the financial collapse was very different. When the
Panic of 1837 began Emerson's instinctive sympathies were with the failing
merchants rather than with the laborers idled by their ruin. His first reference in his journals to the crisis expresses a fear of violence from the kind of
mob that had just burned down the New Orleans stock exchange. But soon a
different note creeps into his voice as he surveys the financial wreckage of the
cities from the relative security of Concord:

Behold the boasted world has come to nothing. Prudence itself is at her wits' end.
Pride, and Thrift, & Expediency, who jeered and chirped and were so well pleased with
themselves, and made merry with the dream, as they termed it, of Philosophy and Love[:]
Behold they are all flat and here is the Soul erect and unconquered still.

What fills Emerson with joy is the discovery that the world State Street warned him to treat with respect – the "solid" world of thrift, of prudence, of compromise and self-interest – had failed like an overextended bank. When Alcott asked Emerson to take his place as speaker at the opening of a new school in Providence, Rhode Island, Emerson delivered a speech, "Address on Education," that turned into an attack on the immense "hollowness" the financial collapse had revealed at the center of society. Like Brownson, Emerson identifies the "disease of which the world lies sick" as "desperate conservatism," but the struggle Emerson sees played out in the world around him is not the struggle between privileged and underprivileged classes but between the past and the future. Brownson looks at the current world and sees greed; Emerson sees fear – sees "that utter unbelief which is afraid of change, afraid of thought."

One may wonder whether by spiritualizing the conflict in this way Emerson is hiding from himself the hardheaded wisdom of an argument he had made in a lecture on "Politics" earlier that winter – that political power always grows out of *property*. If conservatives have been rendered desperate it is because the Panic threatens their property and the power it confers, not because it threatens their habits or their notions of the world. Replacing class antagonisms with temporal ones masks this hard fact and makes a hopeful outcome to the present conflict seem inevitable – for when has the past ever defeated the future? Emerson's refusal to conceive of historical conflict as a clash of irreconcilable interests makes it possible for him to achieve an elevation above the scene that feels like power. "Let me begin anew. Let me teach the finite to know its Master. Let me ascend above my fate and work down upon the world."

He was to have his first opportunity very soon. Cornelius Felton, the professor of Greek at Harvard, wrote to Emerson at the end of June asking him to give the annual address to the Phi Beta Kappa Society during Harvard's August commencement week. The British author Harriet Martineau had attended the Phi Beta Kappa Society meeting two years earlier and had been shocked both by Harvard's air of indolence and privilege and by the Phi Beta Kappa address she heard then. She was startled, "among a people whose profession is social equality, and whose rule of association is universal self-government," to hear "the contempt which the few express for the many, with as much assurance as if they lived in Russia or England." Granted, scholars in America formed their notions of virtue from the aristocratic literatures of Europe, but Martineau was still surprised that "within the bounds of the republic, the insolence should be so very complacent, the contempt of the majority so ludicrously decisive as it is."

Emerson's topic for the address – America's lack of an indigenous literary tradition – was by now a familiar one. Explanations for the nonexistence of American literature were so common in postrevolutionary America as to constitute a genre of their own. But "The American Scholar" derives its power from a confluence of forces more powerful than a sense of provincial inferiority. Emerson's memories of loneliness and boredom as a Harvard undergraduate, his anger at the way Alcott had been savaged by some members of the Cambridge establishment and abandoned by others, and the recent lashing he himself had gotten from Francis Bowen all made him eager to puncture the complacency of the college whose commencement ceremonies he had been invited to improve. At the same time, his pride in the success of his recent course of lectures and his barely suppressed glee when in the general financial collapse the businesses of State Street shattered all around him like towers of glass gave him a prophet's conviction that his reading of history was correct. Hence "The American Scholar," though written at a time of national crisis, is buoyed by an exhilaration almost continuous. In its conviction that nature and tradition can both be made transparent by the enlightened mind, Emerson's address gives us a sense of what an indigenous humanism on the German model might have been like had there been an academy capable of supporting it; and the shrewd advice Emerson includes for learning to tap the richness of past literary tradition without being bankrupted by a sense of inferiority to it marks the beginning of the modern phase of American literary history.

The address begins by conceding what foreign critics had delighted to assert – that there was in America no native intellectual tradition worth speaking of, that the "sluggard intellect" of this continent had as yet produced little more than "the exertions of mechanical skill." But this satirical view of American dullness quickly gives way to a vision of what the American scholar ought to be: *"Man Thinking."* This heroic figure confronts power incarnate in the circular processes of nature, and he matches it with a tyrannizing instinct to classify: piercing phenomena, reducing multiplicity to unity, inspired by the conviction that natural objects "have a law which is also a law of the human mind."

That same conviction should give the American scholar courage when he confronts a more intimidating incarnation of eternal law – "the mind of the Past." The books written by geniuses have a tendency to warp the reader out of his own orbit, making him "a satellite instead of a system." He must fight against this gravitational pull by becoming an inventor himself; he must use books only to inspire and seek in them only those words he had nearly said himself. In this way, he transforms masters into servants and makes someone else's words the key that will unlock his own thoughts and so acquaint him with himself. This is the "creative reading" without which there can be no "creative writing," the endlessly profitable trade that carries out wealth to bring wealth home. "When the mind is braced by labor and invention, the page of whatever book we read becomes luminous with manifold allusion." Such "self-trust," the only virtue Emerson ever really cared for, will cure literary imitativeness as it cures maladies far more dangerous, maladies whose effects were beginning to be visible everywhere.

Less than a month after Emerson delivered "The American Scholar," a series of events in a distant state seemed to offer a particularly vivid example of the heroism of self-trust. In Alton, Illinois, a mob stormed the offices of Elijah Lovejoy, editor of the *Alton Observer,* and smashed the press. Lovejoy had already lost presses to mobs who objected to his criticisms of slavery and of lynching; the press smashed on September 21 was his third. Undaunted, he ordered a fourth press. When the prominent men of Alton tried to persuade him to cease publishing and leave town, he replied that he feared God more than he feared man. The fourth press arrived by riverboat on November 6 and was spirited ashore at midnight to be guarded by Lovejoy's friends. But a mob the next evening attacked the newspaper offices. They were at first repulsed by Lovejoy's guard but returned hoping to set fire to the roof. During a lull in the firing Lovejoy himself stepped out to see where the attackers had gone. He was shot through the chest and killed.

According to the critic and historian John Jay Chapman (1862–1933), "nothing except John Brown's Raid ever sent such a shock across the continent, or so stirred the North to understand and resist the advance of slavery as Lovejoy's murder." A memorial service was held for Lovejoy a month later in Faneuil Hall, and, in the lecture "Heroism," Emerson went out of his way to praise "the brave Lovejoy" for his death in defense of free speech. Such willingness to honor defiance like Lovejoy's was one of the qualities that led James Freeman Clarke to praise Emerson's insistence upon "the *needed* truth" to Margaret Fuller. In a letter written to her from Louisville, Clarke said of Emerson: "He asserts the necessity of self-reliance in an age when imitation and sympathy predominate; he defends the individual man, when we all get melted together in masses" (Clarke to Fuller, March 29, 1838).

Orestes Brownson, however, remained unconvinced that free speech was all that an individual needed in this time of severe deprivation. Brownson took the shocking step (shocking to most of the Transcendentalists, anyway) of joining the Democratic party, and in the winter of 1837–8, he started his own journal, the *Boston Quarterly Review.* Brownson wanted an outlet for his overflowing energies, and the aggressiveness of printed polemical discourse suited his temperament as well as the lecture platform's alternating current of seduction and challenge suited Emerson's. In its first number Brownson frankly confessed that although no Unitarian journal had ever refused to print his work, the mere act of submitting his work for someone else's possible censoring involved a submissiveness he could no longer tolerate.

In one sense the *Boston Quarterly Review* stood as a shining illustration of Emerson's doctrine of self-trust. As Ripley later pointed out, "It was undertaken by a single individual, without the cooperation of friends, with no external patronage," and most of its pages were filled by Brownson himself. But Brownson's political education had carried him beyond the point where he thought that self-trust alone could solve the problems of the urban poor. He had already delivered a Fourth-of-July oration to a thousand people at a Democratic mass meeting on Bunker Hill. Now he publicly announced his sympathy for the Locofocos, the most radical members of the Democratic party, who advocated schemes for outlawing inherited property and for distributing government-owned lands free to needy immigrants. Henry David Thoreau, who had boarded with Brownson while he was teaching school in Canton, wrote to offer his praise for the *Boston Quarterly Review,* but some of the older members of the Transcendental Club were distressed at Brownson's affiliation with a political party whose contempt for high culture and willingness to use techniques of mass political appeal made it quite as distasteful to them as it was to their conservative Unitarian critics.

The stresses along this particular fault line were to be felt in tremors throughout the next few years. Transcendentalism placed absolute faith in the integrity of the soul's intuitions; when these intuitions were hostile to established institutions Transcendentalism appeared revolutionary. But in its relentless pursuit of spiritual gain and its corresponding contempt for the world of the Understanding, Transcendentalism was of little immediate use to reformers who wanted to feed the hungry or free the slave; indeed, the quietism the movement fostered and the self-absorption it encouraged favored existing institutions, even the ones that the Transcendentalists criticized. Moreover, the principle of association so necessary to effective political action was distasteful to the Transcendentalists because of the necessary loss of perfect sincerity involved in compromise and negotiation. Solitary heroes like Lovejoy (and later, John Brown) always appealed to Emerson's imagination; canvassers and founders of societies repelled him. He saw clearly enough that any kind of association was bound sooner or later to involve some degree of coercion or cant, and to coerce someone to obey the will of a reformer was only to replace vice with fear. Yet the earnest labors of the philanthropists troubled his conscience, and though he tried to shoo away doubts by describing himself as a man who "only loves like Cordelia after his duty," he admitted that the sense of shame he felt when reformers came calling was itself the best proof that the claims they had on him were real.

Emerson always insisted that he was a reformer too, though of a different kind, visiting souls in prison and bringing news of release. His words did indeed affect members of his chosen audience powerfully – particularly the generation of younger disciples that the original Transcendentalists were beginning to acquire. But the excitement they aroused was not always controllable, as the strange exaltation of a young Harvard tutor of Greek would shortly demonstrate. Jones Very (1813–80) – the son of a Salem sea captain and his wife, a freethinking and aggressive woman who did not scruple to express her doubts of God's existence – was in the spring of 1837 completing his first year at Harvard Divinity School. He was supporting himself during his theological studies by serving as Greek tutor to the freshmen of Harvard College, from which he himself had just graduated the year before.

Very was ten years younger than Emerson but had entered Harvard late, so that his Harvard class (1836) graduated a full fifteen years after Emerson's. But if Very belonged to a different generation, his college experiences followed a familiar pattern. He studied the required curriculum and at the same time immersed himself in poetry; he was intensely shy, studious, and ambitious of literary fame. An early fascination with Byron gave way to a reverence for Wordsworth, Coleridge, and "the Germans" – Goethe, Schiller, and Schegel. Victor Cousin introduced him to ideas derived from German Idealist philosophy. For his entry in the Bowdoin Prize competition his senior year in college he submitted a long essay (it won the prize) entitled "What Reasons Are There for Not Expecting Another Great Epic Poem?," in which he argued that the progress of human history and the advent of Christianity had made the epic impossible by making its traditional subjects unimportant. By "transferring the scene of action from the outward world to the world within," Christianity had made the consciousness of the individual the scene of all significant action. Far from lamenting the demise of traditional epic, Very hailed it as "the greatest proof of the progress of the soul – and of its approach to that state of being where its thought is action, its word power."

Very's own soul suffered intensely at times. Besides an instability of mood that made him subject to periodic depressions, he felt himself (he confessed much later) tormented by sexual desires that made him long for a spiritual regeneration in which his own will would be wholly lost in the will of God. After months of scarcely endurable distress he felt that he had experienced a "change of heart" that gave him great joy. Very's change of heart bore a close resemblance (as one of his classmates noticed) to the conversion of the Calvinists, in which a sense of election replaces an overpowering conviction of sinfulness. But the carnal man within him kept reasserting himself, despite Very's resolution to allow no occasion for sin. He took a vow not to speak to, or even look at, a woman – a decision he called his "sacrifice of Beauty."

Because thought was temptation and temptation sin, he resolved to banish thought and eliminate all traces of individual will.

By obliterating all traces of individual will Very may have hoped to find peace from his rebellious desires. Instead he propelled himself into an ecstatic sense of divinity. Signs of the change were already evident in the way Very marked up the copy of Emerson's *Nature* he read in the fall of 1836. Very's biographer points out that the chapter "Idealism" in *Nature,* which contained Emerson's insistence that the transference of nature into the mind leaves matter behind like an outcast corpse, interested Very the most. He sensed the apocalyptic impulse behind Emerson's Idealism and glossed the text with references to Revelation. Next to the Wordsworthian maxim – "Infancy is the perpetual Messiah" – Very wrote "R12," probably a reference to the twelfth chapter of Revelation, where a woman clothed with the sun gives birth to a male child who is later revealed to be the Christ. Next to Emerson's innocent remark that riding in a carriage or looking at the landscape upside down through one's legs affords a "pleasure mixed with awe" because it suggests that the world is only a spectacle while something in the self is stable, Very wrote "Rev XX:II," a verse that describes the fleeing of heaven and earth before the face of "a great white throne, and him that sat on it."

Throughout 1836 and 1837 Very pursued his theological studies and tutored his Harvard freshmen in Greek, making himself popular with them (and unpopular with the professors) by actually trying to interest them in the literature they were reading. He gained the reputation on campus of being the only teacher of classical languages who insisted on accurate translations. But he also tried to inspire students with a love of literature, speaking to them enthusiastically of Shakespeare and Milton and urging them to find moral instruction in the true representations of human nature given by all poets. News of his gifts for making literature attractive had spread sufficiently that by the winter of 1837 he was invited to speak on epic poetry at the lyceum in Salem, Massachusetts, where he caught the attention of Elizabeth Peabody (who had moved back there after the furor following the publication of *Conversations with Children on the Gospels* had ended her teaching career in Boston). She befriended Very and discovered that he was an "enthusiastic listener to Mr. Emerson" and wrote to urge Emerson to invite him to lecture at the Concord lyceum; she also introduced Very to Nathaniel Hawthorne, who liked him but found the intensity of his loneliness alarming.

On April 4, 1838, Very walked twenty miles from Salem to Concord to deliver his "Epic Poetry" lecture and to dine with the Emersons. Very poured out to Emerson all his theories about poetry and particularly about Shakespeare (with whom he had come to believe he had achieved a perfect identification); he asked Emerson to inscribe his copy of *Nature*. Emerson thought him remarkable. When Very came back to Concord a few days later with some Harvard friends, Emerson invited them all to dinner. Promise in young men was making Emerson feel hopeful again about the state of the country. Very's "Epic Poetry" was published in the *Christian Examiner* early in May 1838; in the same month Very came as Emerson's guest to the Transcendental Club, where the subject for discussion was "the question of Mysticism." Very explained the history of his own "change of heart," its partial success, and the continued effort he was making to eradicate his selfish will. Indeed, by the end of the school year in 1838 he began to be sensible of a change for the better in himself, a certain lightness and effortlessness in the performance of his duties, a great peace and contentment.

Emerson, on the other hand, was finishing a spring full of vexations, some of them self-inflicted. He had long wanted to get out of the position he still held as supply preacher to an East Lexington congregation, and he now began to take formal steps to find a replacement for himself. At the same time his dissatisfaction with organized Unitarianism reached new heights. At home he chafed under the wretched preaching of the Concord minister Barzillai Frost. Frost was a glaring example of what was wrong with theological instruction at Cambridge. When Emerson visited him at home and inspected his library, the works of historical criticism and proofs of the Christian religion from "internal and external evidences" ranged on his shelves made Emerson shiver. A year earlier Frost had preached the sermon when Emerson's son Waldo was christened: it had been a dismal performance delivered in a "ragged half screaming bass" that showed how thoroughly Frost had failed to learn the capital secret of the preacher's profession – "to convert life into truth."

Even the venerable Dr. Ripley, Emerson's step-grandfather and a man he usually venerated as a link with the Puritan past, now provoked Emerson's impatience. "This afternoon the foolishest preaching – which bayed at the moon. Go, hush, old man, whom years have taught no truth." Dr. Ripley's confusion when he mislaid his glasses reminded Emerson of the stupid stare of squash bugs suddenly exposed to light under the rotten leaves of vines. Myopia seemed in fact the curse of the established churches, which clung to shreds of historical evidence, writing laborious volumes seeking to demonstrate that the Godhead had once dwelled on earth – when all around them its epiphanies were perpetual.

When Emerson received an invitation from the small senior class at the Harvard Divinity School to deliver an address at its graduating ceremonies in July he was at first reluctant. The young men of Cambridge were just setting out in the profession he had renounced. But the forces impelling him were

[margin notes, top: suffering of poor / Chronic malaise of Educated / Church dogma / anti Historical Christ]

greater than the forces restraining him. His old distaste for "historical Christianity" and the archaic epistemology upon which it was based, his anger at
the bigotry that had quashed Alcott's innocent attempt to find new evidences
of Christianity in his students' souls, his growing sense that the church was
helpless to suggest any remedy for the recent sufferings of the poor or the
chronic spiritual malaise of the educated classes, for whom the faith of the
fathers had vanished as completely as melted snow, and most of all his sense
that the traditionary preaching of the church was driving away entire congregations who desperately needed saving, all combined to provide enough
indignation to fuel a jeremiad.

Yet the speech Emerson delivered at the Divinity School on July 15, 1838,
also reflects the powerful sense of joy he was beginning to feel in his achievements as a lecturer and literary man and as father to a growing band of
younger disciples. He had been disengaging himself gradually from the
Unitarian ministry ever since 1832, when he resigned his pastorate. Giving
up the East Lexington supply position completed this process of disengage-
ment. In February 1838 he had written to ask his wife whether the step he
was taking distressed her. His teasing letter suggests how strongly orthodox
Christianity was becoming identified in his mind with something at once
feminine and Oriental, with the archaic. "But does not the eastern Lidian my
Palestine mourn to see the froward man cutting the last threads that bind
him to the prized gown & band the symbols black & white of old & distant
Judah?" His solicitude was greater for her loss than for his. He believed that
the lecture platform was providing him with a more powerful and less
encumbered pulpit than any that the church had offered, and the arrival of
candidates for his influence and affection like Jones Very made him feel sure
that his secular ministry could also promise a harvest of souls.

Emerson began his Divinity School Address by expressing adoration for
the beauty of nature and the "more secret, sweet, and overpowering beauty"
that appears to man when his heart and mind open to "the sentiment of
virtue." Following the laws revealed by this sentiment brings us nearer to
divinity; indeed, the man who is just at heart *is* God and dispenses "good to
his goodness, and evil to his sin." To the man who beholds the sovereignty of
law, "the worlds, time, space, eternity, do seem to break out into joy." The
history of civilization is constituted by successive apprehensions of the moral
sentiment, and the immense influence of Jesus upon the world stems from his
fierce determination to speak for that sentiment without qualification or
compromise. But "historical" Christianity has made a killing mistake. It
deifies the *person* of Jesus and in so doing reduces itself to another ancient
Near Eastern mystery religion, a "Mythus" whose stilted language represents
Jesus as "a demigod, as the Orientals or the Greeks would describe Osiris or

[margin notes, bottom: adoration of NATURE / Christianity "reduces" Jesus To myth / Historical Christianity]

I maginatin

Apollo." The Reason hears Jesus say "I am divine" and understands it as an exhortation to every soul to achieve spiritual perfection; the Understanding hears the same words and says, "This was Jehovah come down out of heaven. I will kill you, if you say he was a man."

So far Emerson has not really left behind traditional Unitarian accounts of the corruptions of Christianity, though in the violence of his language he sounds more like Carlyle than like Channing. But his declaration of independence from formal Unitarianism is more than stylistic, as he quickly makes clear. Perhaps most immediately wounding were his scathing attacks upon the dessication of the churches. Only thirteen years after the founding of the Unitarian association, every parish was feeling the loss of faith and the waning of piety. "Where shall I hear words such as in elder ages drew men to leave all and follow, – father and mother, house and land, wife and child?" The public worship now "has lost its grip on the affection of the good, and the fear of the bad." We inhabit our own religion like peasants stirring in the ruins of civilizations they did not create. "The prayers and even the dogmas of our church, are like the zodiac of Denderah and the astronomical monuments of the Hindoos, wholly insulated from anything now extant in the life and business of the people. They mark the height to which the waters once rose." The power a Congregationalist minister once commanded in his community has vanished. "In the street, what has he to say to the bold village blasphemer? The village blasphemer sees fear in the face, form, and gait of the minister."

This "bold village blasphemer" who intrudes into the Divinity School Address is more than a fiction. During March and early April 1838, the four-year-long judicial ordeal of an irrepressible freethinker named Abner Kneeland (1774–1844) was coming to a conclusion. The sixty-four-year-old Kneeland had begun as a Baptist, next had joined the Universalists and preached for twenty-five years there, and finally had become involved with Robert Owen and Frances Wright. In 1829 he announced in a New York lecture that he had rejected Christianity after what he said was a final review of its evidences (the book he then published on the subject went through six editions in ten years). In 1830 he moved from New York to Boston to take charge of Boston's First Society of Free Enquirers, where he was given the official title "Lecturer to the Free Enquirers." He also founded the *Boston Investigator,* a weekly journal of free thought, in 1830, and used it to campaign for rationalism, working-class rights, the abolition of slavery, racial equality, equal rights for women, and birth control.

Abner Kneeland

In 1833 a particularly frank number of the *Boston Investigator* got Kneeland arrested for blasphemy (he had already spent time in jail for distributing his treatise on birth control). Challenged by one of his former Universalist colleagues to explain how he differed from them, Kneeland referred to God as "a chimera of the imagination," judged the story of Christ to be as much "a fable and a fiction as that of Prometheus," and denied the existence of miracles and the resurrection of the dead. Because an act passed July 3, 1782, had clearly made blasphemy an offense punishable by law, Kneeland was convicted in 1834. But appeals dragged the case out interminably, and there were many among Boston's leading liberal clergy who worried about the constitutionality of persecuting a man for exercising his rights of free speech, no matter how distasteful they might find Kneeland or his doctrines. The Lowell *Advertiser* called the case an "outrage upon *human* rights, upon *expediency,* upon the *freedom of the press,* and of *speech,* upon *mercy,* upon *truth,* upon *Christianity,* and upon the *Spirit of the Age.*"

Meanwhile Kneeland had soared to new heights of popularity; his Sunday services at the Federal Street Theater drew audiences of two thousand or more, and as many subscribed to the *Investigator.* Kneeland's alarming popularity was one reason that George Ripley had been so eager to bring Orestes Brownson to the Boston area, where Brownson's working-class background and familiarity with the free-thought movement might help him win back converts from those classes genteel Unitarians rarely could reach.

In April 1838 Kneeland's request to appeal his case to the U.S. Supreme Court was denied by the attorney general of Massachusetts; on June 18 he began serving his two-month sentence in the county jail, accompanied by throngs of supporters. The Reverend William Ellery Channing drew up a petition asking for Kneeland's pardon and circulated it among sympathetic clergy; Emerson was one of the signers. Channing's petition failed. Kneeland remained in his Boston cell until his release on August 17, 1838. While in jail he wrote an open letter reminding his fellow citizens that he was suffering imprisonment for the very liberty their fathers had fought to win.

Kneeland's case reminded everyone that congregationalism was losing its hold on congregations. "In the country, neighborhoods, half parishes are *signing off,* – to use the local term," Emerson reminded his hearers when he spoke on that July evening at the Divinity School. "The Church seems to totter to its fall, almost all life extinct." Why? Why had the confidence of the Unitarians of 1805 or of 1815 given way so quickly to complacency and then to ossification? The Unitarians did not see that the "historical Christianity" whose empirical proofs they clung to as a defense against sectarian bigotry was fatal to the belief it was meant to protect. "Men have come to speak of the revelation as somewhat long ago given and done, as if God were dead. The injury to faith throttles the preacher; and the goodliest of institutions becomes an uncertain and inarticulate voice." Worshipping Christ as if he were a demigod means thinking of virtue and truth as already "foreclosed and monopolized." Worse still, we are encouraged to believe in the doctrines of Christianity by means insulting to our dignity as spiritual creatures—by the report of miracles. "To aim to convert a man by miracles, is a profanation of the soul."

This last assertion turned out to be the one that generated the most explosive controversy, and it helps to remember just what was at stake. Traditional Unitarians looked on the miracles reported in the New Testament as the one place where the spiritual world erupted into the world of ordinary sense perceptions with effects the senses could perceive. Miracles were empirically verifiable and universally persuasive – a powerfully attractive combination in an age deriving its notions of rationality from empirical science and its notions of human nature from Enlightenment universalism. To dismiss miracles as either unverifiable or unimportant meant relegating faith to the wholly private world of the individual soul and its fitful "contact" with God – uncertain, unsteady, dangerous. Miracles were like Newton's laws, only better; they testified to a power above nature yet accessible through it, pores in the fabric of time and space through which eternal power once leaked down to men and women.

Emerson had read Hume's attack on the credibility of miracle testimony and found it irrefutable on its own terms. He felt that he had liberated himself from the need for such empirical proofs by his discovery that God was to be found within the self, here and now. He now was seeking to proclaim that happy news, preaching from the soul, not from the church. Emerson's *ecce homo* looks forward to a hero still unincarnated, not back to Jesus of Nazareth. "In the soul then let the redemption be sought. Wherever a man comes, there comes revolution. The old is for slaves. When a man comes, all books are legible, all things transparent, all religions are forms. He is religious. Man is the wonderworker. He is seen amid miracles." This new Teacher, when he comes, will preach moral law with a new authority, one not derived from miracles and prophecies and manuscripts and testimony, but rather one that flows from his power to see "the identity of the law of gravitation with purity of heart."

It is difficult to know from the surviving evidence whether Emerson knew his address to the Divinity School would prove to be as incendiary as it in fact was. His journals and letters written near the day of delivery betray no particular militancy; he seems far more preoccupied with the speech entitled "Literary Ethics" he was scheduled to deliver at Dartmouth College a few days later. When he returned from Dartmouth he found a letter waiting for him from Henry Ware, Jr., once his predecessor at the Second Church in Boston, now the professor of pulpit eloquence and pastoral care at the Divinity School. Ware (who had been in the audience when Emerson delivered the address and who had discussed it with him afterwards) found some of Emerson's ideas impossible to agree with.

Ware's mild strictures were nothing compared to the blast of fury that came from Andrews Norton when Emerson published the Divinity School Address on August 27. Norton could not wait for a quarterly like the *Christian Examiner* to appear; he published his review in the *Boston Daily Advertiser* (a newspaper that had recently applauded the sentencing of Abner Kneeland). Norton's diatribe, "The New School in Literature and Religion," blasts the arrogance and presumption of the whole Transcendentalist movement and its foreign progenitors, the "hasher up of German metaphysics," Cousin, and "that hyper-Germanized Englishman, Carlyle." Norton treats with raucous contempt the self-confidence of the Transcendentalist visionaries who announce a new future of glorious transformation but never tell us how it is to be achieved, who advance their intuitive convictions as indisputable, who barbarize language with neologisms and "coarse and violent" metaphors. But he reserves his special fury for the graduating class of the Divinity School, who saw fit to invite Emerson to insult religion in their presence. Any minister who agreed with Emerson was a menace to the Christianity he was hired to teach, a situation equally "disastrous and alarming."

Three days after Norton's article appeared in the *Advertiser*, Emerson attended the meeting of the same Phi Beta Kappa Society at whose festivities he had delivered "The American Scholar" the year before. That he found himself there the object of hostile curiosity can be inferred from the shaken tone of his journal entry the next day. "Yesterday at Φ.B.K. anniversary. Steady, steady. . . . The young people & the mature hint at odium, & aversion of faces to be presently encountered in society. I say no: I fear it not." But he did fear it, and for obvious reasons. He had left the ministry for good in the spring of that year, and no Unitarian parish would have him now even if he wished to return. He now depended upon popular favor in the form of lecture tickets for at least half his income. The grim example of Alcott was there to remind him of what happened to people who offended popular taste. Would Emerson announce his winter lectures only to find the tickets unsellable? In his journal he gloomily recorded thoughts about economic self-sufficiency that look forward to Thoreau's experiment at Walden Pond: "It seems as if a man should learn to fish, to plant, or to hunt, that he might secure his subsistence if he were cast out from society & not be painful to his friends & fellow men."

In September Henry Ware, Jr., preached a sermon entitled "The Personality of the Deity" expressly designed to refute Emerson's chilly brand of impersonal theism by insisting that we must think of God as a Father if we are not to be cast into a loveless universe. Ware sent the sermon to Emerson asking for his comments and got in reply a letter full of calculated innocence. "I could not give account of myself if challenged," Emerson wrote.

I could not possibly give you one of the "arguments" on which as you cruelly hint any position of mine stands. For I do not know, I confess, what arguments mean in reference to any expression of a thought. I delight in telling what I think but if you ask me how I dare say so or why it is so I am the most helpless of mortal men.

But Emerson's affectation of unconcern, almost indeed of dandyism, masked real anxieties, as his journals of the period make clear. "Steady, steady!" is an exhortation (from Emerson to himself) that recurs more than once.

Emerson nevertheless kept out of the controversy his Divinity School Address had generated, partly from principle, partly from a deep instinct for imaginative self-preservation. The minute an opponent can compel you to begin wasting your time in parrying and defense he has won, Emerson thought, because he has diverted your energies from promulgating the gospel you were sent to preach. Any temptations he might have had to enter the debate were quickly squelched by his second wife, Lidian (Lydia Jackson Emerson) — who, upon being told by her husband that he had things to say to his critics that were too good to be lost, replied, "then there is some merit in remaining silent."

Emerson did not lack defenders in this time of distress, though some of these were such allies as he probably could have spared. A disciple of Kneeland hailed Emerson as a fellow "free enquirer" in the pages of the *Boston Investigator*, and Kneeland himself later threw in a word of praise. In the October 1838 issue of the *Boston Quarterly Review* Brownson protested the abuse heaped on Emerson (though his criticism of the "Address" itself was almost more devastating than Norton's). Brownson then turned his attention to Norton's own summa, *The Evidences of the Genuineness of the Gospels,* savaging it by reducing it to absurdity. What do the postulates of Norton's "historical Christianity" amount to but a counsel of despair? Norton argues, in effect, that "religious truth never springs up spontaneously in the human mind; there is no revelation made from God to the human soul; we can know nothing of religion but what is taught us from abroad, by an individual raised up and specially endowed with widsom from on high to be our instructor." Norton believes that we cannot even recognize God's legitimate messengers unless they perform miracles, for without miracles we should not be able to tell whether the messenger comes from heaven or hell. The records describing those messengers thus become our only link with the divine, without which we should be "plunged into midnight darkness," left in gloom no light of reason or faith could illumine.

Meanwhile, Emerson was discovering, much to his relief, that the citizens of Boston and New York were willing "to allow much to the spirit of liberty" and to buy tickets to his winter lecture series despite his new fame as a heretic. He could be glad that at least he had not recanted in the face of opposition, and in the presence of nature's soothing influences he even managed to forget that he had been (and he underlined the word in his journal) "reviewed." But a disturbing drama beginning to play itself out during the fall of 1838 suggested to Emerson that conservatives who hated his philosophy might be far less menacing than disciples who embraced it with too much enthusiasm.

In September 1838 Jones Very began his third year of tutoring in Greek at Harvard. Very had always involved himself in the lives of his students, but now his spiritual advice became more urgent. He told his students to submit their wills wholly to God, then act as conscience prompted; God would then take up his abode in them. Such advice might not have sounded odd in an orthodox seminary like Andover, but at Harvard rumors began to circulate that Very had gone mad. On September 13 Very became sensible of a change in himself. His biographer reports that he felt he had completed the "identification with Christ" he had been urging on his students. And even though this sense of perfect identification wavered in its intensity, Very felt moved to proclaim that the coming of Christ was at hand.

Very called on Henry Ware, Jr., and announced that he had an interpretation of the twenty-fourth chapter of Matthew he had to give. When Ware tried to silence him, Very accused him of disobeying God and cried in frustration when Ware continued to oppose him. The next day in class, a student reported, Very declared to one of his Greek sections "that he was infallible: that he was a man of heaven, and superior to all the world around him" and then cried out a verse from the chapter of Matthew he had wanted to expound to Ware: "Flee to the mountains, for the end of all things is at hand." That evening he attended the Divinity School debating club and calmly announced that, because "the Holy Spirit was speaking in him," whatever he said was "eternal truth."

At this point the president of Harvard, Josiah Quincy, intervened, summoning Very's younger brother Washington (a Harvard freshman) to take Very home to Salem. Before Very left Harvard he mailed Emerson a recently completed essay on Shakespeare along with a letter calling on Emerson to rejoice and give thanks that the Father and Christ had taken him to themselves. "I feel that the day now is when 'the tabernackle of God is with men, and he will dwell with them, and they shall be his people.' " In Salem Very continued his proselytizing. He visited a startled Elizabeth Peabody, announcing that he was "the Second Coming" and offering to baptize her with fire; he visited several ministers, who were considerably less sympathetic than she had been. One angrily demanded to see Very perform some miracles to validate his mission; another threw him out of the house; a third — a good friend of Andrews Norton and an enemy of the Transcendentalists — vowed to have him committed by force to McLean Hospital for the Insane at Charlestown, a threat he in fact carried out.

Elizabeth Peabody offered a guess at the etiology of Very's insanity by supposing that it came from "overtaxing his brain in an attempt to look from the standpoint of Absolute Spirit." A modern clinician would be more likely to diagnose acute mania. Very's rapid transition from mild euphoria to exaltation, his immediate conviction of identity with the divine, his extreme lability of mood and sudden bursts of anger when frustrated, and the endless volubility he displayed both before and after he was committed to the asylum — these are all recognizable symptoms of mania. But the folio sheet of sonnets Very gave Peabody the day before he was hospitalized contains material very unlike the loosely associative or enigmatically discontinuous material produced by most writers in the manic state. On the contrary, the sonnets are highly organized and formally precise; in strictness of organization and in spiritual intensity they resemble the seventeenth-century English religious poetry the Transcendentalists admired.

After Very had been in the hospital for a month the doctor at McLean decided to dismiss him, judging him to be no danger to himself or others, though he still refused to renounce his beliefs. (The other patients are reported to have thanked Very as he left.) Very now determined to call on Emerson, whom he had wanted to see at the time of his removal from Harvard. His nearly week-long visit with Emerson at Concord was both intense and disturbing. Emerson at first found Very far less "mad" than he had expected; the things Very said about society, the church, and the college struck him as "perfectly just." When Very confronted the presiding preacher at a meeting of Sunday School teachers held in Emerson's house and "bid him wonder at the Love which suffered him to speak there in his chair, of things he knew nothing of," Emerson gleefully reported that Very "unhorsed" the desperate, dogmatizing minister "and tumbled him along the ground in utter dismay." It is not hard to see why Emerson should have enjoyed and even tacitly encouraged naked aggression by a younger and less inhibited self against the forces that were ranged against both of them. When he said goodbye to Very at the end of the visit Emerson felt — the words are revealing — as if he had "discharged an arrow into the heart of society."

Nevertheless, Emerson had to bear much abuse himself during the visit. Very accused Emerson of coldness, of being willing to receive the Truth but not to obey it. Emerson suddenly found himself playing Henry Ware to Very's Emerson, as he tried to argue with Very only to be met with flat refusals to engage in dispute. "It is the necessity of the spirit to speak with authority," Very said. Very could not have known it, but the problem of the source of spiritual authority had plagued Emerson throughout his own career in the ministry. Very's perfect sincerity and his passionate conviction gave him authority, and even if Emerson refused to become a convert he was moved to make an extraordinary confession nevertheless, and one that would return to haunt him.

I told J. V. that I had never suffered, & that I could scarce bring myself to feel a concern for the safety & life of my nearest friends that would satisfy them; that I saw clearly that if my wife, my child, my mother, should be taken from me, I should still remain whole with the same capacity of cheap enjoyment from all things.

After he had returned to Salem, Very sent Emerson some of his sonnets, and Emerson responded with interest and admiration. (Emerson published a volume of Very's poetry and essays in 1839.) Very continued to publish his sonnets in the Salem *Observer* and in James Freeman Clarke's *Western Messenger* and to circulate them in manuscript among the members of the Transcendental Club.

Clarke's periodical was coming to play an increasingly important role in the life of the Transcendentalists. The *Christian Examiner* was now closed to them, but the *Western Messenger* of St. Louis – nominally Unitarian but under the editorship of Clarke, and at safe distance away from the pressures of public opinion in Boston and Cambridge – could print what it chose. In November 1838 the *Western Messenger* devoted two articles to a survey of the controversy surrounding the Divinity School Address, pointing out that the Unitarian hierarchy was making itself a laughingstock by hurling at Emerson precisely those epithets the orthodox once delighted to hurl at the Unitarians. More importantly, it took the sneer "new school" over from Norton and turned it into a term of praise. The New School is made up of all those members of the clergy and laity who are "dissatisfied with the present state of religion, philosophy, and literature. The common principle which binds them together and makes them if you choose a school, is a desire for more of LIFE, soul, originality in these great departments of thought." Members of the New School are not any one person's disciples; they choose which doctrines and virtues to admire in their spokespersons. They agree only in their conviction "that life should not be a mechanical routine, but be filled with earnestness, soul, and spiritual energy." Early in 1839, Orestes Brownson continued his attack upon the conservative position by pointing out in the

Boston Quarterly Review that it was more truly "skeptical" to require sensory evidences before believing Jesus' teachings than to believe without such evidences. In this sense, Norton is the skeptic, Emerson the faithful believer.

Norton was not finished. A year after Emerson delivered his address, the newly formed "Association of the Alumni of the Divinity School" invited Norton to speak. His "Discourse on the Latest Form of Infidelity" attempts to present systematically the position he had argued the preceding year in his newspaper blast immediately following Emerson's address. Against those who argued that miracles were no necessary proof of the truth of revelation Norton pointed out that Jesus himself always referred to his miracles as attesting his divine mission, and that modern theologians who refuse to accept miracles as testamentary must therefore believe either that Jesus was lying or that he was deluded. Christianity, being a revelation from God, is inherently miraculous, and requires a miraculous confirmation of its doctrines.

Nothing is left that can be called Christianity, if its miraculous character be denied. Its essence is gone; its evidence is annihilated. Its truths, involving the highest interests of man, the facts which it makes known, and which are implied in its very existence as a divine revelation, rest no longer on the authority of God.

The intensity of Norton's language suggests how threatening he found the Transcendentalists' attempt to sever the link between truth and history and how repugnant he found their attempt to ground on "undefined and unintellible feeings." Men who refuse to accept the indispensably evidentiary quality of miracles have no right to call themselves Christian teachers.

More than one spectator of the conflict must have been struck by its irony. Norton, the aggressive young iconoclast who had wanted to smash the strongholds of Calvinism and build new temples of liberal religion was now hurling charges of heresy at the younger members of his own sect. As John White Chadwick (author of a 1900 biography of Theodore Parker) noted:

The situation was a vivid reproduction of that which existed twenty years before, more irrational and less ethical than that, because the Calvinists of 1819 believed great truths to be in danger, − the Trinity, the Atonement, the Deity of Christ − while Mr. Norton and his friends had only to object that their great truths were not believed for their own particular reasons.

In attempting to insist that one must believe in miracles in order to be a Christian, Norton had let himself be pushed into arguing (as Chadwick put it) that "the unpardonable sin was belief in Christianity upon the grounds of its intrinsic excellence."

Yet what Norton was attempting to defend was not, after all, negligible. Miracles are important not just as sensible events but as historical events, as part of the many signs and wonders strewn through history to mark a series of covenants binding the people of God to God and assuring them of their eventual triumph. Getting rid of "historical Christianity" meant giving up a promise that history itself unfolded in the direction of fulfillment. How great a void this left became apparent every time the Transcendentalists tried to imagine the "church of the future." After a journey to New Hampshire in September 1839 Emerson wrote to Margaret Fuller confessing his weariness with existing denominations and his helplessness to come up with an alternative.

We heard in one place blue sulphureous preaching, in another the most ominous shaking of Unitarian husks & pods out of which all corn & peas had long fallen, the men were base the newspapers base, & worse, the travellers did not find in themselves the means of redemption. I see movement, I hear aspirations, but I see not how the great God prepares to satisfy the heart in a new order of things. No church no state will form itself to the eye of desire & hope.

The oracle refuses to enlighten us as to the mode of our redemption. "A thousand negatives it utters clear & strong on all sides, but the sacred affirmative it hides in the deepest abyss" (Emerson to Fuller, September 6, 1839).

When Harrison Gray Otis Blake, one of the students who had been in the fateful graduating class at the Divinity School the previous year, wrote to express his doubts about continuing in the ministry, Emerson could only urge him to choose his path by the light of "a greater selfreliance, – a thing to be spoken solemnly of & waited for as not one thing but all things, as the uprise & revelation of God." And he struggled to express his sense of the impermanence of all forms before the living soul. "Man seems to me the one fact; the forms of the church & of society – the framework which he creates & casts aside day by day. The whole of duty seems to consist in purging off these accidents & obeying the aboriginal truth" (Emerson to Blake, August 1, 1839). Blake can hardly be blamed for wondering how a practicing minister might implement such a program, particularly because in the Divinity School Address Emerson had warned that all attempts to contrive new systems of worship seemed to him as vain as the devotions to the Goddess of Reason introduced by the French revolutionaries – "today pasteboard and fillagree, and ending to-morrow in madness and murder." If the new forms are facticious and the old good for nothing but to be sloughed off, what kind of worship can be true?

Emerson was by this time too detached from the problems of the ministry to devote much time to considering the problem, and George Ripley, who waded into the battle with a series of thick pamphlets attacking Norton and replying to Norton's counterattacks, was also headed for separation from his ministry. His parish was poor to begin with and had continued to decline; the part he had played in the recent controversy had caused at least some of his parishioners distress. In a letter to them dated October 1, 1840, he looked back sadly over the excitement of the early days of the Unitarian controversy, when the liberal clergy "asserted the unlimited freedom of the human mind, and not only the right, but the duty of private judgment." Young people raised in such a heady atmosphere "had been taught that no system of divinity monopolized the truth, and they were no more willing to be bound by the prevailing creed of Boston or Cambridge, than their fathers had been by the prescription of Rome or Geneva." But now some clergy feared the forces of unlimited inquiry. "Liberal churches begin to fear liberality, and the most heretical sect in Christendom to bring the charge of being so against those who carried out its own principles." The suggestion by some of the church's proprietors that Ripley avoid all controversial topics in his sermons seemed to him depressing and embarrassing. "Unless a minister is expected to speak out on all subjects which are uppermost in his mind, with no fear of incurring the charge of heresy or compromising the interests of his congregation, he can never do justice to himself, to his people, or the truth which he is bound to declare." He offered his resignation to the proprietors of the church and preached his farewell sermon in March 1841.

Some Transcendentalist ministers, however, refused either to leave or to be driven out of the church. One of Ripley's close friends from the Transcendental Club was Theodore Parker (1810–60), a Unitarian minister who could trace his belief in intuitive religion back to his boyhood, when something in him rebelled at hearing a minister preach that the Resurrection of Jesus was the only proof we had of the immortality of the soul. He was unable at the time to explain to himself why he thought that a historical event could not prove a universal proposition, but some version of that problem was to recur in the work he did in his maturity.

Parker was the grandson of the captain who commanded the minutemen at the battle of Lexington in 1775. He was the youngest of eleven children. His father, a farmer, could not afford to send him to Harvard, but Parker applied for admission anyway and, once admitted, satisfied every requirement for the bachelor's degree except tuition and residency. (The university eventually granted him an honorary master's degree in 1840.)

Parker turned to schoolteaching in Watertown to earn enough money to enter the Harvard Divinity School, all the while pursuing an ambitious personal course of reading in literature, philosophy, and mathematics that kept him occupied ten or twelve hours a day besides the six hours that he spent in school. He had already begun to study Hebrew with a tutor and to borrow German books from his Watertown pastor, Convers Francis (1795–1863).

Francis was the oldest member of the Transcendental Club and the author of the suggestively named *Christianity as a Purely Internal Principle* (1836), which argued that Christianity was remarkable among religions chiefly for its independence of rituals and creeds. Francis was already well known for his extensive knowledge of German theological literature and for the size of his library; he would become a professor at the Divinity School in 1842.

Parker entered the Divinity School in 1834. At the time of his entrance his beliefs appear to have been unexceptionable by Unitarian standards, and he was chosen to help edit a magazine of biblical interpretation for the Unitarian faithful called the *Scriptural Interpreter*. But in the same year the teacher who had taught him Latin and Greek at the Lexington district school, Dr. George Noyes, published an article in the *Christian Examiner* questioning one of the traditional "evidences" of Christianity. Noyes argued that it was difficult to point out *any* predictions in the Old Testament that were fulfilled in the life of Jesus – an opinion deemed shocking enough by the attorney general of Massachusetts for him to demand Noyes's prosecution for blasphemy (proceedings were begun but the charges were later dropped).

Parker was inclined to agree with his old teacher. His labors for the *Scriptural Interpreter* had brought him into contact with modern critical investigators of the Bible. For the *Interpreter* he translated Jean Astruc's revolutionary *Conjectures* (1753) about the two sources of the book of Genesis (Parker's translation appeared in 1837 in the May and August issues). But he also began to read the more recent German criticism; in fact, he undertook in 1835 to prepare a "Report on German Theology" for the Divinity School's Philanthropic Society. Originally instituted to promote good works for prisoners and the poor, the Society had become by the mid-1830s a forum for the discussion of ideas both intellectually and socially radical. Students would meet to hear reports and debate resolutions on everything from the Abner Kneeland case to antislavery and labor reform.

Parker immersed himself in German theology and biblical criticism for the report and began to discover what a truly critical approach to the Bible entailed. He became acquainted with the man whose work he was to spend so many years of his life translating, Wilhelm Martin Leberecht De Wette (1780–1849). De Wette's voluminous works include an *Introduction to the Old Testament* in which he argues, among other things, that Moses was not the author of the Pentateuch, which is itself not a single document but a collection of fragments with little connection to one another assembled many hundreds of years after Moses was supposed to have lived; that the books from Exodus through Numbers have more than one author; and that the account of the origin of Israelite ceremonial religion given in the book of Chronicles is wholly unreliable. In fact, the whole dream of the rationalist critics of the

Bible – which is to separate the truly "historical" elements in it from the supernatural – is doomed to failure, because the Bible is not a historical document at all but rather a poetic or mythological expression of the hopes and beliefs of the Jewish people at the time when the various fragments of the text were written.

Parker decided to translate this work of de Wette's, which one recent scholar has called the beginning of modern criticism of the Old Testament; the project, begun in 1836, was not brought to completion until 1843, when it was published in two volumes in Boston by Little and Brown. (Another work by De Wette, the autobiographical novel *Theodore; or, The Skeptic's Conversion*, was translated by James Freeman Clarke and published first serially in the *Western Messenger* and then in Ripley's series of foreign standard books in 1841; it was particularly interesting to the Transcendentalists in giving an account of the hero's struggles to discover a satisfying faith as he leaves behind orthodoxy to pass successively under the influence of the ideas of Kant, Schelling, Fries, and Schleiermacher.) But the effects of Parker's study of German criticism were apparent long before the De Wette translation appeared.

Parker questioned the messianic interpretation of the fifty-second chapter of Isaiah in an article for the *Scriptural Interpreter,* to the great distress of one of its subscribers. When he was ordained and settled as a minister to a small congregation in West Roxbury, Massachusetts, he continued his heterodox researches. He wrote a long and detailed review of David Friedrich Strauss's *Das Leben Jesu* (1835) for publication in the *Christian Examiner* in 1840. The beginning of the review, which is taken up with a summary of Strauss's own introductory survey of the history of biblical interpretation since Origen, allows Parker the opportunity to explain how Strauss arrived at his radical argument. Strauss asserted that the New Testament did not merely contain mythological elements (like the Nativity story or the Ascension) but was itself fundamentally mythological in character. Most interpreters have rested their belief in the historicity of the Gospels upon the tradition that the Gospels were written by eyewitnesses, but Strauss "finds little reason for believing the genuineness or the authenticity of the Gospels," regarding them instead as "spurious productions of well-meaning men, who collected the traditions that were current in the part of the world, where they respectively lived."

Parker calls this the weakest part of Strauss's argument, but whether he really thought so is harder to determine. He wrote in his journal that he could not say all that he thought in the *Christian Examiner* review, but only what the readers of the journal would bear, and he wrote to Convers Francis to say that he was inclined to agree that Strauss might be right "in the main" when he calls the New Testament a "collection of Mythi" (Parker to Francis, March 22, 1839). In any case, Parker quickly proceeds in his review to give Strauss's definition of "myth" – it is not a history but "a fiction which has been produced by the state of mind of a certain community" – and to summarize with zest the main points of Strauss's attack upon the credibility of the Gospels, particularly the more than two hundred and fifty pages *Das Leben Jesu* devotes to the subject of miracles. By the end of Strauss's attack not a single miracle – not even the Resurrection itself – is left standing.

Does Parker accept Strauss's conclusions? At the end of his review he lists several deficiencies in the logic of *Das Leben Jesu:* first, that Strauss begs the miracles question by assuming from the outset that miracles are utterly impossible; next, that he refuses to believe that the Ideal can ever be incarnated in a single individual; next, that he assumes but never proves that the Gospels are not genuine and authentic; finally, that in his determination to find myths everywhere he makes the effect precede the cause. "He makes a belief in the resurrection and divinity of Christ spring up out of the community, take hold on the world, and produce a revolution in all human affairs perfectly unexampled; and all this without any adequate historical cause." Parker dismisses Strauss's attempt in his "Concluding Treatise" to save the "eternal truths" of Christian faith by seeing them as unconscious projections of the whole human race. "If there was not an historical Christ to idealize," Parker points out, "there could be no ideal Christ to seek in history."

Where in history do we then seek for Christ, if the tales about his life and resurrection are myths? Strauss leaves the authenticity of one element in the Gospels unchallenged. Parker quotes Strauss's contention that a comparison of the synoptic Gospels will show that "the granulary discourses of Jesus have not been dissolved and lost in the stream of oral tradition, but they have, not rarely, been loosened from their natural connexion, washed away from their original position, and like boulders rolled to places where they do not properly belong." One suspects that Parker was drawn to this sentence less for its critical than for its affirmative force: The discourses of Jesus, though granulary and dislocated, have survived the dissolving powers of time, oral transmission, and blundering apostolic redactors. On these small rocks Parker would found his mature faith.

When the miracles controversy broke out between the Transcendentalists and the traditional Unitarians, Parker naturally took part. He was by far the best linguist (he read some twenty languages, including Syriac and Coptic) and best biblical scholar among the Transcendentalists, and his familiarity with recent German criticism enabled him to meet the professional theologians on their own ground. His first contribution was a review in the *Christian Register* of a pamphlet edited and introduced by Andrews Norton.

The pamphlet was a reprinting of an attack by three Princeton scholars writing in the *Princeton Review* upon the Transcendentalists in general and Emerson's Divinity School Address in particular. They were particularly incensed by the assumption of the New School that

the truths declared by Christ and his Apostles were from God only in the same sense in which all our own intuitions of truth are from God. The Koran is of equal authority with the Bible; all pretended revelations have one and the same authority, that is, the self-evidence of the truths which they contain. The Gospel of Christ is thus stripped of its high prerogative as a special message from God; and holy prophets and apostles, nay, our Saviour too, were deceived in supposing that they had any other kind of communication with God, than that which every man enjoys.

Andrews Norton had liked their argument so well that he reprinted their two essays as a pamphlet in Cambridge in 1840 and affixed a commendatory notice to it.

Parker attempts to crush this production with superior scholarship, showing that the Princeton scholars are shallow and dependent on secondary sources for knowledge of the philosophy and theology they attack. But his long piece sinks under the weight of its own learning and contains only one really memorable sentence: "Our countrymen are now wandering in the wilderness, parched with thirst, and pinched by hunger; we look longingly, – not back to the flesh-pots, and leeks and garlics of Locke, and the Egyptian bondage of sensualism, but forward to the promised land of Truth, Liberty, and Religion."

Parker's experience with theological niggling must have made him understand why Emerson refused to engage in it. In any case, he began to believe that the debate about miracles was fraying into squalid accusations and depressing occasions for self-display. In his journal he expressed his wish that someone would "move the previous question" – in other words, stop arguing about credentials and ask what everyone really wanted to know: *"How does man attain to Religion?"* He decided to attack Norton head-on in a pamphlet he published under the pseudonym of "Levi Blodgett." Blodgett presents himself as a plainspoken Yankee and addresses an open letter to the gentlemen of Cambridge asking them to explain what he cannot for the life of him understand – why a true Christian needs to be convinced of the truth of Jesus' doctrines by miracles. The truths of Jesus, being self-evident, are in no need of miraculous confirmation. To argue as Norton did that miracles constitute the sole proof that the relation between God and humanity is *real* makes us rest our "moral and religious faith" on "evidence too weak to be trusted in a trifling case that comes before a common court of justice." Besides, the Bible in which these miracle stories occur is frankly acknowledged by Unitarians to be full of fabulous material. Norton himself concluded in 1840 that the first two chapters of Matthew (the Davidic genealogy of Jesus and the story of the Annunciation) were spurious. How then can perfect historical accuracy be claimed for any part of a document so riddled with interpolations and embellished with myth?

This was bad enough, but Parker's real heresy lay less in the critical weapons he turned against Scripture or the logical ones he turned against testimony than in the quiet relinquishing of Christianity's claim to exclusive possession of truth. "All religions are fundamentally the same," Christianity being only "one religion among many, though it is the highest." Hence all religions must appeal to the "primary essential truths of religion, which are innate with man." Religious geniuses like Jesus appeal to these innate truths, and their utterances become the scriptures of nations.

These principles were already implicit in the Divinity School Address, but in his pamphlet Parker was willing to state them with particular frankness and in so doing reveal what the underlying quarrel concerning "miracles" had really been about all along. What miracles offer us is proof that our revelation is *the* revelation, that we are not merely children of God but inheritors of his blessing — Jacobs rather than Esaus. Remove miraculous confirmation from the teachings of Jesus and Christianity becomes merely "one religion among many." Trinitarians had always warned that denying divinity to Jesus would end in this diffuse sort of Theism anyway, and they naturally were quick to point out that the Transcendentalists had taken the final step beyond Christianity that the Unitarians had initiated.

Despite his attempt at anonymity Parker soon found himself the object of hostile speculation. His defense of the Transcendentalists in the *Christian Register* and similarly disturbing articles in *The Dial* attracted the hostile attention of his clerical colleagues. At an annual meeting of Unitarian ministers in May 1840 Parker discovered that the question to be debated was "Ought differences of opinion on the value and authority of miracles to exclude men from Christian fellowship and sympathy with one another?" Parker held his peace at this meeting, where older liberals like Frederic Henry Hedge and George Ripley defended the Unitarian tradition of allowing the widest possible latitude of opinion. But Parker went home and confided to his journal his outrage that such a question should be raised. "This is the nineteenth century! This is Boston! This among the Unitarians!" And he added, "For my own part, I intend in the coming year to let out all the force of transcendentalism that is in me, come what will come." By the end of the year he had already started to suffer that polite freezing out that was Boston's only form of excommunication: his colleagues in the ministry began refusing to exchange pulpits with him.

Whether Parker was sufficiently stung by this treatment to decide that he might as well be hanged for a sheep as for a lamb or whether his growing sense of intellectual power simply made him ready to emerge from tutelage and anonymity, he very soon seized an opportunity offered him to move from minor irritant to major scandal. In May 1841 Parker was invited to deliver the sermon at the ordination of Charles C. Shackford at the Hawes Place Church in South Boston. Thirty-two years earlier Channing had made the ordination of Jared Sparks the occasion to define "Unitarian Christianity." Now Parker would use the opportunity provided by Shackford's ordination to redefine Christian truth in his own way. As a recent scholar has pointed out, the title of Parker's sermon, "A Discourse of the Transient and Permanent in Christianity," translates the title of an article by Strauss – though few people besides Parker himself were learned enough to get the complicated point of the allusion. In 1838 Strauss had replied to wholesale lament about the destructiveness of *Das Leben Jesu* by offering a rare "positive" appreciation of Jesus, whom Strauss praises as the greatest genius in history, devoted not to outward works but to the creation of a perfect soul. Strauss called his article "Uber Vergängliches und Bleibendes im Christenthum" and reprinted it in a volume called *Zwei friedliche Blätter* (Two peaceable papers).

Parker's division of Christianity is not quite the same as the one Strauss proposed in his article; rather, it returns to the distinction suggested in *Das Leben Jesu* between the granulary discourses of Jesus and the stream of myth and oral tradition in which they are embedded. But Parker's conscious intentions are peaceable. He simply wishes to rescue Christ's Word from his churches. He begins his discourse with fervent and glowing praise of the preaching of Jesus. He praises Jesus' words as simple, lucid, and self-explanatory. In the opening paragraphs he describes their miraculous survival in a world of constant change, where empires rise and fall:

The philosophy of the wise, the art of the accomplished, the song of the poet, the ritual of the priest, though honored as divine in their day, have gone down a prey to oblivion. Silence has closed over them; only their spectres now haunt the earth. But through all this the words of Christianity have come down to us from the lips of that Hebrew youth, gentle and beautiful as the light of a star, not spent by their journey through time and through space.

Nothing is more "fixed and certain" than this "real Christianity," the religion Jesus taught. "The old heavens and the old earth are indeed passed away, but the Word stands."

Yet Parker soon turns from the "permanent" element in Christianity to attack the "transient," and here the havoc wreaked by his critical faculty upon theological history must have left his audience gasping. For in the remainder of his relentlessly argued discourse Parker focuses the whole force of his richly stocked mind toward demonstrating that *no* doctrine advanced or ritual celebrated by any Christian sect can proclaim itself free of inherited error or local prejudice. An honest study of the history of religions forces us to confess that the Unitarians, with their two modest sacraments and their tiny collection of dogmas (that Jesus was divinely commissioned, as his miracles show; that after his death he rose again and ascended into heaven), are no more safe from critical analysis than the *Summa Theologica* or the Byzantine church.

Any one who traces the history of what is called Christianity, will see that nothing changes more from age to age than the doctrines taught as Christian, and insisted on as essential to Christianity and personal salvation. What is falsehood in one province passes for truth in another. The heresy of one age is the orthodox belief and "only infallible rule" of the next.

We now smile at the obsolete systems of the past, but how can we know that "our Christianity" will not share the same fate? "Many tenets that pass current in our theology seem to be the refuse of idol temples, the off-scourings of Jewish and heathen cities, rather than the sands of virgin gold which the stream of Christianity has worn off from the rock of ages." The Bible itself has suffered a loss of its authority, its texts unraveled by critics, its sacred canon revealed to be the product of "caprice or accident." With unfeigned delight Parker slyly enlists Andrews Norton on his side. "One writer, not a sceptic, but a Christian of unquestioned piety, sweeps off the beginning of Matthew; another, of a different church and equally religious, the end of John. Numerous critics strike off several epistles. The Apocalypse itself is not spared, notwithstanding its concluding curse."

How then can we be sure the Apostles themselves "were not sometimes mistaken in historical, as well as in doctrinal matters"? What then? Christianity does not stand or fall with the doctrine of the infallible inspiration of "a few Jewish fishermen, who have writ their names in characters of light all over the world." The truth of Jesus' Word is not dependent upon the infallibility of the document in which they are preserved, nor on the personal authority of Jesus, any more than the axioms of geometry are dependent upon the personal authority of Euclid.

So if it could be proved – as it cannot – in opposition to the greatest amount of historical evidence ever collected on any similar point, that the Gospels were the fabrication of designing and artful men, that Jesus of Nazareth had never lived, still Christianity would stand firm, and fear no evil. None of the doctrines of the religion would fall to the ground; for, if true, they stand by themselves.

And, in case any members of the audience balked at this willingness to jettison the founder of Christianity in the name of Christian truth, Parker proclaims boldly, "Christ set up no Pillars of Hercules, beyond which men must not sail the sea in quest of truth." Real Christianity is the source of life. "It makes us outgrow any form or any system of doctrines we have devised, and approach still closer to the truth."

In his South Boston sermon Parker manages to combine those two qualities he said he admired most in theologians like de Wette and Schleiermacher – criticism that is "bold, unsparing, and remorseless" with a spirit of "profound piety." Parker's sermon is as radiant with the love of Jesus as it is scornful of the narrowness of the theologians who have sought to define him. "If ever I wrote anything with an *Xn* zeal," Parker wrote after the storm of protest had broken, "it was that very discourse" (Parker to Ezra Stiles Gannett, June 17, 1841). In this respect Parker's sermon is strikingly different from the Divinity School Address, where Emerson's attitude toward Jesus fluctuates between strained expressions of admiration and outbursts of unmistakable resentment.

The piety that informs Parker's South Boston sermon might have protected it if three outraged Trinitarian ministers who attended the ordination had not published a two-page precis of its argument in the orthodox *New England Puritan* with an accompanying challenge to Unitarians to comment on it. Although the Unitarian clergy who replied directly to this challenge hewed to the position that Unitarians recognized no creed or covenant that interfered with individual liberty, Unitarian publications – the *Christian Register, Monthly Miscellany,* and *Christian Examiner* – published attacks upon the South Boston sermon. Parker replied to their charges in a series of five lectures at the Old Masonic Temple in the winter of 1841–2. Unfortunately, the habit Parker had of branding his opponents with the most opprobrious of epithets only increased their alienation from him, and they began to refuse pulpit exchanges.

Parker was hurt that so few of his friends were willing to stand by him; by 1842 only eight ministers would still exchange with him. The remainder doubtless felt with Frederic Henry Hedge that progressive Christian minds must be *in* the church and not out of it. Hedge wrote to Convers Francis in 1843 to express his worry that "if the principle of dissent from existing institutions & belief continues to spread at the rate it has done for the last two years, the entire *Clerus,* professional and parochial, will be ousted in ten years" (Hedge to Francis, February 14, 1843).

When Parker compounded the offense of the South Boston sermon by publishing the Masonic Temple lectures as *A Discourse of Matters Pertaining to Religion* (1842), his colleagues in the Boston Association of Ministers invited him to a "tea" in January 1843 to inform him that many felt they could no longer bear the "vehemently deistical" tendencies of his writing and preaching. A minister named Chandler Robbins tried to convince Parker that "since the feeling in respect to him is so general," it was his "duty" to withdraw from the association, an argument seconded by others.

It cannot have been easy for a thirty-one-year-old man to stand up to the collective disapproval of his senior colleagues, but Parker refused to withdraw from the association, saying that what was at issue was the right of free inquiry. Then one of Parker's friends spoke up in defense of his sincerity; others (including some of his original attackers) hastened to join in that sentiment; and Parker broke into tears and left the room. Afterwards Robbins wrote to say that he "felt most deeply the delicacy and hard trial of your situation" and that he thought that Parker had acquitted himself nobly. But, he added, "It would have been unjust to you to have been less frank than we were" (Robbins to Parker, January 24, 1843).

In the end, Parker refused to be silenced or ousted from the church. He finally published his massive edition of De Wette's *Introduction to the Old Testament* in 1843 and then left for a tour of Europe made necessary by the cumulative exhaustion of the preceding years. Before departing he preached a sermon to his West Roxbury congregation thanking them for their fidelity to him in his time of trial. "Fear in the churches, like fire in the woods, runs fast and far, leaving few spots not burned," he told them. "I thought you would do what others did; others had promised more but fled at the first fire."

This sense – of what it takes to stand fast in the time of trouble – may be the most enduring personal legacy of Transcendentalism's period of challenge. Alcott and Emerson and Parker survived public immolations, but the same lesson was learned by those whose circumstances were necessarily more obscure. From her exile in West Newton, where Elizabeth Peabody had gone after the publication of *Conversations with Children on the Gospels* had ended her teaching career, Elizabeth wrote to her sister Sophia to explain what she meant by the "new light" she had attained by her experience at the Temple School.

I feel as I never felt before that to be true to one's self is the first thing – that to sacrifice the perfect culture of my mind to social duties is not the thing – that what we call disinterestedness of action is often disobedience to one's *daimon* – that one's inward instinct is one's best guide – that selfdenial may encroach on the region of the spiritual.

Her biggest mistake in Boston lay in not insisting upon a room of her own. "Something must be allowed to one's self for the infirmities of nature & it is better to be called selfish and oldmaidish than to lose one's own soul" (Elizabeth Peabody to Sophia Peabody, July 31, 1838).

6

LETTERS AND SOCIAL AIMS

TRANSCENDENTALISM WAS from the beginning a literary movement as well as a religious and philosophical one. The Transcendentalists kept journals and wrote poetry; they wrote long letters about
literature to one another; they tried their hand at prose sketches and Oriental
fables; they delivered lyceum lectures and commencement speeches; they
held "conversations" on topics like Beauty and Mythology; they reviewed
books for the *Christian Examiner* and the *North American Review*. But few of
the Transcendentalist texts that managed to find their way into print before
the 1840s could be classified strictly as belles lettres. Perhaps only Emerson's
Nature could really qualify as polite literature, a "prose poem" – though its
review by Francis Bowen in the *Christian Examiner* in 1837 suggests that even
Nature in its home territory was read more as a part of the philosophical
skirmishing going on between the Lockeans and the spiritualists than as a
work of the imagination.

There were many reasons for this state of affairs. The strong New England
prejudice against fiction made writing novels or short stories out of the
question for most of the Trancendentalists, even supposing that they had any
talent for plot or dialogue or any interest in the social complexities novelists
thrive on. Emerson ridiculed Jane Austen for her "vulgar boardinghouse
imagination," and Thoreau devoted a good part of the chapter "Reading" in
Walden to abusing those readers who read with saucer eyes and digest with
unwearied gizzards the latest romance about the Middle Ages. Poetry was
considered more respectable, but the kind of Wordsworthian Romanticism
practiced by William Cullen Bryant and the senior Richard Henry Dana
seemed too derivative to appeal to the fiercely independent Transcendentalists, and the vogue for Byronic imitations that had marked the 1820s in
America had died away without leaving much in its wake.

Some of the liveliest writing in the period was unpublished – the letters of
Emerson, Margaret Fuller, James Freeman Clarke, and Elizabeth Peabody;
the journals of Emerson and Thoreau. To think of these writings as really
"private" is not quite accurate, because both letters and journals were regularly passed around among the circle of friends – in fact, at one point Emer-

son had to borrow back one of his own letters from Margaret Fuller so that he could extract from it a passage for the essay he was writing, "Friendship." In these intimate reflections and exchanges the Transcendentalists could write with an exuberance their sense of decorum kept out of their published works; in letters particularly they could be witty, malicious, and seductive as well as high-minded and devoted to truth. Shortly after Emerson had completed his "Human Life" lecture series at the Concord Lyceum in 1839 the Reverend Barzillai Frost wrote to inform him that some Concord gentlemen who wanted to express their thanks for the lectures had gathered contributions to buy books for his library – the works of Sir Thomas Browne, Victor Cousin's twelve-volume translation of Plato, and the letters of Horace Walpole. Emerson enjoyed the Walpole as much as he did the Plato and Browne; to Margaret Fuller he boasted that Walpole had effected a change in his own style: "If I were in earnest to write you a letter, you would be forced to shade your eyes from my glitter."

Other Transcendentalists found in George Ripley's series, *Specimens of Foreign Standard Literature,* opportunities to translate works that had meant much to them. The spirit that moved these enterprises is best summed up in the words from John Milton's *History of Britain* that Margaret Fuller used as the epigraph to her 1839 translation of Johann Peter Eckermann's *Conversations with Goethe:* "As wine and oil are imported to us from abroad, so much ripe understanding, and many civil virtues, be imported into our minds from foreign writings; – we shall miscarry still, and come short in the attempts of any great enterprise."

Periodicals remained, however, the most tempting form of publication for the Transcendentalists in the 1830s and 1840s. Magazines and reviews offered beginning authors the pleasure of seeing something quickly in print; they also offered the stimulus of deadlines and the excitement of working with a group of like-minded contributors. (Getting contributors to submit manuscripts and printers to print issues on time or subscribers to pay for the numbers they had received was another matter, as most editors soon discovered.) When the young James Freeman Clarke wrote to Margaret Fuller in the early 1830s declaring his confidence that she will found a "New School" of American literature in which he plans to enroll himself, he thinks of her as the editor of a magazine, a "Maga" that will "make the North Americans and American Quarterlies" fly like chaff before an angry wind.

In the early 1830s many of the Transcendentalists published their position papers in the form of reviews for the *Christian Examiner,* but as the group began to acquire a distinct identity the notion of publishing a magazine of its own naturally arose. As early as 1835, Frederic Henry Hedge and George Ripley were planning a "journal of spiritual philosophy" in which they hoped to enlist the aid of "all the Germano-philosophico-literary talent in the country." Emerson even tried to persuade Thomas Carlyle himself to come to America and assume the editorship, an offer Carlyle declined.

At the same time, a group of Unitarian clergy who had emigrated to cities in the Ohio Valley were determining to publish a magazine of their own, partly to disseminate Unitarian theology, partly to serve as a forum for discussion of western issues and a showcase for western literary talent. Ephraim Peabody, the Cincinnati editor who was responsible for putting together the first issues of their magazine, the *Western Messenger,* wanted to make the journal a forthright defense of Unitarian doctrine in a region dominated by varieties of Calvinism; he was wary of material too obviously recondite. But Clarke, now pastor of a congregation in Louisville, Kentucky, clearly hoped to find room in the *Messenger*'s pages for the works of his eastern friends as well, for he was soon pleading with Fuller to send him anything she had written to help fill the magazine, whose first issue appeared in May 1835.

Peabody was reluctant to publish Fuller's pieces, reminding Clarke that other magazines had perished from trying to satisfy tastes they had not yet created. For his part Clarke was furious that the pieces he had solicited had been treated cavalierly. He wrote to Peabody to demand that at least ten or twelve pages of each issue be given to him to do with as he wished. In those pages, at least, he could feel himself *"unlimited & absolute."* His appetite for dominion was soon to be satisfied, for by the end of 1835 ill health and family tragedy had forced Peabody to offer Clarke the sole editorship of the *Messenger.*

Clarke quickly discovered that the life of an editor is no despotism of unlimited and absolute power but a trial by petty miseries, particularly when a magazine's editors and subscribers alike are scattered over a vast territory and its finances are always approaching ruin. Still, the pleasure of being able to shape the journal at least partly as he pleased was considerable. By the spring of 1836 Clarke was publishing defenses of Goethe and Schiller, reviews of Wordsworth and Tennyson, and selections from the journals of John Keats, whose brother George had emigrated to Louisville, where Clarke met him and became his close friend.

One persistent source of disappointment for Clarke lay in the failure of the eastern church to contribute to the support of his magazine or even to buy subscriptions to it. He angrily accused his eastern brethren of indifference, yet in September 1836 he was forced to appeal to their charity to keep the *Messenger* alive. The trip he made back to Boston, where he preached at Dr. Channing's Federal Street Church, was successful in raising donations, and it had an unexpected benefit as well for the chronically homesick Clarke. He was on hand for the first two meetings of the Transcendental Club and was in

Cambridge to discuss the books that were published that season by the club's members.

How much this might have meant to Clarke can be guessed from the letters he sent Margaret Fuller from the very beginning of his Louisville ministry. His decision to move to the West had resulted in part from his sense that the atmosphere of Boston and Cambridge Unitarianism was stultifying and oppressive. In the West he had indeed found freedom, but it was a freedom so capacious that it devalued everything he had to say. "Intellectually speaking I am at present dead," he complained to Fuller in a long letter written in December 1834.

You know why I came West. I thought that here was real freedom of thought and opinion, and that it was therefore a more favourable scene for the development of a mind which wished to have the power to express individual convictions. I have so found it. We are free to speak here whatever we think — there is no doubt of it. Public opinion is not an intolerant despotism, for there is no such thing as Public Opinion. The most opposite and contradictory principles, notions, opinions, are proclaimed every day. Every variety of human thought here finds its representative. All is incongruous, shifting, amorphous. No spirit of order broods over this Chaos. (Clarke to Fuller, December 15, 1834)

Rebellion needs something rigid to overthrow, Clarke was discovering, and if he could not find it in Louisville he could enlist in the wars back home. Returning to Louisville in November 1836 he eagerly declared his allegiance to the New School by publishing largely favorable reviews of Furness's *Remarks on the Four Gospels* (in December 1836), Emerson's *Nature* (in January 1837), Brownson's *New Views of Christianity, Society and the Church* and Alcott's *Conversations with Children on the Gospels* (both in March 1837), and Ripley's *Discourses on the Philosophy of Religion* (in April 1837). Clarke did not write all of these reviews himself, but he did write the defense of Alcott, and in April he began writing letters to Boston periodicals protesting the savagery of Alcott's treatment by the press there. Alcott was grateful that anyone had the courage to praise him and noted in his journal that the young men of the Boston area "grow sturdy and free as soon as they leave the enervating influences of this region of shackle & authority."

The summer of 1837 proved to be a depressing one for Clarke. He had lost eastern subscribers not only for his championing of the New School but also for some of his tactless remarks about the lassitude of the American Unitarian Association. His own congregation, he thought, cared little for the ideas he was trying to import from the East, whereas Cambridge conservatives fumed at the way he had taken over a respectable Unitarian publication and used it to puff the works of the Transcendentalists. Moreover, the sense of isolation that Clarke had complained about in his letters to Fuller ever since his arrival at Louisville was particularly hard to bear when so much seemed to be happening back home.

Still, Clarke's distance from the "region of shackle & authority" would soon prove useful. His "Letter on the State of Unitarianism at the East," which appeared in the June 1838 number of the *Western Messenger* and announced the "death" of Unitarianism through its own coldness and indifference, happened to reach subscribers shortly before Emerson delivered his Divinity School Address. Clarke had published the letter anonymously but as editor of the magazine he could hardly avoid taking responsibility for it, and he now found himself permanently linked with the "New School" in the public mind.

If he were a young minister in Boston who had expressed himself with this degree of freedom he might have expected the same treatment that Emerson or Theodore Parker received — threats of social ostracism, denial of Christian fellowship, even accusations of blasphemy. Mild as these forms of persecution were, Emerson and Parker were distressed (though not silenced) by them at the time. But Clarke's distance from Boston rendered him immune from such pressures. His fellow editors at the *Messenger* were mostly young liberals like himself, and the members of his congregation cared little about what the Harvard Divinity School or the Boston Association of Ministers thought of Clarke or the *Messenger,* though they did resent the amount of time he spent visiting the East and writing about the theological battles there.

Clarke's frustrating distance from the intellectual life of Boston turned out to give him a freedom of expression no Bostonian could enjoy — a perfect example of what Emerson would come to call the Law of Compensation. Clarke was quick to take advantage of his freedom. When Andrews Norton, nine days after the Divinity School Address, published his intemperate attack "The New School in Literature and Religion" in the *Boston Daily Advertiser* and included the *Messenger* in his general condemnation as a "professedly religious work" that nonetheless declined to condemn "the atheist Shelley," Clarke treated the diatribe with insouciance. To Fuller he wrote, "What a lot of twaddle they have uttered about Mr. Emerson! I think of writing something in the next *Messenger* about his oration, and the New School. I am seized with an industrious qualm since I got well, and write much" (Clarke to Margaret Fuller, September 30, 1838). And in the next letter to Fuller he was able to announce, "I shall have an article in the next *Messenger* about Mr. R[alph] W[aldo] E[merson], and the New School. Why not? As well as the professor" (Clarke to Fuller, October 7, 1838).

This tone of insouciance surfaces in the published articles Clarke wrote as well. "R. W. Emerson and the New School," which appeared in the November 1838 issue of the *Messenger,* professes to be surprised that anyone could find Emerson's Divinity School Address dangerous.

Parts seemed somewhat obscure, and for that we were sorry – in places we felt hurt by the phraseology, but we bounded carelessly over these rocks of offence and pit-falls, enjoying the beauty, sincerity, and magnanimity of the general current of the Address. As critics, we confess our fault. We should have been more on the watch, more ready to suspect our author when he left the broad road-way of commonplace, and instantly snap him up when he stated any idea new to us, or differing from our pre-conceived opinions.

Clarke denies the existence of the kind of cabal Norton fears. What holds the members of the New School together is their dissatisfaction with the current state of affairs in literature, philosophy, the church, and the professions. "The common principle which binds them together and makes them if you choose a school, is a desire for more of LIFE, soul, energy, originality in these great departments of thought."

In his own way Clarke had tried to foster these qualities in the *Messenger,* publishing essays and sketches by Margaret Fuller, poetry by Emerson, Jones Very's mystical sonnets, and (in serial installments that threatened to extend to infinity) Clarke's own translation of W. M. L. De Wette's *Theodore; or, The Skeptic's Conversion,* a religious novel tracing the passage of a young man from doubt to intuitive faith. But Clarke had grown weary of the demands of the editorship and frustrated by his congregation's refusal to offer him a perma-nent call. His homesickness for Boston had never left him, and when his Cincinnati coeditors suggested transferring the magazine back to its original home he eagerly accepted. He had recently married Anna Huidekoper, the daughter of a wealthy western Pennsylvania landowner who had been one of the earliest patrons of the *Western Messenger,* The allowance of one thousand dollars a year given to the couple by her father made it possible for Clarke to contemplate leaving his position in Louisville without having a firm offer of another post elsewhere.

The role money played in underwriting Transcendentalist experimentation is considerable. Emerson, for instance, had a legacy from his first wife's estate when he resigned the ministry at the Second Church. He was certainly aware of (and bothered by) the possibility that his brave defiance of convention might be founded more on security than on courage. After returning from one lecture in which he had preached the gospel of self-reliance to young men he worried in his journal that it might be his twelve hundred dollars a year speaking and not him. In a similar way, the wealth of the Huidekoper family made possible James Freeman Clarke's break from a situation he had long found frustrating.

Both men still needed to find additional sources of income, but at least they could not be frightened into submission or compromise.

The Transcendentalists' endless obsession with issues of "manliness" is usually read by modern students as the expression of anxieties about gender — loss of masculinity or failure to attain it. But in its own time such language was easily recognizable as a part of a code that had more to do with livelihood than with manhood — or rather with the relationship between livelihood and manhood. The opposite of "manliness" in this code is not "effeminacy" but "servility." To be dependent on another person for one's livelihood places the strongest possible check on freedom of thought or speech. Transcendentalist ministers felt this check with particular irritation, because they were beholden both to the members of their own churches and to the ministerial organizations that might declare them heretical enough to be unworthy of sharing in pulpit exchanges.

Orestes Brownson would later explain in his own periodical, the *Boston Quarterly Review,* why New England ministers were likely to feel the temptation to compromise their principles. Very few congregations could support a minister if the three or four richest pew owners withheld their subscriptions or pew tax; hence these three or four individuals – who were always conservatives – dictated to the clergyman what doctrines he should preach.

If they are distillers, he must not speak of the sin of manufacturing and vending ardent spirits; if they are factory owners, the iniquities of the present factory system he must not point out; if they are merchants, he must not censure the unchristian spirit of trade which the mercantile world fosters; if slaveholders, he must labor to prove that slavery is sanctioned by all laws human and divine . . . ("The Laboring Classes" [Part 2] October 1840)

Leaving the religious for the secular pulpit, as Emerson did, is a partial solution, but many of the same dilemmas remain. An orator is before all else *a man who prays,* and a professional orator is obliged to confront his own tendencies toward complaisance in ways that producers of more tangible commodities need think about only on market day. To reach an audience at all one must please them enough to hold them, for – as Chaucer's Harry Bailly long ago pointed out to the tedious Monk, "Whereas a man may have noon audience / Noght helpeth it to tellen his sentence." Yet to please an audience too much is to do it no good, for only by awakening it to a sense of its own danger can it be saved.

Emerson remembered a clerical ancestor who liked to castigate his parishioners freely from the pulpit; when they rose, offended, to leave the church, he would cry out after them, "Come back, you graceless sinner, come back!" But Transcendentalist ministers had renounced claims to an authority like that, and Transcendentalist writers had not yet discovered how to acquire its equivalent in print – hence their sometimes uneasy veerings between flattery and excoriation.

To speak the truth and go on speaking it is no easy matter, and the man or woman who plans to speak truth habitually needs not only a tough soul but also a steady income. Increasingly, the Transcendentalists, as they left established posts in the church or had careers closed to them (as Alcott and Peabody were driven out of teaching by the furor following publication of *Conversations with Children on the Gospels*), had to find new ways of making a living. Alcott became a day laborer and conductor of "conversations," Emerson a lecturer, Thoreau a surveyor, Peabody the owner of a bookshop, Ripley the organizer of a communal organization, Brownson the writer and editor of a quarterly review. Even those who stayed in the church, like Clarke and Parker, felt the need to create new forms of church organization that would free them from financial dependence upon church members whose allegiance to the congregation depended upon their ownership of a pew in the church building rather than upon spiritual agreement with the minister and the rest of the congregation.

Clarke would eventually found such a church in Boston when he returned there – the Church of the Disciples, organized in 1841 and made up of spiritual seekers from all over the city who had found no sustenance in the established churches. But for now Clarke and his wife rested on the Huidekoper estate in Pennsylvania while Clarke preached at the local Unitarian church and tried to decide what to do about his future. Meanwhile, the magazine he had edited for three years was about to founder through its determination to discuss the growing problems of the urban poor.

The new editors of the *Western Messenger* in Cincinnati were William Henry Channing (a nephew of the Unitarian leader, who had arrived in Cincinnati in 1839 to become pastor of its First Unitarian Church) and James Perkins, both of whom were more concerned with problems of social reform than Clarke had been. Perkins in particular had become convinced that the human tragedies he witnessed in his ministry-at-large to Cincinnati's poor came not from individual failure but from the failure of social institutions. In October 1839 one of the magazine's nominal coeditors, a Cincinnati lawyer named John Vaughan, published in the *Messenger* an article, "Chartism," on the British movement for working-class rights, in which he hailed Chartism as a "glorious sight" and maintained that economic inequalities were in themselves sufficient justifications for revolution.

Needless to say, prosperous and conservative Unitarians like Clarke's father-in-law, Harm Jan Huidekoper, angrily denounced Vaughan's article. Huidekoper called it "Jacobinical" and expressed his regret that Clarke was no longer the *Messenger's* editor. He prepared his own rebuttal of the idea that the sins of the rich are responsible for the miseries of the poor, which the *Messenger* published in the summer of 1840. Its title — "The Right and Duty of Accumulation" — might serve as the motto for the kind of conservative Unitarianism that frequently bankrolled Transcendentalist enterprises and endured Transcendentalist scorn. Huidekoper argued that wealth represents the power to do good and that the desire to accumulate it is the parent of industry among the poor.

The *Messenger,* however, was not repentant, and when Carlyle's 1839 pamphlet *Chartism,* with its savage attack on the ineptitude of the British governing classes, was published in America by Emerson in 1840, Vaughan reviewed it in a three-part article that praised Carlyle's love of liberty and refused to criticize his proposals for reform. At the same time, back in Boston, a far more famous review of the same pamphlet was being published in the *Boston Quarterly Review* — Brownson's manifesto "The Laboring Classes." Brownson's prediction of imminent class warfare and his call for the outlawing of inherited property provoked a torrent of abuse not only from the Whigs but also from the Democrats whose cause he had embraced and who were now desperate to disown him.

The *Western Messenger* was willing to come to Brownson's defense. In October 1840 one of the editors published a review of "The Laboring Classes" that derided the "howling and shrieking of Conservative men and women" against Brownson and compared it to "the uproar by which the Peruvians tried to stop the moon's eclipse." Though the *Messenger* strongly disagreed with Brownson's proposals for eliminating inequality, deeming them unchristian in spirit and unwise in thought, it nonetheless declared its belief that the man himself was "as honest as Luther, as fearless as Knox, and as capable, either for good or evil, as any writer of our day."

If the *Messenger's* editors hoped to arouse sympathy for Brownson by likening him to the heroes of the Reformation they failed, for angry subscribers deluged them with letters protesting their support of Brownson. Huidekoper wrote to protest that the radicals rarely subjected their own ideas or the ideas of their friends to the same kind of "severe scrutiny" that they turned on conservative doctrines. "Either from the love of novelty, from the fear of appearing to be behind the age, or from a blind partiality for the innovator, these new opinions are often treated with a criminal indulgence."

The *Messenger* refused to back down. W. H. Channing, who had just returned from a visit to Boston, reported with heavy irony in the December 1840 issue that he had visited the "cave of this Cyclops" (Brownson) and had found no human bones. If he had offended his readers he could only repeat his determination to offend them again. "We became editors of this periodical, supposing ourselves to be freemen, and the Western Messenger an organ of Freedom; and, so long as we continue editors, we shall assuredly act on this supposition." Channing did not have long to act, for the magazine soon expired; the April 1841 number was the last.

Many lessons could be drawn from the *Messenger's* demise. Subscribers to any periodical are likely to resent bewildering changes of editorial direction and to punish editors for ideological shifts by cancelling their subscriptions. Liberals will tolerate radicalism only so long as it does not interfere with the property relations from which they derive their income; it is one thing to assent to the doctrine that the evidences of Christianity are inward and spiritual, quite another to contemplate allowing the state to seize and redistribute one's estate in the interests of greater social equality. The writer who would speak his opinions on all subjects with perfect fearlessness and with scorn for consistency must either give up periodical publication altogether or vow to publish a periodical alone.

"Men like to make an effort," Orestes Brownson asserted in one of his early essays for the *Christian Examiner*. The proposition may not be true of the human race as a whole, but it certainly is true of the man who advanced it. Brownson's biographer calculates that he wrote nearly 150,000 words a year during the first two years of the *Boston Quarterly Review*'s existence, when he was filling the magazine he had started with every imaginable kind of material – long disquisitions on the theory of democracy, reviews of everything from the latest works of Carlyle and the novels of Bulwer Lytton to a series of cookbooks by a vegetarian (a cousin of Alcott's) who thought that roast beef was the Devil and who aimed to fight him with a diet of mush, apples, cold boiled potatoes, and desserts of parched corn.

The task of putting together four times a year a review each of whose issues was well over a hundred pages in length (one issue is 228 pages long) would have flattened most men, but the impression the early volumes of the *Boston Quarterly Review* make on anyone willing to read them straight through is one not of the founding editor's exhaustion but of his exuberance. Brownson does not so much review books as devour them and convert them to power. He is the only American who sounds like the *Edinburgh* reviewers – like Jeffrey, Brougham, and Hazlitt. His prose has the kind of aggressiveness and relentless logic that can make watching him conduct an argument a source of pleasure. It is a pity that Hazlitt did not live to read him, for Brownson has the quality of intellectual fearlessness that Hazlitt had found sadly lacking in William Ellery Channing's essays when he reviewed them in 1829.

Brownson's achievement is all the more impressive when one remembers that he had only the shortest contact with formal schooling, a brief stint at a country academy when he was fourteen. For the rest, he was self-taught and learned the journalist's trade by editing or contributing to a variety of religious and political journals whose titles chart his turbulent course through various denominations, cities, and political movements — from the Universalist *Gospel Advocate and Impartial Investigator* of Auburn, New York, through the New York *Free Enquirer* of Frances Wright and Robert Dale Owen, to the Genesee, New York, *Republican and Herald of Reform*. When Brownson had left in turn both the Universalist ministry and the Workingmen's party and declared himself a Unitarian, he signaled his change of heart by starting yet another journal, the short-lived Ithaca, New York, *Philanthropist*.

By the summer of 1832 Brownson had become a Unitarian minister in Walpole, New Hampshire. He soon began sending articles to the leading Unitarian journals in Boston. George Ripley, the editor of the *Christian Register*, struck up a friendship with him and tried to persuade him to come to Boston. Eventually Brownson's powerful articles began appearing in the prestigious *Christian Examiner* where others besides Ripley took notice of them. Emerson learned a great deal from Brownson's early pieces. In Brownson's 1834 review of Benjamin Constant's history of religion, for instance, there is a distinction between the religious sentiment and the succession of forms it inhabits that sounds like an early draft of Emerson's essay "Circles," with its evocation of the endless proliferation and decay of the spirit's various incarnations.

By July 1836 Brownson had moved to Chelsea and had become the editor of yet another journal, the *Boston Reformer*. William Ellery Channing, whom Brownson revered (hearing a friend read Channing's famous sermon "Likeness to God" had converted Brownson to Unitarianism), hoped that Brownson's experience preaching to working-class congregations might help him bring the Unitarian doctrine of salvation through self-culture to groups usually reached only by the fiercer consolations of evangelicalism on the one side or the anticlerical radicalism of Abner Kneeland on the other.

Still, Brownson longed to have a magazine free from the entanglements of denominational allegiance. He wanted to escape the kinds of compromises forced on writers by the expectations of editors; he was equally determined to avoid the miseries faced by editors whose contributors were dilatory or otherwise unreliable. And it seems clear that he nursed the ambition of providing an American alternative to the British reviews that had played such an important role in the self-education of his whole generation. Finally, he felt a prophet's sense of urgency to speak out on "the problem of the Destiny of Man and of Society," as he declares to his readers in the "Introductory Remarks" to the first issue of the *Boston Quarterly Review*. "I must and will speak. What I say may be worth something, or it may be worth nothing, yet say it I will. But in order to be able to do this, I must have an organ of utterance at my own command, through which I may speak when I what I please. Hence, the Boston Review." A farewell note at the bottom of the last page of the first number is similarly uncompromising. Brownson sends his magazine forth to make its own fortune. "If the public like it and want it, they will support it, and if they do not, – then of course they will not."

This blunt self-reliance was as far as possible from the gentility of Cambridge, and Brownson (whose rough manners and contentiousness grated on the Transcendentalists quite as much as it did on traditional Unitarians) lost no opportunity to flaunt his independence from every group that might think it could claim his allegiance. The longest piece in the first number of the magazine is the address that Brownson had delievered in September 1837 to the Democratic State Convention at Worcester, Massachusetts. Brownson had used the occasion not so much to glory in his new political allegiance as to lecture his fellow party members about their too-facile equation of "democracy" with "the sovereignty of the people."

Tocqueville himself could not have attacked the "tyranny of the majority" more ferociously. "Are the people the highest?" Brownson demands.

Are they ultimate? And are we bound in conscience to obey whatever it may be their good pleasure to ordain? If so, where is individual liberty? If so, the people, taken collectively, are the absolute master of every man taken individually. Every man, as a man, then, is an absolute slave. Whatever the people, in their collective capacity, may demand of him, he must feel himself bound in conscience to give.

The real object of democracy is not to replace the sovereignty of the privileged classes with the sovereignty of the people but to restore to individuals their natural rights and to teach them to "perform those duties, and those duties only, which everlasting and immutable Justice imposes."

Yet if Whigs were gladdened by the severe lesson Brownson preached to the Democrats at Worcester they were likely to be brought up short by his scathing attack upon Francis Bowen, the young philosophy tutor at Harvard whose review of Emerson's *Nature* had turned into a denunciation of the Transcendentalist movement. Brownson treats Bowen as too muddled to be worthy of refutation, but the aristocratic pretensions of Harvard come in for a pounding. Followers of Locke, like Bowen and the Harvard school, see the mind as a *tabula rasa* capable of being inscribed only from without, and they very naturally imagine themselves the only trustworthy inscribers. "But in point of fact, the masses are not so poor and destitute as all this supposes. They are not so dependent on *us,* the enlightened few, as we sometimes think them." Brownson is most passionate when (as here) he speaks in anger to the class that has temporarily adopted him about the class from which he rose;

nothing infuriates him as much as the condescension of the educated classes toward the poor and ignorant. "Philosophy is not needed by the masses: they who separate themselves from the masses, and who believe that the masses are entirely dependent on them for truth and virtue, need it, in order to bring them back, and bind them again to universal Humanity."

Brownson's literary criticism is quite as vigorous and prickly as his political and philosophical theorizing. Even the Transcendentalists he had defended against Bowen's strictures had no particular reason to rejoice when it was their turn to come under Brownson's scrutiny. Emerson's utter disregard of logic exasperated Brownson, who valued logical consistency over life itself. And this attitude was shared by the young reforming minister to whom Brownson gave the task of reviewing "The American Scholar." William Henry Channing's review appeared in the January 1838 number of the *Boston Quarterly Review,* a year before Channing left for Cincinnati and his short-lived stint as editor of the *Western Messenger.* But he lamented that Emerson's conclusions are only "hinted, without the progressive reasonings through which he was led to them."

Brownson sounded a similar note when he reviewed the commencement day oration Emerson had delivered to the combined literary societies at Dartmouth College on July 24, 1838, shortly after the Divinity School Address. "Literary Ethics," like the Divinity School Address itself, had been published as a pamphlet in 1838, and Brownson attempted to review it in the January number of the 1839 volume. He tries at first to give a synopsis of Emerson's meandering oration, but the piece quickly turns into parody, and finally Brownson breaks off in exasperation:

But we give it up. We cannot analyze one of Mr. Emerson's discourses. He hardly ever has a leading thought, to which all the parts of his discourse are subordinate, which is clearly stated, systematically drawn out, and logically enforced. He is a poet rather than a philosopher – and not always true even to the laws of poetry.

Brownson rejects Emerson's contention that Americans are imitative rather than creative; the Patent Office furnishes proof enough to the contrary. As for the ritual laments about American acquisitiveness, Brownson dismisses them with the exuberance and largeness of sympathy that make the *Boston Quarterly Review* delightful: "It is said, that the whole nation has been absorbed in the pursuit of wealth. We admit it, and rejoice that it has been so. It is a proof of the unity of our national life." And he adds, more seriously: "The very intensity with which we pursue wealth is full of hope. It proves that the pursuit of wealth can be only a temporary pursuit, that we must soon satisfy our material wants, and be ready to engage with similar intenseness in providing for the wants of the soul."

Brownson reviewed the Divinity School Address in October 1838. There he had more serious charges to bring against Emerson than illogicality. The address strikes him as dangerous. Emerson, he says, tells us to obey our instincts and scorn to imitate even Jesus. But which instincts are we to obey? "How shall we determine which are our higher instincts and which our lower instincts? We do not perceive that he gives us any instructions on this point. . . . We are to act out ourselves. Now, why is not the sensualist as moral as the spiritualist, providing he acts out himself?" Worse still, Emerson appears to recognize no higher good in the universe than the perfection of the individual soul. Such "transcendental selfishness" provokes Brownson to genuine anger. "Are all things in the universe to be held subordinate to the individual soul? Shall a man take himself as the centre of the universe, and say all things are for his use, and count them of value only as they contribute something to his growth or well-being?" According to this system "I am everything; all else is nothing, at least nothing except what it derives from the fact that it is something to me."

This tendency to "pure egotism" Emerson shares with his masters Carlyle and Goethe. "The highest good they recognise is an individual good, the realization of order in their own individual souls." Can a person who adopts this moral rule really be called moral? "Does not morality always propose to us an end separate from our own, above our own, and to which our own good is subordinate?" It is indeed necessary to achieve harmony within the individual soul, but this is only a preliminary step. "Above the good of the individual, and paramount to it, is the good of the universe, the realization of the good of creation, absolute good." The man who forgets himself is "infinitely superior to the man who merely uses others as the means of promoting his own intellectual and spiritual growth."

Emerson encourages us to recognize ourselves as God, but in doing so he is unwittingly destroying the religious sentiment he professes to venerate, because that sentiment springs from our sense of our own dependence and of God's infinite power. If Emerson is right in seeing God only in the soul, present in potentiality as the oak is in the acorn, who is there to depend on? "Is there really and actually a God? Is there any God but the God Osiris, torn into pieces and scattered up and down through all the earth, which pieces, scattered parts, the weeping Isis must go forth seeking everywhere, and find not without labor and difficulty?"

Brownson cannot believe that we are justified in dispensing not only with "historical Christianity" and the use of miracles as evidence for faith but even with Jesus himself. Nor can he really believe that the Gospel records are of no further use in the church, that they have become merely a "let and a hindrance." We need more faith than our own. "We want that record, which is to us as the testimony of the race, to corroborate the witness within us. One witness is not enough." If the church has recently erred in giving us only the historical Christ, "let us not now err, by preaching only a psychological Christ."

Brownson's criticisms of the Divinity School Address were all the more telling because they proceeded neither from a desire to defend Lockean epistemology and the rickety structures of historical evidence nor from a fear of the murderous instincts of the lower classes who needed to be kept under control by a system of threats. And Brownson's questions must have hurt doubly because they came close enough to some of Emerson's own recent self-reproaches to sound like confirmation of his worst suspicions. Yet for Emerson, unlike for Brownson, one witness to spiritual truth *was* enough, and its radiance made all external aids superfluous.

Yet if Brownson did not hesitate to attack Emerson when he thought Emerson was wrong he was willing to retract his whole attack on the Divinity School Address half a year later — not because he had changed his mind about its shortcomings but because the abuse heaped on Emerson by other critics awakened his sympathies. In an article in the April 1839 number defending Bulwer Lytton (whose novels Brownson loved) from the usual charges of immorality Brownson suddenly speaks of a quarrel closer home:

Let the odds be against a man, and he may call us his friend, and count upon our taking up the cudgels in his behalf. Since the world has turned against our friend Emerson . . . we heartily repent of having appeared among his opponents. We were as much out of our place as Saul was among the prophets. Heavens! only think of the Boston Quarterly Review joining with grave doctors and learned professors to write down a man who has the boldness to speak from his own convictions, from his own free soul! It was a great mistake on our part, and one which, alas! we perceived not till it was too late. Honor to every man who speaks from his own mind, whatever be his word. He is an Iconoclast, a servant of the true God, even though it be a left-handed one.

Brownson was himself soon to discover what it felt like to be an iconoclast needing support from friends. Like the editors of the *Western Messenger* Brownson was deeply affected by Carlyle's *Chartism* with its indictment of the laissez-faire economic philosophy that first created and then justified the sufferings of the working class. "Is the condition of the English working people wrong; so wrong that rational working men cannot, will not, and even should not rest quiet under it?" Carlyle asks and proceeds to heap page after page of evidence to show how very wrong it is. With bitter urgency he tries to make his complacent readers understand that the condition of the laboring poor has become so intolerable and so degrading that unless some government capable of relieving their miseries and answering their demand for simple justice can be found to replace the "No-government" (the law of the marketplace, the economics of supply and demand) that presently ruled England, the working class will necessarily be moved to seize the government for itself in an upheaval as violent as the French Revolution.

Carlyle's indictments of the English government and the capitalist system were devastating, but the practical remedies he proposed to alleviate misery – education and emigration – were worse than useless, Brownson thought. Brownson reviewed Emerson's 1840 American edition of *Chartism* for the *Boston Quarterly Review* in July 1840. Carlyle is "good as a demolisher, but pitiable enough as a builder. No man sees more clearly that the present is defective and unworthy to be retained . . . but when the question comes up concerning what ought to be, what should take the place of what is, we regret to say, he affords us no essential aid, scarcely a useful hint."

Brownson in fact confesses that he always rises from reading Carlyle so disheartened and exhausted that he almosts dreads to encounter a new Carlyle text. But the example of *Chartism* helped precipitate Brownson's translating into literary form his growing dissatisfaction with the Unitarian response to the suffering of the poor in the United States. To preach self-culture or self-improvement in such circumstances is complacent to the brink of cruelty. Brownson turned his review of Carlyle, entitled "The Laboring Classes," into the occasion for his own version of *Chartism,* his own analysis of the class struggle.

First, Brownson laughs at Carlyle's fear that the English working class is close to revolution. The plight of the working class in England is the worst in Europe precisely because in England the middle class is more numerous and powerful than anywhere else on earth. "The middle class is always a firm champion of equality, when it concerns humbling a class above it; but it is its inveterate foe, when it concerns elevating a class below it." Brownson despairs for the workers of England because their enemies are impossible to escape. "Their only real enemy is their employer."

To prescribe education as a cure for the condition of men and women who work twelve to sixteen hours a day is also laughable, and emigration can afford only temporary relief, "for the colony will soon become an empire, and reproduce all the injustice and wretchedness of the mother country." Besides, the problem in Europe is not overpopulation but maldistribution of property. Workers now labor for the benefit of their employers, and Brownson offers a new economic principle, Brownson's Law: "Men are rewarded in an inverse ratio to the amount of actual service they perform."

Few laborers in modern factories can ever hope to achieve more than subsistence wages. Individuals born poor do sometimes become rich, but if they attain wealth it is not by accumulating wages. A rich man is a man who has "contrived to tax for his benefit the labor of others." Southern planters confess that it would be cheaper to abolish slavery and hire laborers by the hour; what greater proof is there of the injustice of the current wage structure?

As for Dr. Channing's self-culture, it is a very good thing, but "it cannot abolish inequality, nor restore men to their rights." It may restore to laborers their sense of dignity and hence give them the courage to contend for those rights, but as a "remedy for the vices of the social state" it is powerless. Self-culture is for the Abbott Lawrences who own the cotton mills, not for the girls who tend the spindles until their health breaks and then go home to their villages to die. The priestly class represented by Channing is in fact the historical oppressor of mankind, and mankind can never be liberated until it abolishes religion as a profession. "What are the priests of Christendom as they now are? Miserable panders to the prejudices of the age, loud in condemning sins nobody is guilty of, but silent as the grave when it concerns the crying sin of the times. . . . As a body they never preach a truth till there is none whom it will indict."

The only way to establish the kingdom of God on earth is to do away with all monopolies that keep the laboring classes poor. The government must be wrested from the control of the banks, for the banks represent the interests of the employers. But the reforms must be even more radical than that. All hereditary descent of property must be abolished, for it represents "the privilege which some have of being born rich while others are born poor." Brownson realizes that this measure will never be carried without "the strong arm of physical force." The war in which this transformation will be effected will be "the like of which the world as yet has never witnessed, and from which . . . the heart of Humanity recoils with horror."

"The Laboring Classes" is one of the most powerful and disturbing documents produced by the Transcendentalist movement. Its vision of the inevitability of class struggle and the murderous war of class interests is a far cry from the woolly benevolence that usually passes for Transcendentalist social thought. But with Brownson's attack on Channing, the man he had called his "spiritual father," and on the bankruptcy of Channing's "self-culture" as a way of erasing class differences, some deep personal bitterness suddenly seems to propel Brownson back to the working-class anticlerical radicalism of his days with Frances Wright and Robert Owen's *Free Enquirer.*

As for Brownson's curious vision of the kingdom of God on earth, it resembles a strange kind of casino where the management would collect all the winnings at the end of each evening and redistribute them anew for the next day's gaming, not the kingdom of love and mutual solace described in the New Testament. It is significant that Brownson never stopped to ask himself what would happen to a man's wife and children if his property were confiscated by the state at his death – a flaw in his argument, as he admitted in his later "defense" of the article, and one which led him to champion (briefly) the cause of property rights for women.

Brownson's real desire is not for a social state at all. At one point in his analysis he speaks of the "savage state" from which civilization emerged and commends it for its lack of inequality. "The individual system obtains there. Each man is his own centre, and is a whole in himself. There is no community, there are no members of society, for society is not." If it were possible to combine this state with "the highest possible moral and intellectual cultivation" it would be "the perfection of man's earthly condition." But human beings must take a long detour through history before they can reach again the perfect isolation of the self-centered individual.

Without realizing it Brownson has revealed his kinship with the Emerson of the Divinity School Address, the Emerson he had abused. Brownson, too, places the individual above all else, and "The Laboring Classes" finally leaves an impression not of class solidarity but of personal isolation. Brownson's ideal men, all born equal, some rising to great wealth but yielding that wealth back to the state at their death, seem an incarnation of Tocqueville's worst fears about Americans – cut off from ancestors, cut off from descendents, isolated forever within the solitude of their own hearts.

Loneliness, of course, was not what Brownson's critics feared as the worst result of his polemic. He was denounced on all sides as a Jacobin, a socialist, a hater of religion and a destroyer of society. The Whigs eagerly reprinted "The Laboring Classes" as campaign propaganda designed to show what the Democrats would do if they won the presidency; the Democrats quickly disowned him. Contributors to Brownson's magazine stopped sending their articles (the journalistic equivalent of a refusal of pulpit exchanges). Brownson replied to some of their objections in a later article with the same title ("The Laboring Classes," October 1840), but by then the election was almost upon the country, and the Democratic party went down to crushing defeat.

Almost the only sympathy expressed for Brownson in his home territory during the contentious summer of 1840 came from his closest friend among the Transcendentalists, George Ripley. Ripley had prepared an article on Brownson and the *Boston Quarterly Review* for *The Dial,* the magazine that the members of the Transcendental Club had long been planning. *The Dial*'s first number appeared in July 1840, the same month as "The Laboring Classes." This coincidence linked the two magazines in the public mind much more closely than the facts of the case warranted, for *The Dial* was as different from the *Boston Quarterly Review* as could be imagined. (Brownson put his finger on the most obvious difference when he reviewed the first volume of *The Dial* in the January 1841 number of the *Boston Quarterly Review.* "The Dialists belong to the genus *culottic,* and have no fellowship with your vulgar *sans-culottes,"* he wrote, quite well aware that most of the people who wrote for *The Dial* did not share his sympathy for the laboring classes – or, for that matter, for him.)

The Transcendentalists' plan to have a journal of their own, first broached in the mid-1830s, was revived again in earnest after the Divinity School Address and the controversy surrounding it, when established journals like the *Christian Examiner* were closed to the group. At the May 1839 meeting of the Transcendental Club, Alcott complained about the poor quality of contemporary journals, which seemed to him to be empty and lifeless. Again, in September 1839, club members discussed the possibility of starting a journal that should be "the organ of views more in accordance with the soul." Alcott suggested the title, which was meant to suggest both the magazine's openness to the light and its ability to mark the passage of current events.

An aim at once so lofty and so vague might seem an unpropitious one for a magazine, but *The Dial*'s planners could take heart from the flourishing state of the periodical press in the United States at the time. Periodicals of all kinds sold well – religious magazines, political journals, critical reviews, and ladies' magazines that mixed fiction and poetry with engraved fashion plates. The historian of the *The Dial*'s rise and fall points out that by 1842 nearly three million numbers of various periodicals were produced every year. Surely in a country so hungry for magazines there was room for one that aimed to look at life in a way more in accordance with the soul.

The connection with the Transcendental Club seemed to promise a healthy list of contributors, but finding an editor for *The Dial* was not easy. Emerson, who was engaged in the laborious process of reworking material from his lectures and journals to make up a volume of essays, flatly refused the post. He wrote to Margaret Fuller on October 16, 1839, to promise his assistance as a contributor but to decline any editorial position. "I should heartily greet any such Journal as would fitly print these Journals of yours, & will gladly contribute of my own ink to fill it up. But unless Mr. Ripley would like to undertake it himself, or unless you would, I see not that we are nearer to such an issue than we have been these two years past."

Emerson's willingness to suggest to Fuller that she herself consider the position may have come from his enthusiastic response to her translation of Eckermann's *Conversations with Goethe,* recently published as Volume 4 of Ripley's *Specimens of Foreign Standard Literature.* In the "Translator's Preface" Fuller spoke with an authority and simplicity that seemed to mark her coming of age as a writer. Emerson, to whom she had sent a copy of the book, wrote back in June 1839 to thank her and praise her "decision and intelligence." He told her that her translation was "a beneficent action for which America will long thank you," and the preface he praised as a "brilliant statement" that filled him with "great contentment & thanks" (Emerson to Fuller, June 7, 1839). When Ripley proved to be both too deeply embroiled in his pamphlet war over miracles with Andrews Norton and too occupied with his work as editor of the *Specimens of Foreign Standard Literature* series to consider editing *The Dial* as well, Emerson persuaded Fuller to take on the task, promising that Ripley would serve as coeditor to help with the business details.

For Fuller the editorship meant many things: a move from her role as occasional guest at Transcendental Club meetings to a position of authority; a chance to see her own work published and to invite contributions from her friends; a chance to work out her own aesthetic theories and explain them to the world. She had, it is true, long carried on correspondences with Hedge and Clarke and finally with Emerson that had allowed her to display her brilliance and exercise her peculiar powers of intrusion and caress. (In a letter of June 3, 1839, she had urged Emerson to visit her at her temporary residence in the Boston suburb of Jamaica Plain: "If you will come this week I will crown you with something prettier than willow, or any sallow. Wild geranium stars all the banks and rock clefts, the hawthorn every hedge. You can have a garland of what fashion you will Do but come.")

The learned Hedge treated her with respect; Clarke, from his exile in Louisville, adored her and tried desperately to amuse her; and Emerson, though he was startled by the impertinence of her first letter to him, soon found himself seduced by the way she invaded his reticences and demanded his responses. But her early "public" prose was disappointing even to her closest friends. Clarke could hardly conceal his surprise and dismay at the first pieces she sent him in response to his request for material to fill the *Western Messenger*. They were very unlike her letters; the style was Latinate and heavily mannered and the tone seemed alternately arch and patronizing.

All the Transcendentalists had problems with tone: their attempt to speak from the Reason rather than the Understanding led them to strain after effects that lent themselves to ridicule (one thinks of Norton's pardonable exasperation at being told by Emerson in the Divinity School Address that the religious sentiment is "myrrh, and storax, and chlorine, and rosemary"). But most of the male Transcendentalists had professions that obliged them to try their productions out on live audiences, those chastening critics of style. Clarke reported to Fuller in humiliating detail the disastrous reception of his first sermons in Louisville; still, he was getting an education in practical oratory no classroom could provide. Fuller knew all this and felt frustrated by her inexperience. If women's minds, as men complained, lacked precision and focus, it was partly because their "accomplishments" were meant for show rather than for use. In a world that denied them higher education, most kinds of employment, and entrance into the professions, women had little experience of the sharpening or toughening that takes place in the to-and-fro of public debate.

In the summer of 1839, Fuller consulted Bronson Alcott about how to hold a series of "Conversations" for women in Boston that might help bring women out of their habitual reticence. Fuller needed the money she could earn from the "Conversations" to help pay the rent on her family's house and to send two of her brothers to Harvard, and she wanted to avoid having to return to schoolteaching, which exhausted her and left her little time for writing. But she also wanted to oblige women to think for themselves, to examine their ideas as they discussed topics like "mythology" and "the fine arts" and to learn to revise, qualify, and defend what they had said. Notes taken by Elizabeth Peabody show how the process worked. To one young woman who had offered a definition of "life," Fuller replied, "Good, but not grave enough. Come, what is life? I know what I think; I want you to find out what you think." Such pedagogy hardly strikes anyone as revolutionary now, but to women who had scarcely ever been asked to do anything except repeat by rote, it seemed electrifying.

Fuller held a series of "Conversations" each winter between 1839 and 1844. The two-hour meetings were held at Elizabeth Peabody's house in Boston. Each of the twenty-five to thirty women who attended the meetings paid ten dollars for the thirteen-week session, enough to net Fuller almost five hundred dollars per year. The women who attended the "Conversations" came from different groups: Fuller's close friends, young women who were married to Transcendentalists or social reformers, and women who were themselves social activists, as well as older women from Boston's traditional Unitarian elite. (Men were invited to join during the second year, but they tended to dominate the conversation, and Fuller dropped the experiment after one attempt.) The women who paid to attend came to listen to Fuller's brilliant opening monologues, then to be coaxed out of their reticence by Fuller's kind yet insistent questioning. The way their stumbling replies were transfigured in her generous rephrasing made them feel transfigured as well. Ednah Dow Cheney (1824–1909), a young woman who attended the "Conversations," gave the best account of the way the love she felt for Fuller during the "Conversations" flowed back into confidence in herself.

I found myself in a new world of thought; a flood of light irradiated all that I had seen in nature, observed in life, or read in books. Whatever she spoke of revealed a hidden meaning, and everything seemed to be put into the true relation. Perhaps I could best express it by saying that I was no longer the limitation of myself, but I felt that the whole wealth of the universe was open to me. (*Reminiscences of Ednah Dow Cheney*, 1902)

Fuller's experience as editor of *The Dial,* on the other hand, involved her from the outset in a tangle of frustrations. She wrote to her old friend Frederic Hedge asking him to contribute something to the magazine's first number, but after a series of evasions he confessed that he now feared to associate himself in print with the Transcendentalists, whose recent wars with the Unitarian establishment during the miracles controversy had made his Bangor congregation uneasy. Fuller wondered whether her own contributions were "pertinent to the place or time." The material she had so far gathered – two of her own essays, extracts Emerson had made from the papers of his dead brothers Edward and Charles, an article on the Roman satirist Persius by Thoreau (taken at Emerson's insistence) – hardly seemed earth shaking, and she feared that those who looked to *The Dial* for the "gospel of transcendentalism" would be badly disappointed and would begin to blame her for what they could not find in the journal.

Her anxieties and the reactions they generated must have been intense, for the "Introduction" to *The Dial* that she drafted and sent to Emerson in April struck him as both arrogant and defensive. He volunteered an introduction of his own, which Fuller accepted. The correspondence between them makes clear that Emerson felt embarrassed by his need to intervene; it seemed to take away the authority he had urged her to assume. In fact Fuller's introduction, however callow or ill-judged it might have been, could not possibly have drawn as much ridicule down upon *The Dial* as another of Emerson's editorial suggestions did.

For several years Emerson had served, unhappily, as Bronson Alcott's chief manuscript critic and rejecting editor – telling him, for instance, that the manuscript of "Psyche" (Alcott's account of his daughters' childhood education) was simply not publishable even after three massive revisions, or sending back with similar discouragement a collection of "Orphic Sayings" Alcott had tried to pattern after Goethe's. Nothing is more irritating than a hopeless writer who dutifully revises what no amount of revision can save, but Alcott was incapable of taking hints, and by late April 1840 he had given his revised "Orphic Sayings" to Emerson in hopes of seeing them in *The Dial.* What made it worse was that Alcott had just moved with his family to Concord.

Emerson can be pardoned for wanting to get Alcott off his back, but the letter he sent to Fuller telling her that the revised "Orphic Sayings," though still bad, were not as bad as he had expected and might "pass muster & even pass for just & great" (Emerson to Fuller, April 24, 1840) shows how desperate he had become to find something of Alcott's he could publish. *The Dial* had been planning to publish pieces without identifying authors, but Emerson suggested that Alcott's name be printed over the "Orphic Sayings," because at least to people who knew Alcott they might then have a "majesti-cal sound" (Emerson to Fuller, May 8, 1840).

Emerson of all people should have known that the *ethos* of the speaker in a printed text can be constructed only from the text. For the readers and review-ers who encountered *The Dial* without any prior reverence for Alcott, the "Orphic Sayings" quickly became not only famous but hilarious. Transcenden-talist writing was always in danger of either rising unballasted into the clouds in its pursuit of the Ideal or descending into obscurities in its drive to solve the mysteries of existence. Alcott's "Orphic Sayings" does both at once.

"The poles of things are not integrated," Alcott complains in an Orphic Saying entitled "Genesis." "Yet in the true genesis, nature is globed in the material, souls orbed in the spiritual firmament. Love globes, wisdom orbs, all things. As the magnet the steel, so spirit attracts matter, which trembles to traverse the poles of diversity, and rests in the bosom of unity." The popular press could hardly resist the temptation to deflate such pretentious-ness. The New York *Knickerbocker* published in its November 1840 number a selection of "Gastric Sayings": "The poles of potatoes are integrated; eggs globed and orbed. . . . As the magnet the steel, so the palate abstracts matter, which trembles to traverse the mouths of diversity, and rest in the bowels of unity." A writer to the *Boston Post* compared the "Orphic Sayings" to "a train of fifteen railroad cars with one passenger."

Alcott gave *The Dial* a reputation for silliness and unintelligibility it found difficult to live down, particularly when Fuller, reluctant to hurt Alcott's feelings, took another batch of "Orphic Sayings" for the January 1841 number. But a more serious charge than obscurity began to be leveled at *The Dial* even by its friends. The magazine was too dreamy, too aesthetic, too unreal; it lacked a backbone; its verse was saccharine or vaporous; it ignored the real world. Orestes Brownson reviewed *The Dial* and found it "vague, evanescent, aerial." Emerson himself, though he had chosen or sug-gested a good deal of the material for the first number of *The Dial,* began to look enviously at the notoriety Brownson's journal was achieving. Shortly after the first *Dial* had appeared Emerson tried (unsuccessfully, as it turned out) to interest Fuller in printing a tract by Edward Palmer, the reformer who argued against the use of money. Emerson even offered to act as "godfa-ther" to the tract and introduce it himself. "O queen of the American Parnassus," he pleaded, "I hope our Dial will get to be a little *bad*. This first number is not enough to scare the tenderest bantling of Conformity" (Emer-son to Fuller, July 21, 1840).

Emerson returned to this theme in subsequent letters. A week later he was pestering Fuller to allow a friend named George Bradford to write on "the Abolition question" for the magazine. "He is the properest person to write on that topic, as he knows the facts, has a heart, & is a little of a Whig & altogether a gentleman" (Emerson to Fuller, July 27 and 28, 1840). In early August he confessed that he was beginning to wish for a different kind of *Dial* from the one he had first imagined. "I would not have it too purely literary. I wish we might make a Journal so broad & great in its survey that it should lead the opinion of this generation on every great interest & read the law on property, government, education, as well as on art, letters, & religion." He himself was trying to work on a paper that would treat the great subject of Reform. "And the best conceivable paper on such a topic would of course be a sort of fruitful Cybele, mother of a hundred gods and godlike papers. That papyrus reed should become a fatal arrow" (Emerson to Fuller, August 4, 1840).

The androgynous image Emerson conjured up to symbolize his ideal *Dial* essay — a Great Mother armed with a fatal arrow — may have been an attempt to appeal to Fuller, but it also suggests the difficulty he had deciding what kind of journal he wanted *The Dial* to be. Like others in the Transcendental Club Emerson feared that there was something "effeminate" about American art. It is not always clear whether Emerson thought American art lacked manliness because it was imitative or whether he feared that all art lacked manliness. But his anxieties ran deep. At the very first meeting of the group back in 1836 he had voiced his fear that the best talents of the day — Washington Allston, Horatio Greenough, William Cullen Bryant, William Ellery Channing — had a "*feminine* or receptive" cast rather than a "masculine or creative" one, and the idea troubled him repeatedly throughout the late 1830s when he was preoccupied with the problem of America's cultural dependence. Any journal of American *belles lettres,* then, was in danger of seeming effeminate, and *The Dial* particularly so because Emerson and Ripley had given the task of editing it to a woman.

Certainly Theodore Parker saw *The Dial* in this way. Parker, who disliked Fuller, wrote a letter to Convers Francis after the first two numbers of *The Dial* had come out complaining that *The Dial* bore about the same relation to the *Boston Quarterly Review* that "Antimachus does to Hercules, Alcott to Brownson, or a band of men & maidens, daintily arrayed in finery . . . to a body of stout men, in blue frocks, with great arms, & hard hands & legs — like the pillars of Hercules." Parker imagines an allegorical conflict in which the men and maidens of *The Dial,* bearing a banner with a cradle and pap spoon, confront the stout men in blue, led by Brownson "dressed like David; with Goliath's sword in one hand, & that giant's head in the other" (Parker to Francis, December 18, 1840).

If Fuller lacked something that Brownson and his hard-legged men obviously had, she also had something he lacked, as Emerson's comment about

George Bradford's projected article on abolitionism makes clear. Emerson wanted articles about reform, but most reformers were not gentlemen, and abolitionists were worst of all. To genteel ex-Unitarians, whose notions of self-culture necessarily included great stress upon personal refinement, offenses against taste were almost as serious as offenses against the spirit. When Emerson read "The Laboring Classes" he was surprised and delighted by its vigor. Brownson "wields a sturdy pen which I am very glad to see. I had judged him from some old things & did not know he was such a Cobbett of a scribe." But the catty remark he immediately adds says much about the impassible gulf between the culottic and sans culottic: "Let him wash himself & he shall write for the immortal Dial" (Emerson to Fuller, December 21, 1840).

Fuller's hopes for the new journal differed from Emerson's in significant ways. The prospectus printed on the back cover of the first number made it clear that under her editorship *The Dial* would aim at "the discussion of principles, rather than the promotion of measures" and that it would try to promote "the constant evolution of truth, not the petrifaction of opinion." At the same time she wanted to redefine literary receptivity in a way that removed it from the self-defeating terms in which Emerson had cast it. If all provincial or peripheral cultures must begin by importing their ripe understandings from foreign writings before they can attempt any great enterprise, as Milton had argued, then to be receptive is to be invigorated rather than emasculated.

In her manifesto in the first number of *The Dial,* the "Short Essay on Critics," Fuller describes the critical process in terms that make it seem anything but passive. Only the bad or "subjective" critic, who simply gives his impressions as laws, is feminine or receptive in Emerson's sense. The two good kinds of critics — the *apprehensive* critics, who "can go out of themselves and enter into a foreign existence," and even better the *comprehensive,* who actually "enter into the nature of another being and judge his work by its own law" — have learned how to turn receptivity into domination. As the Latin root of both words suggests — *prehendere,* "to seize" — both apprehensive critics and comprehensive critics are aggressive even when they are most sympathetic; they begin as emigrants but end as lawgivers at home in their own courts.

Fuller had every intention of remaining the lawgiver for *The Dial;* she insisted on making the magazine a reflection of her own interests and tastes, rejecting manuscripts Emerson had solicited, sometimes to his considerable exasperation. She looked with benevolence on the products of her own pen, publishing critical essays such as her forty-one-page survey of Goethe's life and works (July 1841); a "Dialogue" between Poet and Critic (April 1841); romantic fables like "Meta" and "The Magnolia of Lake Pontchartrain" (January 1841); and a good deal of her own poetry. And she gave generous amounts of room to the poetry of her girlhood friend Caroline Sturgis. But she also published some of Thoreau's essays and poems (though she rejected others), and she accepted as much material as she could from Parker, Emerson, Clarke, and Clarke's charming friend, Christopher Pearse Cranch (a poet and translator now perhaps best remembered for his cartoon of Emerson's Transparent Eyeball).

Fuller edited *The Dial* for two years. In April 1842 she announced her intention to resign. Her health, always poor, had suffered from the responsibilities of the job, and the salary she had been promised at the outset (two hundred dollars a year) had never materialized. Ripley, her coeditor, had become deeply involved with planning his community at Brook Farm and had announced in October 1841 that he was withdrawing from *The Dial*. Fuller needed to support her fatherless family, and *The Dial* could scarcely support itself.

After a few days deliberation Emerson decided to assume the editorship. The financial success of his recent lecture series, "The Times," meant that he could contemplate taking on a time-consuming job without pay. Under his editorship, many features of the magazine remained the same, and Emerson continued to solicit a good deal of material from Fuller (whose first article for him he hastened to praise as "manly"). Her most famous submission to *The Dial* after she had left the editorship was also her most militant. For the July 1843 *Dial* she sent Emerson a passionate article into which she distilled her pride and her anger. "The Great Lawsuit" speaks for the multitudes of women who were now, as never before, "considering within themselves what they need that they have not, and what they can have, if they find they need it." What they want is nothing less than "the intelligent freedom of the universe." What a woman wants is not the power to rule but the freedom "as a nature to grow, as an intellect to discern, as a soul to live freely, and unimpeded to unfold such powers as were given her."

Fuller has no wish to blot out difference between the sexes, so prominent in the mythologies she studies and loved. It may be true that "male and female represent two sides of the great radical dualism." But mythology seems to teach that these opposites are endlessly passing into one another: "Man partakes of the feminine in the Apollo, woman of the masculine as Minerva." It is therefore folly to set bounds to the limits of either sex. As for the argument that the highest bliss lies in the union of the two sexes, Fuller tartly replies: "Union is only possible to those who are units." Love to be strong must come "from the fulness, not the poverty of being." Fuller scornfully rejects Byron's arrogant belief that love is woman's whole existence. "Woman, self-centered, would never be absorbed by any relation; it would be only an experience to her as to man. It is a vulgar error that love, *a* love to woman is her whole existence; she also is born for Truth and Love in their universal energy."

As editor Emerson did more than offer Fuller a platform for the expression of her ideas. He began to bend *The Dial* in the direction he thought it should grow. He printed more poetry and solicited articles about social reform. He printed some selections from a Hindu text that had interested him the previous summer, *The Heetopades of Veeshnoo-Sarma;* in later numbers of the magazine he made selections from the holy books of other nations a regular feature entitled "Ethnical Scriptures," thus helping to encourage that religious syncretism that marks Transcendentalism's second phase.

Although Emerson still hated anything that looked like personal controversy he finally accepted for the October 1842 number an article by Theodore Parker entitled "The Hollis Street Council," so called after a recent meeting of the Boston Unitarian Association. The association's members had supported the dismissal of a minister who had angered his congregation by pointing out the contradiction between their pious condemnation of drinking and their willingness to profit from the liquor trade. Parker accused the association of hypocrisy and interference with freedom of conscience.

Emerson complained to Parker that his article was on a "most unpoetic unspiritual & un Dialled" subject (Emerson to Parker, September 8, 1842), but he accepted the piece as a way of honoring Parker, whose "Discourse on the Transient and Permanent in Christianity," delivered the previous winter, had brought down the wrath of the Unitarian establishment upon his head. Emerson could not bring himself to read Parker's manuscript completely through or to read proof for it. He instructed the printers to set it in type and send the proofs to Parker directly. This curious behavior says much about Emerson and his view of *The Dial;* he thinks of controversy as something that defiles the magazine's pages yet is unwilling to reject an author like Parker when the rest of the world is attacking him.

Emerson contributed a good many of his own poems and essays to *The Dial:* poems like "The Sphinx," which became almost as famous as the "Orphic Sayings" as an emblem for Transcendentalist unintelligibility; several of his lectures from the recent series "The Times"; an essay called "Transcendentalism" and one on modern literature; "The Chardon Street Convention," a wickedly funny account of a recent Boston convention of reformers and come-outers; an essay on Walter Savage Landor, woven out of journal passages from Emerson's 1833 visit to Landor in Italy, which drew an angry response from Landor himself. But Emerson had already published one complete book of essays when he began editing *The Dial* and was completing a second; he did not need the magazine to make his writings known. What he wanted to do with *The Dial* was to give space in it to talented young writers who needed encouragement and shepherding. Some of his enthusiasms are difficult to share. The verse of William Ellery Channing (Dr. Channing's nephew and Margaret Fuller's brother-in-law) is mostly weak and derivative, and the first installment of the murky allegory "The Two Dolons," by Charles King Newcomb, left no one but Emerson longing for the second (which never arrived). But Thoreau actually had the talent that Emerson ascribed to him, and in *The Dial* we can witness him becoming a major writer.

Henry David Thoreau (1817–62) was a Concord native, descended on his father's side from French Huguenots who had settled on the Isle of Jersey. Like Emerson, Thoreau had attended Harvard and like Emerson he had failed to distinguish himself there, graduating nineteenth in a class of forty-five. During his college years (1833–7) he nevertheless managed to acquire a rich education in Transcendentalism. He met and boarded with Orestes Brownson during a summer in Canton; he was tutored in Greek by Jones Very; he eagerly read Emerson's *Nature* and Emerson's edition of *Sartor Resartus;* and he was in the graduating class in 1837 for which Emerson delivered "The American Scholar" at commencement.

Some of the battles the first generation of Transcendentalists had waged seemed already won by 1837, and the battle they were about to wage over biblical miracles probably meant little to a young man whose first act upon returning to Concord was to *sign off* of the local parish. But the problem of finding work appropriate to the spirit – or any work at all – was acute in an economy made hostile by the recent financial panic, with its resultant deflation and mass unemployment. A job as a schoolteacher in the Concord public schools ended after two weeks. After that Thoreau applied unsuccessfully for teaching positions in a number of New England towns, then opened a small private academy in Concord, which soon grew large enough to need a second teacher. Thoreau asked his brother John to join him. He lived at home.

Emerson had come briefly into contact with Thoreau as early as 1835, when he examined a group of college students on rhetoric. But the two did not become friendly until the autumn of 1837, when Emerson's famous question to the twenty-year-old graduate – "Do you keep a journal?" – set Thoreau off on a literary project that would last almost as long as his life. Throughout the following years their friendship intensified. Acquaintances began to notice that Thoreau was imitating Emerson's style, his manner of speaking and gesturing, his handwriting – even (so one observer alleged) his nose. For his part, Emerson valued Thoreau's simplicity and directness, his union of intellectual brilliance with physical grace and strength, and his natural and instinctive nonconformity.

Thoreau served as curator of the Concord Lyceum from 1838 to 1840. He had delivered his first lecture there in 1838 on the subject of society. (The lecture, "Society," no longer survives, but the notes for it in Thoreau's journal suggest that it contained a lament over the insincerity of ordinary society and a plea for a better state that would foster ideal friendships.) Emerson may have realized that Thoreau would never make a successful platform lecturer; in any case he was eager to see Thoreau publish. When *The Dial* began, Emerson lobbied Fuller shamelessly (and not always successfully) to accept Thoreau's essays and poems. When Emerson took over he began accepting Thoreau's work in quantity.

To watch Thoreau develop from the first of his essays in *The Dial* ("Aulus Persius Flaccus") to the last ("Homer. Ossian. Chaucer.") is exciting, because it allows us to witness something that provincial literary magazines exist to foster and rarely do − the development of an immature writer into a powerful and confident one. Thoreau did a great deal of writing during the four years of *The Dial*'s existence, and only a portion of that was submitted to the magazine. Still, the experience of being accepted by (and rejected by) *The Dial* helped Thoreau understand what it meant to adopt letters as a profession and how that decision could shape prose.

"Aulus Persius Flaccus," the essay Thoreau gave to Emerson in the early months of 1840 and that Emerson finally badgered Margaret Fuller into accepting for the magazine's first number, starts out by sounding like hardly more than a college exercise, like the brief essays "The Greek Classic Poets" or "T. Pomponius Atticus" that Thoreau wrote at Harvard. In the "Thursday" section of *A Week on the Concord and Merrimack Rivers* Thoreau calls the essay (which he reprints there) "almost the last regular service which I performed in the cause of literature," and he would have us believe that he took Persius with him on that 1839 trip because "some hard and dry book in a dead language, which you have found impossible to read at home, but for which you still have a lingering regard, is the best to carry with you on a journey."

This affected indifference explains why Thoreau might have taken Persius to read in a country inn but hardly why he should have chosen to write about the experience; indeed, he begins the essay by lamenting that Persius seems "a sad descent" from the Greek poets and ends it by saying that there are scarcely twenty lines worth remembering from Persius's six extant satires. In what sense is this a service either to Persius or to the cause of literature? No wonder Fuller wanted to squelch the essay by pocket veto; it is hardly the sort of apprehensive or comprehensive criticism she was advocating in her "Short Essay on Critics." Instead, it seems a throwback to the kind of neoclassical essay in which gentlemen wandered through the classics pointing out beauties and faults.

Yet Emerson was right to see more in "Aulus Persius Flaccus" than that, for many passages give a startling glimpse into the future. So Thoreau, after blaming satire in general and Persius in particular for his "unmusical bickering," suddenly breaks out into a plea for true music in poetry whose paradoxes might fit neatly into *Walden:*

When the Muse arrives, we wait for her to remould language, and impart to it her own rhythm. Hitherto the verse groans and labors. . . . The best ode . . . has a poor and trivial sound, like a man stepping on the rounds of a ladder. Homer, and Shakespeare, and Milton, and Marvell, and Wordsworth, are but the rustling of leaves and crackling of twigs in the forest, and not yet the sound of any bird. The Muse has never lifted up her voice to sing.

There are also passages of Thoreau's familiar wit, as when he points out that the satirist always ends by arousing our suspicions. "We can never have much sympathy with the complainer; for after searching nature through, we conclude that he must be both plaintiff and defendant too, and so had best come to a settlement without a hearing." And in the final section of the essay Thoreau turns Persius's sneer at the sluggard who lives from moment to moment (*ex tempore*) into a matter for praise with a bilingual pun. "The life of a wise man is most of all extemporaneous, for he lives out of an eternity that includes all time."

If the Persius essay manages to mine wisdom and poetry from unpromising materials, Thoreau's next piece, "The Service," takes a subject very dear to Thoreau's heart – bravery – and makes a muddle of it. Like many young people of his generation, Thoreau had been moved by Emerson's writings about the possibility of military valor in civilian life, and "The Service," with its three portentously titled subsections ("Qualities of the Recruit," "What Music Shall We Have," and "Not How Many But Where the Enemy Are"), is meant to sketch the contours of the possible hero. But Thoreau had been reading too much Alcott and too much Emerson, and the result was a disaster. Some of Thoreau's sentences seem to call out for illustration by Edward Lear: "Mankind, like the earth, revolve mainly from west to east, and so are flattened at the poles."

Margaret Fuller rejected the essay in a letter of December 1, 1840. Writing rejection letters to a young man who is the protégé of one's own mentor is never easy, and under the circumstances Fuller tried to be diplomatic, casting her response in the military terms Thoreau had employed in the essay. She told Thoreau that she agreed with Emerson that essays not to be compared with Thoreau's had already been published in *The Dial;* but she added that she thought that his essay was "so rugged that it ought to be commanding." Although she offered to look at it again, Thoreau never resubmitted it or tried to publish it elsewhere.

Thoreau continued to publish poems in *The Dial*, but the next original prose composition he wrote did not find room there until Emerson assumed the editorship in 1842. By then much had changed in Thoreau's life. He had moved into Emerson's house in 1841 to serve as what one of his biographers calls a "transcendental handy man, combining manual and intellectual skills." He worked in the garden and tried to teach Emerson to graft apples; he managed *The Dial* when Emerson was away on lecturing tours; he became the close friend of Emerson's wife and children. Though Emerson never became the ideal friend Thoreau sought – one who would be "like wax in the rays that fall from our own hearts" and who could confer benefits without expecting gratitude in return – at least he gave Thoreau time to write and the patronage of an editor who was also his host.

Thoreau's happiness at finding a home and an environment suited for work was soon interrupted by tragedy. On the first day of 1842 Thoreau's beloved brother John cut himself while stropping a razor. Nine days later he developed the first symptoms of lockjaw, and, after suffering spasms and agonizing pain, died in Thoreau's arms shortly thereafter. Thoreau himself soon fell ill with symptoms that mimicked his brother's, though he slowly recovered. His native stoicism helped him pull out of the worst period of grief, and by the middle of March he speaks in his journal of a sudden access of "superfluous energy." The pattern is eerily reminiscent of Emerson's response to the death of his brother Charles in May 1836, when a period of numbness suddenly gave way to a burst of creative energy that produced the apocalyptic closing chapters of *Nature*.

Emerson helped find an outlet for Thoreau's renewed energy when he returned from Boston with a collection of wildlife reports commissioned by the Massachusetts state legislature and asked Thoreau to review them for *The Dial*. On the face of it, the task Emerson set Thoreau looked as unpromising as Lady Austen's suggestion to William Cowper that he write a poem about a sofa, but the very dryness of T. W. Harris's *A Report on the Insects*, C. Dewey's *Report on the Herbaceous Flowering Plants*, D. H. Storer's *Reports on the Fishes, Reptiles and Birds*, A. A. Gould's *Report on the Invertebrata*, and E. Emmons's *A Report on the Quadrupeds* liberated something in Thoreau's imagination that his attempts to write conventional literary reviews and essays had failed to do. "The Natural History of Massachusetts," published in *The Dial* for July 1842, is the first of Thoreau's works to reveal his gift for evoking natural scenes in luminous, precise language.

In an opening section Thoreau praises the cheering effects of reading books of natural history, particularly in the winter, when their "reminiscences of luxuriant nature" restore health to the soul. He recommends keeping such books as "a sort of elixir, the reading of which should restore the tone of the system." With a high good humor Thoreau dismisses the whole of the practical and political world and even pokes fun at "the trumpeted valor of the warrior," preferring to it the complacency of Linnaeus setting out for botanical expeditions in Lapland with his leather breeches and gnat-proof gauze cap. He has discovered a new kind of heroism. "Science is always brave; for to know is to know good; doubt and danger quail before her eye."

Then comes one of those passages that show how far Thoreau had already advanced beyond the creakily scholastic notion of "correspondences" that had guided Emerson's quizzing of nature. Thoreau writes:

Entomology extends the limits of being in a new direction, so that I walk in nature with a sense of greater space and freedom. It suggests besides, that the universe is not rough-hewn, but perfect in details. Nature will bear the closest inspection; she invites us to lay our eye level with the smallest leaf, and take an insect view of its plain. She has no interstices; every part is full of life.

The remainder of the review alternates between a quiet recital of statistics ("Of fishes, seventy-five general and one hundred and seven species are described in the Report") and long cadenzas made from Thoreau's own observations of animals, insects, birds, and fishes. These observations convey a sense of sheer delight at the energy and grace displayed by the state's creatures, such as the fox, whose pace is a sort of "leopard canter" and whose course is "a series of graceful curves," conforming to the shape of the land's surface. Even when Thoreau pursues it the fox maintains its self-possession. "Notwithstanding his fright, he will take no step which is not beautiful."

Such regard for beauty permeates the whole kingdom of nature. "In the most stupendous scenes you will see delicate and fragile features, as slight wreaths of vapor, dew-lines, feathery sprays, which suggest a high refinement, a noble blood and breeding." Even man, who had seemed so corrupt when viewed in his "political aspect," turns into a graceful enchanter when he sets his nets to catch fish.

The small seines of flax stretched across the shallow and transparent parts of our river are not more intrusion than the cobweb in the sun. I stay my boat in mid-current, and look down in the sunny water to see the civil meshes of his nets, and wonder how the blustering people of the town could have done this elvish work. The twine looks like a new river-weed, and is to the river as a beautiful memento of man's presence in nature, discovered as silently and delicately as a footprint in the sand.

Two mottoes that sum up the rest of Thoreau's writing can be mined from "The Natural History of Massachusetts." The first and better known, which comes from the opening pages of the essay, is "Surely joy is the condition of life." But the second is just as characteristic. Admitting that the publications he has reviewed might seem dry to the general reader, Thoreau cautions: "Let us not underrate the value of a fact. It will one day flower into a truth."

Throughout 1842 and 1843 Thoreau continued his high rate of productivity, writing in his journal, working on translations from the Greek (his translation of "Prometheus Bound" appeared in *The Dial* for January 1843, and later numbers carried translations from Anacreon and Pindar), and helping to excerpt material from translated Hindu, Confucian, and Buddhist texts for the "Ethnical Scriptures" department of the magazine. But he also experimented with a new form, the "excursion," a kind of small-scale travel literature recording impressions and thoughts during a trip on foot or by boat.

"A Walk to Wachusett," the first of these excursions, was not published in *The Dial* but in the *Boston Miscellany of Literature* for 1843. It records Thoreau's thoughts and perceptions as he goes on an expedition with Richard Fuller (Margaret's brother) to climb a mountain that was visible from Concord. "A Walk to Wachusett" blends autobiographical detail, observations of nature, and literary rumination in a style that would find its fullest expression in *A Week on the Concord and Merrimack Rivers*. When, as Thoreau reports, he reached the summit of Mount Wachusett, he read Virgil and Wordsworth in his tent, and wondered (like a nineteenth-century version of the "rising glory" poets of the early Republic) whether "this hill may one day be a Helvellyn, or even a Parnassus, and the Muses haunt here, and other Homers frequent the neighboring plains."

"A Winter Walk," Thoreau's next attempt to blend observation and thought, was published in the October 1843 number of *The Dial*. Here no distant peak serves as the destination; the essay records instead the strangeness and beauty of a day's walking in the neighborhood of Concord, from the sky's first lightening before dawn, when Thoreau unlatches his door to face the cutting air, till the winter evening when "the thoughts of the indwellers travel abroad" and the farmer, secure in the warmth his providence has insured, looks out with satisfaction at the glittering landscape around and the glittering stars above. As we accompany Thoreau in his stroll through the woods, and his examination of a glade in which a covering of snow is "deposited in such infinite and luxurious forms as by their very variety atone for the absence of color," or glide on ice skates deep into a frozen marsh that summer's heat will make inaccessible, or listen to the "faint, stertorous, rumbling sound" the rivers make beneath their surfaces of ice, we are invited to enjoy the exhilarations of winter.

Thoreau is mostly content to leave his countryside unmoralised, though in his praise of the "sort of sturdy innocence, a Puritan toughness," that he finds in all "cold and bleak places," like the tops of mountains, we find a constitutional attraction to a landscape that the painter Washington Allston would have called the objective correlative of Thoreau's stoicism. Such places, according to Thoreau, strike us as belonging to the original frame of the universe, "and of such valor as God himself."

In the next-to-last number of *The Dial* Emerson printed a lecture Thoreau had given at the Concord Lyceum the preceding November. "Homer. Ossian. Chaucer." attempts to consider poets who lie "in the east of literature," at once the earliest and latest products of the mind. Thoreau's Homer and Ossian are primitive bards, whose portrayal of the "simple, fibrous life" of warlike heroes makes our civilized history appear "the chronicle of debility, of fashion, of the arts of luxury." They speak "a gigantic and universal language." (The editors of Thoreau's translations remind us that classical education at Harvard in Thoreau's day gave the student "a distinctly romantic view of classical antiquity" and was based on European scholarship "openly primitivist in orientation.")

In the "Homer" and "Ossian" sections of his lecture, Thoreau scarcely departs from the Romantic commonplaces he shared with his contemporaries. But the "Chaucer" section – by far the longest part of the piece – is a surprise: Not only is it a shrewd and sympathetic appreciation of the beauty of Chaucer's poetry and of the deeper appeal of his humanity, but it is also a thoughtful meditation on the nature of literary history. Thoreau had studied both ancient and modern languages assiduously at Harvard, adding Italian, French, German, and Spanish to the required four years of Latin and Greek. He read Chaucer with E. T. Channing and studied literary history with George Ticknor, the historian of Spanish literature; he attended Henry Wadsworth Longfellow's lectures on northern European literature, Anglo-Saxon literature, and English medieval poetry.

Thoreau had a far wider knowledge of European literature and a far more sophisticated understanding of literary history than most of the other Transcendentalists, whose learning, although sometimes impressive, tended to favor philosophical or hermeneutical texts. In the fall of 1841 he seems to have been toying with the idea of compiling an anthology of earlier English poetry; he was reading every poetic text and anthology he could find in the Harvard library – ballads, romances, metrical tales, saints' lives. Though Thoreau never completed the anthology project, the effort of reading through a great deal of English and Scottish poetry of the Middle Ages gave him an understanding of Chaucer's peculiar excellences that few of his contemporaries shared. Even though Chaucer, in Thoreau's view, is not a heroic bard like Homer or Ossian, he is still, in many respects, "the Homer of the English poets" in being the wellspring of English literature, the most original of its origins. "Perhaps he is the youthfullest of them all." Modern poetry is mournful and reflective, but in Chaucer we still find "the poetry of youth and life, rather than of thought; and though the moral vein is obvious and constant, it has not banished the sun and daylight from his verse." Anyone who reads Chaucer can appreciate his humor, his perception of character, his "rare common sense and proverbial wisdom," but only someone who had approached him "through the meagre pastures of Saxon and ante-Chaucerian poetry," as Thoreau had just done, could understand how great Chaucer's contribution to the creation of literary language in England really was.

Chaucer, in fact, "rendered a similar service to his country to that which Dante rendered to Italy," for "a great philosophical and moral poet gives permanence to the language he uses, by making the best sound convey the best sense." And this was true even though Chaucer sought no part in the turbulent political strife of his century. He was a literary man and a scholar, not a man of action. "There were never any times so stirring, that there were not to be found some sedentary still." If we read him without criticism, it is because in his fidelity to his craft he has "that greatness of trust and reliance which compels popularity." And is that fidelity not a kind of heroism? The true poet is "a Cincinnatus in literature," weaving into his verse both "the planet and the stubble."

The nearly ten years spanned by the main Transcendentalist periodicals – the *Western Messenger* (1835–41), the *Boston Quarterly Review* (1838–44), and *The Dial* (1841–4) – were the formative and maturing years of the movement itself. Most of the contributors are now forgotten, and the thought of the time and energy spent in publishing such ephemera makes one want to exclaim (as Thoreau did of ante-Chaucerian poetry) that "it is astonishing to how few thoughts so many sincere efforts give utterance." Yet the work the periodicals did was important. They gave their editors and major contributors a sense of what the profession of letters was like; they provided a forum for the free expression of ideas; they let beginning writers like Thoreau experiment with forms and ideas. Their editors insisted on the right of free expression, even when they found one another's ideas distressing or repellent.

Most of all these periodicals cooperated in the great work of making midcentury American prose as flexible an instrument as the neoclassical prose of the Founding Fathers had been. Clarke's generous enthusiasm, Brownson's fierce logic, Fuller's critical sophistication and her feminist scorn, Parker's indignation, Thoreau's precision, Emerson's alternations between oracular statement and dry wit, and even Alcott's vaporous apothegms and the parodies they generated all helped to turn the language into something very different from the Unitarian prose of the 1820s and 1830s – made it sharper, tougher, more powerful; polished it for use and kept it ready to hand.

7

THE HOPE OF REFORM

R ELIGIOUS CONTROVERSY and the publishing of periodicals absorbed much of the Transcendentalists' energy during the early
1840s. But larger movements caught their attention as well. The
various reform movements sweeping the country seemed to offer support to
the theory that a new age was indeed at hand, an age when the mountainous
obstructions of inherited evil would be forced to yield to the pure force of
spirit. Life would learn to conform itself to the idea in the mind; a new
church and state would flow outward from the wellsprings of regenerate
souls. In an 1839 lecture, "Literature" (from a series entitled "The Present
Age"), Emerson had predicted that the genius of the time would soon "write
the annals of a changed world and record the descent of principles into
practice, of love into Government, of love into Trade. It will describe the
new heroic life of man, the now unbelieved possibility of simple living, and
of clean and noble relations with men."

The sense that great things were taking place or were about to take place
in the world often made Emerson at once hopeful and chagrined. He wrote to
his young friend Caroline Sturgis in October 1840 that he felt that he and his
friends were "the pets & cossets of the gracious Heaven, have never known a
rough duty, have never wrestled with a rude doubt, never once been called to
anything that deserved the name of an action. . . . I am daily getting
ashamed of my life."

Yet the antislavery and temperance crusaders, the organizers of the factory
workers, and the defenders of the poor, the imprisoned, the insane, were not
likely to make many recruits among disciples of the newness, as Emerson
himself acknowledged in a lecture entitled "The Transcendentalist," delivered in December 1841. "The philanthropists inquire whether Transcendentalism does not mean sloth. They had as lief hear that their friend was dead as
that he was a Transcendentalist; for then he is paralyzed, and can never do
anything for humanity."

The causes of this paralysis were several. At the heart is the old split
between the life of the Understanding and the life of the Reason, which
makes action seem either ineffectual or supererogatory: "One prevails now, all

buzz and din; and the other prevails then, all infinitude and paradise; and, with the progress of life, the two discover no greater disposition to reconcile themselves." But less metaphysical causes were at work too. A patrician dislike of reformers — who were often evangelical in religion, crude in expression, peremptory in their demands for commitment — often crops up in Emerson's public and private writings from the period, and not only in Emerson's. When Fuller, who had migrated to New York in 1843 to take up a job reviewing books for Horace Greeley's *Tribune,* was called upon to review *The Narrative of the Life of Frederick Douglass,* she rebuked William Lloyd Garrison for the strident preface he had written for the book:

We look upon him with high respect; but he has indulged in violent invective and denunciation till he has spoiled the temper of his mind. Like a man who has been in the habit of screaming himself hoarse to make the deaf hear, he can no longer pitch his voice in a key agreeable to common ears.

To this Garrison might have replied that he was indeed screaming to make the deaf hear, and that Emerson and Fuller were the sort of deaf people he was particularly desirous of reaching.

A more serious obstacle in the way of their embracing any particular reform movement grew from the Transcendentalists' intense dislike of all forms of association. Any group of people gathered together to work toward good or to eradicate evil will find themselves obliged either to suppress dissent in the interests of solidarity or to endure endless ideological squabbling. Both of these alternatives were hateful to the Transcendentalists, who had just emerged from the old hypocrisy of Unitarian civility and had no wish to exchange it for a reformer's bullying or a reformer's cant. In his introductory lecture to the series entitled "Lectures on the Times," delivered in December 1841, Emerson asserts that the reformers of his own day are indeed "the right successors of Luther, Knox, Robinson, Fox, Penn, Wesley, and Whitfield. They have the same virtues and vices; the same noble impulse, and the same bigotry." The denouncing abolitionist who castigates the reluctant Northerner is himself a slaveholder in his habits and thoughts. "He is the state of Georgia, or Alabama, with their sanguinary slave-laws walking here on our north-eastern shores."

Yet in another mood Emerson could identify the various reform movements of the day as upwellings of the eternal life force. In a lecture entitled "Man the Reformer," delivered in January 1841, he asks:

What is man born for but to be a Reformer, a Re-maker of what man has made; a renouncer of lies; a restorer of truth and good, imitating that great Nature which embosoms us all, and which sleeps no moment on an old past, but every hour repairs herself, yielding us every morning a new day, and with every pulsation a new life?

Boston bankers who sneer at the idea of a juster world only show how corrosive is the national skepticism. "The Americans have many virtues, but they have not Faith and Hope."

How might a juster world be brought into being? Without coercion, without violating "the sacredness of private Integrity"? As he states in the lecture "Reforms" from which that phrase is taken, Emerson thought he glimpsed an answer.

Our doctrine is that the labor of society ought to be shared by all and in a community where labor was the point of honor the vain and the idle would labor. What a mountain of chagrins, inconveniences, diseases, and sins would sink into the sea with the uprise of this one doctrine of labor. Domestic hired service would go over the dam. Slavery would fall into the pit. Shoals of maladies would be exterminated, and the Saturnian Age revive.

The mixture of hyperbole and worldliness in this passage is a clue that Emerson was not taking this prescription for universal reform with entire seriousness, though he was probably not the only Massachusetts burgher to dream occasionally of returning to an agrarian simplicity, when a New Englander did not need to worry about either servants or slaves. In any case, a life devoted to labor would at least be *genuine,* not a tissue of conventions and hypocrisies. Would you live the heroic life? "Write your poem, brave man, first in the earth with a plough and eat the bread of your own spade."

At the end of this lecture Emerson carefully distances himself from the recruiters for any particular reform. "Though I sympathize with your sentiment and abhor the crime you assail yet I shall persist in wearing this robe, all loose and unbecoming as it is, of inaction, this wise passiveness until my hour comes when I can see how to act with truth as well as to refuse." Yet Jesus allowed himself to be persuaded to that first miracle at Cana, and hopeful reformers could hardly be blamed if they took Emerson's reluctance as an implicit invitation. Ellen, Emerson's elder daughter, remembered that about this time "all sorts of visitors with new ideas began to come to the house, the men who thought money was the root of all evil, the vegetarians, the sons of nature who did not believe in razors nor tailors, the philosophers, and all sorts of come-outers." Feeding this menagerie was no easy task; her mother's recipes began with instructions like "take 3 pts. of sour milk" or "beat 2 doz. eggs." At the dinner table the vegetarians tended to bolt their squash and potatoes and glare at the slower meat eaters, eager for the pudding to come. One guest responded to an offer of tea with an exclamation of astonished outrage. "Tea! I!!!" When butter was offered to him a moment later his response was the same. "Butter! I!!!"

Understandably Emerson's patience sometimes wore thin, and on one occasion desperation pushed him into an unlikely feat. A certain "new light" had come to visit him in the morning, announcing that he planned to leave on the afternoon stage for Boston. When the stage drew near and the guest showed no signs of leaving, Emerson said, "Here comes the stage. I'll stop it for you," and he took off in a run after the departing coach while his amused wife looked on from the balcony. "My running," he said after the guest was safely dispatched, "was like the running of Ahimaaz the son of Zadok."

In the fall of 1840, however, Emerson received a visit from a reformer he could not so lightly dismiss. George Ripley had gradually come to believe that the Unitarian ministry could no longer serve as a platform from which to preach spiritual perfection or social reform. His battles during the miracles controversy with the conservatives in his own denomination had disheartened him, because they seemed to reveal a growing rigidity and intolerance in what had once been the most liberal of denominations. His continued preaching on social issues had wearied some members of his congregation. On October 4, 1840, he wrote a letter of resignation in which he vigorously castigated all his opponents but expressed renewed hope that a practical Christianity would eliminate suffering throughout society.

However tiresome they had sometimes found his preoccupation with issues of reform, Ripley's parishioners were finally reluctant to let him go. They prevailed upon him to stay through the beginning of the next year, but he remained determined to leave. On March 28, 1841, he preached his farewell sermon, reaffirming his faith in the obligation of all Christians to work toward establishing the kingdom of righteousness on earth.

Liberation from a pulpit where he had never felt truly competent as a preacher or comfortable as a would-be reformer gave Ripley an exhilaration that made this normally sober man look as if he were "fermenting and effervescing" (as James Freeman Clarke put it) with plans for the reformation of the world. Nor was he alone. Emerson wrote to Carlyle that there was not a man in New England but had the plan for a new social order in his pocket. The despair caused by the economic depression during the late 1830s had not succeeded in extinguishing the millennial zeal of the earliest days of the Transcendentalist movement; hope merely took a new form. Instead of assuming (as Emerson had in the closing sentences of *Nature*) that the redemption of the soul will cause the kingdom of God to organize itself around the beholder's sight, individuals like Ripley became convinced that only a reorganization of existing social structures could nurture the regeneration of the soul.

In recent years Ripley had felt himself drawn more and more strongly toward practical reform. He visited several English and German pietist communities and attended several conferences sponsored by "The Friends of Universal Reform" where he heard Christian socialists speak. In Albert Brisbane's *The Social Destiny of Man* (1840), an American exposition of the doctrines of the French social theorist Charles Fourier, Ripley came across the idea that a single perfectly organized community could by its example convert the whole society. The idea sounded enough like the old Puritan doctrine that the redeemed community should be a "city on a hill" to appeal to a man who had begun life as an orthodox Congregationalist, yet Fourier made it seem modern, scientific, secular. Fourier's plans for his ideal community wedded the prestige of French social science to the visionary arithmetic of the Book of Revelation. His carefully plotted phalanxes of 1,620 souls would rid the world of hunger and class hatred and would put an end to the ennui of the intellectual and the brutalization of the manual laborer.

Ripley could hardly hope to assemble a full phalanx, much less build the huge edifice that Fourier insisted was necessary to house it. For now his plan was simpler and more American. A corporation would be formed. Shares would be sold at five hundred dollars apiece, shareholders to be promised dividends of 5 percent from the profits of the enterprise. Land would be bought for farming. A school would be established to provide cash income. The shareholders and their students would live in buildings on the farm and take their meals together. The duties of running the farm, of feeding and washing for the inhabitants, and of caring for the residences would be shared, as far as possible, by everyone equally. All labor – teaching Latin, boiling vats of laundry, or cleaning out stalls – would be recompensed out of the expected profits of the enterprise at the same hourly rate.

As one of Ripley's early biographers puts it, however unlikely it seemed that a bookish parson should choose to exchange dignity, leisure, and elegance for toil and rudeness, and the works of Kant, Schelling, and Cousin for muck manuals, Ripley had come to think of it as the only possible solution to the alienation of the intellectuals and the misery of the poor. The Boston intellectuals' heads had become as distant from their own bodies as the whole scholarly class had become from the suffering workers. To labor in conditions of social equality would restore health to the body and the body politic at once. It would demonstrate to the world that the kingdom of heaven *was* possible on earth.

This sense that the planned community must be exemplary as well as functional explains why Ripley tried so hard to persuade Emerson to join. Ripley had brought up the idea of the community that would become Brook Farm at a meeting of the Transcendental Club in October 1840, where it was earnestly discussed. But no one was willing to enlist. Ripley visited Emerson again later in the month, this time accompanied by his wife, Sophia, and by Margaret Fuller. The famously ill-tempered judgment Emerson recorded in his journal after that visit, alleging that Ripley's planned community would be "not the cave of persecution which is the palace of spiritual power, but only a room in the Astor House hired for the Transcendentalists," reflects Emerson's lifelong distaste for using material means to produce spiritual ends. Its vehemence also suggests that he was chagrined at being challenged to live up to his recent call for an honest life, in which a true man will eat the bread of his own spade. Ripley's earnest request for aid continued to trouble Emerson; as late as December 2 he was still toying with the possibility of joining the community, as a letter he wrote to his brother then makes clear.

When he finally declined Ripley's invitation in a carefully drafted letter of December 15, 1840, Emerson gave his reasons in terms that recall his objections to the Lord's Supper many years before. What chiefly weighs with him is "the conviction that the Community is not good for me" (Emerson to Ripley, December 15, 1840). Ripley sent Emerson several more earnest letters, but in the end the small group of people who followed the Ripleys to West Roxbury had to begin life without either Emerson's presence or his financial support.

Their spirits nevertheless were high as they set out in April 1841 and remained so even through years of increasing discouragement and privation. The sandy ground beneath the picturesque meadows that Ripley had purchased proved stubbornly difficult to farm, and the community's small craft shops and greenhouse proved to be more drains upon their treasury than sources of profit to it. Indeed, whoever studies the accounts of the Brook Farm Association marvels that it managed to survive its natural and self-created difficulties for as long as it did – from the spring of 1841 until the autumn of 1847.

Yet an account of Brook Farm that told only of its financial difficulties would find it difficult to explain why the letters written by Brook Farmers during their years at the farm (even during the grimmer late years, when the various "retrenchments" had reduced the fare at table severely) and the reminiscences that many wrote later rarely complain of deprivation. They speak instead of joy – in the beauty of nature, in the exuberance of the young resident scholars coasting the snow-covered hills or going out before breakfast to gather spring wildflowers for the tables, in the constant flow of jokes and nicknames and execrable puns that enlivened their dinner-table conversations, in the dances and tableaux they staged in the evenings, in the feelings of robust health they got from working, in the camaraderie that freed them from isolation, and in the sense of purpose that freed them from aimlessness and despair.

To read these testimonies to the power of Brook Farm to create joy in its inhabitants is to understand why its residents continued to believe that they had found the remedy for all social evils – for poverty, hunger, ignorance, ill health, boredom, class hatred, sexual inequality (at Brook Farm the women voted and received the same pay as the men, and the men wiped dishes and shelled peas). They looked forward to the day when the land would be dotted with Brook Farms modeled on their own. In the autumn of 1842 Georgiana Bruce, a young resident at Brook Farm, wrote a glowing letter to a friend and concluded by saying that she thought that if their grandchildren collected the letters written from Brook Farm they would be able to "trace the history of the *first community*."

John Codman, a Brook Farmer who arrived in 1843 at the age of twenty-seven, remembered how intoxicating the collective prospect seemed. "It was for the meanest a life above humdrum, and for the greatest something far, infinitely far beyond. They looked into the gates of life and saw beyond charming visions, and hopes springing up for all." In the memoir he wrote fifty years later he tried desperately to communicate some sense of the time when it was bliss to be alive:

Imagine, indifferent reader of my story, the state of mind you would be in if you could feel that you were placed in a position of positive harmony with all your race; that you carried with you a balm that could heal every earthly wound; an earthly gospel, even as the church thinks it has a heavenly gospel – a remedy for poverty, crime, outrage and over-taxed, hand, heart, and brain.

Is it any wonder that the Brook Farmers seemed a little giddy with joy? "And, after sound sleep, waking in the rosy morning, with the fresh air from balmy field blowing into your window, penetrated still with the afflatus of last night's thoughts and reveries, wouldn't you be cheerful? Wouldn't the unity of all things come to you, and wouldn't you chirrup like a bird, and buzz like a bee . . . ?"

Individual joy was valuable only insofar as it could be patented and distributed. The life the Brook Farmers led – milking the cows, haying the meadow, teaching in the school, laboring in the laundry or kitchen, cleaning the rooms – and the pleasantly Bohemian attire they adopted, with beards and belted tunics with Byron collars for the men, flowing tresses and broad-brimmed hats for the women, were obviously improvements over the dreary life of the "civilizees" (as the Brook Farmers contemptuously called them). But Ripley and his band of devoted associates thought of themselves as social reformers, not merely escapers from reality; they continued to insist that their community was a pattern upon which a new social reality could be built. Egalitarian, courteous, cultured, healthy, respectful of individuality yet suffused with the spirit of love, Brook Farm would show the way to a culture at once democratic and refined, where young men and women could hoe melons or scrub floors in the morning, study Greek at midday, and join the glee club in the evening to sing masses by Haydn and Mozart.

How far did the ideal correspond to the reality? Already during the first six months of operation Brook Farm had created its most famous critic. Nathaniel Hawthorne, fresh from his job at Salem's custom house, had joined the first settlers in hopes of finding a way to live cheaply and get time for writing. His letters to his fiancée, Sophia Peabody, during the spring of 1841 were at first full of enthusiasm. "I am transformed into a complete farmer," he boasts in a letter of May 3, 1841. "The whole fraternity eat together; and such a delectable way of life has never been seen on earth, since the days of the early Christians. We get up at half-past four, breakfast at half-past six, dine at half-past twelve, and go to bed at nine."

A month later, however, he is apologizing for not writing and complaining that "this present life of mine gives me an antipathy to pen and ink, even more than my Custom House experience did" (Hawthorne to Peabody, June 1, 1841). Though he tries to amuse Sophia with descriptions of the eloquence of the Brook Farm pigs, by August of 1841 he had already decided that the dream of *combining* labor and thought was a vain one.

Even my Custom House experience was not such a thraldom and weariness; my mind and heart were freer. Oh, belovedest, labor is the curse of this world, and nobody can meddle with it, without becoming proportionably brutified. Dost thou think it a praiseworthy matter, that I spend five golden months in providing food for cows and horses? Dearest, it is not so. (Hawthorne to Peabody, August 12, 1841)

By November Hawthorne had left the community.

In *The Blithedale Romance* (1852), the novel he set in a community modeled loosely on Brook Farm, Hawthorne's narrator and alter ego Miles Coverdale lodges a more serious charge against the practices of the community. Behind the boasted egalitarianism of Brook Farm – members of the finest Boston families working and eating side by side with mechanics and servants – lay an unquestioning snobbery, which took it for granted that the manners of the lower classes would be refined and softened by such contact. Many of the Brook Farmers testified to the sense of excitement they got from crossing class boundaries, though only Hawthorne subjected the emotion to later analysis. Here is how he describes the first supper at Blithedale, as the members of his imaginary community join the local couple they have hired to teach them how to farm.

We all sat down – grisly Silas Foster, his rotund helpmate, and the two bouncing handmaidens, included – and looked at one another in a friendly, but rather awkward way. It was the first practical trial of our theories of equal brotherhood and sisterhood; and we people of superior cultivation and refinement (for as such, I presume, we unhesitatingly reckoned ourselves) felt as if something were already accomplished towards the millennium of love. The truth is, however, that the laboring oar was with our unpolished companions; it being far easier to condescend, than to accept of condescension.

Indeed, the "equanimity" with which the aristocratic Blithedalers bore "the hardship and humiliations of a life of toil" owed much to their knowledge that they could choose at any time to leave their humble surroundings and return to lives of comfort. Coverdale concludes: "If ever I did deserve to be soundly cuffed by a fellow-mortal, for secretly putting weight upon some imaginary social advantage, it must have been while I was striving to prove myself ostentatiously his equal, and no more."

If the real Brook Farmers occasionally did show signs of the kind of condescension Coverdale blushes to remember – one elderly lady who had been a student at Brook Farm during its early days remarked that "the noble, sweet simplicity of the life there" and its lessons in the unimportance of worldly distinction helped her later to treat her servants "as if they were really equals" – it would be a mistake to dismiss the whole enterprise because of it. The Brook Farmers took seriously their mission to replace the greed and cruelty of the "civilized" economic system with a society founded upon the principles of generosity and love. A visitor to Brook Farm in the first summer of its existence gave this rendering of the motives that actuated the residents:

How *dare* I be a drone when others are drudges? How dare I sacrifice not only my own, but others' health, in sequestering myself from my share of bodily labour, or neglecting a due mental cultivation? How dare I have superfluities, when others are in want? How dare I oppose the unfolding of the spiritual progress of my whole race, by all the force of my personal selfishness and indolence? In short, is it not the sin against the Holy Ghost, with this new-found insight, to hesitate to enter immediately upon the immortal life?

The writer of this letter goes on to point out that the Brook Farm community has achieved "in the most peaceable manner in the world" the very "rectification of things which Mr. Brownson, in his Article on the Laboring Classes, is understood to declare will require a bloody revolution."

Surprisingly, Orestes Brownson (who sent one of his sons to the Brook Farm school) agreed. A long article he published in the *U.S. Magazine and Democratic Review* in November 1842 surveys all the current proposals for ending social misery and disposes of them all briskly. Only Ripley's attempt to found a community on love wins Brownson's approval. Brownson thought Ripley had succeeded where other communitarians like Robert Owen and Charles Fourier had failed, because he had avoided elaborate theorizing and organized Brook Farm around "the simple wants of his soul as a man and a Christian." The rule of that community is

the Gospel LAW OF LOVE and the rule to be honored is HONOR ALL MEN, and treat each man as a brother, whatever his occupation. In other words, the community is an attempt to realize the Christian Ideal, and to do this by establishing truly Christian relations between the members and the community and between member and member.

Emerson, too, followed the goings-on at Brook Farm with interest and amusement. But his own life was moving in a different direction, toward a vocation more literary, less local. A few weeks before Ripley's band departed for Brook Farm in the spring of 1841, Emerson published in Boston a book of twelve essays: "History," "Self-Reliance," "Compensation," "Spiritual Laws," "Love," "Friendship," "Prudence," "Heroism," "The Over-Soul," "Circles," "Intellect," and "Art." Each of these essays consisted of passages from Emerson's store of unpublished writings – his journals, letters, sermons, and lectures – that had been worked and reworked to increase their concision, vividness, and power.

We know from the letters Emerson wrote to friends when he was working on this book that he found the processes of revision and assembly painful. If his daily work for many years had been a labor of joy – reading, thinking, writing in his journal – the task of selecting and concatenating journal passages to make up lectures and essays forced him to play the role of editor to his own inspirations and be cold hearted and critical where he had once been excited and inspired. He often felt despondent as he tried to cobble his passages together into something larger than the one- or two-paragraph shape his thought seemed naturally to take in the journals, particularly because he was aware that the associative rather than strictly logical patterns of his discourses left many in his audience bewildered, as if they found themselves (to use his own comparison) in a house without stairs.

By the time Emerson had begun to work seriously at compiling a book of essays for publication he had already been writing professionally for thirteen years – first as a minister, then as a lyceum lecturer, and finally as an independent entrepreneur producing courses of ten or eleven lectures almost every year for the winter season. And he had learned that his unorthodox method of text making *worked,* at least in the opinion of his audiences. If it made his lectures elliptical, it also made them strangely stimulating. If his transitions were abrupt and his imagery startling, he managed to exhilarate as much as he puzzled. James Russell Lowell remembered what it was like to be part of that audience, to walk in from the country to the Masonic Temple on a crisp winter night to enjoy lectures whose "power of strangely subtle association" startled the mind into an attention almost painful, relieved only by "flashes of mutual understanding between speaker and hearer" that reminded Lowell of sheet lightning.

In the summer of 1839 Emerson set about revising material from these lectures to make the book of essays he had long hoped to publish. Work went slowly, partly because he had to write a new series of winter lectures for the 1839–40 season to pay the publishing costs for a collection of Carlyle's essays and reviews (four volumes of which Emerson edited and published between 1838 and 1840), partly because he found himself obliged to help Margaret Fuller as an unofficial coeditor of the fledgling *Dial*. But by the spring of 1840 he could look forward to an autumn of uninterrupted work. He wrote to a friend: "My chapter on 'Circles' begins to prosper and when it is October I shall write like a Latin Father" (Emerson to Elizabeth Hoar, September 12, 1840).

The pruning and revising that Emerson's journal passages underwent to become lectures became still more severe. Emerson understood very well that compression in a written text must create the intensity a lecturer can supply with his voice. He set out to prune empty repetitions, tighten syntax, sharpen images; he tore down bridges between ideas to leave gorges leapable only by the reader's wild surmise.

The resulting volume surprised even those who thought they knew Emerson well. Orestes Brownson, who had mocked or attacked Emerson for nearly everything else he had written, found that the *Essays* moved him not just to admiration but to reverence. In a brief notice written for the April 1841 number of the *Boston Quarterly Review* Brownson praised the book's transforming power. "He who reads it will find, that he is no longer what he was. A new and higher life has quickened in him, and he can never again feel, that he is merely a child of time and space, but that he is transcendent and immortal."

What kind of essays were these, that they were able to please even the ferocious Brownson? Some of them ("Prudence"; "Compensation") offer solid wisdom about the world of the senses, while others ("Intellect"; "The Over-Soul") rise insistently beyond it. Some essays celebrate personal courage ("Heroism"; "Self-Reliance"), while others urge a wise passivity and an entire trust in the self-executing laws of the universe ("Spiritual Laws"). Some examine the records of human civilization and human achievement ("History"; "Art"), while at least one ("Circles") celebrates time's power to swallow all traces of civilization and achievement alike as it ceaselessly generates new forms and new men. Against this energy individual men and women can oppose only the difficult love that binds strangers into fluctuating societies of affection ("Friendship") or the even more mysterious intoxication that begins with the erotic binding of one man to one woman and ends by connecting them both to society and to the race ("Love").

The essays are arranged for maximum contrast: a meditation on the collective experience of the race ("History") is followed by an intense focus upon the individual ("Self-Reliance"); a look at the hard economic balance of the universe ("Compensation") is followed by a hymn to the endless expansiveness of the soul ("Spiritual Laws"); and advice for achieving worldly success ("Prudence") is followed by exhortations to despise it completely ("Heroism").

Yet the effect of such juxtapositions is anything but self-canceling. On the contrary, what Emerson urges on every page is that we grasp the underlying principle of unity that binds together both the eternal laws and the phenomena that manifest them. "Let a man keep the law, – any law, – and his way will be strown with satisfactions," he says in "Prudence." Even the hard Law of Compensation – that nothing is got for nothing; that in nature nothing is given but everything is sold – had attracted him since boyhood, he says, because he thought a discourse on the subject might show human beings "a ray of divinity, the present action of the Soul of this world, clean from all vestige of tradition" and so would bathe their hearts in "an inundation of eternal love."

So great is the force of love that its effects are visible in evil and disorder as well as in harmony and virtue. "Truth has not single victories: all things are its organs, – not only dust and stones, but errors and lies," Emerson says in "Spiritual Laws." In the same essay he suddenly breaks out into an apostrophe that would startle if it did not stem from a real sense of the unbelief that Emerson detected beneath the conventions of society and the rituals of religion. "O my brothers, God exists. There is a soul at the centre of nature, and over the will of every man, so that none of us can wrong the universe."

It sounds strange to reassure readers that they cannot wrong the universe; but Emerson realized that guilt, like unbelief, was an enemy to the kind of radical self-culture his *Essays* promoted. He announces the project in the book's first essay, "History": "The world exists for the education of each man." As historians refuse to be condemned to ignorance by the pastness of the past but strive to replace the "preposterous There or Then and introduce in its place the Here and Now" by reflecting that all history was made by the same mind that is now trying to read it, so every reader must approach the imposing richness of tradition as merely a portrait gallery "in which he finds the lineaments he is forming. The silent and the eloquent praise him, and accost him, and he is stimulated wherever he moves as by personal allusions."

Yet Emerson points out that the muse of history will never utter oracles to those who do not respect themselves and that the obstacles to self-respect in the Boston of 1841 are many and formidable. "Self-Reliance," the second essay in the book, is an assault upon those obstacles, the greatest of which is fear of opinion – fear of appearing foolish or selfish or insignificant or inconsistent. As Emerson says toward the close of the essay, "The sinew and heart of man seem to be drawn out, and we are become timorous desponding whimperers. We are afraid of truth, afraid of fortune, afraid of death, and afraid of each other." Against this primary disease Emerson fights back with epigrams designed to stiffen the backs of those poor, obscure young men he always thought of as his primary audience. "Trust thyself: every heart vibrates to that iron string." "Whoso would be a man must be a nonconformist." "A foolish consistency is the hobgoblin of little minds, adored by little statesmen and philosophers and divines." "The centuries are conspirators against the sanity and authority of the soul." "Check this lying hospitality and lying affection." "Insist on yourself: never imitate." "Nothing can bring you peace but yourself. Nothing can bring you peace but the triumph of principles."

Emerson's insistence upon self-assertion even to the point of rudeness has an unpleasant ring in the present day, when boorishness flourishes and self-forgiveness is an article of faith. Not surprisingly, a chorus of moralists has recently arisen to blame Emerson for all the woes of modern society – narcissism, infantilism, self-indulgence, the breakdown of marriage, the withdrawal from political life. It may be true that the pendulum has swung so far in the direction of the self that we almost long for a return to deference and repression – though one wonders how long these critics (urban intellectuals, most of them) could actually bear the stifling atmosphere of small-town intrusiveness that was Emerson's target in "Self-Reliance." Such critics should be encouraged to remember the fate of the Parisian in Stendhal's *The Red and the Black* who yearned to be the proprietor of a country estate, only to discover that rural life was a "hell of hypocrisy and petty vexations." Chastened, he returned to seek solitude and rustic tranquillity in "the only place where they exist in France – in a fourth-floor flat overlooking the Champs Elysées." (When Emerson visited Paris in 1848 he understood immediately why every young man from the provinces wanted to move there – to be *free from observation*.)

In fact, Emerson does not wish to leave the self in sterile isolation, endlessly contemplating its own magnificence. The essay "Love" opens with an unqualified hymn to Eros, builder of cities. Emerson praises love because it is a divine rage that

seizes on man at one period, and works a revolution in his mind and body; unites him to his race, pledges him to the domestic and civic relations, carries him with new sympathy into nature, enhances the power of the senses, opens the imagination, adds to his character heroic and sacred attributes, establishes marriage, and gives permanence to human society.

But union is only possible to those who are units. And most men in Emerson's society are not units, only fragments and pieces of men; not sturdy oaks but "leaning willows."

Transforming willows into oaks will take more than exhortation. You cannot urge someone to absolute self-reliance without addressing the question of the self's constitution, for if the self is evil then absolute self-reliance is absolute death. Emerson's refusal to answer this question at first, except by saying "If I am the Devil's child, I will live then from the Devil," recalls in its irritation at being badgered some of Jesus' retorts to the Pharisees, but the question refuses to go away, and Emerson finally addresses it in a passage that rises up in the middle of the essay like a great mountain.

The magnetism which all original action exerts is explained when we inquire the reason of self-trust. Who is the Trustee? What is the aboriginal Self on which a universal reliance may be grounded? What is the nature and power of that science-baffling star, without parallax, without calculable elements, which shoots a ray of beauty even into trivial and impure actions, if the least mark of independence appear?

A star without parallax or calculable elements would defy astronomists and chemists alike in their attempts to analyze or place it, would be something irreducible to the terms of any known system.

That irreducible something Emerson calls, rather oddly, "Spontaneity or Instinct" – an *intuition* rather than a *tuition*. "Spontaneity" suggests activity and "instinct" passion, yet Emerson clearly is thinking of something quite different from both, for he goes on to describe a surprisingly passive primal self, a "sense of being" rising in our calm hours assuring us of our unity with things. "We lie in the lap of immense intelligence, which makes us receivers of its truth and organs of its activity." At its source, self-reliance turns into its opposite, self-abnegation. "When we discern justice, when we discern truth, we do nothing of ourselves, but allow a passage to its beams."

In this hour of vision we feel neither gratitude nor joy, but only a sense that "all things go well." From this height Emerson can even confess the inadequacy of the title of his essay. "Why then do we prate of self-reliance?" The word "reliance" is "a poor external way of speaking," focusing attention upon the dilapidations of the empirical self instead of upon the power that shoots through it in those precious moments of spontaneity or instinct. "Speak rather of that which relies, because it works and is."

If "Self-Reliance" is an attempt to look at truth from the perspective of the empirical self striving to attain it, "Spiritual Laws" looks at truth from truth itself, an effort that leads Emerson to write proverbs of the pure Reason, mysterious statements that are meant to sound like fragments of Eastern wisdom. "The soul's emphasis is always right." A man "may see what he maketh." He "may have that allowance he takes." "He may read what he writes." "He shall have his own society."

These odd little bits of gnomic wisdom are as far as possible from the militant exhortations of "Self-Reliance." Instead of telling us what to do they tell us that no doing is necessary. Emerson quotes an exclamation of Confucius – "How can a man be concealed!" – to point out the fruitlessness of sham. But he also points out the needlessness of worry, for the universe of "Spiritual Laws" is that lap of immense intelligence we only glimpsed in "Self-Reliance." "Place yourself in the middle of the stream of power and wisdom which animates all whom it floats, and you are without effort impelled to truth, to right, and a perfect contentment."

Do not choose is Emerson's advice to us now, as long as we realize that the puny activity of the conscious will is insignificant beside the perpetual choosing represented by our lives.

A man is a method, a progressive arrangement; a selecting principle, gathering his like to him, wherever he goes. He takes only his own, out of the multiplicity that sweeps and circles round him. He is like one of those booms which are set out from the shore on rivers to catch driftwood, or like the loadstone amongst splinters of steel.

For this reason we cannot go astray so long as we trust our fascinations. "What your heart thinks great, is great. The soul's emphasis is always right."

And this is so because, as Emerson finally asserts openly in "The Over-Soul," the book's ninth essay, "There is no bar or wall in the soul where man, the effect, ceases, and God, the cause, begins." The individual soul is distinct enough from the universal soul that it feels a "shudder of awe and delight" when they blend together, yet united enough that Emerson can quietly redefine "Revelation" as "the disclosure of the soul," without bothering to say whose soul is being disclosed. "Man is a stream whose source is hidden. Our being is descending into us from we know not whence." If there is something terribly frightening about Emerson's description of union with the divine – "The soul gives itself alone, original, and pure, to the Lonely, Original, and Pure" – at least the soul, like Moses, returns at last to other men. "More and more the surges of everlasting nature enter into me, and I become public and human in my regards and actions. So I come to live in thoughts, and act with energies which are immortal."

Such energies are necessary, because the world we live in is still a fallen one, however brilliantly its defects illustrate the workings of the moral law. Prudence is needed to manage the world of the senses, heroism to endure its cruelties, and a firm sense of the Law of Compensation to reassure us that the universe, though fatally flawed, is still thoroughly moral in its workings. It is a pity that the tough and often funny essays that treat these virtues are so rarely anthologized for modern students, because they show Emerson as the brilliant practitioner of a tradition of wisdom literature that includes both the book of Proverbs and the maxims of Epictetus.

Perhaps the most deeply felt of all the advice Emerson offers in these essays comes in "Prudence," where he warns against the folly of engaging in religious controversy. "If they set out to contend, Saint Paul will lie, and Saint John will hate. What low, poor, paltry, hypocritical people, an argument on religion will make of the pure and chosen souls!" Instead of arguing, Emerson urges a more generous (and more devious) tactic. "Though your views are in straight antagonism to theirs, assume an identity of sentiment, assume that you are saying precisely that which all think, and in the flow of wit and love, roll out your paradoxes in solid column, with not the infirmity of a doubt." Does not the Bible tell us that by doing good to our enemy we shall heap his head with coals of fire?

Avoiding controversy has a deeper value as well. In "Intellect" Emerson explains why. "God offers to every mind its choice between truth and repose. Take which you please, − you can never have both." The man who loves repose will accept whatever creed he inherits, but the man who loves truth will "abstain from dogmatism, and recognize all the opposite negations between which, as walls, his being is swung." Dogmatizing forces us to defend some momentary apprehension of truth until it becomes falsehood and "incipient insanity."

Why should truth be so elusive? If we can lie in the lap of an immense intelligence, why cannot we repose on the bosom of an unchanging truth? In "Circles," the shortest essay in the book as well as one of the latest to be written, Emerson tries to answer this question. Alone of all the *Essays* "Circles" has no source in an earlier lecture, and it moves with a logical directness rare in Emerson. It is, as one critic has said, an attempt to measure the depth of the universe by the rapidity with which it swallows up institutions. "Our culture is the predominance of an idea which draws after it this train of cities and institutions. Let us rise into another idea: they will disappear."

If this instability were merely chaotic one might have cause for despair, but Emerson sees each culture's attempt to draw a new circle around the old one it inherited as a symbol of "the moral fact of the Unattainable, the flying Perfect, around which the hands of man can never meet, at once the inspirer and the condemner of every success." In every effort we strive to reach, or to represent, the Oversoul, and the detritus left by our failures is what we know as civilization.

Yet the dominant tone of the essay is anything but bitter or despairing. On the contrary, Emerson's standpoint within the eternal gives him a giddying look down at the universe below, vibrant with life and energy. "The life of man is a self-evolving circle, which, from a ring imperceptibly small, rushes on all sides outwards to new and larger circles, and that without end." For if each circle we form naturally tends to solidify into "an empire, rules of an art, a local usage, a religious rite," still the soul is strong and bursts over the boundary it has just formed. "Step by step we scale this mysterious ladder: the steps are actions; the new prospect is power."

The reason we can bear this endless self-overcoming is that, like God, we are circles whose circumference is everywhere and whose center is nowhere. If our empirical selves are ceaselessly tossed in the flux, our transcendental selves abide in the center. "Whilst the eternal generation of circles proceeds, the eternal generator abides. That central life is somewhat superior to creation, superior to knowledge and thought, and contains all its circles." All efforts at self-culture are inspired by this central life, laboring to create "a life and thought as large and excellent as itself, suggesting to our thought a certain development."

Still, the products of that thought can never be as valuable as the energy that throws them off. "Nothing is secure but life, transition, the energizing spirit. No love can be bound by oath or covenant to secure it against a higher love. No truth so sublime but it may be trivial tomorrow in the light of new thoughts." And then, in a final joke directed against all poor youths who hunger after a permanent position, Emerson sums up the wisdom he has learned so far. "People wish to be settled: only as far as they are unsettled, is there any hope for them."

Essays is still unsettling to read, and not merely in those passages where Emerson speaks as "the Devil's child." Yet the overwhelming impression the essays make is of faith and hope and if not quite of charity, at least of incandescent desire. Because God exists, nothing can be lost that matters to the soul, and everything should be jettisoned that hinders it. Or, as Emerson says in the final paragraph of "Circles": "The way of life is wonderful: it is by abandonment."

As if to prove that he meant what he said, Emerson tried to make some alterations in his own way of living – inviting the Alcott family (once again in financial trouble) to move into the house, acquiring habits of regular manual labor, and abolishing domestic service or at least abolishing the invidious class distinctions domestic service created. But his efforts to make the Emerson house into a little Brook Farm were mostly doomed to failure. Mrs. Alcott, foreseeing what might happen if two such transcendental egos as her husband and Emerson occupied the same house, turned down Emerson's offer of help. Emerson's wife and mother refused to do without domestic servants. And the cook and housemaid firmly declined to eat at the Emerson family table.

Anxious to salvage at least one plank in his reform platform, Emerson turned to Thoreau. "Henry Thoreau is coming to live with me & work with me in the garden & teach me to graft apples," he informed Margaret Fuller in April 1841. By the first of June he was writing to his brother William to say that the arrangement seemed to be working:

> He is thus far a great benefactor & physician to me for he is an indefatigable & a very skilful laborer & I work with him as I should not without him. and expect now to be suddenly well & strong though I have been a skeleton all the spring until I am ashamed. Thoreau is a scholar & a poet & as full of buds of promise as a young apple tree.

The contrast between youthful energy and skeletal age would come to dominate the new lecture series that Emerson planned for the winter of 1841–42 in Boston, the last complete series he would manage himself. Called "Lectures on the Times," the series represents Emerson's clearest attempt to address the problem of reform directly. "These Reforms are our contemporaries; they are ourselves; our own light, and sight and conscience; they only name the relation which subsists between us and the vicious institutions which they go to rectify," he said in the introductory lecture of the series. Yet he is careful to give conservatism its due. In "The Conservative" he lets an imaginary defender of the established order rebuke the visionary. "The existing world is not a dream, and cannot with impunity be treated as a dream; neither is it disease; but it is the ground on which you stand, it is the mother of whom you were born." Reform deals in possibilities, "but here is sacred fact."

To this a reformer replies (in a lecture entitled "The Transcendentalist"): "You think me the child of my circumstances: I make my circumstance." What is mere fact before the dissolving power of consciousness? "I – this thought which is called I, – is the mold into which the world is poured like melted wax." In a radiant final lecture that bears the same title as the last chapter of *Nature*, "Prospects," Emerson leaves little doubt where his heart lies. "I hate the builders of dungeons in the air," he says. "We were made for another office, professors of the Joyous Science, detectors and delineators of occult symmetries and unpublished beauties, heralds of civility, nobility, learning, and wisdom, affirmers of the One Law." How can the conservative dispirit us with his facts? "The last fact is still astonishment, mute, bottomless, boundless Wonder."

There is nothing at last but God only. "All perishes except the Creator, the

Creator who needs no companion, who fills the Universe . . . , and instantly and forevermore reproduces Nature and what we call the world of men, as the sea its waves." The man who has learned to regard all his possessions and relations as mutable has put himself out of the reach of skepticism. "All its arrows fall far short of the eternal towers of his faith." We must be content to watch whatever spectacle the great spirit sends us, "to see it, and hold our tongues. Who asked you for an opinion?"

If this indeed was Emerson's mature faith it was about to be put to a severe test. He returned home to Concord to find Henry Thoreau suddenly ill with hysterical symptoms of lockjaw, the disease that had killed his brother a week earlier. Emerson was frightened until Thoreau's symptoms gradually abated. But a worse trial yet was in store. Emerson's five-and-one-half-year-old son, Waldo, came down with scarlet fever on Monday, January 24. By Thursday he was delirious. When his mother Lidian asked the attending doctor when she could expect her son to get better, the doctor could only reply, "I had hoped to be spared this." Waldo died shortly after eight o'clock that evening.

Grief left Emerson with a numbness he found more terrible than agony, but he hardly had time to reflect upon his sensations. The receipts for the Boston lecture series had been disappointing, and Emerson's bank had failed to pay its usual dividend. He calculated that he needed to earn another two hundred dollars by lecturing to meet his family's expenses. And he was still trying to find some way to help Alcott, whose move to Concord had brought him neither prosperity nor peace. Emerson thought that a trip to England, where Alcott's writings had acquired for him a band of enthusiastic disciples among reformers interested in education, might lift Alcott's spirits and improve his health; but his efforts to raise money for this "Alcott-Voyage-fund" among the wealthy citizens of Boston were unsuccessful.

Emerson had better luck in Providence, Rhode Island; a liberal friend of Alcott's gave money toward the voyage. But his own lecture audiences in Providence were so small that he sometimes earned as little as nine dollars for a lecture. Reluctantly, he decided he had to take the series to New York. Fortunately, audiences there were larger and his profits greater. (He was reviewed in New York by a young reporter for the Brooklyn *Aurora,* Walter Whitman.) By the time Emerson returned to New England in mid-March he had earned enough money both to cover his family's needs and to contribute to Alcott's voyage.

But that voyage, like almost everything else that involved the man Emerson had once, in an exasperated mood, called "Plato Skimpole," ended badly. It set in motion forces that would give rise to the shortest lived of all the reform efforts and would end by depositing Alcott and his family once again on Emerson's doorstep. Alcott sailed from Boston on May 8, 1842. In

London he was greeted by two admirers, Charles Lane and Henry Wright, who took him immediately outside of London to a school named after him, Alcott House. Lane and Wright were communitarians; they wanted to establish what they called a "New Eden." Like Brook Farm, it would invite laborers who would live on and work the land, both to provide subsistence for themselves and to achieve harmony between body and spirit. A society of people with chaste minds in healthy bodies would be able to achieve the perfection once thought lost by the Fall; strict vegetarian diets, cold baths, and exercise would undo the corruption and decay Alcott saw everywhere around him in England.

Alcott returned to America on October 21, 1842, bringing with him Wright, Lane, and Lane's nine-year-old son, who moved in with the Alcott family. By January 1843 Wright's enthusiasm for the New Eden had evaporated under the fanatical regimen of diet and cold bathing that the tyrannical Lane imposed on everybody; Wright took ship for England again. Lane and Alcott continued to proselytize and to look for a suitable farm to purchase.

Finally, in May 1843, Lane found a ninety-acre farm he liked in the Massachusetts village of Harvard. Only eleven of the farm's acres were arable, and these promised to be difficult to cultivate without the use of animal labor and animal manure, both of which Alcott and Lane scorned as exploitative or unclean. But the prospect from the farm, with woods behind and mountains in the distance, was lovely, and when "the consociate family," as they called themselves, set out on the first of June for Fruitlands (as they had decided to name their community, though ten ancient apple trees were all the orchard they had), their spirits were high. In the July issue of *The Dial* Alcott and Lane proudly announced their escape from the bondage of the cash nexus. "We have made an arrangement with the proprietor of an estate of about a hundred acres, which liberates this tract from human ownership."

Most of the people they had tried to persuade to join them had declined to come. The group they did attract was a motley one. There were two discontented Brook Farmers, a cooper who had once been imprisoned in a madhouse, a former nudist from England, and a mild revolutionary who had endured a year in the Worcester jail rather than pay the small tax then levied on men who wore full beards. Only one woman joined the group to help Abba, Bronson's long-suffering wife, with the cooking and the domestic chores. This woman, Ann Page, deserves to be remembered, if only for the acerbic comment she made about all such reform efforts. A woman may live a whole life of self-sacrifice and die saying meekly, "Behold a woman," whereas a man who passes a few years in experiments of self-denial says "Behold a *god.*"

Louisa May Alcott, who was ten when her family moved to Fruitlands, later wrote a brief account of her experience there; it was published in 1873 as

Transcendental Wild Oats. She gives a good idea of what life in this fantastic commune was like:

Such farming probably was never seen before since Adam delved. The band of brothers began by spading garden and field; but a few days of it lessened their ardor amazingly. Blistered hands and aching backs suggested the expediency of permitting the use of cattle till the workers were better fitted for noble toil by a summer of the new life.

But in other areas their determination to purge their lives of evil dictated severe measures:

Unleavened bread, porridge, and water for breakfast; bread, fruit, vegetables, and water for dinner; bread, fruit, and water for supper was the bill of fair ordained by the elders. No teapot profaned that sacred stove, no gory steak cried aloud for vengeance from her chaste gridiron; and only a brave woman's taste, time, and temper were sacrificed on that domestic altar.

Clothing was similarly ascetic. "Cotton, silk, and wool were forbidden as the product of slave-labor, worm-slaughter, and sheep-robbery. Tunics and trowsers of brown linen were the only wear."

Alcott and Lane proved fonder of talking about farming than of actually farming; during the harvest season they were off on a pilgrimage through New York and New England trying to enlist more members for Fruitlands, without success. Abba, three of her daughters, and Lane's son were the only crew on hand when an October thunderstorm menaced the grain stacks; they managed to get the crop in using clothes baskets and sheets, but the harvest was meager at best.

By the end of October 1843 Fruitlanders were drifting away, and tensions began to rise between Lane and Alcott. Lane, who had put up the money for the enterprise, believed that he had been misled by Alcott's optimistic assurance that America would yield cohorts of recruits for the consociate family. In early January 1844 Lane (who had long-standing objections to the nuclear family as a hotbed of selfishness and an obstacle to true association) left with his son to join a nearby Shaker community. Alcott, exhausted by work and hunger, moved his family to board with a nearby farmer. Deeply depressed, he refused to eat for several days, and only the presence by his bedside of his wife and daughters finally persuaded him to take food again. Louisa remembered that he emerged from his sickroom a "wan shadow of a man, leaning on the arm that never failed him." But the crisis had passed, though the few possessions they still had left had to be sold to pay Fruitlands debts.

Emerson had tried to prevent the Fruitlands debacle by writing to Alcott's English admirers warning them that Alcott was not to be trusted in practical matters (a letter he sent in care of Alcott himself, who dutifully showed it to the intended recipients). During the long months in America when Alcott and Lane were trying to gather a flock Emerson was impatient with them. In November 1842 he had written in his journal: "This fatal fault in the logic of our friends still appears: Their whole doctrine is spiritual, but they always end with saying, Give us much land and money." He was half-inclined to say, as the world would, "Let them drink their own error to saturation, and this will be the best hellebore." But now that Alcott was thoroughly saturated with his error Emerson felt pity at Alcott's despair. Alcott was, after all, being true to his principles, and if they led him to ruin in the world it was the world's fault. When Alcott moved back to Concord, Emerson joined with the trustee who managed Abba May Alcott's estate in buying a farm for the Alcotts in Concord. This time they made sure that the property would be held in trust, safe from Alcott.

Not all of Emerson's time during this busy period was taken up with caring for Alcott, lecturing to earn income, or editing *The Dial*. Slowly during the summer and fall of 1843 Emerson began to return to the literary project he had long planned – putting together a second volume of essays for the press. He found it difficult to find time to work. To Margaret Fuller he complained in a letter of December 17, 1843, that "the felon Dial, the felon lectures, friend, wife, child, house, woodpile, each in turn is the guilty cause why life is postponed." The tales he heard of the feats of the German scholars who studied eleven and twelve hours a day filled him with envy. He could scarcely manage five hours (Emerson to Fuller, November 5, 1843). Yet when the new year came he could at least rejoice that one source of distraction was ending. On April 1, 1844, he wrote to his brother William that proof sheets for the last *Dial,* that "perpetual impediment" to his new book, had been sent to the printer. Three chapters of the new book were almost ready for the printer. Work on the remaining five chapters and the concluding lecture took up the rest of the summer, and it was not until October 4 that he could write to William that he had been "released at last from months of weary tending on the printers devil!" In a moment of giddiness he agreed to buy eleven acres of land (at $8.10 an acre) on the shore of Walden Pond from some men who accosted him there on one of his solitary walks; he then bought a few more acres of neighboring pine grove. He was now "landlord & waterlord of 14 acres, more or less," and could raise his own blackberries. (A mention of Alcott later in the same letter made William fire back a warning against pouring any more money down that "Orphic sieve.") *Essays, Second Series* was published on October 19, 1844.

Like the first series of essays, the book was loosely arranged in groups of contrasting essays. The godlike power of discernment celebrated in "The

Poet" is followed by the bewilderment of "Experience"; an investigation of daimonic power in "Character" yields to studies of social relations in "Manners" and "Gifts." "Nature" shows the world as it appears to the solitary contemplator, whereas "Politics" studies men as they behave in senates and caucuses. The final essay in the book, "Nominalist and Realist," does not so much seek to reconcile all these opposites as to make them spin too rapidly to be distinguishable. The last piece in the book, included because Emerson's publisher had told him the book was too short, is a lecture Emerson had delivered in March 1844 entitled "New England Reformers," a witty survey of the various reform movements Emerson had witnessed with varying proportions of amusement and respect.

That Emerson chose to place "The Poet" first suggests how willing he had become to accept a merely symbolic transformation of his world. *Nature* had predicted the actual renovation of the world through the influx of spirit; the Divinity School Address had looked forward to a Teacher who could bring glad tidings of a gospel proclaiming the identity of science and law. "The Poet" celebrates the intoxications of perception itself. The poet stands nearer to that spot "where Being passes into Appearance, and Unity into Variety"; he "sees the flowing or metamorphosis; perceives that thought is multiform; that within the form of every creature is a force impelling it to ascend into a higher form; and, following with his eyes the life, uses the forms which expresses that life, and so his speech flows with the flowing of nature." This power to mimic by a flux of tropes the flux of nature "has a certain power of emancipation and exhilaration for all men. . . . We are like persons who come out of a cave or cellar into the open air." Emerson's theft of a famous image from Plato is no accident, for he means to insist upon the centrality of true poets to his ideal republic. "Poets are thus liberating gods." Unlike the mere men of talent, who imitate the contours of the phenomenal, or the mystics, who stop the free play of symbols by a premature quest for meaning, true poets give us the "cheerful hint of the immortality of our essence" by their refusal to be pinned down.

That "fugacity," which seems in a moment of joy the gift of an expansive universe, can seem in another mood a sign of the universe's mockery and retreat. In "Experience," now regarded as one of the greatest of his essays, Emerson attempts to describe what it feels like to live in a universe not merely in flux but in flight from the perceiving self. The essay begins by evoking a nightmare world of endless staircases and a speaker who feels drugged. It might almost be the beginning of a story by Edgar Allan Poe, except that the horror Emerson seeks to describe is simply everyday life as it is experienced by ordinary men and women as they try to gain wisdom and love in a world where the very condition of subjectivity seems to preclude

both. We do not know where we are or where we are going; our temperament
shuts us in a prison of glass we cannot see; the stream of moods is so powerful
that we cannot long anchor in any affection or belief; and grief itself can only
teach us how shallow it is. "That, like all the rest, plays about the surface,
and never introduces me into the reality, for contact with which we should
even pay the costly price of sons and lovers."

The numbness Emerson felt after the death of his son now seems a
synecdoche for a greater impenetrability. "The Indian who was laid under a
curse, that the wind should not blow on him, nor water flow to him, nor fire
burn him, is a type of us all. The dearest events are summer-rain, and we the
Para coats that shed every drop." It is difficult to avoid the doubt that begins
to surface toward the end of the essay. "Perhaps these subject-lenses have a
creative power; perhaps there are no objects." Yet the perceiving subject is
not allowed even the comfort of a consistent skepticism, because at any
moment the reality that has eluded us will manifest itself once again and
make it clear that it had never really vanished. "Underneath the inharmo-
nious and trivial particulars, is a musical perfection, the Ideal journeying
always with us, the heaven without rent or seam." In the end, our journey
must continue with a hope that we can neither fulfill nor relinquish – that
victory will follow justice, that genius will be transformed into practical
power.

In "Character" Emerson suggests that one means of achieving this transformation might be through the kind of daimonic power manifested in oratory,
the "river of command" that flows from stronger natures into weaker ones.
"Manners" concerns itself with that combination of manhood and gentleness
the man of character will use toward his fellow human beings. The composure and self-content that are his trademarks are what might be called the
social manifestation of self-reliance, and his motto is "Let us not be too much
acquainted." Suddenly, toward the close of the essay, Emerson considers the
very different manners he wishes to see in women. The whole passage is
remarkable as a concealed tribute to the two women whose assaults upon the
fortress of his shyness had precipitated him into such delicious confusion in
the half-decade just past – Margaret Fuller and Caroline Sturgis. Margaret
Fuller is clearly the woman whose generosity "raises her at times into heroical
and godlike regions, and verifies the pictures of Minerva, Juno, or Polymnia."
Sturgis, on the other hand, fills Emerson's vase with wine and roses and breaches
his walls of habitual reserve until his tongue is unloosed and he says things
he otherwise never would have thought to say – though this seduction (in
which Emerson seems to be playing the feminine role) finally ends in regression
to asexual innocence: "We were children playing with children in a wild field
of flowers."

"Gifts" contains no passages so revealing, though it does have some very funny maxims about the dangers of being a benefactor, a role Emerson had played at one time or another to most of his friends. "It is a very onerous business, this of being served, and the debtor naturally wishes to give you a slap." What makes the essay engaging is Emerson's complete sympathy with the indignation of the beneficiary. "It is not the office of a man to receive gifts. How dare you give them? We wish to be self-sustained. We do not quite forgive a giver. The hand that feeds us is in some danger of being bitten."

"Nature" turns back from the world we make to the world we inhabit. The first half of the essay concerns itself with the beauty of phenomena, *natura naturata,* the second with the "efficient nature," *natura naturans,* "the quick cause, before which all forms flee as the driven snows." Throughout the essay Emerson sees nature as an evolutionary process, shaping species slowly through the vast stretches of geologic time, equipping them to occupy particular ecological niches and, at the same time, equipping enemies to destroy them. Yet the essay is still closer in spirit to Genesis than it is to *The Origin of Species,* for this vast panoply still centers on us. "By fault of our dulness and selfishness, we are looking up to nature, but when we are convalescent, nature will look up to us." "The world is mind precipitated, and the volatile essence is forever escaping again into the state of free thought."

"Politics," though it is suffused with nostalgia for the old Federalist idea that property should make the law for property and people for people, at least admits that there is something injurious, something "deteriorating and de-grading" in the influence property has on people. Although Emerson says that he refusess to despair of the republic, he finds little comfort in the current political scene, with radicals who are "destructive and aimless" and conservatives who are "timid, and merely defensive of property."

"Nominalist and Realist," the final essay in the book, attempts to find some virtue in polarities. "Jesus would absorb the race; but Tom Paine or the coarsest blasphemer helps humanity by resisting this exuberance of power." Even the scurrilousness of political campaigners opposes flaws in their oppo-nents that would otherwise remain hidden; hence Emerson gives perhaps the best defense of the two-party system ever mounted: "Since we are all so stupid, what benefit that there should be two stupidities!"

Our awkwardness in this life comes from the fact that we are weaponed for two elements, the particular and the universal. "We must reconcile the contradictions as we can, but their discord and their concord introduce wild absurdities" in our speech. Nor are our psyches any less riven. We no sooner state a proposition than we wish to turn and rend it; no sooner expound a doctrine than we recant, saying, "I thought I was right, but I was not." Like the Zimri of John Dryden's *Absalom and Achitophel,* we are everything by starts, and nothing long. Emerson had said something similar in "Experience," but here the tone of the assertion is not elegiac or despairing. Instead it is indulgent, amused, even Augustan. Inconsistency is part of the human condition; indeed, it *is* the human condition; and it guards us against the fanaticism of bigots whose very single-mindedness is the best sign of their insanity.

The final piece in the book is not listed as one of the essays, but instead is presented with its original title: "New England Reformers: A Lecture Read before the Society in Amory Hall, on Sunday, 3 March, 1844." The Amory Hall Society was a very radical group indeed, organized when an eloquent Philadelphia antislavery editor named Charles Augustus Burleigh gave three lectures on social reform in Boston during January 1844. His auditors were unwilling to let the inspiration of the moment pass; they formed a society on the spot and deputized a committee to hire speakers to address them on similar topics for the next twelve Sundays. William Lloyd Garrison spoke there; so did Charles Lane and Adin Ballou, cofounder with Garrison of the New England Non-Resistance Society. There was even an address by a Jewish immigrant freethinker named Ernestine Rose, a convert to the communitarian ideals of Robert Owen.

Both Emerson and Thoreau delivered lectures in this series, although both dissented strongly from the principles of association most of the other lecturers espoused. Emerson begins his lecture with an amused survey of the schismatic frenzy that has taken over New England in the last twenty-five years. There are societies for the reform of everything. "In these movements, nothing was more remarkable than the discontent they begot in the movers." The "spirit of protest and of detachment" drives the members of the movements away from established institutions, then away from the conventions called to protest these institutions, and then from their colleagues in protest. "The country is full of rebellion; the country is full of kings. Hands off! let there be no control and no interference in the administration of the affairs of this kingdom of me." What these "solitary nullifiers" often forget is that the would-be renovators must themselves be renovated before they can regenerate the world around them.

Those who hope to cure evils too big for single men and women to attack by joining together in associations will find that they are diminished, not expanded, by proximity to one another. Associations and rules will never liberate us. "We wish to escape from subjection, and a sense of inferiority, — and we make self-denying ordinances, we drink water, we eat grass, we refuse the laws, we go to jail; it is all in vain." Only when we obey our genius freely does an angel arise before us and lead us by the hand out of all the wards of the prison. "The union is only perfect, when all the uniters are isolated."

It is one of the ironies of history that Emerson made this familiar plea for the centrality of the individual at the time when his old friend George Ripley was attempting to lead his community in precisely the opposite direction. Even though Brook Farm to all outward appearances was happy and thriving in 1843, with a student population of thirty in a larger community of seventy, a study of its books in November of that year revealed a deficit of $1,160.84. Brook Farm was not a commune but a joint-stock company; those who wished to become full-fledged Associates needed to purchase at least one five-hundred-dollar share in the Brook Farm Association, which promised to pay a yearly dividend of 5 percent. Not enough new members with sufficient capital to buy the five-hundred-dollar shares in the Brook Farm Association were applying for admission (though Ripley was deluged with applications from people with no money, in poor health, and with large families). The task of bringing previously uncultivated soil into agricultural production proved to be far more difficult than Ripley had anticipated, and though he and his associates worked heroically, they were able to produce few marketable commodities besides milk and hay. They were not able to supply all of their own needs from the gardens, no matter how many luxuries they agreed to do without. The school itself was profitable, attracting students from as far away as Cuba and the Philippines; and the thousands of visitors who yearly descended upon Brook Farm became a modest source of income when the governing council finally decided to charge fees for entertaining them. But real self-sufficiency eluded them, and without real self-sufficiency how could they hope to regenerate the world?

At just the point when the Brook Farmers were longing to attract more members so that they could become truly self-sufficient, they were visited by proselytes for a new scheme of social regeneration. Albert Brisbane (1809–90), a well-to-do young New Yorker who had become a convert of the doctrines of the French social visionary Charles Fourier (1772–1837) during a six-year tour of European intellectual centers, had returned to America in 1834 determined to win converts to his master's doctrines. In the fall of 1840 he published *The Social Destiny of Man*, his own summary and exposition of Fourier's doctrines; it was one of the books Ripley had read when he was planning the Brook Farm Community. Brisbane also attracted the attention of New York publisher Horace Greeley (1811–72), who allowed him, for a fee of five hundred dollars, to write a front-page column in the New York *Tribune*. Brisbane's column, which ran from March of 1842 to September of 1843 and was titled "Association: or, Principles of a True Organization of Society," tried to suggest how Fourier's theories could be applied to American circumstances.

Fourier's voluminous writings aimed to explain how the economic misery of contemporary societies could be eliminated by reorganizing human living and working conditions completely. Instead of living in isolated houses and engaging in cutthroat economic competition that is as inefficient as it is cruel, people should be organized into "phalanxes" of 1,620 members. They would occupy a vast building called a "phalanstery," shaped like Versailles, which would contain everything necessary for human life. There carefully organized groups of laborers would raise food, manufacture needed objects, educate children, and provide arts and entertainment. Since Fourier believed that labor is made hateful through tedium, he argued that tasks should be broken down into shifts lasting no more than two or three hours, at which groups of laborers would never have to work until they were weary.

Such "attractive industry," where group replaced group in ordered succession, would provide material support for residents of phalansteries and would at the same time afford ample scope for the exercise of their passions, which Fourier tabulated with French precision: five "sensitive," four "affective," three "distibuting and directing." Because our passional attractions participate in a divine order, they therefore predict their own ultimate satisfaction; even apparent social disharmonies exist only to be resolved into a larger harmony. Indeed, Fourier was so strongly convinced of the correspondence between microcosm and macrocosm that he insisted that workers should form groups only in "harmonic" numbers – three, five, seven, or twelve. He believed that his discovery of the harmony of the passions deserved to be ranked with Newton's laws, and he expressed its fundamental law in the formula *Les attractions sont proportionelle aux destinées* (the attractions are proportional to the destinies). Life in the harmonious phalansteries would be so blissful that those outside would clamor to build phalansteries of their own, and soon the earth would be covered with a network of over two million interlocking and interconnected phalansteries, and a sixty thousand year period of creativity and happiness would commence.

It may seem odd that a doctrine so baroque in its complications and foreign in its terminology should ever have appealed to people in the United States. But Brisbane's proselytizing coincided with a period of severe economic stress and psychic dislocation. Many artisans were being displaced by the factory system, the economy seemed unable to recover from the disastrous crash of 1837, and recent immigrants to the cities often suffered from nostalgia for the more intimate world of the village and farm. Fourier claimed that his precise calculations were based upon social laws as immutable as the law of gravity. Suppose he were right? As many as thirty-five small phalanxes were formed in the United States during the 1840s.

Brisbane and Greeley visited Brook Farm during 1842 and 1843, urging

Ripley and others among the Brook Farmers to convert their community into a phalanx. By doing so Brook Farm could at once make itself more successful economically, attract members from a wider range of social classes, and offer hope to potential phalansterians still imprisoned within "civilization." The arguments sounded persuasive to the Brook Farmers, whose experiments so far had been mostly agricultural or educational rather than commercial, and who tended to underestimate the difficulties involved in the production of goods. Anna Russell, a well-traveled woman from a distinguished Boston family who had joined the association around 1843 and remained with it almost until the end, thought that the conversion to Fourierism was directly connected to naïveté about trade among the governing members: "Unused to commercial pursuits, the slow process so often needed to establish and successfully prosecute a business was to them a mystery; and I really believe that some of us thought that to place men in a workshop was sufficient to make our fortune."

The surviving documents from the Fourierist period that began roughly when Ripley and two associates drew up a new constitution for Brook Farm in 1844 make clear that far more was at stake than attracting more artisans in hopes of making a profit. Fourier's ambitions had been cosmic, and those of his American disciples were no less so. "Association" was meant to heal a wound in consciousness, even a wound in nature; Brisbane aimed (as one scholar put it) at nothing less than "the rehabilitation of the universe." In February 1844 John Sullivan Dwight, a Brook Farmer and former Unitarian minister, gave a lecture entitled "Association in Its Connection with Education" to the New England Fourierist Society. His lecture begins with an exposition of Fourierist theory and ends with an anguished cry from the heart, whose cadences Emerson himself would one day imitate.

We are harmonies; every man is a microcosm, or world in miniature, reflecting all the laws of all things; and each mortal child is as indispensable to the balance and completeness of the world into which he comes so small an atom, as is each planet in the system of our sun, or each sun in the celestial sphere, or each note in the great music of God. How comes it, then, that we clash? that our noblest aspirations prove our keenest misery? that we cannot put forth our hands to accept the promises of life without stealing food and joy from our neighbor? that we cannot seek our neighbor's good without being trampled under foot ourselves?"

If Fourier should be right, then these miseries will vanish when our children are gathered into phalanxes, laboring for one another's benefit rather than for one another's harm. Nor do we need to wait for these New Jerusalems to descend to us from heaven; we can start to build them now, and hasten that final consummation we so earnestly desire. Is it any wonder that Fourier displaced Kant and Schiller as the subject of Ripley's evening lectures? The Brook Farmers began to celebrate Fourier's birthday with festivities in which a bust of Fourier, flanked by azure tablets inscribed with "UNIVERSAL UNITY" and the motto *Les attractions sont proportionelle aux destinées,* presided over a room that also contained an inscription from the New Testament suggesting that the blessed Comforter would confirm the hopes of those who believe that association would bring down upon earth the kingdom of heaven. Someone even proposed the toast, "Fourier, the second coming of Christ."

Needless to say, this strange pasteboard-and-filigree religion did not appeal to everyone, nor did an exegesis of the works of Fourier much satisfy those who had preferred Kant and Schiller. Many of the original settlers did not choose to follow Ripley into the promised land of association, and some of the new working-class men and women who replaced them were markedly less willing to be gentrified than their predecessors had been. One student remembered that a group of "discontented mechanics" used to shout "Aristocrats!" as the Education Group passed by; things reached such a point of tension in January 1846 that Ripley had to threaten some residents with expulsion unless they stopped trying to create class conflict. For Anna Russell, such measures were fruitless as soon as they were thought necessary, for they proved that the old unity of heart was gone forever.

Still the exuberance of the old "Transcendental days," as the Brook Farmers themselves referred to the pre-phalanx association, did not wholly disappear. Fourier's frankly stated belief in pleasure as the end of human existence, though it gave rise among the "civilizees" to rumors of sexual license that damaged the school's ability to attract pupils, was friendly to the spirit of play that continued to enliven Brook Farm. And new members continued to fall in love with the joys of associated life.

A remarkable series of letters written during the later years of Brook Farm shows how much delight it still could generate. In 1844 a young woman named Marianne Dwight came to Brook Farm and began sending letters to Boston describing her experiences there back to her friend Anna Parsons and to her brother Frank. Marianne was the sister of John Sullivan Dwight, one of the original Brook Farmers and its teacher of music. Their parents and another sister were also Brook Farmers – Dr. John Dwight, the father, served as the group's doctor. It was natural that Marianne should feel a strong commitment to an enterprise in which her entire family was so deeply involved. Her sense of gratitude to Brook Farm produced a loyalty to it that never wavered throughout the darkest months of its existence, and her determination to record its life produced the only record we have of events written as they were happening during those last tumultuous years.

Women had more to gain from Brook Farm that anyone else, as John Codman argued in his own memoir.

It is often stated that the home circle is the sphere of women, but at times it is a very narrow circle — a very narrowing circle to its occupants. There are thousands who enter it as brilliant young ladies, and come from it at the end of a few years morbid, harassed, depressed; sunk in all the graces and powers that make a woman's life beautiful and distinct from a man's. The circle in many cases is so narrow that there is no room for growth.

At Brook Farm, in contrast, women were encouraged to expand and aspire, and they improved the opportunity. They were released from the isolation of the home; their labor was valued; there was even a Nursery Group designed to free women with small children for work elsewhere, or simply to give them temporary relief from the demands of child rearing. And women responded with devotion. Codman repeatedly praises the faithfulness of the Brook Farm women, their sacrifices and love of principle.

Marianne Dwight certainly proved herself capable of sacrifice and devotion. But she makes it clear that Brook Farm offered women something else — a sense of their own power. Marianne had been a teacher before coming to Brook Farm, but the association's chronic need for money prompted her to join with other women there in a "fancy group" devoted to making "elegant and tasteful caps, capes, collars, undersleeves, etc., etc." for sale in Boston shops. The experience of making money on her own triggered a frank and delightful explosion of feminism in her, along with a shrewd insight into the way liberation must be achieved.

In a letter to her friend Anna dated August 30, 1844, Marianne writes with amusement:

And now I must interest you in our fancy group, for which and from which I hope great things, — nothing less than the elevation of women to independence, and an acknowledged equality with man. Many thoughts on this subject have been struggling in my mind ever since I came to Brook Farm, and now, I think I see how it will all be accomplished. Women must become producers of marketable articles; women must make money and earn their support independently of man.

She sees what must be done: borrow some capital; purchase materials; turn out high-quality articles — the Boston distributors have already agreed to take all she can produce. When funds accumulate they may start other branches of business, but all proceeds (she swears) must be "applied to the elevation of women forever." She urges her friend to "take a spiritual view of the matter. Raise woman to be the equal of man, and what intellectual developments may we not expect? How the whole aspect of society will be changed! And this is the great work, is it not, that Association in its present early stage has to do?"

In fact Marianne did become a significant earner of capital for the association – her delicate watercolors of flowers and birds, painted onto lampshades and fans, sold so well that she was often painting eight hours a day. But Brook Farm proved to be a greedy consumer of all the capital she could generate, and the liberation of women had to be postponed (not for the last time in history) to the common good. Still, she was happy to have escaped women's ordinary lot among the "civilizees." To her brother she wrote, "For myself, I would not exchange this life for any I have ever led. I could not feel content with the life of isolated houses, and the conventions of civilization" (September 19, 1844).

Like Codman, Marianne Dwight is constantly entranced by the beauty all around her. The sight of the landscape after an ice storm makes her exclaim to Anna,

Oh, this day and yesterday! Was ever earth clad in such beauty? Would you were here to slide and coast over our hills of glistening white marble, – to admire the glittering coral branches that border our paths, and the trees of crystal, of silver and of diamonds, that make magnificent this fairy palace. Have I seen such beauty in a former existence, – or is it the realization of some dream or fancy – that it continually *reminds* me of something, I know not what?

Quite as fiercely as Emerson she scorns the notion that salvation must be achieved in a grim struggle with temptation; strength comes through happiness.

Look into your inner life. Did you ever feel that sorrow in itself gives you strength? Wasn't it rather an obstacle, an enemy, that, from some higher and happier source, some *hope* or *faith* or *joy* that was in you, you must draw strength to conquer? Have you not sometimes felt almost omnipotent from the impulse of some *joyful* emotion? (January 19, 1845)

The strength she got through hope Marianne wanted to devote to the cause of association, which was quite as holy an idea to her as it was to her brother John. In May 1845 she tells Anna:

The great doctrines of Association fire my soul every day more and more. I am awed at the vastness of the schemes it unfolds, I am filled with wonder and ecstasy. . . . A deep, solemn joy has taken possession of my soul, from the consciousness that there is something worth living for. In the hopes and views that the associative life has disclosed to me, I feel that I have a treasure that nothing can deprive me of. (May 19, 1845)

Nevertheless, conditions at Brook Farm were worsening. "Retrenchments" at the dinner table were called for so often that little was left to sacrifice. A kind neighbor had to supply the Thanksgiving turkeys; coffee and cakes put out for someone's wedding party seemed like unimaginable luxuries to the hungry Brook Farmers who clustered around the table. Throughout the grim autumn of 1845 and the outbreak of smallpox that affected twenty-six of the Brook Farmers in November (no one died, but two were severely scarred) Marianne tried to keep her hopes up. But by December 7 she is beginning to come to the same conclusion that Anna Russell had reached. Cautioning her friend to keep what she writes confidential, Marianne admits that Brook Farm has reached its severest crisis. "We are perplexed by debts, by want of capital to carry on any business, – by want of our Phalanstery or the means to finish it." The new building, started the preceding summer, was supposed to provide accommodations for fourteen families as well as for single people, but the construction costs were saddling the already strapped association with heavy debts, and the building was still less than half-finished when work had to stop for the winter. "I think here lies the difficulty, – we have not had business men to conduct our affairs – we have had *no* strictly business transaction from the beginning, and those among us who have some business talents, see this error, and feel that we cannot go on as we have done." A sad article by her brother John Sullivan Dwight in the November 1846 *Harbinger,* an associationist journal published at Brook Farm, imploring readers not to consider Brook Farm a failure "because in one point of view it has failed," already sounds like an epitaph.

Still, after a bleak winter things seemed to be looking up in the early spring of 1846. Sympathetic Fourierists were helping to raise money to complete the Phalanstery; work on it had begun again after the winter break. On the evening of March 1, 1846, most of the Brook Farmers decided to celebrate this renewal of hope with a dance. Suddenly someone broke in and shouted that fire had broken out in the Phalanstery. People seized buckets and ran in the direction of the fire, but the whole building was consumed in flames; they had all they could do to keep the surrounding buildings from going up in flames as well.

"Would I could convey to you an idea of it," Marianne wrote to her friend Anna three days after the fire. "It was glorious beyond description.... An immense, clear blue flame mingled for a while with the others and rose high in the air, – like liquid turquoise and topaz. It came from the melting glass. Rockets, too, rose in the sky, and fell in glittering gems of rainbow hue." All the onlookers were awed by the sublimity of the scene.

There was one moment, whilst the whole frame yet stood, that surpassed all else. It was fire throughout. It seemed like a magnificent temple of molten gold, or a crystallized fire. . . . The smoke as it settled off the horizon, gave the effect of sublime mountain scenery; and during the burning, the trees, the woods shone magically to their minutest twigs, in lead, silver, and gold. (March 4, 1846)

When John Codman ran to fetch buckets of water from the greenhouse where flowers were raised for the Boston trade he found the flowers there "lighted up with a heavenly glow of color, and so startlingly beautiful that in spite of my haste I lingered a moment to look on them. Roses and camellias, heaths and azaleas – whatever flowers there were in bloom looked superbly glorified in the transcendent light, and I uttered an exclamation of surprise at the lovely display." The fire lit up the sky for miles around. Crowds gathered from nearby towns, for the huge blaze was visible as far away as Boston. The Brook Farmers somehow contrived to feed two hundred of them on bread and cheese. Ripley even managed a few gallant jokes as he thanked the firemen who had driven out from Boston only to discover that their engines were useless.

No one wished to admit that the Phalanstery fire spelled the end of Brook Farm. But the financial loss had been severe – seven thousand dollars had been invested in the building, which was not insured. Though Ripley and his loyal supporters tried to keep the farm going through another summer and another winter, most people realized that the cause was lost. Brook Farmers began to drift away, so slowly that when Codman tried to remember it in later life the closing months of Brook Farm seemed "dreamy and unreal," like a skein of wool unraveling, or apple petals falling softly to the ground. In the spring of 1847 Ripley let the farm grounds for a year, and later on he and Sophia left Brook Farm for a furnished room in Flatbush, Brooklyn, where he tried to eke out a living by teaching school and by writing book reviews for Horace Greeley's *Tribune*. Sophia, seeking a firmer faith than association, converted to Roman Catholicism. Though Ripley eventually worked his way out of poverty, paid off the remaining Brook Farm debts, and became an influential literary critic in post-Civil War New York, he remained silent about his Brook Farm experiences – telling a friend who pressed him that he had not yet reached his "years of indiscretion." When Ripley reviewed *The Blithedale Romance* he contented himself with remarking that only the funny parts of the book would seem recognizable as portraits of the real Brook Farm to those who had actually been there.

For Marianne Dwight the sorrow of Brook Farm's end was tempered by private joy. On December 26, 1846, she had married John Orvis, a Brook Farmer who had been a tireless worker on the farm and a lecturer for association – a cause to which, in various forms, he devoted the rest of his life. That she and her husband were leaving together made her feel confident that the love of humanity she had learned at Brook Farm would continue strong in them, and neither feared poverty or hard work. Still, it saddened her to leave the place where she had been so happy. In her last letter from Brook Farm in March 1847 she writes that she hates to think of the green-house plants being sold off, and then, the Eve of this small Eden, gives way to momentary grief:

Oh! I love every tree and wood haunt – every nook and path, and hill and meadow. I fear the birds can never sing so sweetly to me elsewhere, – the flowers can never greet me so smilingly. I can hardly imagine that the same sky will look down upon me in any other spot, and where, where in the wide world shall I ever find warm hearts all around me again? Oh! you must feel with me that none but a Brook Farmer can know how chilling is the cordiality of the world.

Almost half a century later, Codman would remember his experience at Brook Farm with gratitude for the variety of his satisfactions there. "I had tasted of actual farm work. I had planted beans, potatoes, and melons. I had hoed corn, and on my knees weeded, in the broiling sun, the young onions. I had driven horse to plough, and side by side with others, trying to hoe my row with them, disputed, discussed social questions and ideas . . ." Had he been happy? "I loved the daily round of life. All were kind to me. I was well mentally and physically. I was in the bud of youth. I was like the pink rhodoras in spring, callow of leaf or fruit but brightly covered with promis-ing blossoms. There remained one thing for me – to know I was happy. Did I know it? Yes, I did."

What lessons could be drawn from the collapse of Fruitlands and Brook Farm? For Emerson, the defeat of so much hope testified to the irreconcilabil-ity of the world of desire and the world of actuality. In the essay "Montaigne" he writes Brook Farm's epitaph: "Charles Fourier announced that 'the attrac-tions of man are proportioned to his destinies;' in other words, that every desire predicts its own satisfaction. Yet all experience exhibits the reverse of this; the incompetency of power is the universal grief of young and ardent minds." Every man was born with a raging hunger, an appetite that could eat the solar system like a cake, yet as soon as he tried his strength, his senses gave way and refused to serve him. "He was an emperor deserted by his states, and left to whistle by himself or thrust into a mob of emperors, all whistling: and still the sirens sung, 'The attractions are proportioned to the destinies.'"

A younger person, however, might draw a different conclusion. Although Thoreau's own (still unpublished) Amory Hall lecture in 1844 had been quite as passionate as Emerson's in rejecting collective solutions to the problem of reform, his aim was not so much to reject the project of reform as to transform it into a personal quest. In the lecture Thoreau scorned most reforms as death presuming to give laws to life, and suggested that the sun, who does most of his reforming in the spring, was the kind of reformer we ought to emulate. The trouble with Fourier was that he wanted more civilization; Thoreau wants less. Only in Nature is there hope and freedom, and only when we are rooted in her soil can we spring again refreshed.

The cabin Thoreau built on Emerson's new property at Walden Pond in the spring of 1845 and the life he lived there for the next two years sought to combine the best features of the two communities Thoreau was most familiar with while avoiding the mistakes that destroyed them. Like the Fruitlanders, he was a vegetarian and devoted to cold-water bathing. (He was also celibate, something John Lane believed in but never persuaded Alcott to agree to.) Like the Brook Farmers, Thoreau believed in the principle of "attractive industry," in the healthful alternation of mental and physical labor, in joyous recreation, even in obsessive punning. He was free of the personal and ideological squabbling that had split Fruitlands, free of the class tensions that had marred Brook Farm. Thoreau built the only successful phalanx in America: a phalanx for one. What would he later say he had learned?

I learned this, at least, by my experiment; that if one advances confidently in the direction of his dreams, and endeavors to live the life which he has imagined, he will meet with a success unexpected in common hours. He will put some things behind, will pass an invisible boundary; new, universal, and more liberal laws will begin to establish themselves around and within him. . . . In proportion as he simplifies his life, the laws of the universe will appear less complex, and solitude will not be solitude, nor poverty poverty, nor weakness weakness. If you have built castles in the air, your work need not be lost; that is where they should be. Now put the foundations under them. (*Walden,* "Conclusion")

8

DIASPORA

THE 1840S WITNESSED the slow fragmentation of the Transcendentalist movement and the departure of its members upon paths of their own. The last meeting of the Transcendental Club was probably the meeting held in September 1840. *The Dial* ceased publication in 1844. The members of the group continued to meet and talk with one another, to write letters to one another, to attend one another's lectures, and to read one another's books; but they had begun to break into smaller groups defined by interest, personal affection, or ideology and to regard one another with friendly curiosity rather than with feelings of solidarity. Some of them returned to the Boston area after years of exile; others departed from it on long journeys. Some remained within the Unitarian church (two even become professors at the Harvard Divinity School); some left it for other religions or for a "church of the future" they hoped would materialize. Most found themselves being drawn into one of the practical reform movements of the day – association, prison reform, opposition to the Mexican War, antislavery. Two witnessed the European revolutions of 1848, for Emerson crossed the channel from England to witness the celebrations on the Champ de Mars during the French uprising, and Margaret Fuller ran a hospital during the siege of Rome.

Convers Francis slid gently from his position as the elder statesman among the Transcendentalists (he was five years older than Alcott, eight years older than Emerson) to a Harvard professorship. Francis had been ordained as minister to a congregation at Watertown in 1819 and remained in that post until he was invited to become professor of pulpit eloquence and pastoral care at the Divinity School in 1842. Although he was one of the charter members of the Transcendental Club, serving as its moderator when he was in attendance, and was a friend and mentor of Theodore Parker, he had no desire to leave the Unitarian church, but rather sought to accentuate its historic preference for the moral over the dogmatic, for internal principles rather than for rituals or forms. When the club met in early September 1840 to discuss "the organization of a new church," Francis joined Frederic Henry Hedge and another member in supporting the existing Unitarian Association, despite

Theodore Parker's complaint that they were wedded to the past and Emerson's stronger charge that such distrust of the divine soul amounted to atheism.

If Francis could not follow Emerson in all of his flights, he still remained one of Emerson's sincerest admirers. In his journals he left a vivid account of the exhilaration he felt at Emerson's lectures, where the speaker seemed less a speaker than like the place from which truth radiated. If he had any criticism to make, it was that Emerson's lectures contained such a "succession of the best things in condensed sentences, that we can scarcely *remember* any of them" (January 9, 1839). Or, as Francis complained elsewhere, "I find that his best things are *slippery,* and will not stay in my mind" (February 16, 1837).

Francis attended the Divinity School Address and heard not a blasphemous tract but a discourse "full of divine life." Its accuracy and even its humor in portraying the "downfallen state of the church" Francis appreciated, and though he did not agree with everything Emerson said in the discourse he did not think that Emerson valued Jesus less than other people did, merely that he valued humanity more (Francis to Frederic Henry Hedge, August 10, 1838). The subsequent outbreak of wrath after that address he attributed to the long-smoldering jealousy felt by the *dii majores* of the pulpits and Divinity School against Emerson because of his popularity among the "brightest young people" (Francis to Frederic Henry Hedge, November 12, 1838).

Another first-generation Transcendentalist was blunter than Francis at expressing dismay about the direction the movement was taking in the 1840s. Hedge's 1833 article on Coleridge had been one of the early manifestos of Transcendentalism, and his June 1836 letter to Emerson had been instrumental in getting the Transcendental Club started. But he had never been as enthusiastic a believer in the newness as some of his fellow club members, and his constitutional tendency to value old institutions and traditional practices set him apart from those who, as he later remembered, "saw in every case of dissent, and in every new dissentient, the harbinger of the New Jerusalem." "My historical conscience, then as since, balanced my neology, and kept me ecclesiastically conservative, though intellectually radical" ("The Destinies of Ecclesiastical Religion," 1867). At one of the last meetings of the Transcendental Club in September 1840 he stoutly defended the American Unitarian Association against attacks by Parker, Ripley, Fuller, and Emerson.

Hedge's congregation in Bangor, Maine (where he was pastor from 1835–50), was a difficult team to drive, containing as it did both "*ultra* liberal" and "*ultra* conservative" factions, and at one point he offered to resign his position there because he was aware that some conservatives, doubting his orthodoxy, were trying to unseat him. At the same time, he was alarmed by what seemed to him the real skepticism underlying Transcendentalist radicalism. In a letter to his good friend Convers Francis in 1843 he complained that Emerson and Parker were publicly advancing doctrines that had been considered infamous a few years ago when associated with names like Fanny Wright or Tom Paine. Worse still were the social radicals, "that numerous class of persons, with large ideas & small faculty, who have not obtained what they covet from existing institutions & who think they shall find their account in a general overturn." Radicals trying to escape human evil reminded him of dogs with tin pots tied to their tails.

When Margaret Fuller wrote to Hedge in 1840 urging him to submit something to *The Dial,* he refused politely. When she pressed him, he admitted that he did not wish to be publicly identified with the Transcendentalists lest he be considered "an atheist in disguise." The same anxiety wells up in a letter he wrote to Convers Francis in February 1843. Francis had recently resigned his Watertown pastorate to accept a position at the Harvard Divinity School, a move Hedge encouraged. But Hedge feared that their friendship would suffer, as Francis would no longer feel free to enjoy genial "pernoctations and confumations" with someone who had "incurred the stigma of transcendental & heretical tendencies. . . . There is a rigid, cautious, circumspect, conservative *tang* in the air of Cambridge which no one, who had resided there for any considerable time can escape."

Yet Hedge was certainly not a conservative in other respects. He reacted with derision when he learned that Andrews Norton had recently stormed out of a sermon advocating religious liberty. "What stronger proof could he give of being pricked in his conscience? . . . The professor actually grows antic as the new age advances. 'And wroth to see his Kingdom fail / Swinges the scaly horror of his folded tail' " (Hedge to Convers Francis, January 26, 1842). Hedge remained true to what he thought were the central doctrines of Transcendentalism – the belief that human beings could perceive truth intuitively, and the hope that every genuine reform is "a step in that progressive incarnation of divine attributes in humankind, which illustrates and fulfills the prophetic prayer of Christ, 'that they all may be one in us.' "

Hedge's opinions on social questions were similarly complex. He considered himself a conservative, and condemned socialism as amoral, irreligious, and "grovelling." But he joined the Cambridge Anti-Slavery Society as early as 1834 and delivered an address the next year on emancipation in the British West Indies (nine years before Emerson did). After the passage of the Fugitive Slave Law in 1850, Hedge fully endorsed the use of force to rescue fugitive slaves from southern slavehunters who had tracked them down, arguing that a mob was better than the enforcement of an unjust law. He advocated women's suffrage and women's right to pursue at least certain

careers outside the home. (He thought women might be doctors, for instance, so long as they treated only their own sex.) In 1866 he delivered an
important address at Harvard urging replacement of the hated recitation
system with an elective system in which the student's choice of material to
study would be "self-determined."

He remained on friendly terms with his old associates and even relented
about writing for *The Dial,* though most of his contributions were translations. He wrote a discerning review of Emerson's second book of essays
(*Essays, Second Series*) for the *Christian Examiner* in 1845, objecting to Emerson's theology but praising the essay "Experience" as the best piece in the
book and likening it to Ecclesiastes in its movement from doubt to affirma-
tion. (He also spoke admiringly of "New England Reformers," probably
because Emerson's skepticism about reform movements in that address
matched his own.)   ·

In 1858 Hedge joined the faculty of the Harvard Divinity School as a
professor of ecclesiastical history; in the same year, he became the editor of the
Christian Examiner, a position he held for three years. In 1859 he began a four-
year term as president of the American Unitarian Association. *Reason in Religion,* his major theological work, which one scholar has called "the definitive
statement of mainstream or moderate Transcendentalism," appeared in 1865.

Like Francis and Hedge, Theodore Parker and James Freeman Clarke chose
to remain within the Unitarian church. But Parker and Hedge insisted upon
trying to transform it radically. Parker's innovations were forced upon him by
the reaction within his own denomination to the furor aroused by both "The
Discourse of the Transient and Permanent in Christianity" and the ambitious
Discourse of Matters Pertaining to Religion (1842). Although his own small
congregation in West Roxbury had remained loyal to him throughout the
controversy, most of his fellow Unitarian ministers refused to exchange pulpits with him – some out of a genuine belief that what Parker was preaching
could no longer be considered Christianity and others because they feared the
obloquy they would suffer if they allowed him in their pulpits. Even Convers
Francis, who had been his friend and mentor, withdrew from a scheduled
pulpit exchange on the advice of a colleague at the Divinity School, though
he later mustered enough courage to supply Parker's Roxbury pulpit when
Parker was in Europe.

The cost of befriending Parker could be severe. In December 1845, when a
young minister named John T. Sargent invited Parker to preach at his Suffolk
Street Chapel, a Unitarian "mission" chapel overseen by the Benevolent
Fraternity of Churches, the officers of the Benevolent Fraternity rebuked
Sargent so sternly that he felt obliged to resign his position. In January of the
next year when James Freeman Clarke invited Parker to exchange pulpits,

fifteen of the wealthiest and most prominent members of Clarke's congregation left his society.

Parker could glory in abuse heaped upon himself, but watching his few courageous supporters suffer for their allegiance to him was another matter. If he were to continue to preach outside of Roxbury it would have to be by other means than pulpit exchanges. Accordingly, in January 1845 a group of Parker's admirers met to pass a single resolution: "That the Rev. Theodore Parker have a chance to be heard in Boston." They engaged to rent space for him in a building quite as unorthodox as his preaching. The Boston Melodeon was a dirty theatrical hall, freezing cold in winter, roasting in summer, redolent with the scents of the variety acts that played there during the week – dancing monkeys, minstrel shows, acrobats. Parker noted in his farewell sermon there in 1852 that he often had looked down when he was preaching upon the spangles left by opera dancers who had performed on the stage the previous night.

But the society was open to all. There were no pews to purchase, no weekly collection (the expenses of the society, including Parker's own salary, were paid by subscriptions). Parker was a powerful and effective preacher, and he now felt free to let out all the length of his reins – to denounce, to uplift, to venerate, or to beseech, just as the spirit moved him. Before long he was drawing a congregation not only from all parts of the city but also from the surrounding suburban towns. By November 1845 there were enough members in Parker's church to organize themselves as the Twenty-Eighth Congregational Society of Boston; eventually his parish register contained seven *thousand* names (the largest congregation in Boston, possibly even in the United States). William Lloyd Garrison and Samuel May were members of the Twenty-Eighth, for Parker became increasingly vocal as a critic of slavery. In 1852 the growth of the congregation necessitated a move to the Boston Music Hall, an ample space illuminated from above by a row of gas jets in a way that reminded one visitor of Milton's Pandemonium.

James Freeman Clarke, though younger than Parker, was far more conservative theologically: He believed in miracles, in Christ's supernatural character and mediatorial role, and in the depravity of humanity and the consequent need for a Redeemer. In fact, when Parker's *Discourse of Matters Pertaining to Religion* had appeared in 1842, Clarke published a review denouncing it as "the new gospel of shallow naturalism." Nonetheless, Clarke refused to cancel pulpit exchanges with Parker even though some members of his congregation were upset with his decision, and he spoke out vigorously against the growing tendency among Unitarians to deny the free speech that they had so long regarded as sacred. When he persisted in his determination to exchange with Parker in 1845, the church members held a meeting at which they tried to persuade Clarke to cancel. Clarke remained unmoved. He stated that he was now determined to exchange with Parker even if *Parker* refused. The attempt to crush heresies had destroyed the Roman church and was now paralyzing the Protestant one. Free discussion was the only principle of union that could save it. "I think in this question is involved the question whether hereafter there shall be any Church of Christ on earth."

Clarke's bravery is all the more commendable because he, too, was experimenting with an unorthodox form of church organization. He had come back from Louisville in 1840 dismayed by the bitter rifts within Unitarianism but even more by the lifelessness that seemed to pervade church services. The spiritual distress of the congregants, who looked up like hungry sheep but were not fed, made Clarke determined to found a new kind of church, one in which the members would be bound together by the desire to grow in spiritual perfection rather than by common ownership of a meetinghouse, one in which anyone who wished to could take communion, and one in which the congregation would take an active part in the life of the church — by singing hymns and reading aloud devotional psalms during the Sunday services, by meeting in evening discussion groups or in Bible study groups, and by performing charitable work among the Boston poor. He thought that there were enough discontented worshippers in Boston to form this new church, and in early 1841 he rented a chapel for three evenings in order to preach three sermons that would set forth his own ideas of religion and attract potential worshippers.

Clarke's plan succeeded. By mid-February Clarke had met with a group willing to form a new church. They rented Amory Hall for the Sunday services and began to organize the evening discussion groups. By 1845 there were over two hundred active members in Clarke's Church of the Disciples, enough to force a move to larger quarters in the Masonic Temple. Weekly attendance could run as high as seven hundred. Even the crisis caused by Clarke's refusal to cancel his exchange with Theodore Parker, though it weakened his church financially for a time, failed to stop its growth or damage Clarke's reputation. In May 1845 he was elected to the Executive Board of the American Unitarian Association.

Yet if Francis, Hedge, and Clarke were becoming more firmly entrenched in Unitarianism and Parker was remaining as a kind of spectacular gadfly buzzing around it, another onetime member of the Transcendental Club was about to leave both Unitarianism and Transcendentalism behind. Throughout the early 1840s Orestes Brownson had become increasingly troubled with the view of the world he had worked out in the previous decade. The Transcendentalists had angered him by their misty refusals to face the reality of social injustice. But in 1840 the laboring classes whose interests he had tried to defend in his *Boston Quarterly Review* essays abandoned him to vote for (and elect) the Whig candidate for president, William Henry Harrison, whereas the Democratic party that he had embraced treated him as an embarrassment. As Brownson's biographer points out, such folly and ingratitude made it more and more difficult for him to believe that "the People" were the incarnation of God's spirit. "They could not be close to Him; they must therefore be divorced from Him; they could not be basically virtuous, they must therefore be basically corrupt." And if they were corrupt, the old Unitarian and Transcendentalist project of self-culture was a doomed enterprise, as impossible as a man's trying to lift himself up by his own waistband.

The world could be redeemed only through an infusion of grace. Logically, this conclusion might have pushed Brownson back in the direction of Edwardsean Calvinism, but he had grown increasingly distrustful of the egotism and isolation he thought Protestantism fostered, and Jonathan Edwards's eventual rejection by his own church in Northampton showed the danger of trying to channel grace through the fractiousness of the Congregational parish. Even as far back as his 1836 tract *New Views of Christianity, Society and the Church* Brownson had expressed a theory of history that identified spirituality with the medieval Catholic church and materialism with Protestantism. At that time he had seen Unitarianism as the reconciling term. Now, with Unitarianism found wanting in his eyes, Brownson began to be drawn toward the one church that could claim an unbroken line of succession from the time of the Apostles.

By the spring of 1843 friends began to hear rumors that Brownson was considering conversion to Catholicism, rumors that seemed to be confirmed when he had a brief interview with the Roman Catholic bishop of Boston. For a while Brownson resisted taking the final step. But by July 1844 he believed he had no legitimate reasons for delay. "Our logic allows us no alternative between Catholicism and Come-outerism," he announced, "and we have tried Come-outerism." He began taking instruction, and on October 20, 1844, he formally embraced the Roman Catholic faith. He began a new version of his old quarterly review (which had ceased publication in 1842). The new review was called *Brownson's Quarterly Review,* and Brownson used it to lambaste his former friends in the Transcendentalist movement, threatening them with eternal damnation unless they followed him into the Roman church immediately. They took it calmly enough. James Freeman Clarke merely observed: "No man has ever equalled Mr. Brownson in the ability with which he has refuted his own arguments."

Brownson's chief convert among the Transcendentalists was Sophia Dana Ripley, George Ripley's wife. Sophia had supported her husband throughout years of controversy and disappointment in his ministry; she had been a tireless worker at Brook Farm, even nursing one of the Filipino students through a gruesome attack of leprosy until her own health almost broke down. Emerson said after a visit to Brook Farm that he had never seen her so much to advantage. But she was unable to share her husband's enthusiasm for the conversion of Brook Farm to a Fourierist phalanx; the cause of association, which had filled Marianne Dwight with such joy, left Sophia Ripley unsatisfied and filled with doubts. When Brownson began coming out to Brook Farm to talk to the small community of Catholics there Sophia joined the group, and she soon began going into Boston for Catholic services. In 1846 she became a convert to Catholicism. After Brook Farm had collapsed and the Ripleys had moved to New York she lived a life of intense Catholic piety, devoting much of her time to prayer and to charitable works and concerning herself particularly with New York's large population of prostitutes. She helped raise the money to build a shelter, the Convent of the Good Shepherd, and served on its board of trustees. But George, though he occasionally accompanied his wife to Catholic services, never joined her in her new faith.

If Emerson paid much attention to the controversies in which his former associates were embroiled during the early 1840s, he must have believed that the wisdom of his own decision in the preceding decade to cut all ties with institutions had been amply confirmed. Hedge's unbecoming timidity, Francis's temporary lapse from moral courage, Parker's bitterness and disillusionment, Clarke's battles with his congregation over pulpit exchanges, Brownson's noisy proselytizing – all of these irritants Emerson had escaped by his decision to leave the church, join no party, and form no alliance more binding than any one he might make when he agreed to deliver a lecture series at this hall or that lyceum. Because he never asked his friends for their support he could not be hurt by their defections; because he claimed no authority for his statements except the authority his hearers or readers were willing to concede to them he need not worry whether he was shocking or offending people. They were at liberty to walk out of the lecture hall or throw his books in the fire the minute they were displeased; and in their freedom he found his own.

Emerson's horror of association has brought him into disfavor with modern readers, and he later came to repent that his shrinking from organized reform had kept him out of the antislavery movement far longer than he should have allowed it to. But he had all around him proofs of the vexatiousness of attempting to achieve anything through institutions. Brook Farm, Fruitlands, and the Unitarian squabbles of the 1840s were object lessons in the folly of attempting to reform the world by changing the behavior of people. If Emerson (and Thoreau) kept insisting on the need for *self*-emancipation, even to the point of arguing that evils as recalcitrant as slavery would somehow melt away before the righteousness of a few redeemed souls, it should be remembered also how few examples of success from associated action they had actually witnessed.

At the end of the essay "Experience" Emerson says that he had not found much that was gained by "manipular attempts to realize the world of thought." The people who try it "acquire democratic manners, they foam at the mouth, they hate and deny. Worse, I observe, that, in the history of mankind, there is never a solitary example of success, – taking their own tests of success." In the book *Poems,* which he published on Christmas Day 1846, Emerson included "Ode," inscribed to W. H. Channing, the unofficial Brook Farm chaplain and an enthusiast for most kinds of organized reform. The poem begins with a compliment to Channing and an apologia for Emerson's refusal to connect himself with any movement, ecclesiastical or political. "Though loath to grieve / The evil time's sole patriot, / I cannot leave / My honied thought / For the priest's cant, / Or the Statesman's rant." No amount of reforming activity – not even joining in Garrison's famous cry "No Union with Slaveholders" and rending the northern states from the south – would make the commonwealth virtuous as long as it remained devoted to the protection of property (as all commonwealths are). "Boston Bay and Bunker Hill / Would serve things still; – / Things are of the snake."

This mood of bitterness, brought on partly by the spectacle of the war President James K. Polk had recently declared on Mexico, surfaces in Emerson whenever he considers the increasingly squalid political situation in the United States. But bitterness is not his dominant mood. Indeed, while many of his former colleagues were embroiled in controversy or entangled in collapsing utopian schemes, Emerson was radiating a new sense of confidence. Although his "calling" of itinerant lecturer, journal editor, and mentor to the young might have seemed eccentric to a Boston banker, it *was* a calling and not merely a condition of alienation from society. He deposited his thoughts in his "savings bank," as he called his journals, and withdrew the interest in the form of lectures and essays. As for the banker, was not he too bought and sold? He built his countinghouse on Quincy granite, but the web of credit and speculation that supported him was no less a creation of the human imagination than the *Orlando Furioso,* and he himself was as subject to ecstasies, panics, and despairs as was any heroine of romance.

When it came time to consider possible lecture topics for the 1845–6 season, then, Emerson turned to a more inclusive look at the human condition. Unitarian humanism had always delighted to contemplate in Jesus the perfect man, though Emerson, in his youth, had refused to concur in the estimation. Now he begins to fill his journal with praises of an imagined being he calls "the central man," a Jesus without local or historical limitations, as the Oversoul is a Jehovah without personality and without wrath (though inaccessible and silent as the Sphinx). Emerson imagines the "varying play of his features" as the central man's face dissolves into a series of faces famous for either genius or sanctity – Socrates, Shakespeare, Raphael, Michaelangelo, Dante, Jesus.

There are limitations, however, to the attractions of a composite Redeemer. Instead, Emerson is drawn toward another model of human perfection, one he had adumbrated in "Nominalist and Realist" when he had said that Jesus would absorb the race unless Tom Paine or some other coarse blasphemer "helps humanity by resisting this exuberance of power." Here the model is not religious (as in the different incarnations of Vishnu) but federal, a question of checks and balances. "The sanity of society is a balance of a thousand insanities." This model evokes another one, possibly suggested to Emerson by a treatise he had read at Harvard on the marvelous construction of the human hand, considered as evidence of the Creator's wisdom. In March 1845 Emerson wrote in his journal: "I have found a subject, *On the use of great men.*" A book written on this subject should begin with "a chapter *on the distribution of the hand into fingers,* or on the great value of these individuals as counterweights, checks on each other." Great men *incarnate* various attributes of divinity; their differences *protect* us from excessive reverence for any one variety of incarnation; together they help us *grasp* some aspect of reality otherwise unreachable.

When Emerson received an invitation from the Boston Lyceum in August 1845 to deliver a course of lectures the next winter he hesitated; he liked being an independent lecturer, beholden to no one. But the prospect of being freed from the labor of hiring the hall and selling the tickets was tempting, and Emerson accepted the offer. The course of seven lectures known as "Representative Men" that he began in Boston on December 11, 1845, and repeated in many places during the next three years were revised into a book that was finally published on January 1, 1850.

The opening essay in the book, "The Uses of Great Men," sets the volume's tone. Some sentences from "Nominalist and Realist" might serve as its motto: "We want the great genius only for joy: for one more star in our constellation, for one more tree in our grove." Emerson opens by reminding us that all mythology begins with demigods, and then he explains why this should be so. Demigods, heroes, and great men "satisfy expectation"; they answer the questions we have not the skill to put. Then too, they are representative; they "serve us in the intellect" by embodying particular ideas. In their varying lives we find imaginative compensation for the poverty of our single existence; we are "multiplied by our proxies." For great men represent us not only as symbols represent ideas, but also as congressmen

Plato – dissolve existence back to Essence
Eternal unity
world or order — 175 Linked

represent constituencies, with an authority that derives from the multitudes, not from the skies. We need great men to redress our imperfections and inspire our efforts, but as we grow we discard hero after hero. "Once they were angels of knowledge, and their figures touched the sky. Then we drew near, saw their means, culture, and limits; and they yielded their place to other geniuses." Eventually we will cease to search for greatness in particular men at all, seeing heroes only as "exponents of a vaster mind and will."

Plato, Emerson's first representative man, is the easiest to praise, for he himself tried to dissolve existence back into essence at every turn. He was exactly poised between the world of eternal unity and the world of order and discriminations, in love both with vastness and with limit. Best of all, he brought the good news that these worlds are linked, corresponding to one another in a way that makes reality knowable. Emerson imagines him as saying,

I give you joy, O sons of men! that truth is altogether wholesome; that we have hope to search out what might be the very self of everything. The misery of man is to be baulked of the sight of essence, and to be stuffed with conjectures: but the supreme good is reality, the supreme beauty is reality; and all virtue and all felicity depend on this science of the real.

If Plato has a defect, it is merely that his writings are of excessively literary or intellectual character and hence lack the authority that the Arab and Jewish prophets possess. But all our philosophies are "drift boulders" that have rolled down from his primeval mountain.

From this high tableland of praise we descend into a valley of abuse. "Swedenborg, or the Mystic" presents a figure whom Emerson had once considered an angel of knowledge but who now is discredited. Swedenborg was an eighteenth-century natural scientist of vast ambition who experienced in midlife a mystical illumination that revealed to him the heavens and the hells and suggested to him a method for unlocking the meaning of the Scripture through symbolical interpretation. Emerson still praises Swedenborg as a natural scientist, particularly for his grand unifying vision that tries to tie together the smallest phenomena of nature with the greatest, as when he revealed that the globule of blood gyrates around its own axis exactly like the planet in the sky. "His varied and solid knowledge of the world makes his style lustrous with points and shooting spicula of thought, and resembling one of those winter mornings when the air sparkles with crystals."

Swedenborg's theological works are another matter. Written in language borrowed from the foreign mythology of the ancient Hebrew religion, Swedenborg's books turn the "warm many-weathered passionate-peopled world" into a gloomy "grammar of hieroglyphs or an emblematic free-masons' procession." His hells are nightmares of filth and corruption, vindictive as Dante's but without imagination. His heaven is frivolous – "a *fête champêtre,* an evangelical picnic, or French distribution of prizes to virtuous peasants." Even the beloved doctrine of "correspondence," which to the young Emerson had seemed a possible key to the meaning of nature, is now dismissed with contempt as unworthy of serious consideration: "A horse signifies carnal understanding; a tree, perception; the moon, faith; a cat means this; an ostrich, that; an artichoke, this other."

After the airless universe of the Swedenborg essay, it is a relief to emerge once again into the generosity and urbanity of "Montaigne, or the Skeptic." Montaigne, whom Emerson had loved since his young manhood, stands on the boundary between the world of sensation and the world of morals, but he attempts neither to link them in a scale of knowables (in the manner of Plato) nor to translate one into the other through a dictionary of correspondences (in the manner of Swedenborg). Instead he is there to consider, to weigh; his coat of arms is the balance, his motto "Que sçais je?"; his method an abstention from dogmatizing: "There is much to say on all sides." What prevents this openness from becoming confused with vacillation is Montaigne's own unquestioned probity and hatred of pretense. He enjoys with gusto and writes with utter frankness, and he is the representative of that midworld Emerson had praised in "Experience" and was increasingly coming to value as he reached his own middle age.

Yet even the good sense of Montaigne is finally found wanting in the face of the terrible ferocity of human desire. The end of "Montaigne, or the Skeptic" contains the best description of that desire to be found anywhere in Emerson's writings; that it occurs toward the close of an essay devoted to the joys of temperance suggests why even that venerable solution is helpless to satisfy:

The incompetency of power is the universal grief of young and ardent minds. They accuse the divine Providence of a certain parsimony. It has shown the heaven and earth to every child, and filled him with a desire for the whole; a desire raging, infinite, a hunger as of space to be filled with planets; a cry of famine as of devils for souls.

Art might assuage the hunger for perfection that experience leaves unsatisfied, but neither of the artists Emerson surveys in *Representative Men* quite escapes from his inherited distrust of art as frivolous. Shakespeare, for instance, gets a considerable praise for being the first poet in the world to have mastered the trick of "perfect representation": "Things were mirrored in his poetry without loss or blur; he could paint the fine with precision, the great with compass; the tragic and the comic indifferently, and without any distortion or favour" ("Shakespeare, or the Poet"). Like Daguerre, whose invention for fixing visible images had been announced to the world only six years before Emerson gave his lectures, Shakespeare had learned to make images with absolute fidelity, "and now let the world of figures sit for their portraits." But in the end this miraculous power is used for entertainment alone. With a power of illustration and an understanding of human character that might have done honor to a Hebrew prophet, Shakespeare was content to be a successful actor and playwright only, "master of the revels to mankind."

Goethe, the only modern writer with anything like Shakespeare's comprehensiveness, leaves Emerson even less satisfied. Emerson had never really caught Margaret Fuller's passionate love of Goethe, even though he cribbed many points from her brilliant two-part article on him in *The Dial* for his own essay, "Goethe, or the Writer." Although he praises Goethe for introducing to "Old England" and New England a novel idea – "that a man exists for Culture; not for what he can accomplish, but for what can be accomplished in him" – Emerson ultimately finds this idea wanting. "Goethe can never be dear to men. His is not even devotion to pure truth, but to truth for the sake of culture." This charge resembles Orestes Brownson's complaint about Goethe, Carlyle, *and* Emerson in his review of the Divinity School Address – that all three make "self" the highest aim, that "the highest good they recognize is the realization of order in their own individual souls" – resembles it so closely, in fact, that we must assume the accusation still rankled.

Still, Brownson's insistences that the individual must work to realize universal order, not just order in his or her soul, hit Emerson at what was always his most sensitive spot. He was not laboring in the Unitarian vineyard, like Francis, Hedge, and Clarke, nor proselytizing among the masses, like Parker; he was not constructing a phalanstery, like Ripley, nor even a cabin by a pond, like Thoreau. His 1844 address on emancipation in the British West Indies, however warmly it had been welcomed in Concord, was hardly likely to bring the slave power to its knees. What would it be like to possess power and to wield it effectively?

"Napoleon, or the Man of the World" is Emerson's longest sustained meditation on this topic. Though it is placed second-to-last in both the lecture series and the book, it was the first to be written; Emerson was delivering it as a separate lecture as early as April 1845. Emerson's Napoleon is neither the titanic hero of Romantic mythology nor the demon of Federalist propaganda, but a man whose spontaneity has all the characteristics of genius except its intimate relation to the moral law. Napoleon is an example of "the powers of intellect without conscience" and as such is – sad to say – the most truly representative hero of the book, "the agent or attorney of the Middle Class of modern society," that energetic, industrious, unscrupulous class that runs America as it ran France.

Napoleon had brilliance, courage, tenacity, and freedom from cant, and when we read of his victories we feel encouraged and liberated. Yet the absence of any moral principle in his aims or acts rendered him at last as forgettable as the vapid hereditary monarchs he dispossessed. "All passed away, like the smoke of his artillery, and left no trace. He left France smaller, poorer, feebler than he found it." And in his defeat we can read our own future fate. "As long as our civilization is essentially one of property, of fences, of exclusiveness, it will be mocked by delusions. Our riches will leave us sick, there will be bitterness in our laughter, and our wine will burn our mouth."

The lecture series "Representative Men" was a success, at least if contemporary accounts can be trusted. Convers Francis wrote to Frederic Henry Hedge on January 12, 1846, to report that Emerson was lecturing "with all his usual charm & power." But Emerson himself felt tired at the end of the course. He needed new sources of inspiration, and when a letter arrived from an old acquaintance named Alexander Ireland inviting him to lecture in England he considered the invitation seriously. He was worried that his fame was not sufficiently great to attract an audience that would make the trip worthwhile to him, and he dreaded having his English friends trying to collect an audience for him by "puffing & coaxing" (Emerson to Ireland, February 28, 1847). But Ireland persisted, and Emerson finally agreed to make the British tour. Lidian asked Henry Thoreau to live in the house again while Emerson was away, and he accepted, though the move put an end to his two-year residence at Walden Pond.

On October 5, 1847, Emerson set sail from Boston to Liverpool on the packet ship *Washington Irving,* auspiciously named after the first nineteenth-century American author to win wide popularity in England. At first Emerson's lecturing was limited to Manchester and Liverpool, but he soon expanded it to Nottingham, Derby, and a dozen other towns in the manufacturing regions of England. (Most of the lectures were from the recent series "Representative Men," though he found time to write new ones as well.) Emerson was fascinated by the wealth of the island, by the beefy, self-confident air of the people; but he also noticed the pollution caused by industry and the desperate poverty of an underclass shut out from the wealth that encircled it.

To his surprise and amusement, Emerson found himself a social lion courted by the fashionable and famous, despite the fact that he still considered himself a "parlor Erebus" and dreaded evening parties. In Edinburgh, where he had traveled in February 1848, he met Lord Jeffrey, whose *Edinburgh Review* had filled him with such delight twenty years earlier; Robert

Chambers, whose treatise on evolution, *Vestiges of Creation,* excited him with its proposed solution to the mystery of human origins; and the seventy-year-old Thomas De Quincey, who walked the ten miles from his cottage through a rainstorm to have dinner with him. Emerson then went west to the Lake District, where he called upon Wordsworth once again and went horseback riding with Harriet Martineau. When he reached London he enjoyed the meetings Carlyle had arranged for him with people such as the historian Thomas Macaulay and the geologist Charles Lyell. He met and charmed Crabb Robinson and visited Oxford as the guest of a young admirer named Arthur Hugh Clough.

Emerson's round of brilliant socializing was taking place against a backdrop of revolutionary unrest in England and on the Continent. In France the corrupt, inefficient regime of Louis Philippe, which had planted itself firmly on the side of material interests and had opposed every kind of reform, collapsed in the face of a popular insurrection on February 24, 1848. Louis Philippe abdicated and fled to London; the poet Lamartine proclaimed the restoration of the Republic, and a provisional government dominated by moderate republicans was established. But a group of radicals remained unconvinced that the restoration of civil liberties favored by the bourgeoisie would do anything to alleviate the misery of the poorest citizens. They demanded "national workshops" to guarantee work for the millions of unemployed, as well as universal suffrage to give them political power. They formed a rival government powerful enough to force the provisional government to compromise with them and set up the national workshops.

The apparent success of the revolutionaries in Paris stimulated similar activity all over Europe and awakened fear in the ruling classes – who, as Emerson remarked, were beginning to wonder if their own days were also numbered, and if the "splendid privileges" of their rich houses were not "in too dreadful contrast to the famine and ignorance at the door" (Emerson to Lidian Emerson, March 23 and 24, 1848). They had reason to be fearful. The workers'-rights movement known as Chartism was given new energy by the events in France. Emerson was naturally interested in Chartism, because Carlyle's pamphlet on the movement and Brownson's famous review of it had had such noisy repercussions in America. He attended a March 7 meeting of the Chartists in National Hall and heard the crowd sing the "Marseillaise" in solidarity with the new French government; he listened to revolutionary mutterings among the people there, who hoped that their example might cause the English soldiers to join their cause if an uprising occurred. There were disturbances in Glasgow and smaller outbreaks in Manchester and Edinburgh. Plans for a mass demonstration and march on the houses of Parliament to present Chartist petitions frightened the authorities sufficiently that they called out the military under the Duke of Wellington to prevent the march.

In the event only fifty thousand Chartists assembled on the appointed day, April 10, instead of the half million that had been expected, and the proposed march never took place. But people still feared that revolution was imminent. Emerson scoffed at the idea in the privacy of his journal. There might be a scramble for money, but as long as both sides wanted the same thing – material prosperity – no real *revolution* was possible. The old system would survive, though it might have a new set of masters.

Still, the radicals of Paris were proposing something far more sweeping than the peaceable six-point reform program the British Chartists had wanted to present to Parliament; the Parisians demanded nothing less, Emerson thought, than the "confiscation of France." Though Tennyson warned him he might be risking his life, Emerson decided to cross the Channel and get a closer look at the revolution. He arrived in Paris on May 7, just as events were reaching a crisis. The leaders of the radical clubs of Paris were unwilling to accept the results of the general election that had returned a constituent assembly dominated by moderates. They opened the National Guard in Paris to the workers of the "national workshops" and supplied them with arms. On May 15 a mob assisted by this proletarian militia attempted to invade the National Assembly. They were repelled after a struggle of several hours but not wholly defeated, and the capital still seethed with revolutionary fervor.

Emerson enjoyed himself thoroughly in this scene of passion and rage. He fell in love with Paris, "a place of the largest liberty that is I suppose in the civilized world," as he wrote his wife (Emerson to Lidian Emerson, May 24 and 25, 1848). In the company of another American he visited some of the radical clubs, including those of the revolutionary leaders Armand Barbès and Louis Auguste Blanqui. He admired the "terrible earnest" and "deep sincerity" of the clubs' speakers, who were "studying how to secure a fair share of bread to every man, and to get the God's justice done through the land." And he was fascinated by the "fire & fury of the people, when they are interrupted or thwarted," so unlike anything he had seen in New England even at the most passionate meetings. Every man in the street seemed to be wearing some kind of uniform; they were bearded like goats and lions; they wore red sashes, swords, and brass helmets. He saw "the street full of bayonets, and the furious driving of the horses dragging cannon towards the National Assembly," he boasted to his wife in a letter written two days later (Emerson to Lidian Emerson, May 17, 1848). But he was relieved when the army of shopkeepers who formed that part of the National Guard loyal to the National Assembly drove back the mob and jailed its leaders. In his journal he sternly warned all revolutionaries that they must not contemplate any reforms that would take away the incentive to labor.

After slightly more than three weeks in Paris, Emerson returned to London, where he delivered more lectures and prepared for his return to the United States. He agreed to take a brief trip with Carlyle. Their meetings during this visit had not been happy. Carlyle, deeply in Emerson's debt and too proud not to resent it, had been contentious and on one occasion insulting; after that Emerson had mostly tried to avoid meeting him in private and had taken a small vindictive pleasure in recording other people's cutting remarks about Carlyle in his journals. But he agreed to go with Carlyle to Stonehenge, where they wandered among the giant stones and listened to explanations of their astronomical function from a local antiquary. After a final week of meetings with famous people, including Marian Evans (George Eliot), with whom he was happy to discover a mutual fascination with Jean-Jacques Rousseau's *Confessions,* Emerson sailed for Boston, where he arrived July 27, 1848.

While he was still in London or Paris Emerson had received a half-teasing, half-truculent letter from Thoreau, which apparently amused him; in a letter to his wife he wrote: "Thank Henry for his letter. He is always *absolutely* right, and *particularly* perverse" (Emerson to Lidian Emerson, June 8, 1848). But some of Thoreau's jokes might have warned Emerson about problems to come. Emerson may have suggested to Thoreau in an earlier letter that he consider a trip to Europe; if so, Thoreau firmly rejected the idea.

Who has any desire to split himself any further by straddling the Atlantic? We are extremities enough already. There is danger of one's straddling so far that he can never recover an upright position. There are certain men in Old & New England who aspire to the renown of the Colossus of Rhodes, and to have ships sail under them. (Thoreau to Emerson, May 21, 1848)

Thoreau had in fact been traveling inward during the last half-decade, as he liked to remind his friends. The period had begun miserably enough. Emerson, who had tried to act as his patron and friend, was beginning to doubt that he would ever become a successful writer. In late March 1843, when Thoreau was about to end his nearly two-year stay with Emerson's family and move to Staten Island to take up the tutorial job Emerson had arranged there for him, Emerson recorded in his journal Elizabeth Hoar's comment: "I love H., but do not like him." He then added, in a passage he would incorporate into the essay "Experience": "Young men like H. T. owe us a new world & they have not acquitted the debt: for the most part, such die young, & so dodge the fulfillment."

Not all of Emerson's disappointment was literary. Nathaniel Hawthorne, to whom Emerson confided similar feelings in a conversation the next day, defended Thoreau but noted: "Mr. Emerson appeared to have suffered some inconveniency from his experience of Mr. Thoreau as an inmate. It may well be that such a sturdy and uncompromising person is fitter to meet occasionally in the open air, than to have as a permanent guest at table or fireside." Instead of a disciple to graft his apples, Emerson had — or at least felt that he had — a wolf by the ears. Thoreau was as truculent as he was devoted; indeed, his truculence and his devotion were never easy to tell apart. He demanded perfect and unwavering sympathy yet reserved the right to look with frank contempt upon the middle-class respectability Emerson was traveling to country lyceums and drafty big-city lecture halls to support. There was a time earlier in their relationship when Emerson found this youthful scorn a tonic, but by 1843 the signs of strain are evident.

When Thoreau moved back to Concord he did not return to the Emerson house, but lived with his family and worked in his father's pencil-making business. New York publishers had given him little encouragement, and his hopes of supporting himself by selling his writings now appeared dim. When *The Dial* ceased publication in 1844 he lost the only certain outlet he had ever had for his essays and poems. Thoreau stopped lecturing; he stopped writing regular entries in his journal for a year and a half.

Nor was this all. On April 30, 1844, Thoreau and a younger friend decided to explore the Sudbury River in a rowboat. They stopped for lunch. Foolishly, they built a fire inside of a decaying stump in order to cook their lunch, probably hoping to keep their nascent flame out of the wind long enough to kindle a blaze. But the stump itself caught fire and the fire quickly spread to the surrounding woods, menacing the town of Concord. Thoreau ran to the town and gave the alarm, but by the time the fire had been put out it had destroyed over three hundred acres. Six years passed before Thoreau could even bring himself to mention the incident in his journal.

Still, he had not entirely stopped writing. He was working steadily at attempting to transform his sketchy notes on a boating trip he had taken with his brother John on the Concord and Merrimack rivers in the late summer of 1839 into the kind of "excursion" he had already had success with in two earlier published essays — "A Walk to Wachusett" and "A Winter Walk." The idea of using the tour as literary material was an old one with him; references to it crop up in lists of potential lecture or essay topics as early as 1840, though the brief "Memoirs of a Tour" he began that summer were then abandoned for work on another project. The next year he again listed the tour as a possible subject for compositions.

His brother John's death in January 1842 suddenly made the 1839 journey take on a new significance for Thoreau. By the fall of 1844, when Thoreau appears to have revived his idea for a literary work based on the 1839 trip, he also had begun experimenting with a more ambitious method of composition, one that would allow room for memory to expand outward into meditation. At about this time he acquired a new blank book, larger than his usual journals, to hold transcriptions from his earlier journals. He would copy a passage from an old journal into this new book (which he called the "long book"), then leave a large blank space for future expansions.

Thoreau was more than ever determined to show Emerson that his earlier confidence in him had not been misplaced – that he was capable of producing a major literary work. (The fact that so many of the Transcendentalists were publishing books in 1842–4 only made Thoreau's determination stronger. Parker's *Discourse* appeared in 1842; Ellery Channing's *Poems* in 1843. Emerson's second collection entitled *Essays* and Fuller's account of her western trip, *Summer on the Lakes*, came out in 1844.) Finally Ellery Channing suggested to Thoreau that the only solution to his perennial problem – how to support himself and still find time to write – would be to build himself a cabin on Emerson's newly acquired land at Walden Pond. In March 1845 Channing reminded Thoreau of a field near the pond he had named "Briars" and commanded: "Go out upon that, build yourself a hut, & there begin the grand process of devouring yourself alive. I see no other alternative, no other hope for you." Thoreau proposed to Emerson that he be allowed to live on the land if he would clear it and plant pines on it, and Emerson was happy to agree.

The cabin Thoreau began to build in March 1845 and moved into on the Fourth of July proved to be at just the right distance from Emerson – still on his property, no longer in his house. And the two years spent there were both the happiest and most productive of Thoreau's life. While there he finished two drafts of the book growing out of his 1839 river tour with his brother John, *A Week on the Concord and Merrimack Rivers,* as well as a first draft of *Walden* itself; he also found time to write a long critical piece on Carlyle, an account of his climb up Maine's Mount Katahdin, and a lecture prompted by his one-night's imprisonment in the Concord jail for nonpayment of his poll tax, later published as "Resistance to Civil Government."

The pace of Thoreau's maturation as a writer was equally swift. The prose of the first draft of *A Week on the Concord and Merrimack Rivers* has a limpid, delicate beauty that recalls the best passages of "The Natural History of Massachusetts," allowed now to flower into pure aestheticism (and diffuse eroticism). The Carlyle article exists at the opposite stylistic and intellectual extreme; it is public utterance, hugely self-confident even in the act of paying tribute. Thoreau is fascinated by Carlyle's own boisterous prose style and generous in his estimation of Carlyle's continuing influence on young writers. The story of Thoreau's ascent of Mount Katahdin resembles his accounts of earlier expeditions into nature only in its general subject matter; its tough, polished sentences are far closer to the prose of *Walden* than to that of *A Week,* and it is as bleak in its view of natural power as the earlier text was tender in its cataloguing of natural beauties. Finally, the lecture later called "Resistance to Civil Government" shows a disciplining of anger by logic that would make Thoreau one of the most powerful political writers in the nineteenth century.

The first of these projects to be completed was the first draft of the book that would one day be published under the title *A Week on the Concord and Merrimack Rivers.* At this point, however, Thoreau called it "Excursion on Concord and Merrimack Rivers." Scholars who have studied the relationship between the journals, the long book, and this first draft of the book itself have been able to show that Thoreau reworked and polished his original paragraphs considerably at each stage in the process – shortening them, refining them, pruning out abstractions and concentrating on significant sensory detail. In "Excursion on Concord and Merrimack Rivers," which he completed sometime in the fall of 1845, each water-borne "day" of the original two-week trip serves as a receptacle for these small masterpieces of sensation and reflection.

As the brothers row their homemade green boat with its blue stripe up the lazy Concord to Billerica, then cut via the Middlesex Canal over to the Merrimack River, and then row or sail up the Merrimack into New Hampshire as far as there are locks to take them around waterfalls and rapids, Thoreau notes the things they see, the people they pass, and the thoughts the trip gives rise to. The week-long land journey by stagecoach and on foot that the brothers actually took in 1839 up through the Franconia Notch to the distant northern rivers, together with their climb up Mount Washington, is summarized in a single paragraph; this is meant to be strictly a river book. Land days do not count. We skip from "Thurs. Sept. 5th" (when the brothers left their boat moored in the Merrimack) to "Thurs. Sept. 12th" (when they pick it up again for the rapid trip home).

The narrative thread is slender enough – a passage through a canal as one brother pulls a towrope and the other keeps the boat off the sides of the canal with a pole, an encounter with a young worker, a rise past rapids or falls in an old lock, a mooring at noon for dinner or at night for sleep. Yet on the trip are strung such exquisite moments of perception that the eddies in the narrative are as welcome as the forward pulls. Their silence of the tent at night is punctuated by foxes stepping about over the dead leaves and by "the startling throttled cry of an owl." They know there are pigeons in the woods by "the slight wiry winnowing sound of their wings." The asters of late summer have a "dry ripe scent," and the angular stem of the witch hazel bears "petals like Furies' hair, or small ribbon streamers." Seed vessels of the poppy look "like small goblets filled with the waters of Lethe." Logs rolled down the mountain by lumberers come with a rumbling sound that reverberates on the opposite shore like the roar of artillery. "Dense flocks of bobolinks russet and rustling as if they were the seeds of the meadow grass floating on the wind, rise before us in our walk — like ripe grain threshed out by the wind."

The book is full of remembered joy. "I have passed down the river before sunrise on a summer morning, between fields of lilies still shut in sleep, and when at length the flakes of sun light from over the bank fell upon the surface of the water, whole fields of white blossoms seemed to flash open before me as I sailed along, like the unfolding of a banner." Even the fog and the "genial drenching rain" that surrounds them again and again only increase their "boyancy" (as Thoreau spells it). "On foot indeed we continued up along the banks — feeling our way with a stick through the showery and foggy day. . . . & cheered by the tones of invisible waterfalls — scenting the fragrance of the pines and the wet clay under our feet — with visions of toads and wandering frogs — and festoons of moss hanging from the spruce trees — and thrushes flitting silent under the leaves — The road still holding together through that wettest weather like faith — "

Other men in this river world are also objects of affection as diffuse but intense as Whitman's. A sympathetic lock tender lets the brothers into the Middlesex locks on Sunday against his rules. In another set of locks Thoreau admires a "brawny N. Hampshire man — leaning upon his pole — bare-headed and in simple shirt and trowsers — a rude apollo of a man." The rhythmical poling motions of the boatman must, Thoreau thinks, communi-cate stateliness to his character until he feels the "slow irresistible motion under him" as if it were his own energy. The sight of the rough country boys coming to the Concord Cattle Show fills Thoreau with love for "these sons of earth," so much better prizes than the best specimens of their cattle. Reading Indian lore makes him long for such a friendship as existed in the days of Wawatam and Henry the fur trader, when the Indian, having dreamed of friendship between them, went to Henry's tent and adopted him henceforth.

The many long passages about friendship gathered in the "Wednesday, Sept. 4" section express an intense yearning for personal love. The love of friend for friend is the only thing worth living for, the center from which the rays of the universe radiate. "Our life without love is like coke and ashes." John Thoreau, the brother and companion on the original trip, always pres-ent in the book's "we" but never named or described, was one such friend, "flesh of my flesh bone of my bone." Nostalgia for that perfect union blends seamlessly into longing for an ideal friend who is to come, who will not insult with kindnesses but will trust without reservation and understand completely. "Our whole life is in some sense addressed to that one among men whom we most esteem — and who is most able to interpret it." He must treat us with reverence, give all and demand nothing. "Let him not think he can please me by any behavior, or even treat me well enough."

The imperiousness of that final sentence masks a terrible loneliness. Thoreau says he has heard rumors that the earth is inhabited but has at yet seen no footprint on the shore. "I walk in nature still alone / And know no one. / Discern no lineament nor feature / Of any creature." He cannot bear being discarded, ignored. "Use me, for I am useful in my way, and stand as one of many petitioners from toadstool and henbane up to Dahlia and violet supplicating to be put to my use, if by any means ye may find me serviceable." Batter my heart. "Strike boldly at the head or heart or any vital part — so you may possibly hit. . . . Depend upon it the timber is well seasoned and tough, and will bear rough usage." Nature is not enough. "Though all the firmament / Is oer me bent / Yet still I miss the grace / Of an intelligent and kindred face." In nature I seek the friend who blends with nature: "Who is the person in her mask, / He is the man I ask."

There is much more in "Excursion on Concord and Merrimack Rivers" — the local history Thoreau assiduously weaves in, with its recollections of American Indian life and the colonial past; meditations on the wisdom of the Hindu scriptures; and the allusiveness that links the shores of the Merrimack to Ostia and the Concord Cattle Show to festivals of Bacchus. All of this material would become even more significant in the hugely expanded version of the book that Thoreau finally published in 1849. Yet the confession of longing that occurs at the midpoint of the first draft is a clue to its liberating power for Thoreau himself, because the tenderness it displaces onto perception turns representation into an act of love.

By the fall of 1845 Thoreau is filling his journal with joyous descriptions of his new life, of hoeing the beans he had planted, of studying, and of writing. He appears to have finished "Excursion on Concord and Merrimack Rivers" in the fall of the year. He then turned to another project, one refreshingly external and "objective" after the intense retrospection of his book manuscript. In December 1845 a copy of Thomas Carlyle's edition (with commentary and "elucidations") of *Oliver Cromwell's Letters and Speeches* arrived in Concord. Thoreau now set about writing a lecture for the Concord Lyceum that would be an extended review of Carlyle's writings and an analysis of his remarkable style. The lecture Thoreau delivered at the lyceum on February 4, 1846, was an impressive piece. He hoped to publish it for profit and asked his friend Horace Greeley to help him place it with a magazine. Greeley did persuade his friend George R. Graham of Philadelphia to accept the manuscript for publication, though Graham proved to be dilatory about publishing the piece (and even more dilatory about paying for it). But in March and April of 1847 the two-part article "Thomas Carlyle and His Works" finally made its appearance in *Graham's Magazine.* Emerson quickly forwarded both numbers to Carlyle, who read them with satisfaction and told a friend, "I have got an American review of me."

Carlyle could not have asked for a more generous admirer. Thoreau writes as if his love of Carlyle marks him as one of the elect. "Only he who has had the good fortune to read them in the nick of time, in the most perceptive and recipient season of life, can give any adequate account of them." Conventional literary men are put off by Carlyle's mannerisms, frightened by his raving. "We hardly know an old man to whom these volumes are not hopelessly sealed." To the young, on the other hand, the very wildness and indecorum of Carlyle's speech come like an April thaw. "He has broken the ice, and streams freely forth like a spring torrent." His style "has the rhythms and cadences of conversation endlessly repeated. It resounds with emphatic, natural, lively, stirring tones, muttering, rattling, exploding, like shells and shot, and with like execution." He resembles an advancing army as he crashes through "the host of weak, half-formed, *dilettante* opinions, honest and dishonest ways of thinking" and tramples them into the dust. His humor is "rich, deep, and variegated, in direct communication with the back bone and risible muscles of the globe." Even his invective can be bracing. If he falls short of the highest wisdom, if his spleen becomes wearisome, at least he has one sovereign merit: "Carlyle does not oblige us to think; we have thought enough for him already, but he compels us to act."

Thoreau's desire to replace thought with action would soon be given assistance from an unexpected quarter. One day in late July 1846 when Thoreau was walking into the village to pick up a mended shoe, he was arrested for nonpayment of his poll tax by Sam Staples, the Concord constable and, from 1842–5, collector of taxes, whose contract entitled him to one and one-half cents for every dollar of tax money he succeeded in collecting. The tax (not more than $1.50 per year) was levied on every male inhabitant over the age of twenty, but nonpayment was fairly common and was a continuing problem for the Commonwealth, particularly because communities like Concord seem to have been reluctant to jail people for evading the tax.

Staples, however, had already shown himself willing to jail evaders. Bronson Alcott had stopped paying the tax in 1842 to announce his refusal to take part in the oppressive machinery of the state. No one bothered him the first year, but on January 17, 1843, Staples came to his cottage with a warrant and took him to the Concord jail. Unfortunately, the jailer was nowhere in sight. Staples went off to look for him while Alcott waited peacefully at the jail. In the meantime a friend, Judge Samuel Hoar, paid the tax and the fine for him. Thoreau described this anticlimactic martyrdom shortly after it happened in a high-spirited letter to Emerson, who was then off lecturing in New York. Thoreau announced that he and Charles Lane had been planning to "agitate the State" while Alcott "lay in durance," but their zeal fizzled when Alcott was released, "and the State was safe as far as I was concerned." One detail of the incident particularly amused Thoreau. Staples was used to collaring deadbeats, but Alcott's motives for nonpayment astonished him. Here was a man willing to go to jail, as he said, for "nothing but principle."

Thoreau apparently joined Alcott in his refusal to pay taxes, at least if his statement in the published version of "Resistance to Civil Government" (1849) is correct; there he says he has paid no tax for "six or seven years." Staples took no action against either of them in 1844 or 1845. Because the loss to the tax collector for any particular malefactor was only a cent and a half per year he was sometimes willing to let delinquents go unpunished for several years. But in 1846 Staples apparently decided to try to collect the overdue taxes from the previous years. He warned Alcott in April or May that he would advertise Alcott's land for sale if the tax was not paid, and he took out a warrant for Thoreau's arrest. Fifty years later, Staples told an interviewer that he had just gotten home from locking up Thoreau with the rest of the inmates and had taken off his boots when word was brought to him that a veiled woman had appeared at the jail with "Mr. Thoreau's tax" in an envelope. Unwilling to go to the trouble of unlocking the prisoners he had just locked up, Staples waited till morning to release Thoreau – who, he remembered, "was mad as the devil when I turned him loose." Thoreau's anger is understandable. Having a female relative shamed into paying his taxes was hardly his idea of heroic sacrifice.

What made it worse was that Emerson had no sympathy for either Alcott or Thoreau in this matter. He characterized Thoreau's behavior to Alcott as "mean and skulking and in bad taste." The first two adjectives seem a strange choice, because Thoreau had been perfectly frank about his refusal to pay taxes and had accepted his incarceration uncomplainingly. The last phrase is more revealing and suggests the real source of Emerson's anger. He had always recoiled from the ramping egotism of Garrison and the rest of the antislavery "martyrs" who treated themselves as exemplary sufferers. They were vulgar; they were self-advertising; they were *not our sort*. A gentleman may suffer, but he does not suffer over trifles like a poll tax, nor does he oblige a lady to muffle herself in veils while she ransoms him out of the town jail. Alcott's holy foolishness Emerson had long ago resigned himself to, but to see Thoreau indulging in the same sort of behavior exasperated him.

However much it may have hurt Thoreau to discover this conventionality in his mentor's soul, Emerson's charges drew from him an apologia that has become one of the classic documents of American political thought. In January and February of 1848 (when Emerson was in England) Thoreau read before the Concord Lyceum a lecture he entitled "The Rights and Duties of the Individual in Relation to Government," a lecture he published the next year in Elizabeth Peabody's short-lived periodical *Aesthetic Papers* under the title "Resistance to Civil Government." In the piece he argues that the individual has not only a right but often a duty to resist the government under which he lives, if his conscience tells him that compliance with the will of that government is morally wrong. Such behavior is neither skulking nor tasteless; it is in the original sense of the word, *decorous*. "How does it become a man to behave toward this American government to-day?" Thoreau asks near the beginning of his treatise. "I answer that he cannot without disgrace be associated with it."

Thoreau had witnessed in Wendell Phillips, the abolitionist leader, one example of the kind of conduct he could admire wholeheartedly. Phillips had spoken three times before the Concord Lyceum on the subject of slavery, the last time on March 11, 1845. On March 28 Thoreau published an admiring account of the last speech entitled "Wendell Phillips Before Concord Lyceum" in Garrison's abolitionist newspaper the *Liberator*. Phillips was a Boston aristocrat who had been converted to the cause of "immediate abolition" by Garrison and who shared Garrison's insistence that the individual must consider himself accountable for the monstrous injustice of slavery and must dissociate himself from governments that tolerate and foster it. According to Thoreau, the aim of Phillips's lecture had been to show what the state and church had to do with Texas and slavery, "and how much, on the other hand, the individual should have to do with church and state."

Phillips's willingness to defy the Constitution and say, of the Founding Fathers, "I am wiser than they," endeared him to Thoreau, as did his refusal to let his aims in life be reduced to a single objective. He was not, he said, born to abolish slavery, but to do right. With "soldier-like steadiness" and natural skill at oratory he combined "a sort of moral principle and integrity." His insistence that the individual must withdraw immediately from connection with the state won an admiring tribute from Thoreau. "He at least is not responsible for slavery, nor for American Independence; for the hypocrisy and superstition of the church, nor the timidity and selfishness of the state; nor for the indifference and willing ignorance of any." Phillips is the Red-cross knight, one of the most conspicuous champions of a true church and state now in the field, and at the end of the review Thoreau mockingly wonders if any paynim champion will brave him in the lists.

Phillips's example – to dissociate yourself from the unjust church and state immediately – provided one important strand of Thoreau's argument in "Resistance to Civil Government." "It is not a man's duty, as a matter of course, to devote himself to the eradication of any, even the most enormous wrong; he may still properly have other concerns to engage him; but it is his duty, at least, to wash his hands of it, and, if he gives it no thought longer, not to give it practically his support." Some abolitionists are petitioning the state to dissolve the Union. "Why do they not dissolve it themselves, – the union between themselves and the State, – and refuse to pay their quota into its treasury?" As Carlyle said, it is no good thinking about things endlessly; we have already thought too much. It is time to act. "Action from principle, – the perception and the performance of right, – changes things and relations; it is essentially revolutionary, and does not consist wholly with any thing which was. It not only divides states and churches, it divides families; aye, it divides the *individual,* separating the diabolical in him from the divine."

This secular conversion experience is the fruit of Thoreau's ridiculous stay in the Concord jail. He tells the story of that night in an inset tale full of tenderness and humor: how the prisoners lounged chatting in the doorway until the jailer told them it was time to lock up for the night; how he found himself in a whitewashed room with an amiable companion who gave him the oral history of their cell; how rectangular tin trays of bread and chocolate were shoved under the door for breakfast; how his roommate, leaving to go to his usual morning job of haying, bid farewell to him, expecting him (correctly, as it turned out) to be gone before lunch.

Yet the sudden illumination caused by the night in jail is anything but funny. The constable's willingness to threaten his neighbor Alcott and jail Thoreau went far toward explaining how Massachusetts could support a war it thought unjust and a slave system it claimed to find abhorrent. The view from the deep, grated window of the jail gives Thoreau a new perspective on his town. "I was fairly inside of it. I had never seen its institutions before." He has a new view of the town's residents as well; he understands for the first time what they are about. "I saw yet more distinctly the State in which I lived" – both the state of Massachusetts and the state of man.

The sudden grasp of the interconnectedness of cruelty turns resistance from a right of private conscience into an obligation of citizenship. If William Paley (1743–1805), the English philosopher whose *Moral and Political Philosophy* Thoreau studied at Harvard, had devoted a chapter to explaining the "Duty of Submission to Civil Government," then Thoreau will now devote a chapter to explaining the duties of resistance. "When a sixth of the population of a nation which has undertaken to be the refuge of liberty are slaves, and a whole country is unjustly overrun and conquered by a foreign army,

Wm. Paley, Moral + Political Philosophy   1/6 slaves

and subjected to military law, I think that it is not too soon for honest men to rebel and revolutionize." If the state has become a machine to hold slaves and invade Mexico, then you must let your life become a "counter friction" to stop the machine. Whenever you are obliged to be "the agent of injustice to another, then, I say, break the law."

The state – particularly a democratic state – has no defense against its own tendency to pass unjust laws except the willingness of individual citizens peacefully to resist them. To resist the state when the state is wrong is therefore to save it. "If the alternative is to keep all just men in prison, or give up war and slavery, the State will not hesitate which to choose." The political power of the individual is therefore potentially huge. "A minority is powerless when it conforms to the majority," Thoreau points out, "but it is irresistible when it clogs by its whole weight." Like an Abraham bargaining with the Lord to spare Sodom, Thoreau argues that "if one thousand, if one hundred, if ten men whom I could name," or even "*one* HONEST man" would withdraw from the state-imposed copartnership in slaveowning and let himself be locked up in the county jail "it would be the abolition of slavery in America."

Transcendentalism had always had trouble imagining how to bridge the gap between principle and action largely because it tended to think of action as a kind of sullying – a frustrating and degrading attempt to force pure ideas into a world of corruption and compromise. What Thoreau learned from people like Garrison and Phillips was that if you acted purely from principle to *withdraw* your allegiance from the world of corruption, the world would soon come to you. You would find yourself acting on it and in it as vigorously as Napoleon had and without having to compromise your integrity.

About a month after his night in the Concord jail in 1846 Thoreau left his cabin at the pond for a two-week excursion into the Maine woods with a cousin and two other men. They traveled up the Penobscot River to North Twin Lake, then hiked to the base of Mount Katahdin, at 5,268 feet Maine's highest mountain. The mountain's naked rocks jutted abruptly up, looking like a "blue barrier" formed as one of the ancient boundaries of the earth. While his companions set up camp in the late afternoon light, Thoreau decided to explore the mountain alone through the pathless wilderness, an ascent of such difficulty that it keeps reminding him of Satan's voyage through chaos in *Paradise Lost*. Here the only flocks are the gray silent rocks, "chewing a rocky cud at sunset," regarding Thoreau quietly without a bleat or a low.

The next day his companions join him in the climb. The scenery is quite literally Titanic, reminding him of the rock where Prometheus was bound.

"Some part of the beholder, even some vital part, seems to escape through the loose grating of his ribs as he ascends. He is more lone than you can imagine." The experience is startling, even for Thoreau. He realizes that he has always thought of nature as a place inhabited by humans. Now, descending the desolate side of a mountain burned bare by lightning, he sees nature as "something savage and awful, though beautiful. . . . This was that Earth of which we have heard, made out of Chaos and Old Night."

This sudden encounter with the material sublime triggers a passage of horrified self-awareness, as Thoreau suddenly realizes a kinship between the pure matter of Katahdin's rocks and the equally inhuman matter of which his flesh is made. "I stand in awe of my body, this matter to which I am bound." Each of us is Prometheus, bound to this rock. What is stranger or more mysterious than matter? "Talk of mysteries! – think of our life in nature, – daily to be shown matter, to come in contact with it, – rocks, trees, wind on our cheeks!" Everything we take for granted – "the *solid* earth! the *actual* world! the *common sense!*" – is as mysterious as the inhuman landscape of Katahdin. "*Contact! Contact! Who* are we? *Where* are we?" The things we take for granted are precisely the problems we should pose.

Thoreau quickly turned his notes on the Katahdin trip into a hundred-page manuscript that he would later publish. Horace Greeley helped place "Ktaadn: The Maine Woods" with the *Union Magazine of Literature and Art,* where it appeared in five installments between July and November 1848. But "Ktaadn" was only one of Thoreau's projects. In the next year he would begin work on "Resistance to Civil Government" and write a first draft of *Walden.* He also would write a second complete draft of the book he now called *A Week on the Concord and Merrimack Rivers,* condensing the two weeks' voyage into one week and adding long digressions on a variety of subjects to the seven "days." Earlier, he had delivered a lecture entitled "History of Myself" to the Concord Lyceum, helping to satisfy his neighbors' curiosity about his life at Walden Pond and had seen his long article on Carlyle in print, having the satisfaction of knowing that it was read by the master himself with approval.

By the time Thoreau left the cabin at Walden Pond to move back into the Emerson house (at Lidian's request) to look after things while Emerson was in England, he could feel that his experiment in living and writing was an admirable success. Temporarily freed from concerns about earning a living, living in a house he had built with his own hands, he had proven he could write rapidly and brilliantly. But Emerson had so far been unsuccessful at interesting a publisher in *A Week on the Concord and Merrimack Rivers,* and when Thoreau wrote him in England on November 14, 1847, he had to report that the book had been turned down by still more publishers. "The

Week published Too soon — caused/contributed To Break w/ Emerson

world is a cow that is hard to milk — life does not come so easily," he noted ruefully, "and oh, how thinly it is watered ere we get it!"

Thoreau's response to such discouragement was to expand the book again. He added to the "Sunday" chapter passages learnedly discoursing on "the Christian fable" and frankly avowing his preference for the Greek mythology over the Christian one (a position that raised the hackles of reviewers when the book was finally published) and expanded the dissertation on friendship in "Wednesday." And he completed two more drafts of *Walden*. He submitted both manuscripts to the Boston publishers Ticknor and Company early in 1849 and found to his chagrin that they were willing to publish *Walden* but not *A Week*. Finally James Munroe, Emerson's publisher, agreed to publish the book so long as Thoreau promised to pay the full costs of its publication if it did not sell. The book was published on May 30, 1849.

Greek myth over Christian

The publication of *A Week on the Concord and Merrimack Rivers* apparently precipitated a crisis in Thoreau's relationship with Emerson. Emerson had encouraged Thoreau to risk publishing the book, though he had criticized particular chapters of it. Some time in the half-year following the publication of *A Week,* Thoreau wrote an entry in a notebook complaining that because Emerson had become "estranged" from him he was now willing to shoot "fatal truth" at him on a "poisoned arrow," a criticism he had concealed while the two men were still friends. He notes bitterly that before the book was published Emerson had given him only praise for what was good in it; now he points out all its faults and blames Thoreau for them. This "difference" between the two friends left Emerson feeling wounded too; Thoreau complains in another notebook passage that Emerson had accused him of "coldness and disingenuousness" and in so doing had inflicted a wound too deep to be healed. "I had tenderly cherished the flower of our friendship till one day my friend treated it as a weed." It could not sustain the shock, but "drooped & withered from that hour."

Week on The Concord..

It is difficult to read this last sentence without wincing. Many of Thoreau's earlier journal passages about Emerson contain expressions of longing and reverence so intense that they fill one with foreboding: The young man who wrote them seems headed for terrible unhappiness. And in the summer of 1849 Thoreau was more than usually vulnerable. His sister Helen had died after a long struggle with tuberculosis, and he had just published a book whose failure (should it fail) would plunge him deeply into debt for years. He had been working at high speed for four years but had gotten little recognition to show for it — a few invitations to lecture, a few acceptances by magazines. True, Emerson had praised "Ktaadn" as one of the few pamphlets worthy to save and bind in the last ten years, but what was "Ktaadn" beside *A Week on the Concord and Merrimack Rivers?*

1849

It did not help matters that Emerson was now at the height of his fame, returning from an English tour where he had been flattered and caressed. He had published two books of essays and was about to publish a third, *Representative Men;* he had published a book of poems; and he was in the process of collecting and revising his early writings for publication by the same Boston publisher who refused to print Thoreau's *Week* without a guarantee. (Emerson's *Nature, Addresses and Lectures* appeared on September 7, 1849.) Thoreau complained in his journal that Emerson had become worldly and patronizing. That may have been true, but even if Emerson had remained a model of humility and tact it is difficult to see how fortunes so unequal could have failed to cause strain.

Meanwhile, the book Thoreau had spent ten years writing was proving to be – at least as far as sales were concerned – a disastrous flop. Though some reviewers had praise for parts of it they found its strange combination of narrative, meditation, and learned disquisition frustrating. James Russell Lowell complained in a review that he did not like to be invited to a river party and then preached at. Even Carlyle, to whom Emerson sent a copy of the book, could not get through it, though he had carried it with him all over Ireland. "Tell him so, please," Carlyle wrote brusquely in a letter of August 13, 1849. To his wife, Jane, he wrote that it was "a very fantastic yet not quite worthless book" (September 18 [19], 1849).

The problem with the final version of *A Week on the Concord and Merrimack Rivers* is not that its original charms have been lost in revision or that the material added to it is uninteresting. It is simply that the narrative frame keeps arousing expectations of movement and development that the lengthy meditative passages frustrate at every turn. Reading the book for the second time is much easier than reading it for the first time. But very few of Thoreau's early readers were willing to attempt a second reading, or even to complete the first.

The unbound sheets of Alcott's *Conversations with Children on the Gospels* had eventually been sold to a trunk maker as wastepaper. Thoreau was spared that humiliation, but only because having contracted to pay the publication costs (a two-hundred-ninety-dollar debt it took him four years to pay off) he was now the owner of the edition. In 1853 the publisher asked Thoreau what he wanted done with the unsold copies of his book. He had them sent to him at Concord. In his journal he noted, "I now have a library of nearly nine hundred volumes, over seven hundred of which I wrote myself. Is it not well that the author should behold the fruits of his labor? My works are piled up on one side of my chamber half as high as my head, my *opera omnia.*"

Discouragement did not stop Thoreau from writing. In the fall of 1849 he took a trip with Ellery Channing to Cape Cod. They had planned to take the steamer from Boston to Provincetown, but a violent storm kept the steamer in Provincetown. Handbills in the streets of Boston announced a terrible wreck off the shore at Cohasset. They decided to take the train south to Cohasset and thence to the western end of the Cape. From there they could travel by stagecoach out along its southern arm before heading north on foot to Provincetown. At Cohasset they saw the mangled bodies of Irish immigrants still being washed up on shore from the wreck two days earlier. Crowds were streaming to the beach, either to see the sights or to identify bodies and cart them away. The waves, still cracking the largest timbers of the wreck into pieces, showed how untameable a force was in nature. "I saw that no material could withstand the power of the waves; that iron must go to pieces in such a case, and an iron vessel would be cracked like an egg-shell on the rocks." Yet alongside this scene of tragedy two local residents, an old man and a boy, were gathering kelp and seaweed to use as manure, as if nothing out of the ordinary had happened.

Such contrasts – between the force of the wind and ocean and the obliviousness of the inhabitants – runs through the rest of Thoreau's description of the trip, which is marked by a kind of tough Yankee wit he had never exhibited before in such quantity. The descriptions of the eccentric inhabitants and of their stunted apple orchards and treeless towns, and the unintentional humor of the old histories that record the doings of their ministers, amused the audience at the Concord Lyceum when Thoreau delivered two lectures drawn from his notes of the Cape Cod trip on January 23 and 30, 1850. But the sea itself and the world it generated, the sounds and sights of the ocean and grasses – plover and gull, kelp and poverty grass, sea jellies and clams, crashing breakers and receding foam – are the real theme of the chapters Thoreau was slowly working up for publication. As he stands on the "Backside," the Atlantic side of the northern arm of the Cape, he suddenly realizes he has reached the edge of his continent, the place where America ends. "There was nothing but that savage ocean between us and Europe."

Margaret Fuller, who in 1850 was on the other side of that savage ocean, was preparing to return to America after a voyage of discovery that had taken her farther from her Massachusetts roots than any of the other Transcendentalists had cared to go. The life she lived after leaving Boston and Cambridge for New York and then Europe is so full of incident that any chronicler runs the risk of forgetting what Henry James said about reconstructing someone's past: "To live over people's lives is nothing unless we live over their perceptions, live over their growth, the change, the varying intensity of the same – since it was *by* these things they themselves lived." During the last eight years of her life Fuller grew from a strictly cultural reformer, who had worked out what one scholar has called her own brand of "elite-minded, countercultural proselytizing" but who had found practical reformers like the abolitionists distasteful, into a foreign correspondent, whose firsthand experience with revolutionary upheavals in Europe convinced her that some kind of democratic socialism was the only way of ending the cycle of exploitation and rebellion in which most nations seemed trapped.

Fuller's writings reflect the changes in her ideas; indeed, the activity of writing often brings those changes about, as when a desire to know more about the lives of women for *Woman in the Nineteenth Century* leads Fuller to read journals written by imprisoned prostitutes, and that in turn leads her to rethink the whole relationship between chastity and economic privilege. Such interchange between living and thinking was a Transcendentalist ideal, as it had been a Unitarian one, but Fuller carried it to lengths that would have startled William Ellery Channing, her earliest mentor: writing about prison conditions and insane asylums for a New York newspaper; calling in Paris to pay her respects to that flouter of all conventions, George Sand; becoming the friend of prominent exiled revolutionaries in England and France; getting swept up in the Roman revolution; taking an Italian lover and bearing a child.

Emerson commented on the rapidity with which Fuller always seemed to grow, and certainly many aspects of her life even while she lived in Boston and Cambridge might have helped one predict the sudden eruption of force that took place when she left. Many of the participants in her celebrated "Conversations," those late-morning classes that aimed to liberate women by forcing them to systematize their thoughts and make them public in an atmosphere of mutual sympathy and love, have testified to the power of Fuller's "personal magnetism" and the liberating force of her talk:

Perhaps I can best give you an idea of what she was to me by an answer which I made to her. One day when she was alone with me . . . she said, "Is life rich to you?" and I replied, "It is since I have known you." Such was the response of many a youthful heart to her, and herein was her wonderful influence. (*Reminiscences of Ednah Dow Cheney,* 1902)

No less significant for the shape her development later took was her frankness with herself about the nature of her own sexuality, which was capacious. Most male Transcendentalists tended to be squeamish, saccharine, and icily remote about human desire, even when they were writing in their journals. Fuller was strikingly candid. In a fragmentary journal passage for 1842 she recalls seeing an engraving of the beautiful Madame de Récamier. "I have so often thought over the intimacy between her and Me de Stael," Fuller wrote. "It is so true that a woman may be in love with a woman and a man with a man." This kind of love, she adds, is "regulated by the same law as that of love between persons of different sexes, only it is purely intellectual and spiritual, . . . its law is the desire of the spirit to realize a whole which makes it seek in another being for what it finds not in itself." The love of Socrates for Alcibiades, of Madame de Staël for Récamier, like Fuller's own love for the New Orleans beauty Anna Barker Ward, strikes her as perfectly "natural."

Remembering her own passion for Anna Ward, she muses,

I loved Anna for a time I think with as much passion as I was then strong enough to feel – Her face was always gleaming before me, her voice was echoing in my ear, all poetic thoughts clustered round the dear image. This love was a key which unlocked for me many a treasure which I still possess.

When Anna's husband, Samuel Gray Ward (with whom Fuller had also been in love), was absent on business, Fuller took his place in Anna's bed, though she found it "exquisitely painful" to realize that the "strange mystic thrill" she once felt in Anna's embrace was dwindled into a "sort of pallid, tender romance." With libertine bravado she analyzes her sensations. "I do not love her now with passion, for I have exhausted her idea, and she does not stimulate my fancy, she does not represent the Beautiful to me now, she is only one beautiful object."

Even if Fuller is borrowing her language here from the rakes of eighteenth-century fiction, she makes it clear why she could hardly have stayed in New England even if *The Dial* had ever made enough money to pay her a living wage. Fuller's appetites were continually frustrated in a culture so repressed that a visit to the theater to see the Austrian dancer Fanny Ellsler was considered daring (Fuller went with Emerson, who seemed quite pleased with himself for doing something scandalous). Women responded easily to Fuller's appeal; Elizabeth Peabody once remarked that if Fuller had been a man any one of the fine girls who attended the Conversations would have married her. But the men who surrounded her in Boston and Cambridge could think of nothing better to do with a poor, brilliant, ambitious, high-strung, granite-faced woman than to treat her as a confidante or a prophetess.

Fuller tried to oblige them, but the role of confidante, though she accepted it with apparent relish, was finally a source of pain to her; and the role of otherworldly vestal never really suited someone who was as passionate as a heroine of tragedy and as hungry for experience as a hero of romance. In a famous letter of 1841 to W. H. Channing she described herself as a kind of volcano; she could feel "all Italy glowing beneath the Saxon crust." And she added, "I shall burn to ashes if all this smoulders here much longer. I must die if I do not burst forth in genius or heroism" (Fuller to Channing, February 19, 1841). She sought solace, as she always had, in the imaginative identifications offered by literature. When Tennyson's new two-volume edition of poems came out in 1842 she was impressed with its calm nobility and "still, deep sweetness; how different from the intoxicating, sensuous melody of his earlier cadence!" One of Tennyson's themes, the last expedition of Ulysses, had long been a favorite of hers – "and his, like mine, is the Ulysses of the Odyssey, with his deep romance of wisdom, and not the worldling of the Iliad" (Fuller to W. H. Channing [?], August 1842).

Reading about questers is different from becoming one, however, and though Fuller continued her literary work during the winter of 1842–3, reviewing books for *The Dial,* giving another series of "Conversations" (this time on the subject of education), and preparing her manifesto "The Great Lawsuit" for the July 1843 number of *The Dial,* she began to long for an opportunity to travel. When her old friend and correspondent James Freeman Clarke invited her to join him and his sister Sarah on a journey to the West, she happily accepted. As usual, Fuller had to depend on the generosity of friends to make the trip possible; Clarke supplied some of the money himself. He accompanied the two women to Niagara Falls, where they stayed for a week, and then to Buffalo, where he put them on the steamboat for Chicago. They were met there by another of Sarah's brothers, William, who took them on a tour of the Illinois prairie in an open wagon. After they returned to Chicago they went on to Milwaukee and the surrounding area. Then Fuller, curious to see the annual gathering of the Ottowa and Chippewa tribes to receive their yearly payment from the U. S. government, visited Mackinac Island in the straits separating Lake Michigan from Lake Huron, where she spent nine days alone, watching the Indians and mingling with them as they camped on the beach in front of her hotel. She then rejoined Sarah in Chicago for the voyage back to Buffalo, made a visit to New York, and finally returned to Boston by September 1843.

Partly at Emerson's urging Fuller began to think of turning the journal notes and the letters she had written during the trip into what she called "a little book," though she cautions him not to expect much from it. "I cant bear to be thus disappointing you all the time" (Fuller to Emerson, November 12, 1843). She was disappointed that her materials seemed so scanty; exhaustion during the trip had often prevented her from writing down her impressions as fully as she had wished. Memory helped, but she also sought to make her account of the journey richer and more accurate by consulting reference works dealing with the region – books of travels, accounts of Indian lore and Indian life – a project for which she sought and won the right to use the library of Harvard College (the first woman to do so). The work went slowly, and Fuller availed herself of the travel writer's privilege of filling out the book with sketches and tales – the autobiographical tale of

Mariana; the story of a German clairvoyant known as the Seeress of Prevorst. She finished the book in May 1844; Emerson helped her find a publisher; and by June *Summer on the Lakes* was out, exposing Fuller for the first time in her life to the thing she feared, "that staring sneering Pit critic, the Public at large" (Fuller to Emerson, May 9, 1844).

Fuller's reception was generally friendly, though the book was criticized for its rambling, episodic structure and the apparent irrelevance of some of its embedded tales and poems. Fuller herself claimed no great formal coherence for her book; she seems to have been more concerned to present her impressions freshly to a public already jaded by repeated descriptions of western grandeurs. In that she certainly succeeds. The book begins with Niagara Falls, but Fuller scrupulously avoids any attempt to paint the sounding cataract. Instead, she tells us how much eight days in its company have depressed her. "My nerves, too much braced up by such an atmosphere, do not well bear the continual stress of sight and sound. For here there is no escape from the weight of a perpetual creation." That sound finally inspires in Fuller such dread that she looks nervously over her shoulder, haunted by irrational fears of "naked savages stealing behind me with uplifted tomahawks." One day, as she is seated upon Table Rock, the better to enjoy this sublime spectacle, she sees a man coming to take his first look. "He walked up close to the fall, and, after looking at it a moment, with an air as if thinking how he could best appropriate it to his own use, he spat into it."

The contrast between the continent's sublimities and the vulgar acquisitiveness of the men who are gradually colonizing it continues to trouble Fuller throughout her western tour. There are many things she likes about the West; she admits that she enjoys escaping from the "petty intellectualities, cant, and bloodless theory" of Boston. But if Boston is all thought and no life, the West seems to her all life and no thought. Its men seem blind to the loveliness all around them, preoccupied only with how much wealth they can extract from the earth (Fuller to Emerson, August 17, 1843).

Fuller is naturally sensitive to two groups of people who have suffered most from the acquisitive habits of the men. The women who accompany their husbands out to the West are ill prepared for the hard labor and isolation their frontier existence imposes on them; they do not even have the masculine diversions of hunting and fishing to provide a break from the unrelenting drudgery of the home. The Northern European women used to heavy farm work – Germans, Scandinavians, Dutch – fare better on the whole than the women from the eastern United States, but they too could be left helpless by the illness or death of their husbands.

Even sorrier is the condition of the various Indian tribes Fuller sees on her journey – pushed from their ancestral lands, degraded with rum, and, finally, treated with contempt by the whites who regard them with the natural aversion people feel toward those whom they have injured. Worst of all is the plight of Indian women, bent down from their burdens and walking with a peculiarly awkward gait. The "soft and wild but melancholy expression of their eye" makes Fuller think of the Paraguayan tribe she has read about whose women kill their infant daughters wherever possible to save them from the anguish and weariness of their lives. Yet the Indian women Fuller meets are not coarsened by their lot; on the contrary, she is amazed by their courtesy and natural delicacy. "They used to crowd round me, to inspect little things I had to show them, but never press near; on the contrary would reprove and keep off the children. Anything they took from my hand, was held with care, then shut or folded, and returned with an air of lady-like precision."

These descriptions make *Summer on the Lakes* a sad book, as Orestes Brownson said in his review of it in 1844. But it also contains passages of pure happiness, as when Fuller enjoys the prospect of the "limitless horizon" on the prairie. At first the absence of mountains or valleys disturbs her, but soon she learns to appreciate the exhilaration of unobstructed space.

I would ascend the roof of the house where we lived, and pass many hours, needing no sight but the moon reigning in the heavens, or starlight falling upon the lake, till all the lights were out in the island grove of men beneath my feet, and felt nearer heaven that there was nothing but this lovely, still reception on the earth; no towering mountains, deep tree-shadows, nothing but plain earth and water bathed in light.

On a sunny drive around the shores of Lake Michigan, stimulated by the blue sky and the gold and crimson of the flowers, she felt a kind of "fairyland exaltation" that would recur often as she traveled with her party through the rich landscape. Even raw Chicago, built for nothing but trade, fascinated her when she thought of it as a great valve through which the products of the West made their way to the eastern seaboard and admitted the tide of new immigrants coming from East to West.

Summer on the Lakes did not make Fuller any money, but at least it did not leave her saddled with debt; the publisher had been willing to assume the costs of publication. And the book won the admiration of Horace Greeley, the editor of the New York *Tribune,* who saw in its observations and impressions "an un-American ripeness of culture, and a sympathetic enjoyment of Nature in her untamed luxuriance." Greeley (a frequent visitor at Brook Farm) was already an admirer of Fuller, who impressed him as the "best instructed woman in America." In April 1844, shortly before *Summer on the Lakes* was due to appear, Fuller visited New York, where she spoke with Greeley and may have discussed then with him the possibility of expanding her 1843 *Dial* piece, "The Great Lawsuit," into a book. Prompted by his wife, who had spent much time in the Boston area and had become an admirer of Fuller and a participant in the "Conversations," Greeley invited Fuller to live with them in New York and become a writer for the *Tribune.*

The offer promised an escape from New England and a way of earning a living more stimulating than the drudgery of schoolteaching, but the step was a radical one. Bostonians looked down on New York as raw, vulgar, and vice ridden; and newspaper reporting was not a respectable profession even for a man. Fuller struggled with her decision all summer, even as she was working to revise and expand "The Great Lawsuit." Family troubles continued to plague her, and Emerson was not at all encouraging.

By September, however, Fuller had accepted Greeley's offer to work for the *Tribune* and had left Boston with her friend Caroline Sturgis for a long vacation in Fishkill, New York. She continued to work on her book, now entitled *Woman in the Nineteenth Century,* and to try to widen her understanding of the injustices inflicted upon women of all social classes. Georgiana Bruce, a lively young Englishwoman who had resided for a while at Brook Farm, was now working as an assistant matron in the women's prison at Sing Sing, aiding in an effort to reform what had been a brutal and violent prison. She had encouraged the women inmates (most of them in prison for prostitution) to keep journals, and in the summer of 1844 she had sent some examples to Fuller, who was fascinated by them. "Nothing could aid me so much as the facts you are witnessing[.] For these women in their degradation express most powerfully the present wants of the sex at large" (Fuller to Bruce, August 15, 1844).

The writings of two black women named Satira and Eliza seemed particularly powerful. Fuller was touched by the way Satira managed to maintain an idealized image of herself despite the debasement to which she had been subjected. Eliza gave an account of her "strong instinctive development" that Fuller judged "as clear and racy as Gil Blas." It seemed to her that few white women could have spoken with as much spirit and freedom. The discussion of sexuality among white women was still limited to murmurs and whispers, but Fuller was sure that the sentiments expressed by the black women would find an echo in the boudoirs of the richest mansions.

This thought led Fuller to another question. Bruce had told her that few of the women in Sing Sing had any feeling about chastity. This information made her curious. "Do they see any reality in it; or look on it merely as a circumstance of condition, like the possession of fine clothes?" (Fuller to Bruce, October 20, 1844). Bruce did in fact question the prisoners on this point; they told her that they did not feel "ruined" in the least, whether their sexual experience had been freely chosen or brutally imposed. Even a woman who had been forced into prostitution in a brothel said that she considered the word "ruin" ridiculous as long as the spirit could aspire and the body function. (Bruce decided that the word "ruined" was nothing but "a human, masculine verdict, pronounced by man to further the gratification of his grosser instincts.")

In the fall, Fuller visited Sing Sing with her companion Caroline Sturgis and her friend W. H. Channing. Channing preached a Sunday sermon to the men, and Fuller was allowed to talk with some of the women, whom she found decorous and frank. "All passed much as in one of my Boston Classes" (Fuller to Elizabeth Hoar, October 20 [28?], 1844). She told prisoners that she was writing a book about women and wanted to hear their experiences; they replied with candor, though some asked for a private interview in which they could say things they could not bear to talk about in front of one another. Fuller helped Bruce in her project of improving the dreary prison library (which at that time contained mostly religious tracts) by appealing to her women friends in Boston to send good books. She promised the prisoners she would return and did so, spending Christmas of 1844 at the prison.

These widening sympathies are reflected in the "never-sufficiently-to-be-talked-of pamphlet" that Fuller happily announced she had finished by mid-November 1844 (Fuller to Emerson, November 17, 1844). For once, her usual frustration when trying to put thoughts on paper gave way to fluency. She described to Channing how she had finished the book.

The last day it kept spinning out beneath my hand. After taking a long walk early on one of the most noble exhilarating sort of mornings I sat down to write and did not put the last stroke till near nine in the evening. Then I felt a delightful glow as if I had put a good deal of my true life in it, as if, I suppose I went away now, the measure of my foot-print would be left in the earth. (Fuller to W. H. Channing, November 17, 1844)

The firm of Greeley and McElrath brought out *Woman in the Nineteenth Century* in the spring of 1845. The whole edition was sold off to the booksellers in a week, and a delighted Fuller could report to her brother that she had earned eighty-five dollars from the sale. The book is indeed both the expression of Fuller's true life and the work that won her fame. It has been remarked that *Woman in the Nineteenth Century* represents both the grand summary of the Unitarian belief in self-culture and its widening to include the project of social reform. It is also Fuller's most extensive answer to the brutal reasoning of the passage from Spinoza's *Tractatus Politicus* that she prints in an appendix to the book. There Spinoza considers the question of whether man's supremacy over women is attributable to nature (in which case it is just to exclude women from a share in government) or to custom (in which case such exclusion is unjust). Observing that women nowhere share rule with men but are everywhere dominated by them, Spinoza concludes that women are naturally inferior to men and must be subordinate to them. He adds that because the love men feel toward women is "seldom any thing but lust and impulse, and much less a reverence for the qualities of soul than an admiration of physical beauty," and because physical beauty arouses male jealousy, allowing women a share in government would be destructive of peace and harmony.

Fuller ransacks the entire canon of Western literature and mythology to show that Spinoza's logic is faulty and his view of the relationship between the sexes vulgar and destructive – destructive not only to the happiness of women but also to the happiness of men. As long as women are raised to be frivolous, dependent, weak, and sentimental, men will have contempt for them; as long as women are raised to be wholly ignorant of their own sexuality, men will find themselves faced with the choice between wives whose erotic lives never rise beyond resentful compliance and prostitutes whose greater willingness means only that they have been bought. Greeley remarked that he had never met anyone as gifted at eliciting confidences as Margaret Fuller; people who had just been introduced to her suddenly found themselves pouring out their life stories into her sympathetic ear. The tales of misery she heard from "respectable" women in Boston seemed to her an expression of the same anger she heard in the blasphemies of Sing Sing's prisoners, "for a society beats with one great heart" (Fuller to Bruce, August 15, 1844).

Woman in the Nineteenth Century is finally not as much a book of protest as it is a book of hope, of a hope that one scholar has rightly called "millennial." In "The Over-Soul" Emerson had taught Fuller how to reject all arguments (like Spinoza's) drawn from history. "We give up the past to the objector, and yet we hope. He must explain this hope." To say that women have never played a part in government does not prove that they cannot hope to in the future, for the United States itself exists as a giant challenge to the idea that "the people" are too ignorant to govern themselves.

Besides, even the art and literature created by men bears witness that women have always held a higher place in the reverence of men than political tracts suggest. As Fuller says, "no age was left entirely without a witness of the equality of the sexes in function, duty, and hope." Even in societies where women's social position was low, as in ancient Greece, literature abounds with portraits of female courage and nobility – "Cassandra, Iphigenia, Antigone, Macaria." And mythology everywhere is full of goddesses who radiate mystery and control mighty forces. In another appendix to the book Fuller prints a long passage from Apuleius's *Metamorphoses* (*The Golden Ass*) in which the goddess Isis appears to the hero in a dream, rising from the sea. She wears a crown bearing a shining orb like the moon, a crown wreathed in vipers and studded with ears of grain.

Fuller's effort to develop what one scholar has called a body of female archetypes upon which women can draw imaginatively is made in hopes of reclaiming for women the sense of power that Christian culture has largely denied them. Would you rather be a powerful and even terrifying goddess — Isis, Demeter, Minerva, Artemis, Cybele? Or a meek and Christian wife — "the useful drudge of all men, the Martha, much sought, little prized"?

In the same spirit Fuller urges women to retreat into themselves, to break the habits of dependence and find their strength within. She is even willing to hail as a sign of greater self-reliance the growth of that class contemptuously called "old maids." (No greater proof of Fuller's courage could exist than her willingness to make that claim in print.) Only by being driven back upon herself can a woman hope to be worthy of the salutation with which the unfallen Adam greeted the unfallen Eve: "Daughter of God and man, *accomplished* Eve." And it takes an accomplished woman to join in the only kind of relationship worthy of immortal souls. "Two persons love in one another the future good which they aid one another to unfold."

The writing of *Woman in the Nineteenth Century* brought to a close a period of unusual self-confidence for Fuller. When she had completed her last series of "Conversations" in Boston in the spring of 1844 she looked back with pride upon her six years of "noble relations" with a variety of women's minds and decided, rather to her surprise, that life for once seemed worth living. In a letter to Emerson that summer she was gracious about the dissatisfactions she had always felt with their relationship, realizing that she had been asking him for what was not in his nature to give. But her leave-taking was almost a slap: "Farewell, O Grecian Sage, though not my Oedipus" (Fuller to Emerson, July 13, 1844). Now, at the close of *Woman in the Nineteenth Century,* she feels the fullness of her powers: "I stand in the sunny noon of life. Objects no longer glitter in the dews of morning, neither are yet softened by the shadows of evening. Every spot is seen, every chasm revealed." Yet such realism is perfectly congruent with hope. "Always the soul says to us all, Cherish your best hopes as a faith, and abide by them in action. Such shall be the effectual fervent means to their fulfillment."

This mood of confidence and reconciliation with reality made it difficult for Fuller to read with patience the very first book she reviewed for the *Tribune* — Emerson's *Essays, Second Series.* The preceding summer she had read some of the book in manuscript. At that time she was abashed at the difference between the "rude" piece of her own writing she was sending Emerson (probably a reprint of chapters from *Summer on the Lakes*) and his "great results, sculptured out into such clear beauty" (Fuller to Emerson, July 13, 1844). But by December, with Boston and Sing Sing and *Woman in the Nineteenth Century* behind her, she found she could scarcely bear to read Emerson's book through. The paralyzing sense of unreality described in essays like "Experience," with its emphasis on the isolation of the self and its skepticism about the possibility of reform, grated on her, and the best she could say to Emerson in her thank-you letter to him for the copy of the book he had sent her was that "in expression it seems far more adequate than the former volume, has more glow, more fusion" (Fuller to Emerson, November 17, 1844).

The review Fuller published in the *Tribune* on December 7, 1844, was both a gesture of filial piety toward and a declaration of independence from Emerson. Fuller pays tribute to Emerson as a man of unquestioned sincerity, who worships one god only, the god of Truth. She gives a vivid portrait of Emerson as a public speaker and remarks that the lectures that thrilled the youth of New England "seemed not so much lectures as grave didactic poems, theogonies, perhaps, adorned by odes" and delivered by a speaker who brought to mind the poets and legislators of ancient Greece — "men who taught their fellows to plow and avoid moral evil, sing hymns to the gods and watch the metamorphoses of nature." And she pays him this fine tribute: "History will inscribe his name as a father of the country, for he is one who pleads her cause against herself."

Nevertheless, Fuller also registers disappointment with the lack of cohesion in all of Emerson's essays. Though the second series of essays is better than the first in this respect, "yet in no one essay is the main stress so obvious as to produce on the mind the harmonious effect of a noble river or a tree in full leaf." Worse still is Emerson's neglect of the affections, the glow which is given to a body "by free circulation of the heart's blood from the hour of birth." The ideal region in which he dwells is pure and holy, but it leaves him like an Antaeus cut off from the sources of his strength. "We could wish he might be thrown by conflicts on the lap of mother earth, to see if he would not rise again with added powers."

Anyone who looks at the best of the almost two hundred and fifty columns that Fuller wrote for the *Tribune* in her twenty months of residence in New York might conclude that there was some special magic in the city's soil, for Fuller seemed to acquire added powers almost as soon as she set foot there. To Samuel Gray Ward she wrote that she liked her new position: "It is so central, and affords a far more various view of life than any I ever before was in." Far from feeling overwhelmed by her new duties, she hopes her pen will be "a vigorous and purifying implement" (Fuller to Ward, December 29, 1844). To W. H. Channing, who would serve as her escort through the slums and public institutions of the city, she was even more confident. "I feel as if something new, and *good* was growing" (Fuller to Channing, December 31, 1844).

The effect on Fuller's prose style was striking. As one scholar has pointed out, the contract to write three columns a week forced her to write rapidly and freed her from the paralyzing sense that she should be doing something great every time she wrote. Then too, New York's constantly changing panorama never ceased to interest her. Did she miss Boston? No, she told a friend, "I find I dont dislike wickedness and wretchedness more than pettiness and coldness" (Fuller to Sarah Shaw, February 25, 1845). Best of all was her liberation from the coterie atmosphere of *The Dial* and the inbred literary society of Boston and Cambridge. Fuller quickly realized that it was exhilarating to know that her columns might be read by fifty thousand people. Best of all, they were *anonymous* people. In a long essay on American literature that she wrote for inclusion in a volume of her collected essays in 1846, Fuller explained the chief advantage of writing for newspapers: "We address, not our neighbor, who forces us to remember his limitations and prejudices, but the ideal presence of human nature as we feel it ought to be and trust it will be. We address America rather than Americans."

The prejudices of Fuller's Boston and Cambridge friends about what kind of writing a woman ought to do had affected her adversely. She had tried to be either oracular or intuitively sympathetic and as a result had too often written prose that sounds inflated or cloying. Only in her "Introduction" to her translation of Eckermann's *Conversations with Goethe* had she spoken with the straightforwardness that her *Tribune* articles show. In both places she was sustained by a sense of mission – to bring European literary culture to America – and by the knowledge that she was better qualified to accomplish this mission than almost anyone else in the country.

Fuller quickly embraced her new role. Greeley gave her a free hand to discuss anything she thought significant (his only complaint was that she did not write fast enough). She delighted to rescue authors whom she considered unjustly neglected, like Charles Brockden Brown, a novelist she once called "by far our first in point of genius and instruction as to the soul of things." An 1846 reprinting of Brown's novels *Wieland* (1798) and *Ormond* (1799) gave her a chance to recommend a writer who had become almost inaccessible to the public, though he was far superior in "the higher qualities of the mind" to novelists currently on sale in every shop. Fuller argues that Brown's special genius lies in showing "the self-sustaining force of which a lonely mind is capable." (Fuller naturally likes Brown's decision to make women characters the narrators of several of his books. Brown's willingness to put a "thinking royal mind" in a woman's body makes him the "prophet of a better era.")

If Brown has been unjustly neglected, a poet such as Henry Wadsworth

Longfellow has been praised and glorified all out of proportion to his talent or his achievement. Fuller's notorious and devastating review of Longfellow's *Poems* of 1845 shows how fearless, how merciless, she had become after a year's pursuit of critical truth. She begins her December 1845 review of America's most popular poet by making some discriminations. Between the creators of true poetry and the grinders out of the wretched metrical trash that daily issues from American presses there is a "middle class," composed of persons of little original poetic power but with taste and sensibility, whose function in the realm of the spirit is to develop those faculties in others. Longfellow is such a middle-class poet, "a man of cultivated taste, delicate though not deep feeling, and some, though not much, poetic force." Right now the poetic bouquets he offers us contain "the flowers of all climes, and wild flowers of none." Fuller is sure that Longfellow himself *must* be aware of his relative rank in the kingdom of poetry. But his admirers, by hailing him as a genius, make his poetry usurp the place of better poems, and so prevent the development of that poetic taste that was his only real contribution to the culture of his native land.

Aesthetic issues are impossible for Fuller to separate from moral ones, and some of her most interesting reviews in the *Tribune* are of works that raise moral questions with particular vividness. The publication in 1845 of Carlyle's edition (with commentary) of Oliver Cromwell's speeches and letters allowed her to comment upon Carlyle's descent from a celebrator of spiritual freedom into an admirer of brutality and autocratic rule. Though she praises Carlyle's editorial work, she refuses to admire Cromwell's massacres in Ireland or to find Cromwell's religious holdings forth other than repulsive:

We stick to the received notions of Old Noll, with his great, red nose, hard heart, long head, and crafty ambiguities. Nobody ever doubted his great abilities and force of will. . . . But as to looking on him through Mr. Carlyle's glasses, we shall not be sneered or stormed into it, unless he has other proof to offer than is shown yet. And we resent the violence he offers both to our prejudices and our perceptions.

In some ways the most complex and subtle of Fuller's reviews concerned the religious controversies still agitating the New England she had left behind. On January 26, 1845, Theodore Parker preached a sermon, "The Excellence of True Goodness," in James Freeman Clarke's Boston Church of the Disciples – the pulpit exchange that caused such an uproar and occasioned the defection of fifteen of Clarke's church members. The sermon was printed, and a month after it had been delivered Fuller reviewed it for the *Tribune*. She does not spend much time discussing the sermon itself. Parker avoids controversy in it, and it contains none of his peculiar doctrines. But she has a great deal to say about the controversy within the Boston Association of Ministers and its attempt to freeze Parker out of Boston. Fuller derides the effort of those who call themselves "Liberal Christians" to do away with that sacred tenet of Protestant belief, the right of private judgment. Their failure is part of a larger failure of Protestantism in this country, where "after so many years of political tolerance, there exists very little notion, far less practice, of spiritual tolerance."

The Unitarians promised themselves that they would refrain from such persecution, and as long as the Reverend Channing was alive, they had a leader "who had confidence in the vital energy of Truth, and was not afraid to trust others with the same privileges he had vindicated for himself, even if they made use of them in a different manner." But his followers lack the moral courage of Channing. They were afraid not so much just of Parker himself but of the comments made by other sects about Parker, and "they had not confidence enough in those principles which had been the animating soul of their body" to rise above their fear. Fuller concedes that a minister may exclude from exchanges people with whom he disagrees – though she thinks such exclusion is ill-judged, because it leads to mental petrifaction. But the attempts that were made to coerce Clarke and Sargent into canceling their exchanges with Parker she finds absolutely contemptible. She takes a fierce delight in the failure of the Boston ministers' plots. Denied the church, Parker took to the lecture room, and the congregations followed. "The flock ran out of the fold to seek the wolf."

Fuller necessarily wrote a good many reviews that fall below the standards set by her best ones. She could sound spiteful, and she was not above puffing the negligible poetry of her brother-in-law, Ellery Channing (probably less out of cynicism than out of desperation, for Channing proved as helpless at earning a living as Bronson Alcott had been). But Thomas Wentworth Higginson said of her work for the *Tribune*, "In that epoch of strife which I so well remember . . . she held the critical sway of the most powerful American journal with unimpaired dignity and courage."

Fuller's productivity is all the more remarkable because her personal life during this period was anything but calm. Early in 1845 she met a German-Jewish businessman named James Nathan and began a flirtation that quickly turned (on her side, at least) into love. She showered Nathan with letters and affection; they went on walks together, attended concerts, shared books, left notes for each other. For a while Fuller was blissfully happy. But a crisis soon developed. (Its stages must be reconstructed from Fuller's letters alone because Nathan's do not survive.) Fuller apparently heard through a woman who ran a lodging house that Nathan was visiting a young woman there. She confronted him with the rumor. He almost made a confession, telling her his conscience was suffering, then lost his nerve and told her that the young woman was an "injured woman" whom he was trying to help.

It is a measure of Fuller's innocence and her desperation that she accepted Nathan's story, even telling him she found his conduct "honorable nay heroic." She confessed that she too had done things society would blame her for if she were judged by conventional rules (Fuller to Nathan, April 6, 1845). Fuller may have been thinking of her unconventional passion for Anna Barker Ward, but one can hardly blame Nathan for reading this confession as an invitation to make more explicit advances. He seems to have asked her if he might "hope" for something beyond their present relationship. The word "hope" made her believe at first that he was proposing marriage. When he told her that he could never marry her, Fuller was both shocked and insulted. What was most galling was the feeling that she had brought this humiliation upon herself. They patched up the quarrel, and in the late spring of 1845 they returned to some semblance of their old relationship. But Nathan was clearly puzzled and increasingly bored by a relationship that had all the trappings of passion but none of the usual rewards. He made plans to return to Europe, though he told Fuller only that he planned to travel abroad for a time.

Nathan left in June with his parting gift from Fuller, a copy of Shelley's poems. Before he left she had given him back his letters and asked for her own in return. He refused to give them back, despite her distress and repeated requests by letter after he had left the country. Nathan may have kept the letters because he wanted to ensure Fuller's continued willingness to perform services for him. He may have hoped to use them to extract money either from Fuller herself or from someone interested in her life (his heirs eventually sold them for one hundred and ten dollars). Or he may simply have been flattered to have been the object of such eloquent adoration by a celebrated American woman.

Of course, the immortality Nathan purchased by his refusal to return Fuller's letters turns out to be a dubious one. If her willingness to subject herself to him in these letters is humiliating, his calculating selfishness is repellent. Still, this surviving half of correspondence at least makes clear why Fuller fell in love with him. He may have been a cad, but he was *her* cad (or at least so she thought). By appearing to return her desire, Nathan gave her the chance to move from the periphery to the center of erotic life, if only in imagination. The torrent of generosity, adoration, and forgiveness Fuller unlooses upon him resembles the floods of divine grace poured out upon the unworthy sinner in Puritan theology. No wonder (as Perry Miller said) Nathan fled for his life.

After Nathan left New York, Fuller moved from the Greeleys' place on Turtle Bay into town, where she began to attend parties and gatherings of other literary people. She continued to write for the *Tribune* and began to collect some of her *Dial* and *Tribune* essays for publication in book form (*Papers on Literature and Art*). She composed a long and thoughtful survey of American literature for the book as well. But she was restless and eager for a change. When a wealthy couple, Marcus and Rebecca Spring, Quaker philanthropists who had become friendly with her in New York, suggested that she accompany them to Europe as companion to Rebecca and tutor to their son, she accepted. She reached an agreement with Greeley to continue her writing for the *Tribune;* he would pay her ten dollars for every column she sent back from abroad. Before she left she visited Cambridge to say goodbye to her family and receive from Emerson a letter of introduction to Carlyle.

On August 1, 1846, Fuller sailed with the Springs from New York aboard the steamer *Cambria,* which made the crossing to Liverpool in a new record time of ten days and sixteen hours. After touring the grimy industrial cities of Liverpool and Manchester and making a walking excursion to Chester they set off to visit the Lake District, where they saw a good deal of Harriet Martineau and called on Wordsworth. Then they went on to Carlisle in Scotland, made romantic by its association with Mary, Queen of Scots; next to Edinburgh (where Fuller was shocked to receive a letter from James Nathan informing her of his forthcoming marriage to a woman in Hamburg). Two weeks in the highlands came next, during which Fuller spent a frightening night alone on Ben Lomond, having gotten separated from her companion when both lost their way down the mountain. After Fuller recovered from this incident, the party descended to Glasgow, where the slums were, if anything, more wretched than the ones they had seen in Liverpool and Manchester.

Back in England, the party visited the cathedral at York; saw Walter Scott's home and Warwick Castle; stopped at Birmingham, Sheffield, and Newcastle (where they descended into a coal mine); and finally arrived in London. Fuller met many people in London literary society during the several weeks her party stayed there. *Woman in the Nineteenth Century* and her new book of essays had made her name well known, and she was invited many places. But the two men who meant most to her were Carlyle — whom to her surprise she liked — and Carlyle's close friend, Giuseppe Mazzini (1805–72), the leader in exile of the Italian Republican movement, who continued to try through his writings to agitate for overthrow of despotic regimes and the establishment of republican government in a united Italy.

In November 1846 the Springs left London with Fuller for Paris, where Fuller attended the debates in the raucous Chamber of Deputies, went to the theater, and tried to enter the lecture hall of the Sorbonne to hear a lecture on astronomy, only to be hold that women were not allowed in, even when the hall was empty. She was perpetually frustrated by her difficulties with spoken French but managed all the same to meet artists and literary people, including George Sand, Frederic Chopin, and the exiled Polish poet Adam Mickiewicz (1798–1855). Mickiewicz was an admirer of Emerson and quickly became one of Fuller's closest friends.

Late in February the party left Paris for Italy, passing through Lyons and Avignon (where Fuller visited the tomb of Petrarch's Laura) to board a steamer to Genoa at Marseilles. A tour of Italy followed: Leghorn, Pisa, Naples, and then at last Rome, where they took lodgings on the Via del Corso. Then came an extensive tour of northern Italy, including Florence, Bologna, and Venice. An illness forced Fuller to rest in Venice, where she separated from the Springs, who had decided to return home by way of Germany. When she was well she resumed the tour alone through Vicenza, Verona, Brescia, and Milan (where she met the Italian novelist Alessandro Manzoni, author of *I Promessi Sposi* [*The Betrothed*]). For a while she crossed over into Switzerland, then returned to Italy for two weeks at Lake Como with a new companion, the Marchioness Visconti, another friend of Italian unity recently returned from twenty-six years of exile.

By the middle of October 1847, Fuller was back in Rome. During her previous stay there with the Springs during Holy Week, she had become separated from them while visiting Saint Peter's Church. A young Italian man, fashionably dressed and polite, seeing her anxiety, had offered his assistance. When it proved impossible to locate her companions or to find a carriage, he walked her all the way back to her lodgings. He introduced himself as Giovanni Angelo Ossoli, the son of the Marchese Filippo Ossoli, who held a high position in the papal court.

During the rest of her stay in Rome they became better acquainted. His mother had died when he was a child; his father was ill; his brothers were hostile to him, the last child in the family; he was sad and felt lonely. Fuller's warmly sympathetic nature appealed to him. Ossoli was not the only man in whom Fuller was interested at the time; there is a bold letter from her to the American painter Thomas Hicks in which she invites him to visit her because she is suffering from want of congenial companionship (Hicks politely declined, though he remained her friend and later painted her portrait). But Ossoli was persistent. When she left Rome with the Springs he predicted she would return to him.

Fuller kept the existence of Ossoli a secret from her Boston friends but confided her uncertainties by letter to Mickiewicz, who replied with some blunt advice. In a letter of August 3, 1847, he tells her that he is worried about her tendency to romantic reveries which could exhaust her imagination. He reminds her of what he had said to her in Paris: "I tried to make you understand that you should not confine your life to books and reveries. You have pleaded the liberty of woman in a masculine and frank style. Live and act, as you write." Later he reminded her, "Literature is not the whole of life" (Mickiewicz to Fuller, September 16, 1847). Apparently this was the advice she wanted, for by the middle of October she had returned to Rome, moved into a small apartment on the Corso, and taken Ossoli for a lover.

For a while she was very happy. But her discovery early in 1848 that she was pregnant filled her with despair. Ossoli could not marry a Protestant without a papal dispensation, which required the consent of his family, and his family would hardly consent to his marriage to a poor American woman over ten years his senior who was a Republican sympathizer to boot. Fuller had little money and Ossoli was no richer; in order to survive she had to keep writing for the *Tribune,* though she knew that if any word of her true condition leaked back to New York even the broad-minded Greeley would have to drop her from the paper.

What made her situation more difficult was that Fuller had arrived for her second stay in Rome in the middle of profound political changes. Pope Pius IX had begun his reign in 1846 with a series of reforms that won him the gratitude of the people. In May 1847 Fuller had witnessed a torchlight procession down the Corso celebrating the pope's promise to the people of a representative council; further reforms designed to transfer power in the Papal States from the clergy to the laity followed throughout the year. In February 1848 the pope published a written constitution allowing for secular government of the Papal States. But his reforms never had a chance to take effect, for more radical revolutions suddenly broke out all over Europe. In Sicily the people rose against their king, the hated Ferdinand II; riots broke out in Naples; mobs in Paris forced the abdication of King Louis Philippe; the Milanese rose against the Austrians and drove them from the city. The Venetians had driven out the Austrians as well and proclaimed themselves a republic, followed by Parma and Modena. It seemed a season of hope and joy, but the pope increasingly drew back from a popular revolution he could not control.

At the end of May, Fuller, whose pregnancy could no longer be concealed, left for the country where she remained until her son was born on September 5, 1848. Ossoli stayed in Rome where he was a member of the civil guard. He wrote to her frequently and managed to obtain leave to be with her when the child was born. Because Fuller needed to be in Rome to write her *Tribune* dispatches and the child could hardly be concealed there, they left him with a nurse in the village of Rieti and returned to Rome. There they found the political situation tense. The pope's appointed minister, the Count de Rossi, was assassinated as he tried to open the Chambers, and a mob forced the pope to agree to the formation of a democratic ministry. On the night of November 24, 1848, dressed as a common priest, the pope with the help of his supporters escaped from the palace and fled to Gaeta in the kingdom of Naples.

The pope's flight opened the way to the declaration of a Roman Republic, which the Constituent Assembly decreed on February 9, 1849. But ominous forces were ranged against the new republic. The Austrians had already retaken some of the northern cities; King Ferdinand had suppressed the revolt in the south. The exiled pope appealed to various European powers to help him regain his throne, and the new president of the French Republic, Louis Napoleon, sent French troops under General Oudinot to besiege Rome. Ossoli fought with the civil guard during the siege; Fuller was appointed *regolatrice* (supervisor) of a hospital devoted to tending the wounded. The first assault upon the city on April 24 was repulsed by the Italian patriot Garibaldi and his legions, but the bombardment to which the city was then subjected and the overwhelming numerical superiority of the attacking army finally breached Rome's defenses and forced its surrender. On the Fourth of July, 1849, the French army entered to occupy Rome. With the siege broken Fuller and Ossoli were finally able to reach Rieti, only to find their son Angelino malnourished and dangerously ill. Because it was too dangerous for a former Republican to live in Rome, where harsh repressive measures had been adopted by the authorities, the three of them left for Florence when the child had recovered.

Even the barest summary of Fuller's life story between the time she landed at Liverpool in 1846 and the collapse of the Roman Republic in 1849 sounds impossibly romantic, like a fantasy invented by Fuller when she was a young woman exiled to the boredom of her father's unprofitable farm in Groton. English slums, mist-clad Scottish mountains, coal mines, London literary lions, sensitive exiled revolutionaries, George Sand, Chopin, Italian aristocrats, love, motherhood, political revolution, triumph, siege, resistance, defeat. Even if Fuller had done no more than *live* the life sketched here it would have qualified as a major imaginative achievement. Some sense of what Fuller's life meant to her own generation can be gleaned from a comment made by one of her Boston friends after her death. She said that Fuller had "the most successful woman-life of the nineteenth century." It seems a curious remark, given the amount of suffering and sheer bad luck that dogged Fuller from beginning to end, unless you think of what kind of hope the trajectory of her life offered to the women she had left behind.

Fuller drew upon her experiences to write thirty-seven lengthy dispatches to the *Tribune,* and these dispatches (which run to more than two-hundred-and-eighty pages in the modern edition recently published) form one of the most absorbing, brilliant, and far-ranging of all texts written by the Transcendentalists. The first twelve of the dispatches deal with Fuller's experiences before she got to Italy; the remaining twenty-five with Italy itself. The first twelve belong recognizably to the category of travel writing, but even a cursory reading will suggest how different they are from *Summer on the Lakes.* The excessive subjectivity of the earlier book has been replaced by a speaker whose sense of self, though strong, is not the focus of attention; instead, it is a lens through which events can be clearly seen. Fuller's *Tribune* experience in New York had taught her how to write for an audience, rather than for herself, a discipline that gives her dispatches pace and urgency. And her need for Greeley's ten-dollar payments kept her writing even when she felt desperate or depressed.

This professionalism means that Fuller reports with intelligent curiosity whatever comes into her field of observation: the slums and gin palaces of Glasgow or the "squalid, agonizing, ruffianly" misery of the London poor; boatmen in Walter Scott country singing on beautiful Loch Katrine; the aged Wordsworth, repeating with much expression some lines written by his sister Dorothy and asking Fuller to admire his long avenue of prized hollyhocks; the skeleton of Jeremy Bentham, dressed as in life and equipped with a wax portrait mask, seated companionably in the study of his good friend Dr. Southwood Smith.

Yet Fuller's passages of observation, good as they are, are not as good as her character sketches. The best is that of Carlyle. Fuller wanted to meet Carlyle, as she wanted to meet everyone, but she had not gone to England expecting to like him. She had complained that ever since *Chartism* his works could be reduced to a simple message: "Everything is very bad. You are fools and hypocrites, or you would make it better" (Fuller to R. W. Emerson, June 1, 1843). Her exposure to social conditions in England and Scotland, however, had given her a better understanding of his rage. Now she was simply overwhelmed by his conversation.

"Accustomed to the infinite wit and exuberant richness of his writings, his talk is still an amazement and a splendor scarcely to be faced with steady eyes," she wrote, even though she readily admitted: "He does not converse – only harangues." Carlyle was indeed arrogant and overbearing, with "the heroic arrogance of some old Scandinavian conqueror." But she found herself liking him anyway. His talk seemed like singing, or poetry. "He pours on you a kind of satirical, heroical, critical poem, with regular cadences, and generally catching up near the beginning some singular epithet, which serves as a *refrain* when his song is full." Lonely as the desert, readier than anyone to ridicule all attempts to remedy the evils he deplored, he seemed to Fuller an original, and therefore a source of the most hearty refreshment.

When Fuller moves through France we can see a widening of sensibilities and a growing complexity in her thought about social issues. But the dispatches she sent from Italy show her transforming the genre into something quite different. As her relationship to the revolutionary movements in Italy shifts from sympathetic spectatorship to active partisanship, as the revolutions breaking out all over Italy flower into early successes and then collapse more or less swiftly back into defeats, she begins to add to her descriptive powers political commentary that shows an impressive command of information, understanding of character, and grasp of strategic fact.

This aspect of the dispatches is the one most difficult to convey, because the passages describing the movements of regiments or speculating about the possible motives of dukes or petty kings do not lend themselves easily to summary or quotation. Yet the cumulative impression they make is of a mind both ironic and tough — just as passages about the goals of the revolution and the larger direction of history suggest capacities for passionate indignation and moral absolutism.

Italy's sufferings give Fuller an appreciation for America's amazing luck. As she watched the Romans try to throw off centuries of corruption, brutality, poverty, and ignorance to declare their republic in a world of wolves — tyrannical Austria to the north, the murderous King Ferdinand to the south, the menacing French to the west — the United States seemed more than ever fortunate in the circumstances of its nativity. The infant American Republic was protected by a vast ocean on one side and a wilderness on the other, led by men like Washington and Adams, free of priestcraft, blessedly empty of aristocrats on the one hand and ignorant peasants on the other. It managed to expel the British without becoming the prey of another great power, whereas the poor Roman Republic was menaced from all sides before its independence had even been formally declared.

What angers Fuller is that her native land should have fallen so far from the ideals it espoused at its founding — refusing to do anything about the "cancer of slavery," behaving toward Mexico like the Austrian occupiers of Italy, tolerating a growing gap between the rich and poor that already had begun to reproduce in the New World all the vice and misery of the Old. Her growing awareness of the connection between concentrated wealth and political oppression makes her long for a "reform" that will be more radical than "revolution." Even Mazzini, when he arrives in Rome after his seventeen-year exile, is not radical enough for Fuller; he aims only at "political emancipation" and not at that greater social and economic emancipation of which Fourierism is only a crude prophecy.

The story Fuller tells in her dispatches is a tragedy, and it affects the reader like one. Reading about the celebrations that attend the coming of Roman independence, watching the ominous clouds on the political horizon, hoping against hope that the French will sympathize with the spirit of their own revolutions instead of aid tyrants in crushing one, realizing with fury that the promises of the French General Oudinot are lies, watching the destruction of art and beauty in the city of Rome as the bombardment begins, looking at the mangled limbs of beautiful young men who are brought to Fuller's hospital for treatment, watching the departure of Garibaldi's forces a few steps ahead of the invading French, watching with rage and contempt as the French army enters the city on (a cruel irony) July 4, 1849, Fuller manages to make us feel that we are living through the scenes she describes. By the final dispatch we feel something like that pity and fear tragedy promises to arouse and purge.

Yet the dispatches are not melancholy, as *Summer on the Lakes* was. Fuller's faith in the ultimate direction of the historical process sustains her even during the last awful days of the bombardment of Rome and the collapse of the Republic. She predicts confidently that the age of reaction will be short; by the next century all of Europe will be under democratic governments. The old powers may have triumphed temporarily, but their thrones will either topple or crumble away, and the people will finally claim those rights so long denied them.

From Florence (where she had gone with Ossoli and Angelino after the fall of Rome) Fuller writes of her attempt to recover her spirits and her hope. "I take long walks into the country, I gaze on the beauty of nature, and seek thus to strengthen myself in the faith that the Power who delighted in these creations will not suffer his highest, ardent, aspiring, loving men, to live and die in vain." She breaks off the dispatch (the next-to-last) because she suddenly is offered an opportunity to send it, but not before she concludes with a final rebellious prayer to that other power who inspires revolutions and topples thrones: "O Lucifer, son of the morning, fall not this time from thy chariot, but herald in at last the long looked for, wept for, bled and starved for day of Peace and Good Will to men."

Fuller did not want to return to America. She knew she would be subjected to a "social inquisition" far more daunting than anything she faced in Florence, where her friends accepted (or appear to accept) her story of a secret marriage to Ossoli before Angelino's birth. But she had little choice. Her only marketable commodity was a history of the Italian revolution she had been working on while she was writing the *Tribune* dispatches. Unable to afford steamship fare, the family booked passage on the merchantman *Eliza-*

beth, due to sail from Leghorn under the command of a captain with the reassuring New England name of Seth Hasty.

They set sail on May 17, 1850. But Captain Hasty came down with smallpox shortly after they left Leghorn and died when the ship was off Gibraltar. (Angelino came down with the same disease but managed to recover.) The first mate took over the ship and managed to sail as far as the coast of New Jersey by July 18. He told the passengers to expect arrival in New York the next day. During the night a hurricane arose. Desperate to reach the harbor, the first mate continued to steer for what he thought was the mouth of the harbor. But the wind had driven the *Elizabeth* north and east. At four o'clock in the morning the ship ran aground on a sandbar a few hundred yards off Fire Island. The next wave slammed the ship sideways against the sandbar, and her cargo of Italian marble (including – of all things – a statue of John Calhoun made by an American sculptor in Florence) broke through the hold.

In the morning people were visible on the beach, which was only a few hundred yards away, but the force of the storm prevented lifeboats from being launched or rescue lines from being fired to the ship. During the lull as the eye of the storm passed over the vessel several crew members and a few passengers grabbed planks, jumped overboard, and managed to reach shore. Fuller refused to try unless she, Ossoli, and her child could all be rescued together. At about three o'clock in the afternoon the steward of the boat grabbed Angelino and tried to make it ashore; their bodies were washed up on shore a few minutes later. The incoming tide made the waves larger, and first Ossoli, then Fuller, were washed off the deck of the wrecked ship. Their bodies were never found.

Emerson heard the news of Fuller's death three days later. He dispatched Thoreau to the site of the wreck, hoping to rescue at least the manuscript history of the Italian revolution that Fuller had brought with her. But by the time Thoreau reached Long Island, five days had passsed since the wreck, and by then the huge crowd of wreck pickers who had appeared to scavenge the beach for the *Elizabeth*'s cargo had cleaned the beach thoroughly; no manuscript was found.

9

THE ANTISLAVERY YEARS

IN ITALY MARGARET FULLER had discovered what it felt like to be caught up in historical processes larger than those any individual could control – to be unable to refuse participation, to be forced to watch helplessly the outcome of events. In the winter and spring of 1850 events in the United States Congress would give the other Transcendentalists a similar experience. By the terms of the Treaty of Guadalupe Hidalgo in 1848 Mexico had ceded huge tracts of western land to the United States. The question immediately arose: would slavery be permitted in the new territory? Mexico had abolished slavery, but settlers from the southern United States were determined to reintroduce it, less because they thought slavery likely to flourish there (the arid climate was unsuitable for the crops that needed slave labor) than because they feared they would be encircled by new free states formed from the Mexican Cession, which would upset the balance of power they had up to then maintained in the Senate.

Two years earlier, a freshman Democratic congressman from Pennsylvania named David Wilmot had startled his colleagues in the House of Representatives, which was then debating the possibility of purchasing territory from Mexico, by offering an amendment to the appropriations bill that made it "an express and fundamental condition" to the acquisition of territory from Mexico that "neither slavery nor involuntary servitude shall ever exist in any part of said territory." This famous Wilmot Proviso was never adopted, but under its threat Congress quickly divided – not along party lines (Whig against Democrat) but along sectional ones (North against South) – in a way that seemed ominous for the future of the Union.

By 1848 fortune appeared to favor the South again on the subject of territorial expansion for slavery. The Democratic candidate for preseident, Lewis Cass, was pledged to uphold slavery, and the Whig candidate, Zachary Taylor, was a major slave owner himself. But when Taylor won he quickly disappointed his southern supporters by choosing an antislavery Northerner as his chief adviser and by seeking ways to keep the new territory free. Congress was deadlocked on the subject of whether it had the power to regulate slavery *in the territories;* Taylor encouraged California, suddenly rich in settlers drawn by the Gold Rush of 1848 and badly in need of central government, to apply to the Congress for admission *as a state.* Congress might wrangle endlessly about who had power to regulate slavery in the territories, but no one could deny a state the power to write its own constitution and forbid slavery if it chose to do so. California held a convention in the fall of 1849, wrote a constitution, and sought admission to the Union as a free state.

Southerners were infuriated by Taylor's maneuvers and determined to prevent the admission of California to the Union; young southern radicals called for a convention in Nashville, Tennessee, to be held in the summer of 1850 to discuss secession. Taylor was adamant. He upheld California's right to be admitted and vowed to defend the Union against anyone who would menace it. But Taylor, a war hero drafted by the Whigs because they correctly guessed that his popularity would win the election of 1848, was politically inexperienced and had few ties to the congressional leaders of either party. With talk of secession growing daily louder in the South, Henry Clay, the venerable Whig senator from Kentucky, attempted to devise a series of compromise resolutions that would stave off secession by laying to rest southern fears and threats to the slave system while mollifying the free states by granting them important concessions, including the admission of California.

Most historians agree that the package of eight resolutions put together by Clay had more material benefits in it for the North than for the South. But one of the resolutions in what came to be known as the Compromise of 1850 was a frank concession to the South. A law had been on the books since 1793 stipulating that fugitive slaves who escaped from one state to another must be returned to their owners. But the law was rarely enforced in the North; indeed, some northern states had laws forbidding state officers to assist in capturing or returning fugitive slaves. Now Clay called for a new Fugitive Slave Law, one that provided for federal rather than state administration of the procedures taken to recapture escaped slaves and return them to their owners.

Clay enlisted the help of Daniel Webster, the Whig senator from Massachusetts, in support of his resolutions. Webster had opposed the Mexican War and supported the Wilmot Proviso, but he feared disunion as much as Clay did, and he agreed with Clay that the proposed legislation offered a chance to save the Union from division. On March 7, 1850, Webster delivered one of his most famous speeches in the Senate, "Constitution and Union," throwing his support behind Clay's compromise, including its most obnoxious provision, the Fugitive Slave Law, in the interests of preserving a Union he described as eminently worth the sacrifice of particular sectional interests. Webster was severely criticized in the North by antislavery leaders who regarded his speech of conciliation as a betrayal (Whittier wrote a famous poem portraying Webster as a fallen angel), but there were many among Boston's merchant and professional classes who hailed him as the courageous preserver of the Union. Toward the end of the month they addressed a letter of support to him signed by nearly a thousand citizens.

Four days after Webster's Seventh of March speech Taylor's closest adviser had a chance to reply. William Henry Seward (1801–72) had been governor of New York State and was now its senator. He was a firm opponent of slavery who while he was governor had obtained the passage of laws prohibiting state officials from assisting in the capture of fugitive slaves and guaranteeing the right to a jury trial for fugitive slaves captured by someone else. On March 11 Seward delivered a speech in the Senate opposing Clay's compromise on both Constitutional and moral grounds. It was the second kind of argument that gave the speech the name by which it was popularly known. Seward argued that the moral law established by the Creator was a higher law than the Constitution and that the moral law was working everywhere in the civilized world toward the extirpation, not the extension, of slavery. Though Webster mocked the "higher law" speech, it was popular in the North, where over a hundred thousand copies of it were soon in circulation.

Clay and Webster were unable to secure passage of the compromise during the spring and summer of 1850. Then, suddenly, on the Fourth of July, President Taylor became ill with gastroenteritis; he died five days later. With their strongest opponent out of the way Southerners who were hostile to the terms of Clay's compromise managed to defeat most of its provisions, and by July 31 the compromise appeared dead and Clay defeated. But Stephen A. Douglas of Illinois realized that the Compromise could still be saved by judicious coalition building, and he felt sure that the new president, Millard Fillmore, would sign the measures into law. Douglas succeeded so well that by September 17 he had gotten passage of bills covering most items in the compromise Clay had tried to push through earlier, including two of the most contentious issues. California was admitted to the Union as a free state; and fugitive slaves would have to be captured wherever they fled and rendered back to their owners.

To Emerson the debate seemed at first merely another symptom of the "badness of the times" that was "making death attractive." That his former hero Daniel Webster would throw his weight behind the squalid compromise was bad enough, though by this time Emerson was more or less used to seeing Webster sacrifice principle for expedience. "It seem 'tis now settled that men in Congress have no Opinions; that they may be had for any opinion, any purpose," he wrote glumly in a journal entry headed "D Webster." The rush of Boston's mercantile elite to support Webster, on the other hand, elicited an outburst of contempt. "I think there was never an event half so painful occurred in Boston as the letter with 800 signatures to Webster. The siege of Boston was a day of glory. This was a day of petticoats, a day of imbecilities, the day of the old women." But Webster's mockery of Seward was the unforgivable sin. "The worst symptom I have noticed in our politics lately is the attempt to make a gibe out of Seward's appeal to a higher law than the Constitution, & Webster has taken part in it. I have seen him snubbed as *Higher-Law*-Seward." In "Montaigne," published in January 1850, Emerson had just argued that moral law was the only compass human beings had to steer them through seas of conflicting interests. Webster's ridicule of moral law threatened the one principle in human beings Emerson believed to be divine, and accordingly he called such mockery "atheism" — a term hurled often enough at Emerson during the miracles controversy, but one he almost never used himself.

When the Fugitive Slave Law finally went into effect on September 18, 1850, the abolitionists expressed their determination to oppose it. In October there was a meeting in Boston's Faneuil Hall to express indignation at the law; Theodore Parker and Wendell Phillips were speakers. For a time it seemed as if the new law might be as successfully defied as the old one had been. In the fall of 1850 the members of the Boston Vigilance Committee, which existed to protect black residents of the city from slave catchers and to assist fugitive slaves, got word that two fugitives, Ellen and William Craft, were being menaced by some men from Georgia. Parker called upon the Georgians and managed to persuade them that they themselves were not safe in Boston. Next he married the Crafts at their boardinghouse and then dispatched them to England and the protection of James Martineau.

The next case came closer to catastrophe. On February 18, 1851, Fred Wilkins (nicknamed "Shadrach"), a black waiter in a Boston coffeehouse, was arrested as a fugitive slave. He was being held prisoner in the federal courthouse when a black member of the Vigilance Committee and about twenty associates forced their way into the courthouse, swept Shadrach up into their midst, and got him away. They hid him first in Concord, and then moved him north through Vermont to Canada. Though the liberation of Shadrach looked like another victory, the apparent willingness of Chief Justice Lemuel Shaw of the state supreme court of Massachusetts to enforce the statute was a shock to those who had publicly boasted (as Theodore Parker did a year earlier) that no power on earth could force Bostonians to perpetuate slavery.

Finally disaster arrived. On April 3, 1851, a seventeen-year-old boy named Thomas Sims was captured in Boston and held in the federal courthouse, which was guarded heavily this time to prevent any attempts at rescue. Sims's lawyers tried every argument to persuade Justice Shaw (who was Herman Melville's father-in-law) to free Sims, but in vain. At four o'clock in the morning three hundred soldiers escorted Sims through a jeering crowd who cried "Shame!" at the soldiers but could not block their progress toward the docks, where Sims was put on a ship for Georgia. (As if to drive home the humiliation of Massachusetts, Sims's owner had him publicly whipped in Savannah on the anniversary of the Battle of Lexington and Concord.)

In April 1851 Emerson had formally declared his opposition to the Fugitive Slave Law by sending a letter to the annual meeting of the Middlesex Anti-slavery Society. Emerson apologized for not being able to attend the meeting in person (he was off on a lecture tour), but he declared his determination to oppose the "detestable statute" passed by Congress. He urged everyone to defend fugitive slaves against their owners. The tone of the letter, which was written in mid-March, is one of calm determination rather than anger. Although fugitive slaves had been caught and delivered up to their owners in other states, Emerson may have believed that greater devotion to liberty in Massachusetts would continue to drive the slave catchers out of the state empty-handed. Unfortunately, the day of the Middlesex meeting (April 3) was also the day Thomas Sims was captured in Boston.

The rendition of Sims moved Emerson from controlled anger to white-hot fury. The editors of his journals point out that he filled eighty-six manuscript pages of his 1851 journal with entries devoted to Webster, the Fugitive Slave Law, and the shame both were bringing upon the state that was the birthplace of American liberty. "Boston, of whose fame for spirit & character we have all been so proud. . . . Boston, which figures so proudly in Adams's diary, which we all have been reading: Boston, through the personal influence of this New Hampshire man, must bow its proud spirit in the dust, & make us irretrievably ashamed."

Emerson now had a full-blown case of what John Jay Chapman calls "the disease of antislavery" and felt obliged to take some kind of direct personal action. When the townspeople of Concord approached him on April 26, 1851, requesting that he speak to them on the subject of the Fugitive Slave Law, he agreed. On May 3 he delivered the first of his addresses on the law. The address, which was one of the strongest of his career, draws upon the diatribes with which Emerson had been filling his journals; its reiterated themes are the corruption of the land by the law and the cowardice of the citizens who allowed the law into the land. City and country are "involved in one hot haste of terror," journals are paralyzed with panic, and "one cannot open a newspaper, without being disgusted by new records of shame." The irony of all these attempts to protect property, as Emerson points out, is the loss of its value. The Fugitive Slave Law has caused a collapse in land values all over the nation. "The very convenience of property, the house and land we occupy, have lost their best value, and a man looks gloomily at his children, and thinks, 'What have I done that you should begin life in dishonor?' "

Nevertheless, there is one great benefit to be derived from the recent disgraces. "The crisis had the illuminating power of a sheet of lightning at midnight. It showed truth." All of the protestations of love and the odes to liberty are revealed to be shams, and the poor black boy who has heard of the fame of Boston as he hides in his southern swamp finds out when he gets to the city that "the famous town of Boston is his master's hound" and that he has "taken the risk of being shot, or burned alive, or cast into the sea, or starved to death, or suffocated in a wooden box, to get away from his driver" only to be hunted by the men of Massachusetts and sent back to the dog hutch he had fled.

Yet the loss of state honor pales before the greater skepticism Emerson says has been induced by the law. In a sudden transition to sadness he lists all of the beliefs that the Fugitive Slave Law has caused him to give up, the first being the belief that passage of the law would instantly arouse "all moral beings" to resist it. But if Massachusetts has so far failed to rise up against the law, Webster has been no more successful in using the compromise to silence the debate about slavery. "Mr. Webster's measure was, he told us, final. . . . Does it look final now? His final settlement has dislocated the foundations. The state-house shakes like a tent." In fact, the law has "been like a university to the entire people. It has turned every dinner-table into a debating-club, and made every citizen a student of natural law."

What lessons are taught in this university? First of all, that the Fugitive Slave Law must be resisted. "It must be abrogated and wiped out of the statute-book; but, whilst it stands there, it must be disobeyed." As for the larger question, Emerson argues only that slavery should be kept out of the territories; after that, the free states should help the slave states to make a peaceful end to slavery – if necessary, by buying the slaves, as the British nation bought the slaves of the West Indian planters. "I do not think any amount that figures could tell, founded on an estimate, would be quite unmanageable. Every man in the world might give a week's work to sweep this mountain of calamities out of the earth." This thought revives Emerson's spirits, and the address ends on a note of hope. "We must make a small State great, by making every man in it true."

In a sign of the way that the struggle against slavery was overcoming old antagonisms, Emerson was asked to repeat his Concord address as a stump speech for John Gorham Palfrey, who had been dean of the Harvard Divinity

School at the time of the Divinity School Address and who was now seeking election to Congress on the Free Soil ticket. Emerson agreed, repeating his Fugitive Slave Law address at various places during the spring of 1851. At Cambridge toward the end of May he was hooted and hissed at by Harvard students who shouted the praises of Webster and Edward Everett; he maintained his composure, simply continuing with the next word in his speech when the hubbub died down. Though Palfrey lost the election Emerson found the experience of speaking out against the law in public exhilarating. In a letter to Theodore Parker thanking him for a printed Fast-Day Sermon ("The Chief Sins of the People") attacking the Fugitive Slave Law, Emerson mentions having read five similar speeches and says, "It half exculpates the State, that the protest of the minority is so amply & admirably uttered in the very place & hour of the crime" (Emerson to Parker, April 18, 1851).

The next summer held a bittersweet confirmation of Emerson's belief in the inerrancy of the moral law when Daniel Webster's final try at securing the 1852 Whig nomination for president went down to humiliating defeat. Webster had come to believe that obeying the law was a "Christian duty"; he had encouraged the marshals to arrest fugitive slaves and had accused their rescuers of treason; he had expressed his approval of the rendition of Sims. Now it appeared that Webster's support for the Fugitive Slave Law had been for nothing. Passage of the law had not stopped the agitation of the slavery question in the North, and it had not won the loyalty of the Southerners in his own party. In the Baltimore convention in June 1852 Webster received only 21 out of the 294 Whig votes; the rest of the votes were divided between Millard Fillmore and General Winfield Scott (who finally won the nomination on the fifty-third ballot). Emerson summed up the sad end of Webster's once-glorious career: "To please the South betrayed the North, and was thrown out by both."

Webster did not long outlive his rejection by the Whigs. He died in October 1852. Emerson marked the event by writing in his journal some passages of admiration for the man who had once been his hero. But no tenderness for the dead kept Emerson from cursing Webster for bringing an evil law upon the land. When Emerson was invited in 1854 to deliver an address in New York to mark the fourth anniversary of Webster's Seventh of March speech, he carefully sketched out for his audience the reasons for Webster's previous greatness as a speaker — his manners, his carriage, the simplicity and wisdom of his rhetoric, and the power of his character, which could make his wrath the wrath of the cause he stood for. Yet in the hour of decision Webster had thrown his whole weight on the side of slavery and made the speech that corrupted the country. Its goodness or badness as a piece of logic or rhetoric was not in question. "Nobody doubts that Daniel

Webster could make a good speech. Nobody doubts that there were good and plausible things to be said on the part of the south. But this is not a question of ingenuity, not a question of syllogisms, but of sides. How came he there?"

The need for choosing sides would soon be on everyone's mind again. After the rendition of Sims in 1851 there were no more fugitive slave cases in Massachusetts for several years, and the intense anger aroused by that case gradually dissipated or sought an outlet in more conventional political activity. But on Thursday, May 25, 1854, an escaped Virginia slave named Anthony Burns was seized in Boston, where he had been working in a store. Like Shadrach and Thomas Sims before him, Burns was held prisoner in the federal courthouse in Boston, where he was to be tried on Saturday morning. Antislavery activists planned to hold a protest meeting in Faneuil Hall on Friday night. Members of the Boston Vigilance Committee held a meeting on Friday morning to try to plot some kind of rescue.

Vigilance Committee meetings, however, involved an unruly collection of individualists, completely untrained for revolutionary action and accustomed to follow their own consciences alone in schemes of reform. Thomas Wentworth Higginson (1823–1911), a Unitarian minister who would go on to become the literary mentor chosen by Emily Dickinson and the colonel of the first regiment of black soldiers in the Union army, remembered the Vigilance Committee meetings as "disorderly conventions, each man having his own plan or theory, perhaps stopping even for anecdote or disquisition, when the occasion required the utmost promptness of decision and the most unflinching unity in action." The Faneuil Hall meeting on Friday morning was as unruly as usual, and Higginson despaired of Burns's rescue. The United States marshals guarding Burns would certainly be prepared for a mob assault on the courthouse building after this meeting. Then a Vigilance Committee member named Martin Stowell suggested a plan that contained an element of surprise:

Could there not be an attack at the very height of the meeting, brought about in this way? Let all be in readiness; let a picked body be distributed near the Court House and Square; then send some loud-voiced speaker, who should appear in the gallery of Faneuil Hall and announce that there was a mob of negroes already attacking the Court-House; let a speaker, previously warned . . . accept the opportunity promptly, and send the whole meeting pell-mell to the Courthouse Square, ready to fall in behind the leaders and bring out the slave.

Higginson prepared a box of axes for an assault on the courthouse doors and joined in picking a small band of white and black men to lead the assault. But the plot failed. The Faneuil Hall meeting was so much larger than the Vigilance Committee had expected, filling the galleries, the floors, the stairways, that the chosen messenger could not get into the gallery to shout the prearranged signal. Higginson waited with the other men in Court House Square for a mob that never arrived. Then, just as Higginson had given up hope of rescuing Burns, Stowell appeared and whispered that he and some men were bringing a wooden beam up to the west side of the building and would attempt to hammer down the courthouse door.

At the time of the Sims case Higginson had noted in his journal how difficult it was "to educate the mind to the attitude of revolution. It is so strange to find one's self outside of established institutions . . . to see law and order, police and military, on the wrong side, and find good citizenship a sin and bad citizenship a duty, that it takes time to prepare one to act coolly and wisely, as well as courageously, in such an emergency." Now, three years later, he found himself at the head of a battering party, facing a muscular black man across a wooden beam they were using to try to smash in the doors of the Boston courthouse.

Eventually the door gave way and swung open wide enough for one man to pass through the opening. The black man jumped in; Higginson followed. The six or eight police officers who had been attempting to keep the door shut from within began clubbing them savagely, and one of the marshal's deputies inside the building fell dead — either stabbed by Higginson's black companion or shot by someone in the battering party still outside. Gradually both attackers were forced back across the threshold, where they discovered that their supporters had fallen back to the bottom of the courthouse steps. Though the chances looked slim Higginson still waited near the threshold hoping for reinforcements. Just at that moment Amos Bronson Alcott came forth from the crowd below. "Ascending the lighted steps alone, he said tranquilly, turning to me and pointing forward, 'Why are we not within?' " Higginson answered impatiently that the rest of the people would not stand by them. "He said not a word, but calmly walked up the steps, — he and his familiar cane. He paused again at the top, the centre of all eyes, within and without; a revolver sounded from within, but hit nobody; and finding himself wholly unsupported, he turned and retreated, but without hastening a step."

Alcott's serenity on this occasion seemed to Higginson worthy of Plato or Pythagoras. But if Alcott's trust in absolute spirit represented the driving force behind the antislavery movement, the murder of the marshal's deputy was a better predictor of what was to come. "In all the long procession of events which led the nation through the Kansas struggle, past the John Brown foray, and up to the Emanciption Proclamation, the killing of Batchelder was the first act of violence. It was, like the firing on Fort Sumter, a proof that war had really begun."

Warned by the magnitude of the disturbance, the federal government sent in troops – two companies of artillery and two of marines – to escort Burns back to the ship that took him south on June 2. The sense of outrage and violation now seemed complete. The black residents of Massachusetts were helpless before slave catchers; the white residents who tried to protect or rescue fugitive slaves saw themselves invaded by their own government as if they were a captured nation. The sense of humiliation was intensified when Massachusetts residents learned that the hated Kansas–Nebraska bill had finally passed Congress the day after Burns's arrest. Introduced by Senator Stephen A. Douglas in January, the bill opened the territory west of Missouri to settlement by slave owners and thus repealed the Missouri Compromise of 1820, which had prohibited slavery north of 36°30′ in the territory acquired in the Louisiana Purchase. This repeal violated an agreement the North had come to regard as sacred and raised fears that, as Massachusetts senator Charles Sumner wrote to Emerson, "new outrages are at hand, in the concatenation by which the Despotism of Slavery is to be fastened upon the National Govt." (Sumner to Emerson, June 12, 1854).

When the customary celebrations of the nation's birthday came in 1854 they seemed a mockery. Ellen, the Emerson's daughter, remembered that her mother, Lidian,

considered our country wholly lost to any sense of righteousness, and hearing that there was to be some celebration of the Day, and seeing flags go up, she asked Father's leave to cover our gates with a pall. Father smiled and consented. So she got a quantity of black cambric, and made a great show of it on our front gate and gate-posts.

Henry Thoreau, too, was celebrating an unconventional Fourth of July at an antislavery rally in Framingham, where he read parts of an address entitled "Slavery in Massachusetts." Garrison, who had also spoken at the Framingham rally, printed the whole text of Thoreau's address in the *Liberator* for July 21; it was reprinted again by Greeley in the *Tribune* on August 2 and partially reprinted in the *National Anti-Slavery Standard* on August 12.

"Slavery in Massachusetts" grows directly out of Thoreau's journal passages written during the Burns affair. But Thoreau also used journal passages he had written about the rendition of Thomas Sims three years earlier. The "moral earthquake" in both cases had taken place without awakening the slightest resistance from the elected officials of Massachusetts, who sat tamely by while southern planters transformed them into slave catchers. "The whole military force of the State is at the service of a Mr. Suttle, a slaveholder from Virginia, to enable him to catch a man whom he calls his property; but not a soldier is offered to save a citizen of Massachusetts from being kidnapped!" The trial of Burns (like that of Sims before him) is really a trial of Massachusetts. "Every moment that she hesitated to set this man free – every moment that he now hesitates to atone for her crime, she is convicted."

Where is a slave to turn for comfort? To the courts? They regard him as property. To the governor of Massachusetts? The worst that can be said of him is that in the midst of the crisis nobody bothered to inquire after him or noticed his absence. "The law will never make men free; it is men who have got to make the law free. They are the lovers of law and order, who observe the law when the government breaks it." And again: "Whoever has discerned truth, has received his commission from a higher source than the chiefest justice in the world, who can discern only law. He finds himself constituted judge of the judge."

What should concern the state of Massachusetts is not the Kansas–Nebraska bill but her own "slaveholding and servility." People who think that government exists to protect property should remember that the value of life itself is diminished in a state that has lost its liberties. "I have lived for the last month," Thoreau says, "with the sense of having suffered a vast and indefinite loss. I did not know at first what ailed me. At last it occurred to me that what I had lost was a country."

That sense of collective loss makes "Slavery in Massachusetts" differ markedly from "Resistance to Civil Government," even when the 1854 address borrows arguments and imagery from the earlier essay. Though Thoreau now says that his thoughts "are murder to the State, and involuntarily go plotting against her," his protest is no longer an individual one. He speaks at a rally, not at a country lyceum, and gives his address to the newspapers, not to a fledgling journal of aesthetics that lasted for only one issue and attracted only fifty subscribers. The affectation of indifference to public life cultivated in "Resistance to Civil Government" is gone. Thoreau now speaks as a citizen to citizens, and with a sense of urgency. "We have used up all our inherited freedom. If we would save our lives, we must fight for them."

Yet dark as the times seemed, there were signs of hope. Charles Sumner had been chosen senator by the Massachusetts Legislature after nearly four months of political wrangling in 1851, and though Sumner lacked Webster's genius and Webster's influence he had been a committed opponent of the Fugitive Slave Law since its passage, several times attempting (without success) to move its repeal. In the spring of 1854 he turned his fury upon the Kansas–Nebraska bill. As one of only three Free Soil party members in the Senate he could do little to prevent the passage of the bill, but he could speak against it in lengthy orations that were quickly telegraphed back to his native state.

Sumner found more sympathy even among conservative Whigs than anyone could have predicted six months earlier. The Kansas–Nebraska bill seemed to most people a betrayal of the agreement Webster had persuaded them to accept in 1850. Worse still, it threatened to open to slaveholders northern territories bordering on free states – territories that people in the North believed had been secured permanently for freedom by the terms of the Missouri Compromise of 1820. On May 24, 1854, the day the Senate met to give its final approval to the Kansas–Nebraska bill, Sumner rose to denounce it as the worst bill ever enacted by Congress. But he also praised it as the best – because it "annuls all past compromises with Slavery, and makes all future compromises impossible. Thus it puts Freedom and Slavery face to face, and bids them grapple. Who can doubt the result?" That the reports of Sumner's speech reached Boston the day after the failed attempt to rescue Anthony Burns only gave it more point.

Political parties were thrown into disarray by the outrage over the Kansas–Nebraska bill. Democrats suffered defections because the bill was a Democratic piece of legislation; Whigs, because their dissension had rendered them too weak to prevent the bill's passage. New political parties sprouted all over the country, hoping to gain converts among disgruntled Democrats and Whigs. In Massachusetts the biggest gainers were not the Free-Soilers, as one might have expected, but the anti-immigrant, anti-Catholic party popularly called the Know-Nothings, which had been organized in response to the massive influx of immigrants during the late 1840s and 1850s. In the November 1854 elections the Massachusetts Know-Nothings got 63 percent of the vote; the voters returned a state legislature consisting of 1 Whig, 1 Democrat, and 377 Know-Nothings. That the long Whig dominance of the legislature should have been broken might have been hailed as a cause for celebration by progressives, but that it should have been broken by a collection of disreputable rabble-rousers like the Know-Nothings was dispiriting in the extreme. Rufus Choate, a Whig of the old school, remarked after the election: "Any thing more low, obscene, feculant, the manifold heavings of history have not cast up."

Emerson was inclined to agree, though he thought the inglorious way the two traditional parties had been turned out of office deserved rather to be called an "immense frolic," a mad joke that had gone too far. In a new lecture, "American Slavery," which he first delivered in Boston on January 26, 1855 (and repeated seven times in succeeding months), Emerson tries to make some sense of the moral and political upheavals of the preceding half decade. Many of the themes are familiar. Emerson manifests contempt for the elected northern officials who truckled to the South – "They ate dirt, and saw not the sneer of the bullies who duped them with an alleged state-necessity; And all because they had no burning splendor of law in their own minds." He professes a familiar faith in the "sound healthy universe" that can "rid itself at last of every crime," as a snake casts its skin by spasms. And he still finds the only trustworthy moral compass in the faith of "private men who have brave hearts and great minds." Indeed, "this is the compensation of bad governments, – the field it affords for illustrious men."

Yet there is a new note in the lecture, which tries to take the longest possible view of the question of slavery. "But whilst I insist on the doctrine of the independence and the inspiration of the individual, I do not cripple but exalt the social action," Emerson asserts. Society, it turns out, is more than the joint-stock company he had contemptuously termed it in "Self-Reliance." Now he argues that the state is a reality, and that it is "certain that societies of men, a race, a people, have a public function, a part to play in the history of humanity." And what is America's part? "The theory of our government is Liberty." Liberty is not a fact or a private opinion; it is "a gradual and irresistible growth of the human mind."

It is for this reason that every American is justified, where there is a collision in statutes, to decide in favor of liberty. If the law is unjust, we must be willing to "put the Tea overboard in the Harbor, and hunt the slave hunter, – must destroy the law before the principle." For if it is true that "heaven too has a hand in these events, and will surely give the last shape to these ends which we hew very roughly," it is also true that "our will and obedience is one of its means." In this collective effort even the scholar has a part to play, despite his unfitness for political strife. The curse of America is that its "immense industrial energy" has not been accompanied by "a great imaginative soul, a broad cosmopolitan mind." Hence the frivolity of its politics, the cruelty of its institutions, the superficiality of its culture. In this hubbub of conflicting voices, the scholar alone can recall his fellow citizens to a sense of the ideals they have abandoned, for "God instructs men through the Imagination."

This faith had animated the Transcendentalists from the beginning. In the heady days of the miracles controversy, when public discussion in New England for a time was focused on disputes within the Unitarian church, the Transcendentalists had been the "movement party," full of all the confidence revolutionary zeal generates in its possessors. But the stresses of the 1840s had been hard on them. If like Orestes Brownson they proposed schemes of radical social reform, they were blasted by angry responses clear into reaction and authoritarianism. If like George Ripley they tried to move from theory directly into social practice, they came to grief over the stinginess of nature, the recalcitrance of human beings, and the brusque laws of the marketplace. If like Theodore Parker they remained within the church and tried to reform it, they found the ice of entrenched conservatism depressingly resistant to the flame of zeal.

Refusing to enlist in any of these causes and insisting upon the integrity and authenticity of the individual self, as Emerson and Thoreau largely did, protected both men from this kind of disillusionment. But that carried its own costs: self-reproach, feelings of impotence and sometimes of unreality, and awareness that the proud refusal to be contaminated by inauthenticity could easily look like cowardice or petulance. Even Emerson never really understood what Thoreau was driving at by his night in the Concord jail or his move to the cabin at Walden, and Thoreau was contemptuous of the web of accommodations that allowed Emerson to turn out militant lectures and books in his study while leading a comfortable life in his Concord house.

The political indignities of the early 1850s, however, degrading as they were, confirmed Emerson and Thoreau in their sense that they had been right to insist on private integrity before all else – only in private integrity was there any defense against the stupidity of government or the immorality of law. The health of any democratic government depends upon the virtue of the individual citizen, for when the government has become corrupt only the rectitude of the citizens can restore what it has lost or abandoned. "When the public fails in its duty, private men take its place," Emerson said in "American Slavery." Emerson had not understood in 1846 what Thoreau had hoped to accomplish by his lonely protest against the Mexican War. Now, in 1855, after the Sims and Burns cases, after the Kansas-Nebraska bill, Emerson understands that "we have a great debt to the brave and faithful men who in the hour and place of the evil act, make their protest for themselves and their countrymen, by word and deed." Far from being eccentrics, such men are the genius and future of the tribe.

Emerson thought well enough of "American Slavery" to write to his old friend William Henry Furness that he was willing to deliver it in Philadelphia. "I have a pretty good lecture this time, – good for me, or good 'considering'" (Emerson to Furness, January 26, 1855). But even this minimal confidence slowly evaporated. Though Emerson gave the speech seven more times he refused to write another when Furness asked him for one the next fall. "I believe I make the worst Antislavery discourses that are made in this country. They are only less bad than Slavery. I incline this winter to promise none" (Emerson to Furness, October 1, 1855).

Events though drew Emerson out of retirement. In 1856 open warfare had broken out in Kansas between groups of "border ruffians" from Missouri, determined to organize the new territory as a slave state, and emigrants from the free states, who wanted to keep the territory free. New Englanders raised money to send aid and weapons to the settlers. The struggle was at once depressing and portentous. A letter from Furness to Emerson written in the fall of 1856 expresses the contradictory feelings perfectly. Furness laments the current state of affairs in the United States. "What a mess the country is & how the elements spit & sputter." Yet he also says: "The struggle is tremendous. It is the world's battle. The regeneration of Europe is to be decided here. How grand it is to see the cause of God & man making its way against the passions, the interests, the will of man!" (Furness to Emerson, October 18, 1856).

On May 19, 1856, Senator Charles Sumner began delivering a lengthy speech in the Senate against the "border ruffians" who were ravaging Kansas and the slave powers that supported them. "The Crime Against Kansas" was full of tasteless invective, some of it directed against the dignified elderly senator from South Carolina, Andrew P. Butler, and the state he represented. Sumner finished his speech on the next day. Butler had been absent from the Senate when Sumner spoke, but a young cousin of his, Representative Preston Brooks of South Carolina, had come over to the Senate to hear the speech and was outraged by it. Determined to avenge the insults to both kinsman and state, he waited for an opportunity to give Sumner a thrashing and finally found it when, on May 22, he saw Sumner seated alone at his desk after the Senate had adjourned, franking printed copies of "The Crime Against Kansas" (112 pages long). Brooks began beating Sumner savagely over the head with a cane, giving him about thirty blows during the time it took him to get out from beneath his heavy Senate desk and try to flee. The bleeding Sumner finally tore the desk from the floor as he rose, staggered a few feet, and collapsed. Brooks was still raining down blows when two other representatives intervened to pull him away.

Brooks quickly became a hero to fire-eating Southerners (his constituents voted to give him one gold-headed cane, and the students at the University of Virginia collected money for another). With the same speed Charles Sumner became a martyr to the North, where tens of thousands of copies of his "Crime Against Kansas" speech were distributed. Anger in Massachusetts was intense, particularly because the news of the assault upon Sumner reached the state just as news of a proslavery raid upon the free-state town of Lawrence, Kansas, arrived. Border thuggery and Brooks's cowardly attack upon a defenseless man were denounced together in the protest rallies held in large cities and small towns all over the North.

Emerson spoke at the Concord meeting, held on May 26, 1856. "The Assault upon Mr. Sumner" opens with an admission that the hopes for peaceful reconciliation with which "American Slavery" closed have been dashed by the ugliness of recent events. The time for compromise has ended. "I do not see how a barbarous community and a civilized community can constitute one state. I think we must get rid of slavery, or we must get rid of freedom." Sumner had endeared himself to Emerson as much by his refusals as by his deeds: by his refusal to seek votes during the long months when his first election to the Senate was pending, by his refusal to be hurried by the importunities of his abolitionist friends into speaking on the subject of slavery before he was ready. If he had been hesitant at first on the Senate floor, he has now gone beyond expectation, and "every friend of freedom thinks of him as the friend of freedom."

Kansas claimed Emerson's attention too. He attended meetings of the Kansas Aid Society in Concord, and on September 10, 1856, he delivered his speech on affairs in Kansas. The beginning sounds like propaganda; Emerson writes of "the screams of hunted wives and children answered by the howl of the butchers." But he quickly moves beyond cliché as he contemplates the single lesson history now seems to teach:

I do not know any story so gloomy as the politics of this country for the last twenty years, centralizing ever more manifestly round one spring, and that a vast crime, and ever more plainly, until it is notorious that all promotion, power, and policy are dictated from one source — illustrating the fatal effects of a false position to demoralize legislation and put the best people always at a disadvantage; — one crime always present, — always to be varnished over, to find fine names for, and we free-statesmen, as accomplices to the guilt, ever in the power of the grand offender.

The power of crime to imprison the country is matched by its power to deface language. If wise men pierce rotten diction and fasten words to things, vicious men dislocate innocent words from their referents and paper over cruelty with euphemism. "Language has lost its meaning in the universal cant. *Representative Government* is really misrepresentative; ... the *adding of Cuba and Central America* to the slave marts is *enlarging the area of Freedom.*" Quietly, firmly, Emerson restores an abused word — *anarchy* — to its root when he says, "I am glad to see that the terror at disunion and anarchy is disappearing. Massachusetts, in its heroic day, had no government — was an anarchy. Every man stood on his own feet, was his own governor; and there was no breach of peace from Cape Cod to Mount Hoosac." The real danger is not that the social bonds are too weak but that they are too strong: "Vast property, gigantic interests, family connections, webs of party, cover the land with a network that immensely multiplies the dangers of war." If the defenders of freedom will not make a stand soon, they will find themselves, like the exiles who sought America in 1848, forced "to gather up their clothes and depart to some land where freedom exists."

What Emerson did not know when he gave his speech on affairs in Kansas was that recent events in that territory were to involve him once again in political action, this time on the side not of the victim but of the aggressor. On the night of May 24, 1856, a Kansas emigrant named John Brown, angered by proslavery raiders who harassed free-state settlements like

Lawrence and driven to fury by the news of the assault on Charles Sumner in the Senate Chamber, led seven men from a volunteer free-state militia known as the Pottawatomie Rifle Company to attack men associated with the proslavery forces (one of them a member of the territorial legislature). During their rampage, at each place Brown and his men stopped they shot or hacked to death with broadswords unarmed men. At one cabin they killed a father and two sons; at another they hacked to death a husband in front of his wife. They killed five people in all before rejoining their unit.

Regarding this act of terror, Thomas Wentworth Higginson (who was then in Kansas directing parties of free-state emigrants) claimed he had heard no one among the free-state men who did not approve of its beneficial effects in giving an "immediate check to the armed aggressions of the Missourians." But in fact many free-state residents of Kansas were horrified by Brown's deed, which helped fan what had been disorganized skirmishing into full-scale civil war.

Accurate news from Kansas traveled with difficulty. When Brown appeared in the East early in 1857 to raise money to continue the fight against the proslavery forces in Kansas, the Transcendentalists who heard him speak either did not know of the "Pottawatomie massacre" or chose to believe the antislavery press accounts of it, accounts that tried to place the blame on the proslavery forces themselves. To sympathizers in New England, Brown seemed like a Covenanter imagined by Sir Walter Scott, a man of zeal whose military bearing promised an end to the North's years of humiliation and victimization – in the bungled rescue of Burns, in the beating of Sumner, and in the threat of slave-power expansion in the Midwest and Southwest. In February 1857 Brown came to Concord to speak at the Town Hall about the war in Kansas and to ask for aid. He had lunch with the Thoreaus and there met Emerson, who invited him to stay his second night in town with the Emersons and later wrote approvingly of Brown's speech in his journal.

For the next two years Brown alternated between fund-raising in the East and fighting in Kansas and Missouri, where his band killed a slave owner and led eleven slaves to freedom. But his plans were growing grander. He told the "Secret Six" (a group of northern sympathizers that included Parker and Higginson) of his plans to send armed men into Virginia to set up mountain camps or settlements to which slaves could escape. Here they could either live in freedom or be forwarded along the underground railroad to Canada. To the general public Brown continued to appeal for money to fight slavery in Kansas. Emerson gave fifty dollars, Thoreau a smaller sum.

Even members of the Secret Six were startled when they heard of Brown's seizure of the federal arsenal at Harper's Ferry, Virginia, on the night of October 16, 1859. If (as his prosectors later alleged) he was hoping to start a slave insurrection and then arm the slave with the weapons from the arsenal, his conduct was bizarre: he picked a site impossible to defend, attacked it with only eighteen men (carrying no rations), and made no effort to alert the slaves he planned to free of his presence or of his intentions. Though Brown's men did hold the arsenal for thirty-six hours, a detachment of U.S. marines commanded by Colonel Robert E. Lee easily retook it, killing ten of Brown's men and wounding him. More than one person wondered if Brown were mad, but he appeared lucid and self-possessed during the week-long trial that followed quickly upon his capture. Indeed, his calmness during his imprisonment under sentence of death impressed even Governor Wise of Virginia, who called him "cool, collected, and indomitable."

Brown had been sentenced to death on November 1. His hanging was set for December 2. In the weeks leading up to the execution both Emerson and Thoreau praised his heroism and pleaded publicly for his life. But many people in the North were shocked by Brown's suicidal raid and frightened by the evidence that he hoped to start a slave insurrection. It was partly to counter such a reaction that Thoreau announced on October 30 (the day before the sentence was handed down) that he would deliver "A Plea for Captain John Brown" in Concord, ringing the town bell himself. On November 1 he repeated the lecture at the Tremont Temple in Boston (filling in for Frederick Douglass) and gave it again on November 3 in Worcester. On November 8 Emerson delivered a lecture entitled "Courage" to Theodore Parker's society at the Boston Music Hall, praising Brown, just as his 1838 lecture "Heroism" had praised Elijah Lovejoy. (Parker himself had been driven by his worsening tuberculosis to leave Boston for Europe in quest of better health in February 1859, long before Harper's Ferry.) On November 18 Emerson spoke at the Tremont Temple in Boston at a meeting to raise funds for John Brown's family. When Brown was executed on December 2, Thoreau helped arrange a memorial service in Concord at which he read selections about heroism drawn from his commonplace books, and Emerson read Brown's last speech. In Boston, James Freeman Clarke preached a funeral sermon for Brown to his Church of the Disciples. Emerson delivered a new speech entitled "John Brown" at Salem on January 6, 1860. Finally, Thoreau wrote "The Last Days of John Brown," to be read at a Fourth-of-July "John Brown Celebration" held in North Elba, New York, where Brown was buried and where his widow still resided.

One of the objections to David Friedrich Strauss's hypothesis that the gospels were mythical was that not enough time had elapsed between the death of Jesus and the writing of the gospels for the mythical imagination to transfigure history. In these Transcendentalist orations about John Brown the shaping of history into myth begins while Brown is still alive. Brown is not

merely a hero, he is an "Angel of Light" – saintly as a Puritan, courageous as
the defenders of Lexington and Concord, powerful as Cromwell, romantic as
a figure out of Scott, self-sacrificing as the Redeemer who by his suffering
and death bought again mankind.

What Brown's deed offered to the people of the North was an escape from
the degradation of the last ten years, when every blow, every jeer, every insult
came from the South, and Northerners could do no more than weakly protest
and shamefully concede. "The politics of Massachusetts are cowardly," Emerson said. "We want will that advances and dictates." Thoreau put it even
more strongly: "We aspire to be something more than stupid and timid
chattels, pretending to read history and our bibles, but desecrating every
house and every day we breathe in."

The best proof of Brown's Messiahship, in fact, is the tendency of worshippers to see their own features in Brown's character. To Thoreau, Brown is
the perfect soldier, tough, self-reliant, and ascetic, who can live in swamps
and learn the lore of Indians, and who is full of contempt for the opulent
tables of the rich and for the warriors who believe they can win victories with
words. To Emerson, Brown is the man of courage whose character converts
enemies into admirers and whose radiance sheds grace on circumstances, even
the most ignominious, making the gallows as glorious as the cross. But both
Emerson and Thoreau agree on the quickening power of Brown's practical
demonstration of manhood. "Let us say then frankly that the education of the
will is the object of our existence," Emerson says in "Courage." And Brown is
will incarnate, will confronting the impossible and refusing to quail before
it. Such courage exhilarates and puts a new face on everything. "Everything
feels the new breath except the old doting nigh-dead politicians, whose heart
the trumpet of resurrection could not wake," Emerson says, and Thoreau
remarks that some men who were thinking of committing suicide have now
changed their minds. Brown finally comes in these orations to take on the
characteristics of the Transcendentalist Reason. To Emerson he is "transparent," a "pure idealist, with no by-ends of his own." To Thoreau he is "a
transcendentalist above all." He is "pure spirit himself, and his sword is pure
spirit." Even the brevity of his conquest adds to its glory. "His life was
meteor-like, flashing through the darkness in which we live."

For Northerners, the 1850s began in humiliation, proceeded through shame,
and ended in a desire for revenge, a desire that John Brown both made
conscious and symbolized. But the same decade also saw the publication of
Emerson's *English Traits* and *The Conduct of Life* and Thoreau's *A Yankee in
Canada* and *Walden,* together with parts of his *Cape Cod* and *The Maine Woods,*
and the expansion of Thoreau's journals into a massive project of observation

and representation that contains some of his most brilliant writing. Though the gloom of the political situation sometimes causes these texts to plummet into misanthropy or nihilism, the new conviction of authority that the crisis of the times gave to Transcendentalists as moral philosophers more than compensated for the despair. During the 1840s Transcendentalists had often felt as if they were outside the main streams of human activity, either defiantly or plangently proclaiming their desire to be left alone. Even "Resistance to Civil Government," the most famous political document the movement produced, is full of the imagery of secession; its central statement is probably Thoreau's declaration that he would like to sign off of all societies he had never signed on to, if only he knew where to find a complete list.

For now, however, dragged from the study or the wood to protest the rendition of escaped slaves, the war in Kansas, the assault upon Sumner, or the execution of Brown, the Transcendentalists find that their old gospel – the primacy of the moral law, the innocence of nature, the centrality of intuition – is newly needed in a society corrupted by a deadly combination of material prosperity and moral bankruptcy. If God instructs through the imagination then artists are his prophets. They speak with authority and not as the scribes.

The effects of this transformation are evident in the two books Emerson published during the decade that ended in 1860, *English Traits* and *The Conduct of Life*. Both volumes take up familiar themes – the necessity of self-reliance, the war between impulse and limitation, the saving insanity of egotism, and the adequacy of the moral sentiment as a stay and anchor in a world bereft of the old religions. But both are also shaped by Emerson's need to incorporate into his writing the inevitable changes that time and experience had brought to him as he traveled from a New England giddy with experiments to renovate the world to an England solid with the complacency of achieved empire and to a France agitated by revolution – only to return to a homeland humiliated and debased by its compromises with slavery.

Had Emerson been a younger man he might have called for the overthrow of institutions, but he was forty-six when the decade began, already (as he would put it) "ripened beyond the prospect of sincere radicalism," and his respect for institutions had grown along with his success. Yet it had not grown so great that it pushed him into mere reaction – the immediate revulsion Emerson felt at the Fugitive Slave Law proved that the moral perfection he had followed in his youth was still the only deity worthy of his worship. Indeed, the derelictions of government made every stick of property in the commonwealth worth less, and so prudence and idealism at last pointed the same way.

The Conduct of Life was not published until 1860, but the book grew out of a series of lectures Emerson delivered first in the troubled winter of 1850–1. The book announces itself on its first page as a guide to conduct, as an answer to the question "How Shall I Live?" Several of its chapters – "Wealth," "Culture," "Behavior," "Beauty," and "Considerations by the Way" – offer advice to an audience eager to achieve refinement but not sure how to go about acquiring it in a country with rudimentary notions of civility and scarcely any idea of culture. Emerson refuses to give up his old belief in the principle of compensation, but he now extends its sway beyond the boundaries of the individual life. Thus he notes that the monomaniacs of trade are responsible for netting America with railroads and dotting it with factories, and he points out that the selfish capitalist does more for the welfare of the race than do benefactors like Florence Nightingale. "This *speculative* genius is the madness of a few for the gain of the world." But he also points out that temporary advantages prove in the long run illusory, just as the inflated prices that American traders charged the European nations during the Napoleonic wars serve only to create a glittering prosperity that drew to American shores millions of the European poor who then demanded to be fed and educated.

On a higher plane than behavior is religion. But the essay "Worship," is concerned not with religion itself but with the plight of nineteenth-century men and women facing the collapse of institutional Christianity. "The stern old faiths have all pulverized," Emerson notes, leaving behind "a whole population of gentlemen and ladies out in search of religions." Nearly thirteen years after the Divinity School Address Emerson realizes with amusement and chagrin that the trumpet he had set to his lips to bring down Jericho had been unnecessary; Jericho would have tumbled anyway. The "churches that once sucked the roots of right and wrong . . . now have perished away till they are a speck of whitewash on the wall." A French journal's brief explanation for rejecting an article entitled "Dieu" – "*La question de Dieu manque d'actualité*" – is more devastating than anything in Strauss.

Still, worship was never religion, and religion is in no danger of collapse merely because the old forms of worship are passing away. If the moral crisis of 1850 showed anything, it was that "the moral sense reappears to-day with the same morning newness that has been from of old the fountain of beauty and strength." The spirit that created the old forms will someday create new ones spontaneously, for the moral sense is at once the essence of all religion and "the basis of the human mind." In the meantime, individuals need only concern themselves with their own conduct. "Souls are not saved in bundles."

The individual is aided in the reformation of conduct by the fact that nature no less than mind is saturated with law. "In us it is inspiration; out there in Nature, we see its fatal strength." Essays like "Power" and "Fate" (the final lecture in the original series, though the first essay in the published book) trace the behavior of law in the mind and in nature, showing how the same brutal necessity that lies upon our hopes like a mountain of obstruction in "Fate" turns in the perceiving mind into power, the opposite of fate. "Thought dissolves the material universe, by carrying the mind up into a sphere where all is plastic," Emerson says in "Fate." The famous catalogue of natural disasters near the beginning of the essay – earthquakes, epidemics, wild beasts, ocean storms – leads up to the insight that disarms them. What we call fate is at last "a name for facts not yet passed under the fire of thought; for causes which are unpenetrated." The man or woman who sees the ineluctable web of cause and effect everywhere in nature is no longer a helpless victim of the laws but a sharer in their power. "Thought takes man out of servitude into freedom." Now "we are as lawgivers; we speak for Nature; we prophesy and divine."

"Fate" was initially delivered in December 1851, after Emerson's first lecture against the Fugitive Slave Law; some sentences that sound very much as though they came from this lecture made their way into stray leaves from the manuscript of "Courage," the lecture that Emerson delivered shortly after John Brown's raid on Harper's Ferry: "The statistics show you the whole world under the dominion of the fate or circumstance or brute laws of chemistry. . . . Thought resists and commands Nature by a higher truth, and gives Nature a master." If "Fate" had its genesis in the struggle against slavery, it is hardly surprising that Emerson chose to place it first in the volume he published in November 1860. To take its place at the end of *The Conduct of Life* he now added an essay he had first published in the *Atlantic Monthly* in 1857, "Illusions." A strange intaglio of "Fate," "Illusions" does not so much dissolve fate into thought as reveal that all solidities are illusory to begin with. "Life is as sweet as nitrous oxide." The magazine version of the essay ends with a bit of Persian advice to "be the fool of virtue, not of vice," for folly is inevitable. But for the book Emerson added an Oriental fable that returns the text to the only subject he ever cared about deeply – the nakedness of the soul before God. The young mortal enters the temple where he sees the gods beckon but is instantly distracted by "snow-storms of illusions." He is confused, he is distracted. But when for an instant the clouds lift, "there are the gods still sitting around him on their thrones, – they alone with him alone."

With *English Traits* (1856), the book Emerson based on his two trips to England – the first in 1833, the second in 1847–8 – we are in another universe altogether, where the senses rule. The book is a shrewd but admiring portrait of a land and people superficially so different from Emerson's own that the filial relationship is sometimes difficult to believe, yet the two countries are also united by such deep similarities that Emerson secretly delights in the foreign greatness that dwarfs him – delights because as Britain now is, so shall America someday be.

English Traits opens with an account of the European tour Emerson made as a young provincial just out of the ministry, naively hoping to find in the Old World the personified forms of the books whose genius had so enraptured him. He was courteously received by everyone, but he was disappointed to meet instead of the giants of his imagination, ordinary men: a Landor hospitable but worldly; a Coleridge old, ill, and full of harangues against the Unitarians; a Wordsworth admirable for his "simple adherence to truth" but confined within "the hard limits of his mind." Only Carlyle at Craigenputtock, loosing the floodgates of his talk and boisterous laughter, was the man he had come to find.

Now, in 1847, Emerson is no longer the otherworldly young cleric so devoted to things of the spirit that he sees nothing else. His first view of the land shows the sharpness of his new attention to detail. "Under an ash-colored sky, the fields have been combed and rolled until they appear to have been finished with a pencil instead of a plough." The high finish and artificiality of life fascinates him; "facticious" is a word that recurs constantly in his descriptions. Is British capacity to subdue and manicure these unpromising islands in the cold northern ocean the result of extraordinary racial vigor or were the savage Norsemen who peopled the islands broken into civility by the harshness of the climate and the stubborn resistance of the soil? "The enchantments of barren shingle and rough weather transformed every adventurer into a laborer." However it happened, race and environment worked upon one another to produce a nation beefy, ruddy, valorous, truth-loving, opinionated, prosaic, passionately logical, tenacious of liberty and even more tenacious of property, chilly in company and sentimental in private life, tolerant of eccentricity in behavior and intolerant of it in thought. The contrast between these broad-chested self-confident specimens of Anglo-Saxon humanity and their cautious, spindly, deferential American cousins is so great that it provides an undercurrent of humor throughout the book even though Emerson does not often make the comparison explicit.

For someone who had been preaching against conformity all his life England was almost paradise. "They require you to be of your own opinion," Emerson remarks, and adds: "Everyone does everything without reference to the bystanders, consults only his own convenience, as much as a solitary pioneer in Wisconsin." Even British phlegm comes in for praise. "A saving stupidity masks and protects their perception, as the curtain of the eagle's eye."

Still, these virtues are purchased at the cost of adamantine limitations. The

Englishman is shut in by a horizon of brass the diameter of his umbrella. His universities are somnolent; his church is a doll, whose gospel is "By taste ye are saved." The English church in 1848 is not a persecuting church, but neither is it a believing one. It is "not inquisitorial; it is not even inquisitive." The spirit that animated the theologians, architects, and sacred poets of the seventeenth century has wholly departed, leaving behind only a worship of wealth. And though England is the richest and most powerful nation in the world, Emerson suspects that it has reached its apogee. He cannot help thinking that America, with its unlimited natural resources, in the long run can play the game with immense advantage, and that England must one day be content to be strong only in her children.

Wandering with Carlyle among the buttercups, daisies, nettles, and wild thyme growing around the stones at Stonehenge, "the old egg" out of which all the history and ecclesiastical structures of the British race had proceeded, Emerson thinks back to the continent to which he is returning. "There, in that great sloven continent, in high Allegheny pastures, in the sea-wide, sky-skirted prairie, still sleeps and murmurs and hides the great mother, long since driven away from the trim hedge-rows and over-cultivated garden of England."

By the time Emerson published these words in 1856, his greatest disciple was already more than halfway through a decade of unparalleled literary productivity taking the wildness of that "sloven continent" as one of its central themes. Emerson's failure to acknowledge Thoreau's achievement during these years has always seemed unpardonable to admirers of Thoreau; and certainly Emerson's willingness to puff Ellery Channing's poems while ignoring *Walden* is hard to forgive, even if one takes into account the deep rifts in the relationship between the two men that widened after Emerson's return from England.

Of course, Thoreau himself made it difficult to gauge the magnitude of his labors, because the main work on which he was embarked during the decade — the massive *Journal* — was wholly private until his death, and two other books whose serial publication in journals was begun — *A Yankee in Canada* and *Cape Cod* — were withdrawn by Thoreau before publication was complete in protest against editorial tampering with his text. As for *Walden*, it was in places so savage a denunciation of the kind of life Emerson had chosen to live (and about which the two men had been arguing in private and in print since the early 1840s) that Emerson's silence on the subject of its literary merits is perhaps not really surprising.

The weekly burden of sermon writing and, later, the economic pressures of maintaining a home and family had disciplined Emerson into a rhythm of literary production that lasted most of his life. First the daily work on the journals, thinking and writing; then the culling of passages from the journals for lectures to take on tour; finally the revisions of lectures into a book, negotiations with booksellers, and publication. Emerson was not a particularly canny businessman, and his daughter's memoir of her mother's life reveals how threadbare the household sometimes was. But he wrote steadily enough to keep the family afloat, and his family's demands kept him writing despite his frequent complaints of dessication or dullness.

Thoreau from the beginning had more difficulty finding a steady rhythm of production. He had revised and revised his first manuscript and then (on Emerson's advice) risked publishing it entirely at his own expense, a procedure that gave his publisher little incentive to advertise or sell it, having already recouped the cost of production. In 1850 Thoreau was faced with the fact that his first book had failed to find an audience and had left him with a debt he did not pay off till 1853; that he was forced to turn to surveying, odd jobbing, or helping in the family pencil business to earn money; and that he had no literary role or reputation, other than as an imitator of Emerson and a second-string lyceum lecturer. Yet his response to all this discouragement was not to abandon his literary vocation but to declare it with renewed force.

The first part of Thoreau's literary life to undergo metamorphosis were the journals that he had been keeping (probably at Emerson's suggestion) since 1837. Students of the journals have noticed several distinct phases in Thoreau's practice of journal keeping. Initially his journals are a place to hive transcripts of other writings; then they become more like Emerson's journals, individual meditations with more or less integrity, sometimes used in the published works. But in May 1850 Thoreau begins to write with increasing frequency in his journal, and by June of the next year he has established the habit he will follow until six months before his death: Notes taken down during his daily long walks are worked up into highly polished journal entries in which Thoreau repeatedly attempts the feat of translating natural appearance into language that is both strikingly metaphorical and mathematically precise. Some of these passages find their way into the books and lectures Thoreau writes during the decade, but the sheer bulk of these daily writings (some two million words in all, most written during the last decade of Thoreau's life) suggests that they must have been meant as something more than a source of immediately marketable material.

Whatever prompted Thoreau to begin his new experiment in journal writing – the reading of Wordsworth's recently published *Prelude,* which recorded the mind's relationship to natural phenomena with a fidelity new in English poetry; the need to find a literary work that would keep him constantly practicing his craft; the need to pin down experience that seemed to be vanishing; or even the need to find some source of sanity and health amid America's growing political squalor – by 1851 he has reached the point where *The Prelude* began. "I feel myself uncommonly prepared for *some* literary work, but I can select no work" (September 7, 1851). Gradually it occurs to Thoreau that the journal might be published as it stands rather than plundered for material to make essays of. In early 1852 he writes, "I do not know but thoughts written down thus in a journal might be printed in the same form with greater advantage – than if the related ones were brought together into separate essays. They are now allied to life – & are seen by the reader not to be far fetched" (January 27, 1852). And by July 1852 he is ready to define a journal as "a book that shall contain a record of all your joy – your ecstasy" (July 13, 1852).

Nature in Thoreau's journal is endlessly investigated, followed and recorded in all her seasonal changes. Unlike Emerson, who wanted to decode natural phenomena to release the human meaning hidden within, Thoreau does not ask for human significance in nature and in fact effaces himself as much as possible, except as observer and scribe of a beauty and order not his own. This vocation does not preclude other, more humanly accessible ones; Thoreau was still eager to find an audience in his own time and place, to see his works in print. But the "journal of no very wide circulation" (as he jokes about it in *Walden*) was a secret source of power and assurance for Thoreau that made all kinds of writing easier. The journal was at once a steadying discipline, an act of love, a source of authority, and a secret bid for posthumous fame.

The first half of the decade was a period of extraordinary creativity for Thoreau. In addition to the journal and the antislavery lectures, he wrote the lectures "Walking, or the Wild" and "Life without Principle"; the four chapters of *Cape Cod;* all five chapters of *A Yankee in Canada;* the longest chapter of *The Maine Woods;* and the fourth, fifth, sixth, and final drafts of *Walden.* Of all these texts only *Walden* was published in its entirety during Thoreau's lifetime. (The books we know as *The Maine Woods, A Yankee in Canada,* and *Cape Cod* were published only after Thoreau's death.) Thoreau's willingness to accept Horace Greeley's offer of help in placing his pieces with periodicals hardly suggests a desire to remain unknown, though his determination to withdraw material when it was tampered with shows that he was not willing to accept an editor's decision about what he should be permitted to say.

A Yankee in Canada was the first of Thoreau's excursions to reach publication. Based on a trip Thoreau took to Montreal and Quebec with Ellery Channing during the autumn of 1850, *A Yankee in Canada* describes a round-trip journey by rail through Vermont to Canada, then by boat from Montreal to Quebec and back. The trip was made on a special excursion ticket good for only ten days, so Thoreau's acquaintance with French Canada is ridiculously brief. Moreover, his rudimentary French scarcely allows him to understand most of the residents, much less probe deeply into their thoughts. Still, the contrast between the feudal society of French Canada (its peasant Catholicism overlain by a veneer of British imperialism) and the Yankee democracy he has just left is sharp enough to make him meditate on many matters. And the spectacular valley of the St. Lawrence (particularly as seen from the citadel overlooking Quebec) impresses him with its beauty, while the thought of the country only a little way beyond it, uninhabited by any European, sweeps over him like an "irresistible tide."

The first sight Thoreau visits when he has crossed the river to Montreal is the church of Notre Dame, the largest in North America (it seats ten thousand). The gloom, the solitude, the huge space impress him favorably; it seems "a great cave in the midst of a city," and its altars and candles seem as innocent as stalactites. If only the priest could be omitted from the religion Thoreau concedes that he might visit such a church "some Monday" – though fortunately he does not need to, because the Concord woods make a church "far grander and more sacred."

From Notre Dame Thoreau proceeds to the Champ de Mars, where he watches the British regiments drill, fascinated by the appearance of harmony that made the men look like "one vast centipede," depressed that such cooperation should only exist in the service of "an imperfect and tyrannical government." If free men could only put their hearts and hands together their harmony would in itself constitute "the very end and success for which government now exists in vain."

Yet finally none of the sights of Montreal affects Thoreau as much as the name of a point on the island it partly occupies, the Point aux Trembles, so called from the aspens that once grew there.

There is all the poetry in the world in a name. . . . I want nothing better than a good word. The name of the thing might easily be more than the thing to itself to me. Inexpressibly beautiful appears the recognition by man of the least natural fact, and the allying his life to it. All the world reiterating this slender truth, that aspens once grew here; and the swift inference is, that men were there to see them.

This fascination with the poetry of French names, indeed with the sounds of the French language, grows even stronger as Thoreau leaves Montreal for Quebec. The saint's names on every village fill him with the "intoxication of poetry" and make him dream of Provence and troubadours and think wistfully that if English had only "a few more liquids and vowels" its speakers might "locate their ideals at once." We owe our word "prairie" to the French explorers. Nay, "their very *rivière* meanders more than our *river.*"

The beauty of the St. Lawrence and its tributaries, with their thousand waterfalls, wins Thoreau's admiration, as does the "steel-like and flashing air" of Quebec, garlanded with its late autumnal flowers. And his readings in Canadian history lead him to praise the treatment accorded the Indian nations by the French, who respect their sovereignty and regard them as neighbors and allies, unlike the contemptuous English. But the poverty of the present-day French Canadians, ground between the priesthood and the British soldiery, makes Thoreau long for home, where "it is the most natural thing in the world for a government that does not understand you to let you alone."

The pointless cruelty of the British government, which sets sentinels to guard a wall in a country at peace and then changes them every hour (or even sooner) because of the intense cold, strikes Thoreau as the symbol of military folly everywhere. "What a troublesome thing a wall is! I thought it was to defend me, and not I it. Of course, if they had no wall they would not need to have any sentinel." Far more admirable is the soldier's cat he sees walking back into a high loophole in the wall "with a gracefully waving motion of her tail as if her ways were ways of pleasantness and all her paths were peace." The prosperity of an ordinary white farmhouse he sees on his return through Vermont suddenly shines out as testimony to the health of a country whose greatest blessing (at least for "lucky white men") is that it neither enlists them nor defends them.

Thoreau delivered chapters of his Canada manuscript as lectures during the 1851–2 season; in 1852 he sent them to Horace Greeley, who had asked him if he ever swapped his "wood-notes wild" for cash. Most magazines Greeley tried rejected the manuscript as too long, but Thoreau succeeded in getting his old friend George William Curtis (a handsome boarding student at Brook Farm) to accept it for the new *Putnam's Magazine*. Chapters titled "An Excursion to Canada" began appearing anonymously beginning in January 1853. But Thoreau stopped publication after the third (or March) installment and withdrew the manuscript when he discovered that Curtis felt free to censor his "heresies" without consulting him. (Curtis did pay him seventy-nine dollars for the three episodes he printed.) In 1866 the complete five-chapter manuscript was given the title *A Yankee in Canada* and printed together with Thoreau's antislavery and reform papers.

Another manuscript accepted by Curtis for *Putnam's* was also cut off after several installments, though this time Curtis appears to have been the one responsible for the decision to stop publication. Thoreau had sent Curtis some lectures based upon his Cape Cod journeys of 1849 and 1850 when he sent his Canadian manuscript in 1852. Though he had withdrawn both manuscripts from *Putnam's* in 1853 he remained on good enough terms with Curtis to resume negotiations for the publication of the Cape Cod material in

April 1855. Chapters began appearing in the June 1855 issue. But by
August Curtis had wearied of arguing with Thoreau about the wording of
objectionable passages, particularly because the piece seemed to be arousing
resentment on Cape Cod itself. Thoreau asked for the return of his manuscript. He continued to work on the manuscript at intervals until the time of
his final illness, though he made no more attempts to publish it. *Cape Cod*
was finally published in 1865.

On the first page of *Cape Cod* Thoreau tells us that he has made three
journeys to the Cape. But the narrative in the book follows rather closely the
path of the earliest trip (1849), when Thoreau and Ellery Channing rode the
Cape Cod railroad to its end at Sandwich at the beginning of the Cape. From
there they followed the "bared and bended arm of Massachusetts," at first in a
stagecoach and then on foot, until they reached the end of the Cape at
Provincetown. The Cape's peculiar world of sand and drying cod and stunted
vegetation, where apple trees look like plants in flower pots and orchards are
small enough to leap over, seems like something from a fairy tale about elves
or trolls. Many of its inhabitants in Thoreau's book are grotesques, like the
Nauset woman whose jaws of iron looked as if they could bite board nails in
two, or the old Wellfleet oysterman – petulant, complaining that he was "a
poor good-for-nothing crittur," yet able to hold the two travelers spellbound
with memories stretching back to the battle of Bunker Hill, whose cannon he
had heard booming across the Bay when he was sixteen. They stayed the
night with him, and in the morning he invited them to a Cape Cod breakfast: eels, buttermilk cake, cold bread, donuts, and tea.

The inhabitants' houses and gardens are equally strange. There are octago-
nal windmills affixed to cart wheels that can be turned to face the ever-
changing wind, vats for drying salt from seawater, garden plots where
vegetables thrive in pure sand, crops reckoned not only in bushels of corn
but barrels of clams, and backyards filled with drying cod. Sand is everywhere, pitting surfaces so fiercely that one minister reported having to have
a new pane of glass set every week if he wanted to see out of his house.
Even the name of the ubiquitous beach-grass, *Psamma Arenaria,* combines
the Greek word for "sand" with the Latin for "sandy": sandy sand.

Despite the absence of anything like the woods or streams Thoreau loved
in Concord and admired in Canada, the spit of sand has patches of startling
beauty, where shrub oak, bayberry, beach plum, and wild roses are overrun
by woodbine. "When the roses were in bloom, these patches in the midst of
the sand displayed such a profusion of blossoms, mingled with the aroma of
bayberry, that no Italian or other artificial rose-garden could equal them.
They were perfectly Elysian, and realized my idea of an oasis in the desert."
Just outside of Provincetown they come upon a patch of bushes and shrubs so

startling in their fall colors that they seem like a rich tapestry thrown over the white sand.

For Cape Cod the real source of beauty and terror is, of course, the sea itself. They see evidence of its ferocity before they ever get to the Cape. News of a terrible shipwreck in Cohasset prompts them to take that route to the Cape. When they arrive they find that a brig, the *St. John,* laden with Irish emigrants, had been wrecked on the savage rocks during a storm whose waves were still breaking violently on the shore. One hundred forty-five people have died, and the corpses are being laid out for identification and placed in coffins. When someone lifts a cover from a corpse Thoreau sees a "livid, swollen, and mangled body" of a girl, with bloodless gashes and staring, lusterless eyes. At the close of this first chapter, "The Shipwreck," Thoreau discovers that the humans are not the only victims sacrificed to the power of the sea; he sees a good-sized lake separated from the ocean by only a thin beach and is told that the sea had tossed the water over in a storm and that the fish who swam into the lake were now stranded by the gradual drying up of the water and were dying by the thousands.

The sea wrecks ships, topples lighthouses, and eats away the beaches of Cape Cod; it traps and drowns incautious walkers along the Atlantic beach of the Cape and pulls the strongest swimmers in its undertow or feeds them to sharks. In the ninth chapter, "The Sea and the Desert," Thoreau looks at the seashore — "a wild, rank place, and there is no flattery in it" — as a vast morgue where the carcasses of people and beasts lie rotting, turned by the tide that tucks fresh sand under their bodies. "There is naked Nature, — inhumanly sincere, wasting no thought on man, nibbling at the cliffy shore where gulls wheel amid the spray."

Yet the sea also possesses indescribable beauty and grace, glittering in the sun, rocking delicate sea jellies in its waves, nourishing fantastic shapes of kelp — oar-weed, tangle, devil's-apron, sole-leather, ribbon-weed — "a fit invention for Neptune to adorn his car with, or a freak of Proteus." Indeed, when Thoreau has his first sight of the Atlantic Ocean from the high bluff along the eastern shore of the Cape and then descends to the beach itself, the breakers look to him "like droves of a thousand wild horses of Neptune, rushing to the shore, with their white manes streaming far behind."

He watches the day break over the sea as if it came out of its bosom; on the other side of the Cape he sees the sun set into the Bay, and it makes him think of Homer: "The shining torch of the sun fell into the ocean." *Cape Cod* is full of Greek quotations, not only because the storms and sunrises naturally remind Thoreau of Homer but because Greek has convenient words for things like "the sound of many waves, dashing at once" (*polyphloisboios*). The ocean is still wild and untamed and therefore invigorating. Watching the

Atlantic breakers dash themselves against the high bank on a clear cold day in a gale Thoreau sees a primitive force as dangerous to the schooners anchored off Provincetown as it was to the ships of Odysseus or Aeneas. In the casual daily courage of the mackerel-boat fishermen and lighthouse keepers Thoreau finds ancient virtue surfacing off the shores of America.

The idea that the heroic ages are still accessible in the wild regions of the American continent inspires the happiest of Thoreau's "excursions" from the early 1850s, the lecture "Walking, or the Wild." In this lecture – published after Thoreau's death under the title "Walking" – Thoreau communicates his sudden understanding (brought on by looking at a panorama of the Mississippi) that *this was the heroic age itself,* though we know it not." The wildness and vigor of the earliest ages have not vanished; an afternoon's walk will bring Thoreau into solitary forests and primeval swamps. "I enter a swamp as a sacred place, a *sanctum sanctorum.*"

Not every stroller can make the journey back to innocence. The clerks and shopkeepers who walk for a half hour to get exercise, the preoccupied thinkers who bring their worries with them into the woods, are not true walkers at all, nor will they ever know that deep "recreation" that contact with wildness brings. "If you would get exercise, go in search of the springs of life." And if you would join the ancient and honorable order of walkers you must be willing to leave father and mother, brother and sister, wife and child. "We should go forth on the shortest walk, perchance, in the spirit of undying adventure, never to return, – prepared to send back our embalmed hearts only as relics to our desolate kingdoms." For "every walk is a sort of crusade, preached by some Peter the Hermit in us, to go forth and reconquer this Holy Land from the hands of the Infidels."

Thoreau says that he walks for at least four hours a day and seeks out those places least touched by cultivation. "My spirits infallibility rise in proportion to the outward dreariness." Bogs attract him; given a choice between the best garden and the Dismal Swamp he would always choose the swamp. And he values the same rankness and undisciplined vigor in books and people. "In literature it is only the wild that attracts us. Dullness is but another name for tameness." We delight in "the uncivilized free and wild thinking" in all the scriptures and mythologies, just as we prefer the "awful ferity" of good men and lovers to the polite cultivation that leads in men as in ploughed land to exhaustion of the soil. Do New Englanders complain that the pigeons in the woods grow scarcer every year? "So it would seem, fewer and fewer thoughts visit each growing man from year to year, for the grove in our minds is laid waste, – sold to feed unnecessary fires of ambition, or sent to mill, – and there is scarcely a twig left for them to perch on."

The crowing of the cock reminds us to improve the present moment, to

Expanded, Reshuffled, dismantled Walden 7 Time
1847 1st version — 1854 final edition.

celebrate this instant of time. "Where he lives no fugitive slave laws are passed." If the cock's crowing reminds us how many times we have betrayed our master since we last heard his note, its freedom from all plaintiveness awakens in us a "pure morning joy" that reminds us what innocence is in nature. On a cold November day the sun breaking through the clouds at the horizon gilded an empty meadow – a marsh, a black stream, and a decaying stump – with so pure and bright a light that the place seemed like Elysium, "and the sun on our backs seemed like a gentle herdsman driving us home at evening." "Walking" was one of four essays Thoreau revised during the last months of his life to send to James Fields, the editor of the *Atlantic Monthly,* who had solicited contributions from him. It was published in 1862.

Thoreau's main work of these years, however, was the revision and publication of the long manuscript about his life at Walden Pond whose first draft he had probably completed even before he left his cabin in September 1847. The book, published by the Boston firm of Ticknor and Fields on August 9, 1854, as *Walden, or Life in the Woods* (Thoreau later dropped the subtitle), had been through seven revisions since the first version was completed, revisions that doubled its length and radically changed its structure and tone. Because Thoreau used different kinds of paper each time he revised, a modern scholar is able to reconstruct nearly all of the earliest version from the jumble of almost twelve hundred manuscript pages of work sheets left among Thoreau's papers and to trace the process of growth and alteration that led to the published book.

The story of *Walden*'s composition is nearly as remarkable as *Walden* itself. Few of the Transcendentalists cared much for revision; the forms they favored – the journal, the lecture, the essay, the sermon – emphasized spontaneity and pardoned haste. Even Emerson's lectures, though they often consisted of passages considerably polished and altered from their source in his journals, usually reached their permanent form quickly and there stopped – even when Emerson withheld them from publication for several years. Nothing quite like the wholesale dismantling, reshuffling, expanding, and reconstructing to which Thoreau subjected his original manuscript can be found among the literary works Transcendentalism produced.

Thoreau seems to have written the first version of *Walden* in response to questions from his fellow residents of Concord, who were curious to know why he was living at the pond and how he managed to survive there all alone. He probably began writing it sometime during his second winter there, late in 1846. The draft he wrote then is in many ways like the Brook Farm letters of Marianne Dwight or the reminiscences of John Codman: lyrical, full of wonder and discovery, suffused with a sense of joy. Many of the mocking passages of the later *Walden* are already there in full: the comparison of the ordinary inhabitants of Concord to the Brahmins who do penance in "a thousand curious ways," the suggestion that the worst form of slavery is experienced by the man who is the slave driver of himself. But (like the Brook Farmers who looked with pity upon the civilizees outside) Thoreau seems more eager to convert than to excoriate, and he is careful to include himself in the vices he laments. When he blames Concord's townspeople for their frivolous reading he notes that the Dialogues of Plato lie unread on his own shelf, too. And he underscores the point: "I describe my own case here." A title page he drew up for the second (1848) version of *Walden* addresses the book "To My Townsmen," a gesture in which there seems as much affection as reproach.

Thoreau had begun lecturing on his life at Walden Pond even before he left his cabin there, and he was negotiating as early as 1849 for the publication of *Walden* itself, still a single long essay with no chapter divisions. Ticknor and Company (later, Ticknor and Fields) expressed their willingness to publish *Walden* at their expense but refused to take Thoreau's first book, *A Week on the Concord and Merrimack Rivers,* and he refused to publish the second book first, despite his eagerness to get a book in print.

The disappointment of Thoreau's hopes after the failure of *A Week* and the burden of debt the book left him with coincided with other tests of his faith. His relationship with Emerson was badly strained; he was obliged to earn his living once again by trades like surveying, which always left him feeling vaguely sullied. The willingness to sacrifice principle to profit that led landowners to suggest to Thoreau that he survey their properties to give them the greatest amount of land led on the level of national politics to such abominations as the Compromise of 1850 and Sims and Burns cases.

There were also hopeful signs during these years. Thoreau's determination to make his journal his major literary project meant that he had a steady discipline as well as a rich source of new material to draw upon. His journeys to Canada and Cape Cod had shown him cultures, manners, and scenery different enough to challenge all his powers of representation; his excursions in the neighborhood of Concord had shown him that wildness was accessible within the radius of an afternoon walk.

When he returned to the *Walden* manuscript in full force in 1852 he worked with a new confidence and urgency. Greeley helped him place two pieces of the manuscript with *Sartain's Magazine,* which published them in July 1852 (though with Thoreau's usual luck, the magazine promptly collapsed before it paid him). By 1853 he was experimenting with a new principle of organization, dividing up the manuscript into chapters and adding material to the "winter" chapters to complete the cycle of the seasons hinted at in the first version of the book. After several more revisions Thoreau made a final copy of the manuscript for James Fields of the firm now called Ticknor and Fields, with whom he signed a contract on March 16, 1854. By the end of March 1854 Thoreau was correcting the first batch of partial proofs. He probably finished reading proof sometime in May, the same month in which the escaped slave Anthony Burns was captured and returned to slavery. The angry journal passages Thoreau wrote about that event formed the nucleus of the address "Slavery in Massachusetts," which he delivered on July 4. *Walden* itself was published a little more than a month later, on August 9.

The interleaving of Thoreau's final work on the proofs of *Walden* with the composition of his major political address between "Resistance to Civil Government" and the John Brown speeches is significant. Even though the Burns case came too late to influence the text of *Walden,* the attitudes that permitted Burns's rendition had long been visible in the surrounding culture. To trace the connection between individual folly and social corruption thus becomes one of *Walden*'s main burdens, the source of its frequent rages. This bitterness does not obliterate the memories of pure happiness enjoyed at the pond nor the beauty of the precise observations of nature drawn from the journal of the 1850s. Instead it lashes us in the direction we should go, pointing out the promised land we have stupidly forsaken and reminding us of the paradise still to be had for the asking. And it interrogates the world it describes. Why should nature serve as therapy for a mind diseased? If we crave only reality, what is the reality we crave?

The opening chapter of *Walden,* "Economy," begins by announcing that it will satisfy the curiosity of Thoreau's neighbors about his life at the pond. But before turning to his own life, Thoreau turns upon his neighbors to consider their condition — endlessly contorting themselves into agonies in pursuit of the things they foolishly deem "necessities." They labor under a mistake, and the mistake is costly. "The mass of men lead lives of quiet desperation." *Pursuit of Commodities — Comforts —*

A real survey of the "necessaries of life" will yield only a few, and these cheaply acquirable: food, shelter, clothing, and fuel. The simplest food, inexpensive but sturdy clothes, a cabin one can build for less than thirty dollars (less than the annual rent for a room at college), a few sticks of furniture scrounged from the endless stores in other people's garrets, six weeks of labor a year — Thoreau's formula for successful life involves him in vigorous exercise, endows him with leisure for contemplation, and keeps him in touch with the natural world. Unlike the "saints," whose "hymn-books resound with a melodious cursing of God and enduring Him forever," or the miserable farmers enslaved to the acres they till, Thoreau aims to take up life into his pores and banish dejection. *Exercise Contemplation Nature*

In the next chapter, "Where I Lived, and What I Lived For," he moves both outward and downward: outward into the world of the pond itself, throwing off its nightly clothing of mist until it became a "lower heaven" full of light and reflections. In such surroundings every morning becomes a "cheerful invitation" to make his life of equal simplicity and innocence with Nature herself. But the invitation to renewal has its heroic aspects as well. In a central passage Thoreau declares his reasons for the move to Walden Pond. "I went to the woods because I wished to live deliberately, to front only the essential facts of life, and see if I could not learn what it had to teach, and not, when I came to die, discover that I had not lived." The key to living deliberately is a single commandment: "Simplify, simplify." Instead of three meals eat one; instead of dusting your tabletop decorations throw them out of the window.

Yet the simplified person need not live in poverty. The richness of classical literature and the wisdom hived in the scriptures of the nations are there for anyone willing to read them. In "Reading" Thoreau mocks the romance readers and patrons of circulating libraries who seek escape instead of illumination. They remain imprisoned all their lives in the infantile mother tongue and never subject themselves to the severe discipline of the father tongues, the languages of classical antiquity. Unlike Emerson, Thoreau prefers the written to the spoken word, Latin and Greek to the vernacular. Yet he cherishes the country lyceum and hopes to see it patronize learning and the arts as the nobles of the Old World once did. "To act collectively is according to the spirit of our institutions," he says, and reminds his fellow townspeople how rich they really are. "New England can hire all the wise men in the world to come and teach her."

Below and behind the classical tongues is another language "which all things and events speak without metaphor, which alone is copious and standard." In "Sounds" Thoreau transcribes as many of the dialects of this language as he can — the tantivy of wild pigeons, the whistle of the locomotive, the scream of the hawk, the distant hum of the Sunday bells, the lowing of the cattle, the gelatinous gurgling of the screech owls, and the waterlogged ejaculations of the bullfrogs, who sound like drunken aldermen singing catches in the Stygian lake.

To live in nature this way makes the whole body "one sense," and Thoreau imbibes delight through every pore. In the next chapter, "Solitude," Thoreau answers with grand nonchalance the townspeople who wonder how he can live alone, especially on rainy or snowy nights. "Why should I feel lonely? is not our planet in the Milky Way?" And anyway, is it really space that separates us? "I have found that no exertion of the legs can bring two minds much nearer to one another." Still, in "Visitors" Thoreau declares that he loves society as much as most people do, and entertains visitors either in his cabin or in the most elegant of *withdrawing rooms,* the pine wood behind his house. Chief among the welcome visitors is a certain French-Canadian wood-chopper, a natural man whose humility and contentment seem a gift of Nature, whose glimmerings of original thought are all the more valuable because they so rarely find expression. Girls and boys, children come a-berrying, Sunday morning walkers in clean shirts, occasional runaway slaves, all will find welcome – all but the hopeless invalids and bores, who do not know when their visit has ended.

When the visitors have departed, Thoreau returns to his labors – the writing of his books and the hoeing of his beans. These two activities have much in common. In "The Bean-Field" he describes the "small Herculean labor" involved in making the yellow soil express itself in beans rather than in weeds, "making the earth say beans instead of grass." Pacing back and forth barefoot down the seven miles of bean rows, "filling up the trenches with the weedy dead," he engages in an activity at once heroic and philosophi-cal: "I was determined to know beans." Yet the aggressivity of this declara-tion is misleading; the happiest moments in "The Bean-Field" describe not a burrowing past appearance to reality but a release from self-consciousness that calls into question the very division between subjects and objects. Listening to his hoe tinkle against the stones and the nighthawk swoop and scream, Thoreau harvests an "instant and immeasurable crop. It was no longer beans that I hoed, nor I that hoed beans; and I remembered with as much pity as pride, if I remembered at all, my acquaintances who had gone to the city to attend the oratorios."

Another sound sometimes penetrates the Walden woods, the "faint *tintin-nabulum*" of the trainers readying recruits for the Mexican War. This noise proceeds from Concord, that distant civilization Thoreau visits every few days to hear the news, pay a call, or buy a sack of meal. "The Village" begins humorously enough, with an account of the gossip mongers who remind Thoreau of prairie dogs, each sitting at the mouth of its burrow. He admits that he too finds the gossip as refreshing as the rustle of leaves and the cheeping of frogs, so long as it is taken in small doses, like homeopathic medicine. And the adventures he creates for himself as he sets sail at night from a parlor or lecture room to try to find his cabin again in the pitch-dark woods makes him appreciate anew "the vastness and strangeness of Nature."

Yet the village is also where he was seized because he refused to pay his tax to a state that buys and sells human beings like cattle. He had not set out to run amok against the state. "I had gone down to the woods for other purposes. But, wherever a man goes, men will pursue and paw him with their dirty institutions." Since his release he has lived in peace again, leaving his cabin unbolted and open to any stranger who cares to rest there. If all people lived with equal simplicity robbery would be unknown and fear unnecessary. "I was never molested by any person but those who represented the state."

The village and its institutions represent uncleanness; ponds represent innocence and purity. In "The Ponds" Thoreau gives an account of Walden Pond — a pond of such "crystalline purity" that its bottom may be discerned at twenty-five or thirty feet, with waves of a "vitreous greenish blue," walled in by smooth white rounded stones, dropping off steeply from the shore to a sandy bottom. Without discernible inlet or outlet, pure as a well, it stays cold even in the summer because of its great depth. "It is like molten glass cooled but not congealed, and the few motes in it are pure and beautiful like the imperfections in glass." Its surface reports every motion of insect or fish in circling dimples, lines of beauty, inviting the beholder to days of idleness. A boat on its surface affords the best prospect of the surrounding woods and sky. The area around Walden and its neighboring ponds — Flint's Pond, with its ugly name, sandy waters, and shallow bottom; the little Goose Pond; Fair-Haven, a wide spot in the Concord River; and the distant White Pond, pure as Walden itself — forms Thoreau's own "lake country," of which Walden and White are the chief jewels, more noble than the diamond of Kohinoor and fortunately "secured to us and our successors forever."

Or so Thoreau once hoped. But Walden Pond's purity has been "profaned" not only by Thoreau himself but by the "devilish Iron Horse" who has by now browsed off all the woods on Walden shore and littered it with the sties of Irish workers. In "Baker Farm" Thoreau tells of his visit to one of these shanties, the home of a laborer named John Field who works at bogging a nearby meadow with a hoe. Thoreau tells us he means to help the luckless immigrants with his experience; but his revulsion from the dirty shanty with its "wrinkled, sybil-like, cone-headed infant" sitting upon its father's knee, the "round, greasy face and bare breast" of Mrs. Field, and the chickens wandering freely and pecking at his shoes keeps overpowering him and turning what seems intended as jocularity into something much less pleasant. As he sits lecturing the immigrants on how to save money by cutting out luxuries like meat, tea, and butter, Thoreau sounds priggish and condescending rather than helpful and companionable. Fortunately, the Fields appear to be more tolerant of their guest than he was of them.

The next chapter, "Higher Laws," suggests that Thoreau's disgust at the Irish may stem partly from deeper ambivalences in his attitude toward the body itself and its involvement in materiality. Although Thoreau begins the chapter by declaring that he reverences in himself both an instinct toward a higher or spiritual life and another toward a "primitive rank and savage one," primitivism yields very quickly to asceticism as the chapter proceeds. Eating

Brute Neighbors = Warring ants = Red vs. Black.

Oscillates between acceptance & rejection

is slimy and beastly, ebriosity enervating to men and to nations. The "generative energy" dissipates and makes unclean — unless we manage to stay "continent," in which case it "invigorates and inspires us." Without chastity we are like fauns and satyrs, the divine allied to beasts, and "our very life is our disgrace."

vs Body (sex)

in favor of spirituality

It may be, as some scholars have suggested, that Thoreau had been influenced by the writings of "reformers" like Sylvester Graham and William Alcott, who had advocated a severe vegetarianism and warned of the dire consequences of sexual activity, particularly for consumptives; it may be that "Higher Laws," for all its deference to Eastern scriptures, represents an outcropping of the old Puritan rock beneath the Transcendental sediment. In any case the chapter oscillates uncomfortably between an acceptance of nature, including the appetites that inflame it, and a rigorous rejection of these appetites in favor of a spirituality with which they are perpetually at war.

It is a relief to pass from the condescension of "Baker Farm" and the harshness of "Higher Laws" to the renewed tenderness for nature manifested in the next chapter, "Brute Neighbors." Thoreau happily lets a wild mouse run down his sleeve and eat cheese from his fingers, after which it wipes its face with its paws like a fly. He remarks that the "remarkably adult yet innocent expression" of the eyes of young partridges suggests both "the purity of infancy" and "a wisdom clarified by experience." Two armies of warring ants, small red against large black, fascinate by their savagery and reckless courage. But best of all is the solitary loon who taunts Thoreau as he tries to row close to it one evening on the pond. The loon dives deep; Thoreau tries repeatedly to guess where he will surface, only to hear the demoniac laughter of the loon behind him, holding him in derision — the only satirist more indefatigable than he is.

ANTS
Savagery

7. 4. 1845 - 1847

Thoreau had first taken up residence at Walden on July 4, 1845, and over half of the book seems to refer to a season that might be summer or early fall. But with the chapter "House-Warming" he reminds us of the calendar again. It is October, when the lowering temperatures force him to stop up the chinks in his board shanty with plaster and finish his chimney. The pond is now skimmed over with hard, dark, transparent ice, on which he can lie at full length and observe the pond bottom as if through a pane of glass. Night after night great flocks of Canada geese come, "lumbering in the dark with a clangor and a whistling of wings," bound for Mexico. Thoreau moves inside for good, making a study of different kinds of wood suited for burning, contemplating his woodpile with affection.

Alone in the whirling snowstorms of winter, Thoreau conjures up for company the shades of Concordians past in "Former Inhabitants and Winter Visitors" — slaves like Cato Ingraham, whose carefully planted walnuts survive him; the hospitable Fenda, round and black, who told fortunes; Breed the rum seller; and a loquacious Irish colonel reputed to have fought at Waterloo, with a face red as carmine and a perpetual tremor. They are all dead now, their houses dents in the earth, overrun with weeds, the wells sealed with a stone. But Thoreau is not lonely while a visiting poet (Ellery Channing) makes his house ring with laughter, or a serene philosopher (Bronson Alcott) helps him with endlessly expansive talk building castles in the air "for which the earth offered no foundation."

"Winter Animals" gives affectionate portraits of the companions Thoreau has even in the coldest months – hares, partridges, red squirrels, foxes, thievish jays, and chickadees who make "faint flitting lisping notes, like the tinkling of icicles in the grass." The next chapter, "The Pond in Winter," begins with Thoreau's expedition with ax and pail to harvest his morning's bucket of water through the foot-thick ice on the pond, pauses to pay tribute to the fabulous beauty of the gold and emerald pickerel native to it, then records the results of a series of soundings made by Thoreau through holes in the frozen pond with a cod line and stone to see whether or not the pond was really bottomless, as local superstition had it. The pond proved to be remarkably deep at its deepest point (102 feet) but nowhere bottomless. Thoreau includes in the chapter a map of the pond carefully recording his soundings. He is nevertheless tender to the superstition he explodes. "While men believe in the infinite some ponds will be thought to be bottomless."

At the end of "The Pond in Winter" Thoreau describes the January ice harvesting, when a hundred Irishmen with Yankee overseers came to plough and furrow the ice and take it away in cakes. They build these cakes into a vast blue fort or Valhalla, finally covering it with hay and boards. The thought of where these great emeralds of Walden ice might go leads Thoreau to contemplate trade with an altered eye. It may be that the "sweltering inhabitants of Charleston and New Orleans, or Madras and Bombay and Calcutta" will drink of the water that melts from these cakes. Accustomed to bathing his intellect "in the stupendous and cosmogonal philosophy of the Bhagvat Geeta," Thoreau is pleased to imagine the Walden water mingling with the sacred water of the Ganges, returning purity for purity at last.

Winter at Walden Pond has been full of life, but the joy recorded in "Spring" still seems like a resurrection. First the ice on the pond cracks and booms, then gets honeycombed with bubbles, then (in the last week of March or the first of April) melts in a warm rain. Thawing sand mixed with clay from a deep railroad cut bursts out in streams like lava, flowing down in interlacing streams that look like leaves, or vines, or bowels, or excrements, affecting Thoreau with a peculiar sense that he is standing in the laboratory of the Artist who made the world. Withered wild grasses revealed by the melting snow "are suggestive of an inexpressible tenderness and a fragile delicacy." Faint silvery warblings are heard over the bare fields. The river valley and woods are bathed in "so pure and bright a light as would have waked the dead, if they had been slumbering," and a slight and graceful hawk rises like a ripple and tumbles down again with a strange chuckle, over and over. "And so the seasons went rolling on into summer, as one rambles into higher and higher grass."

The first version of *Walden* ended here, with the year brought full circle. But the final version has a "Conclusion" in which Thoreau tries to tell something not only about what the two years at Walden Pond meant but what they still mean seven years later. "I learned this, at least, by my experiment; that if one advances confidently in the direction of his dreams, and endeavors to live the life which he has imagined, he will meet with a success unexpected in common hours." Living at Walden taught him that much. Working on *Walden* throughout seven long and discouraging years has taught him something else: "Drive a nail home and clinch it so faithfully that you can wake up in the night and think of your work with satisfaction, — a work at which you would not be ashamed to invoke the Muse." And who can ever set bounds to the possibility for regeneration or say that the hopes of youth were wrong? "There is more day to dawn. The sun is but a morning star."

Of course no summary of *Walden* can convey much that is worth knowing about the book. *Walden* is a cascade of wit, Yankee humor, erudition, invective, outrage, exhortation, philosophical rigor, precise observation, lyrical praise, longing, overweening arrogance, disarming candor, and disinterested curiosity. Thoreau once said that the highest goal was not knowledge but sympathy with intelligence, and sympathy with intelligence is what *Walden* best communicates.

Working to complete *Walden* and then "Slavery in Massachusetts" in the spring and summer of 1854 had been exhilarating for Thoreau. But shortly after his birthday on July 12 he seems to have sunk into an irritability made worse by the blistering heat and drought. He was now thirty-seven years old; his second book, upon which he had labored seven years, was about to be published, leaving him both adrift and bereft. He should improve the nick of time, but how? The sound of a thresher's flail late in August made him wonder whether he had spent his time as wisely as the farmer. If the journal was the field he had cultivated assiduously for the last four years, then it was now time to harvest passages from it: thresh them, winnow them, and grind them into something marketable. "The lecturer must commence his threshing as early as August, that his fine flour may be ready for his winter customers."

It was natural that Thoreau (who received his specimen copy of *Walden* from the publishers as early as August 2) should begin to think of the winter lecture season and imagine that the publication of *Walden* might lead to a flurry of lecture invitations for him. Emerson had lectured extensively in New England and New York before his books were published, but the fame of his books had been responsible for the steadily widening scope of his lecture tours. After *Representative Men* came out in 1850 Emerson found himself in demand everywhere. In 1850 he had gone as far as Kentucky and Michigan; in 1851 he toured upstate New York, Maine, and ended in Montreal (where he was wildly popular); in 1852–3 he had gone on the most extensive lecture tour of his career, a trip that had taken him down the Ohio to St. Louis and back up the river to Alton, Illinois, where he boarded a train to Springfield. Illinois seemed to him a "big bog," with mud so deep wagons sank helplessly in it over the wheels, and the stout Illinoians disconcerted him at first by getting up and walking out of his lectures whenever they were bored. But Emerson earned a good deal of money and learned things from his exposure to the crude energy of the West that Concord could hardly have taught him. On the train trip to Springfield an Illinois state senator and a congressman invited him to the baggage car to share brandy, buffalo tongue, and soda biscuit.

Emerson's lecture tours in the early 1850s were grueling feats of endurance; the traveling conditions and lodgings he had to put up with were so primitive that even a man of Thoreau's rigor could look upon them as enviable adventures. In the fall of 1854 Thoreau set about planning a course of lectures that he might take on the road, hoping to put together a tour that would take him West in December and January of 1854–5. His lecture barrel was not very full; he had been devoting most of his time in recent years to *Walden* or to travel lectures (*A Yankee in Canada, Cape Cod*). He had the "Walking, or the Wild" lecture, which could be split in two and the two parts then fleshed out with new journal passages to make two new hour-long lectures. He had a lecture, "Moosehunting," which recounted his adventures on a second journey to Maine in 1853 (it would eventually form part of the book *The Maine Woods*). And he had a rich harvest of passages recently gleaned from the journal on a subject largely ignored in *Walden:* nighttime, the dark, the moon.

When an old Harvard friend named Marston Watson wrote to him in mid-September to invite him to read a lecture in Plymouth to a "private party – social gathering – almost 'sewing circle,' " Thoreau agreed, though the prospect of suddenly embarking on the career of winter lecturer in the Emersonian mold worried him. He realized how much he had enjoyed his life of obscurity and poverty, experiencing the seasons "as if I had nothing else to do but *live* them, and imbibe whatever nutriment they had for me." Such carefree joy was likely to disappear, he believed, if the public started to expect as much of him "as there is danger now that they will." Initial sales of *Walden* had been promising. When Watson wrote again to inquire whether he wished to give one lecture or two, Thoreau responded that he was determined to read only once. "That is as large a taste of my present self as I dare offer you in one visit."

The lecture he titled "Moonlight (Introduction to an Intended Course of Lectures)" and read in Plymouth on October 8, 1854, no longer exists in its original form, though pieces of it are scattered in two later published texts. After Thoreau's death his publisher James Fields put out a volume of his essays and lectures entitled *Excursions* (1863). Fields apparently needed material to fill out a partially empty final "gathering" in the published book; someone (probably Thoreau's sister Sophia, who had custody of Thoreau's manuscripts) selected sheets from the lecture manuscript and assembled them into a brief piece entitled "Night and Moonlight," the final entry in *Excursions.* Some of the remaining lecture sheets and the journal transcripts not used in the lecture eventually found their way into the hands of an editor at Houghton Mifflin, who simply transcribed and published them in a small book titled *The Moon* (1927).

From this desperate jumble it is impossible to be sure about the order of the paragraphs in the "Moonlight" lecture. But the themes of that lecture are discernible even if its shape is not. Thoreau celebrates the strangeness and beauty of the landscape seen or sensed in moonlight. "Instead of singing birds, the half-throttled note of a cuckoo flying over, the croaking of frogs, the intenser dream of crickets." In this strange world shadows are more conspicuous than the objects that cast them. "The smallest recesses in the rocks are dim and cavernous; the ferns in the wood appear of tropical size. The sweet-fern and indigo in overgrown wood-paths wet you with dew. . . . The woods are heavy and dark. Nature slumbers." The sense of sight, so tyrannical by day, yields to the senses of hearing and smell in the darkened landscape. "Every plant in the field and forest emits its odor now, swamp-pink in the meadow and tansy in the road; and there is the peculiar dry scent of corn which has begun to show its tassels."

The night is mystery, the source of the Nile, Central Africa. Why should we not explore it? "Who knows what fertility and beauty, moral and natural, are there to found?" There is something "primal and creative" in the dewy mist that suggests an "infinite fertility. I seem to be nearer to the origin of things." The stalks of the rye fields in the moonlight form an impenetrable phalanx. "The earth labors not in vain; it is bearing its burden. How rankly it has grown! How it tastes to maturity! I discover that there is such a goddess as Ceres."

Above all reigns the moon, Selene, lover of Endymion and of every man who listens to her "weird teachings." The sun is universal, impersonal, but the moon is a "divine creature freighted with hints for me." Watching the moon alternately obscured by a cloud then triumphantly emerging again turns into a game between a queen who conquers and a lover who watches. "The traveler all alone, the moon all alone, except for his sympathy, overcoming with incessant victory whole squadrons of clouds about the forests and lakes and hills."

Erotic, sensual, fascinated by fecundity, worshipful toward goddesses, drawn toward a primitivism not of Indians or French-Canadian woodchoppers but of Central Africa and the Black Nile, "Moonlight" is Thoreau's attempt to write a night hymn to answer the dawn song he had just completed. After delivering his lecture in Plymouth to an appreciative audience that included Bronson Alcott and spending a few days surveying Watson's estate, Thoreau returned to Cambridge to continue work on the "Intended Course of Lectures" to which "Moonlight" was the introduction.

On October 18 a lecture invitation of a different sort arrived from Rhode Island, asking Thoreau if he would participate in a course of "reform lectures" scheduled to begin in November. Thoreau accepted, though he had not much time to write a new lecture on top of the two revised and expanded lectures that he was hoping to get out of his old "Walking, or the Wild" manuscript for a scheduled appearance in Philadelphia. But a search through the journal suddenly turned up a passage that could serve as the nucleus for the lecture he had promised Providence. Dated September 7, 1851, the passage concerned what might be regarded as the subject Thoreau had addressed in all of his works – the art of life. "Was there ever anything memorable written upon it?" Has anyone ever written about the art of getting not a living but a life? All around us are books telling us how to save time, but they are not what we want. "I do not so much wish to know how to economize time as how to spend it, by what means to grow rich, that the day may not have been in vain."

Until December 6, 1855, when he was scheduled to deliver the lecture he called "What Shall It Profit?" at Railroad Hall in Providence, Thoreau worked furiously on the manuscript, copying out passages from the journal to make a working draft, expanding it, revising it, rejecting passages and replacing them with others, carefully placing the rejected passages in a file. This lecture – Thoreau's most frequently delivered – was revised in 1859–60 and given a new title, "Life Misspent." It was revised one final time in the spring of 1862, during Thoreau's final illness, when he responded to an offer from Ticknor and Fields to publish his essays in the *Atlantic Monthly* by sending them the late lecture "Autumnal Tints" and promising to follow it with a piece he now wanted to call "The Higher Law." They objected to the title, possibly (as Thoreau's editor suggests) because it recalled the decade-old controversy surrounding the Fugitive Slave Law; Thoreau was willing to change but said he could think of nothing better than "Life without Principle," the title the published version now bears.

This strange shifting of titles is significant in itself and says something about the complex of emotions the text manifests. "Life Misspent" and "Life without Principle" suggest in different words the pity or contempt Thoreau feels for the majority of his neighbors, employed as they were in ways that degraded them and the country together: scheming, conniving, running to California to dig gold or (even more repulsively) to the Isthmus of Darien to rob graves, solemnly legislating in Congress to *regulate* the trade in slaves and tobacco, risking their lives on the seas to bring home cargoes of rags, juniper berries, and bitter almonds (things Thoreau had found washed up on the shore when he went to look for Margaret Fuller's body). Men who spend their lives in such "business" are accounted "industrious and hardworking"; men who walk in the woods for love of them are called idlers. It is difficult to buy a blank book in the stores to record one's thoughts; most are ruled for dollars and cents. To such mean wisdom Thoreau opposes his own, a Poor Richard's proverb for Richards willing to stay poor. "There is no more fatal blunderer than he who consumes the greater part of his life getting his own living."

So far "Life without Principle" is an angrier version of the "Economy" chapter in *Walden*. But the original lecture title, "What Shall It Profit?," with its explicit allusion to the Gospel of Mark, suggests that Thoreau had another audience in mind besides the burghers whose greed he mocks. Jesus has just predicted his death and resurrection for the first time to his disciples; the shocked Peter rebukes him for saying it. Jesus turns on Peter and rebukes him in turn, saying, "Get thee behind me, Satan; for thou savorest not the things that be of God, but the things that be of men" (Mark 8:33). A few moments later, when he has called the people together, Jesus asks the famous question: "For what shall it profit a man, if he shall gain the whole world, and lose his own soul?" (Mark 8:36)

We know that Thoreau had both of these chapters in mind when he wrote the original lecture, for he makes the former the subject of a joke about greed and the Gold Rush. "Satan, from one of his elevations, showed mankind the kingdom of California, and instead of the cry 'Get thee behind me, Satan,' they shouted, 'Go ahead!' and he had to exert himself to get there first." He dropped this passage from the final text of "Life without Principle," for by 1862 the Gold Rush was no longer news. But the portrait of a different tempter remains. "It is remarkable that among all the preachers there are so few moral teachers. The prophets are employed in excusing the ways of men. Most reverend seniors, the *illuminati* of the age, tell me, with a gracious, reminiscent smile, betwixt an aspiration and a shudder, not to be too tender about these things" – *these things* being the compromises everyone has to make to make a living, the laws of the world. Angrily Thoreau rejects all such advice. "A man had better starve at once than lose his innocence in the process of getting his bread."

It is hard not to see in this passage a portrait of Emerson, whose "Conduct of Life" series included the lectures "Power" and "Wealth" and whose *English Traits* (then being readied for publication) praised the power, wealth, aristocracy, manners – even the complacency – of the British race. Emerson's worship of all things English contains a chapter heaping praise upon the London *Times,* which Emerson credits with stamping out sympathy for the French Republic of 1848 and causing the Chartist rebellion to fizzle. Thoreau demolishes such admiration with a significant pun. "Read not the Times. Read the Eternities." To ignore the center for superficies (as Emerson now seemed to be doing) strikes Thoreau as a betrayal of genius, as a betrayal of truth. "Is there any such thing as wisdom not applied to life?"

Emerson, who was off on a lecture tour in upstate New York when Thoreau delivered "What Shall It Profit?" at the Concord Lyceum on February 14, 1855, would have agreed with that question, at least. Where he differed from Thoreau was not in his diagnosis of the problem – that the world of the senses was fatally severed from the world of the soul – but in his solution to the problem: prudence for the sensible world and spontaneity or instinct for the spiritual one. Thoreau insisted on bringing senses and soul into alignment in every act of his life, whether surveying or writing.

Thoreau's hopes of uniting vocation and avocation by turning his journal passages into lectures had already gone down to defeat. Lecture invitations from the Midwest and Canada had been so sparse that his fees would not have paid for his trip. Even within New England responses to "What Shall It Profit?" had ranged from puzzlement to disbelief (except on Nantucket, whose hardy residents had liked his truculent gospel). After the first reading in Providence, Thoreau believed he had failed to get "even the attention of the mass." Lecturing, he decided, was as violent as was fattening geese by cramming – and in this case the geese refused to get fatter. He had wasted an entire winter writing lectures for audiences that did not want to hear them; he had neglected his journal to turn out work until he felt like a spindle in a factory. He concluded that he would much rather write books.

Thoreau did not give up lecturing after 1855, but he gave up thinking that he might make a living from lecturing. A debilitating bout of illness he suffered in the spring of 1855 suggested that in any case he could hardly hope to stand the rigors of winter lecture tours over a half-savage country as well as Emerson did, though Emerson was fourteen years his senior. Instead he began sending out old manuscripts for publication. But the integrity too prickly for audiences proved too prickly for publishers as well, and the publication of *Cape Cod* that had begun in the June issue of *Putnam's* was ended by August when Thoreau refused to consider eliminating material his editor thought offensive.

Thoreau continued to work on his journal, taking now a more purely scientific interest in subjects like the propagation of plants by seeds or the apparently paradoxical fact that many groves of trees were more hospitable to the seedlings of alien species than they were to their own. A visit to New York in 1856 to see Alcott and Greeley led to a ferry trip across the East River to inspect one of Emerson's new enthusiasms – Walt Whitman. Though the contrast between Whitman's small clutch of mythological engravings (Bacchus, Hercules, a satyr) and the shabby bedroom he shared with his brother was sad, Whitman was then at the high tide of his poetic confidence. Emerson had hailed the first edition of *Leaves of Grass,* and though it sold considerably fewer copies than *A Week on the Concord and Merrimack Rivers* had, Whitman issued a second edition and was convinced that demand for his works would soon be great. Both men were guarded during the meeting, but Thoreau soon began displaying his copy of *Leaves of Grass* in Concord; Whitman later said he admired Thoreau's blazing capacity for dissent.

In 1857 Thoreau took the last of his three trips to Maine. In 1846 he had visited Maine with a group of friends and had climbed Mount Katahdin, a harrowing excursion he described first in a lecture and then in an essay entitled "Ktaadn," published in John Sartain's *Union Magazine of Literature and Art* in 1848. In 1853 he had taken a second trip to Maine's Moosehead and Chesuncook lakes with his cousin, who wanted to go moose hunting, and their Indian guide, the logger Joe Aitteon. When he returned he worked up a lecture for the Concord Lyceum about his experiences and repeated this "Moosehunting" lecture several times over the next few years. In January 1858 he offered an essay derived from his lecture but now called "Chesuncook" to James Russell Lowell, the editor of the new *Atlantic Monthly* magazine, who had asked him for something about his Maine trips. Publication of installments began in June 1858 but was marred by now-predictable quarrels. Thoreau resented editorial tampering with his text and became furious when Lowell deleted a sentence despite Thoreau's insistence that it be printed. When Thoreau discovered the omission in the July number of the magazine he fired off a letter to Lowell so angry and insulting that Lowell never forgave him. (Lowell got his revenge in 1865 with a merciless review of Thoreau's career in the *North American Review;* its famous opening paragraphs rank with Emerson's brief essay on the Chardon Street Convention as the best comic portraits of an era in which self-assertion and lunacy were difficult to tell apart.)

Thoreau's 1857 trip by canoe had taken him up the West Branch of the Penobscot River, then overland to the headwaters of the East Branch for an exhilarating return trip down a swift river corrugated by rapids and waterfalls. The trip furnished material for yet another essay, eventually titled "The Allegash and East Branch," by far the longest of the three Maine pieces. "The Allegash and East Branch" was never printed during Thoreau's lifetime, though he continued to work on it up until the time of his death. (Ellery Channing, who was with Thoreau when he died, said that his last audible words were "moose" and "Indian.") The three essays were published together with an "Appendix" as *The Maine Woods* in 1864. The Appendix contains lists of Maine plants, birds, and animals; two lists of words in the Abenaki language; and advice about how to outfit oneself for expeditions.

"Ktaadn" had recorded Thoreau's startled discovery that the bare rocks of the mountain's top are frightening because they remind us of the materiality of the universe, its alien "thingness," or solidity, a quality shared by the commonest objects and by our own bodies to which we are chained all our lives like Prometheus to his rock. The remaining two chapters in *The Maine Woods* examine forms of otherness less menacing but no less uncanny – the moose, the pine tree, and the Indian.

The last of these is the most important to Thoreau, who confesses in "Chesuncook" that he decided to employ an Indian guide "mainly that I might have an opportunity to study his ways." Joe Aitteon is a twenty-four-year-old Penobscot Indian, a son of the governor, with a broad face and reddish complexion, short and stout, dressed like a logger in a red flannel shirt and black Kossuth hat. Joe takes the stagecoach (with his canoe) from Bangor to Moosehead Lake sixty miles to the northwest; Thoreau and his cousin follow after in an open wagon. They take the steamer up Moosehead Lake – a "wild-looking sheet of water, sprinkled with wild, low islands," rougher than the ocean itself. At the head of the lake they must disembark and carry their canoe and belongings through the forest to the Penobscot River, but lumbermen have made the "carry" a broad straight swath several rods wide through the forest, where the spruce and fir trees "crowded to the track on each side to welcome us" and the wildflowers bloom in profusion.

This happy relationship to nature ends abruptly when they reach the Penobscot, where Thoreau's cousin intends to go moose hunting. Thoreau admits that he feels some compunction about tagging along on the hunt, but tells himself that he wants to see a moose near at hand and see how an Indian kills one. He will go as a "reporter or chaplain to the hunters," not as a hunter himself.

Yet like other reporters and chaplains he discovers that his own detachment ends when the killing is at hand. When at last they surprise a pair of moose in a tributary of the Penobscot, Thoreau finds himself staring at something very different from the majestic bull moose of the hunter's imagination. He sees a cow and her yearling calf peering round the alders at them. "They made me think of great frightened rabbits, with their long ears and half-inquisitive, half-frightened looks." His cousin fires at the larger moose, then at the calf; both animals flee, making no sound on the damp moss that carpets the forest floor. Half an hour later upstream they find the cow dead in the shallow stream, still warm. Thoreau grabs the animal's ears and helps Joe drag it to shore; he measures it carefully and notes the contrast between its "grotesque and awkward" shape and "the delicacy and tenderness of its hoofs."

Then the skinning commences. Whatever appetite Thoreau had to watch native skill with a knife evaporates as he watches the ghastly red carcass emerge from beneath the skin, the warm milk streaming from the rent udder. Though his cousin proudly keeps the ball with which he shot the moose to show his grandchildren, Thoreau feels that "the afternoon's tragedy, and my share in it" has destroyed the innocence and pleasure of his adventure and makes nature look sternly upon him.

Can humans think of no better use for animals than killing them, no better use of pine trees but to turn them into boards? "A pine cut down, a dead pine, is no more a pine than a dead human carcass is a man." Why do so few people ever come to the woods to see how the pine "lives and grows and spires, lifting its evergreen arms to the light – to see its perfect success"? The "higher law" we obey demands reverence for the pine as well as for moose and human beings. "It is as immortal as I am, and perchance will go to as high a heaven, there to tower above me still." (This last is the sentence Lowell found heterodox enough to expunge.)

Throughout the rest of his trip down the Penobscot to Chesuncook Lake and on the return trip to Bangor, Thoreau enjoys the wildness of a landscape still largely untouched by human hands, just as he enjoys the "purely wild and primitive American sound" of the Abenaki language Aitteon speaks with other Indians – something that takes him by surprise and finally convinces him that "the Indian was not the invention of historians and poets." He fills "Chesuncook" with transcriptions of Indian words and pesters Joe endlessly for translations (*kecunnilessu*, the chickadee; *skuscumonsuck*, the kingfisher). These form a vigorous native counterpoint to the flurry of the Linnaean binomials that Thoreau himself habitually uses to identify things (*Parus atricapillus,* the chickadee; *Alcedo alcyon,* the kingfisher).

Though Thoreau admires the woods he does not want to live there, and he confesses that he is relieved at the end of his trip to return to the "smooth but still varied landscape" of Massachusetts, more hospitable to poets than the barren wilderness of Maine. That seems valuable to him as a "resource and a background, the raw material of our civilization." If kings and nobles have their parks why cannot a free people have its "national preserves" where the bear and panther may rove freely and the trees be defended from the logger's saw? Or shall we "like the villains, grub them all up, poaching on our own national domains?"

The last chapter in *The Maine Woods,* "The Allegash and East Branch," records Thoreau's final journey to Maine in June 1857 with his old Concord friend Ed Hoar. They head for the Penobscot village at Oldtown, up the Penobscot River from Bangor, in hopes of finding an Indian to be their guide. The first man they see is an Indian named Joe Polis, who is prosperous (his two-story house looks as neat as one on a New England village street) and a member of the tribal aristocracy. They ask him if he knows of any Indian willing to guide them on their planned circular journey up to Moosehead Lake and across to the east branch of the Penobscot. He answers "from that strange remoteness in which the Indian ever dwells to the white man," that he wants to go himself to get some moose.

Thoreau is fascinated by Polis's remoteness, admiring his refusal to in-dulge in the "conventional palaver and smartness of the white man." Polis ignores attempts to make conversation, or else replies in grunts; such answers as he does give to questions are "vague and indistinct." One morning he is asked, rhetorically, "You did not stretch your moose-hide, did you, Mr. Polis?" Polis responds with irritation at the silliness of the question. "What you ask me that question for? Suppose I stretch 'em, you see 'em. May be your way talking, may be all right, no Indian way." Yet at other moments Polis loves to expatiate upon the history of his tribe or its exploits in battle. When the day's work is done he exhibits "the *bonhomie* of a Frenchman, and we would fall asleep before he got through his periods."

Polis is as hardy and skilled in woodcraft as any wilderness traveler could wish, and he endures without complaint the persecution by flies and mosqui-toes that keep the white men swathed in veils and slathered with repellent lotions by night. Yet some of his attitudes surprise Thoreau. Polis has represented his tribe at the state capital in Augusta and once in Washington (where Daniel Webster was rude to him). He liked Boston, New York, and Philadelphia and would even like to live in one of the cities – though he realizes that in New York he would probably be "the poorest hunter" in the place. He has an enormous appetite for sugar. He loves to challenge Thoreau to contests of speed in carrying or paddling, and, when he wins, admits, "Oh, me love to play sometimes." And he probably understands very well how proud he makes Thoreau when he tells him near the end of the journey that Thoreau paddles "just like anybody."

And the landscape is as beautiful as Thoreau remembers it from his earlier journeys. One morning they drift down one of the many lakes in their path. "The morning was a bright one, and perfectly still and serene, the lake as smooth as glass, we making the only ripple as we paddled into it. The dark mountains about it were seen through a glaucous mist, and the brilliant white stems of canoe birches mingled with the other woods around it." Thoreau hears the wood thrush, then the laugh of some loons, whose echo is strangely magnified by the curving bay in which they ride.

Representing nature in prose so limpid that nothing seems to stand between the reader and the scene represented had been one of Thoreau's great gifts ever since "The Natural History of Massachusetts." The excursions and travel books are full of such passages; many chapters of *Walden* consist of nothing else. But in all these forms the egotism of the organizing fiction is at odds with the perfect self-effacement that representation implies. The speaker must tell us that *he* went on a walk or a river trip, that *he* traveled to Maine or Canada or Cape Cod, that *he* built a cabin and lived by a pond. In the journal such reminders are unnecessary, and that may be one of the reasons Thoreau found the journal an exercise of joy. At once pure enthusiast and pure craftsman, he can record what he perceives without needing to route his language through the petty concerns of the empirical self.

In the early 1850s, when Thoreau's journal expanded into the major literary project of his life, he had expressed frustration that he could not offer the reader his journal passages as they were, without transcription and rearrangement. As the decade wore on he conceived of an even more radical project — letting Nature speak for herself. One kind of work could use as its organizing principle the rhythms of flowering and decay by which trees and plants move in harmony with the seasons. Another could track the curious, prodigal, stochastic ways in which the trees and plants themselves are propagated.

The journal, with its years and years of patiently gathered observations of phenomena, could furnish data for both; the various works of natural history and natural science that Thoreau began reading with voracious intensity in the later 1850s could suggest a method and a stance. These twin projects were left unfinished at the time of Thoreau's death, but the two large bundles of manuscript ("Wild Fruits" and "The Dispersion of Seeds") came to almost a thousand pages. Parts of these longer manuscripts consisted of lectures he had delivered or apparently planned to deliver; along with the John Brown lectures they were the last lectures of his career.

"Autumnal Tints" was the first of these natural history lectures to be delivered. Thoreau had apparently begun working on it in 1857 but first delivered it in 1859, when he read it at Worcester, at the Concord Lyceum, and at Lynn. "Autumnal Tints" begins with Thoreau's confession that he had really dreamed of compiling a book about leaves in which language was unnecessary. He might trace the leaves of each "tree, shrub, and herbaceous plant" at just the moment when it had reached its brightest color as it changed from green to brown, then "copy its color exactly, with paint, in a book." If he could "preserve the leaves themselves, unfaded, it would be better still."

Yet this childlike "memento" of October would still be only a memento — and Thoreau would have the single copy. Description in language is distant from what it describes, but on the other hand, it is easily stereotyped; besides, what Thoreau discovers as he goes along is that the color of the single leaf, however brilliant, means little without the context that makes it beautiful. The earliest tree to redden (the red maple) stands out like a burning bush against the rest of the forest, making the green ones greener; whereas the last great red rose among the deciduous trees (the scarlet oak) depends upon the surrounding evergreens for half its intensity.

But "Autumnal Tints" is more than a series of still pictures. Thoreau wants to convey the excitement of seasonal change itself, as the year moves from late August — when the purple grasses bloom, the pokes redden into great "upright branching casks of purple wine," and the lowly beard grasses on their sterile and neglected soil suddenly amaze the walker with their beauty — through every variety of blaze and flame among the deciduous trees: the red maple, the elm, the sugar maple, and finally the scarlet oak, whose leaves are cut with such precision that a heap of them looks like scrap tin.

What is the purpose of this annual sacrifice? The fallen leaves suggest mortality and self-sacrifice, of course: "They teach us how to die." But a different lesson is taught by the leaves still on the trees. "Did not all these suggest that man's spirits should rise as high as Nature's, — should hang out their flag, and the routine of his life be interrupted by an analogous expression of joy and hilarity?" Trees are as important to villages as town clocks are. Elms form "great yellow canopies or parasols held over our heads and houses by the mile together, making the village all one and compact." Villages without trees fall prey to "melancholy and superstition" — indeed, they soon become the resort of "bigoted religionists and desperate drinkers."

Thoreau is only half-joking here. His growing sense of urgency about the need to preserve wild spaces extended not only to true wildernesses like the Maine woods but also to those humbler wild spaces that used to surround every township but were disappearing as fast as the white pine forests themselves. Fenced off, chopped down, ransacked for profit, the wild fields and forests were disappearing, and with them went the last possibility for a simple and wholesome relationship to nature. In another part of the "Wild Fruits" project Thoreau remarks bitterly that few people care much for Nature and would happily sell their share in all her beauty for a fairly small sum. And he adds, "It is for the very reason that some do not care for these things that we need to combine to protect all from the vandalism of a few." If people can give money to Harvard College, why can they not present a forest or a huckleberry field to the town of Concord? The true wealth of a town lies in its beauty and in the health it creates.

The final lesson "Autumnal Tints" teaches is that beauty is itself a kind of self-transcendence. The lesson that Milton's Raphael gives Adam about how bodies can work up to spirit is also preached by Thoreau's scarlet oaks. "Lifted higher and higher, and sublimated more and more . . . they have at length the least possible amount of earthy matter, and the greatest spread and grasp of skyey influences." Dancing arm and arm with light, the slender leaves with their glossy surfaces trip it so fantastically that "you can hardly tell what in the dance is leaf and what is light."

"Autumnal Tints" is the most beautiful of Thoreau's late natural history essays, and it was also one of the most popular. Ellen Emerson informed her sister that when the lecture was delivered in Concord "there were constant spontaneous bursts of laughter and Mr. Thoreau was applauded" (Ellen Emerson to Edith Emerson, March 2, 1859). Another lecture from the "Wild Fruits" manuscript was also popular. In "Wild Apples" (delivered first at the Concord Lyceum on February 8, 1860, and repeated six days later in New Bedford), Thoreau praises another long-time resident of the New England landscape, the wild apple tree. "Almost all wild apples are handsome. They cannot be too gnarly and crabbed and rusty to look at." The ancestors of all American wild apples are European, but the trees have been in this landscape so long as to seem indigenous – thorny, crabbed, growing fruits "brindled with deep red streaks like a cow, or with hundreds of fine blood-red rays running from stem-dimple to the blossom end, like meridional lines, on a straw-colored ground."

Wild apples are so spicy or tart that only a brisk walk in the November air can make them seem palatable. But Thoreau loves these "wild flavors of the Muse, vivacious and inspiriting" and deplores the vapid grafted varieties that are gradually displacing them, apples with neither *tang* nor *smack*. The temperance reformers have done their best to extirpate the wild apple; Thoreau tells of an orchard owner who cut down his unusually prolific trees for fear the apples would be made into cider. And people who plant grafted apples "collect them in a plat by their houses, and fence them in." Greed and sanctimony alike doom the wild apple to extinction. Thoreau ends with verses (1:5–7, 12) from the prophet Joel (strikingly appropriate, as it turns out, for a land infested with temperance men and women):

Awake ye drunkards, and weep; and howl, all ye drinkers of wine, because of the new wine; for it is cut off from your mouth. For a nation is come up upon my land, strong, and without number, whose teeth are the teeth of a lion. . . . He hath laid my vine waste, and barked my fig tree. . . . The vine is dried up, and the fig tree languisheth; the pomegranate tree, the palm tree also, and the apple tree, even all the trees of the field, are withered: because joy is withered away from the sons of men.

Such denunciation of the greedy and the sanctimonious found ready acceptance in Concord; the records of the lyceum note that there was "loud and continued applause" at the end of the lecture. Alcott noted in his journal that he had listened to it with "uninterrupted interest and delight." As with "Autumnal Tints," the audience seems to have enjoyed the blend of humor, precise description of familiar scenes, and concern for preserving the natural landscape in at least some of its wildness. A concern for preservation and a resolve to understand the mechanisms by which Nature ensures her own survival is even more strongly marked in Thoreau's final lecture in Concord, "The Succession of Forest Trees," which he delivered before the Middlesex Agricultural Society in the Concord Town Hall on September 20, 1860.

In the mid-1850s Thoreau had been struck by the observation made by a neighbor that whenever a pine wood was cut down an oak one would spring up, and vice versa. The folk belief (endorsed even by some naturalists) held that such trees sprang up "spontaneously," but Thoreau knew that trees sprang only from seeds. He began studying the various ways trees and shrubs and plants of all kinds propagated themselves – dispersed to the wind, floated on water, stuck to passing animals or eaten by them, carried by birds, buried by squirrels. This study led to the beginning of his second large unfinished manuscript in natural history, "The Dispersion of Seeds," of which "The Succession of Forest Trees" forms part.

Thoreau explains that when an oak wood is adjacent to a pine one the acorns will be carried into the pine wood by squirrels and other animals every year. A few will take root and spring up into seedlings, which will normally die after a few years. But if the pine wood is suddenly cut down so that light and air reach the oldest oak seedlings they seem to sprout up suddenly into trees. Pines (as the English planters discovered) are the best nurses for oaks, and oak seedlings planted among pines grow more vigorously than oaks planted alone, even though the pines must be pulled out for the oaks to reach maturity. But the greedy American farmer, unaware that he has an oak nursery in his pine wood, cuts the pines down and plows the land under, thinking to sow a crop or two of rye before he turns the land back to woodlot. Of course he kills the healthy oak seedlings ready to shoot into trees; afterwards puzzled that his woodlot remains barren, he complains that his land is "pine-sick."

To cultivate Nature successfully we must adopt the methods she has perfected. "There is a patent office at the seat of government of the universe, whose managers are as much interested in the dispersion of seed as anybody at Washington can be, and their operations are infinitely more extensive and regular." Those operations it is the task of the longer manuscript, "The Dispersion of Seeds," to chronicle. There Thoreau considers the dispersion of seed from every kind of tree, shrub, and plant, all the way from the giant sequoia of the California forests to the lowly thistle, whose ugly head conceals a "hedge of imbricated, thin, and narrow leaflets" enclosing the "delicate downy parachutes of the seed, – like a silk-lined cradle in which the prince is rocked." Everywhere there is immense waste, immense care, immense trust. The slender and brittle black willow sheds cotton from its catkins until it forms a thick white scum on the pond; the minute brown seeds in the cotton float downstream to anchor in new mud and begin new life. Touch-me-not seed vessels explode and shoot their seed like shot. The pod of the milkweed contains in a "little oblong chest" around two hundred little pear-shaped seeds packed in layers like scales, seeds launched by the wind to fly over hill and dale. "Who could believe in prophecies of Daniel or Miller that the world would end this summer, while one milkweed with faith matured its seeds?"

Throughout the autumn and winter of 1860 Thoreau pursued his botanical studies, examining the growth patterns of trees by studying tree rings. After one such expedition on December 3 he came down with a severe cold, which he had probably caught from Bronson Alcott a few days earlier. He forced himself to keep an engagement to read "Autumnal Tints" to an audience in Waterbury, but his cold – now bronchitis – made him read in a monotone and the evening was not a success. It was in fact his last lecture. He returned to Concord exhausted and seriously ill. The tuberculosis that had killed his sister in 1849 and his father a decade later now involved him in a long, slow decline that a trip to Minnesota in the spring of 1861 did nothing to arrest.

He worked as long as he could, employing his sister Sophia as amanuensis when he could no longer write. When James Fields took over the editorship of the *Atlantic Monthly* he asked Thoreau to submit essays, and Thoreau worked to get "Autumnal Tints," "Wild Apples," "Life without Principle," and "Walking" ready for the printer. He persuaded Fields to buy from him the unsold copies of *A Week on the Concord and Merrimack Rivers*. He talked or whispered to the friends who came by to see him – Alcott, Emerson, Channing, Sam Staples (his old Concord jailer, now Emerson's neighbor). Thoreau was touched by the affectionate concern of his townspeople, but he resisted any attempts by the conventionally religious to catechize him on the state of his soul, telling one old friend who wanted to know how he stood with Christ that a snowstorm was more to him than Christ and retorting to an aunt who wanted him to make his peace with God that he did not know that he and God had ever quarreled.

Thoreau died on the morning of May 6, 1862. He was forty-four years old. Emerson insisted that the funeral be held from the First Parish Church, despite Thoreau's well-known antipathy to institutional Christianity. Alcott was in charge of planning the service, which was to consist of a hymn written by Ellery Channing, an address by Emerson, and selections from Thoreau's works read by Alcott. Louisa May Alcott reported to a friend that she thought Emerson's address "good in itself but not appropriate to the time and place." Far better, in her opinion, were the "wise & pious thoughts" from Thoreau read by her father, or the funeral procession to the churchyard where Thoreau's father and brother lay. "It was a lovely day clear, & calm, & spring like, & as we all walked after Henry's coffin with its fall of flowers, carried by six of his townsmen who had grown up with him, it seemed as if Nature wore her most benignant aspect to welcome her dutiful & loving son to his long sleep in her arms" (Louisa May Alcott to Sophia Foord, May 11, 1862).

What may have seemed inappropriate to Louisa in Emerson's address was its frankness, a frankness even more evident in the revised and expanded version of the address that Emerson published in the August 1862 number of the *Atlantic Monthly*. The anger that had divided the two men a decade earlier had long ago given way to peace – the two men spent long afternoons together in a rowboat Emerson bought; Thoreau larded his late natural history lectures with affectionate allusions to Emerson's works; Emerson hired Thoreau to survey his land and plant pines for him on the Walden lot. But looking through his old journals for passages about Thoreau made Emerson relive again the unhappiness of their long relationship:

There was somewhat military in his nature not to be subdued, always manly and able, but rarely tender, as if he did not feel himself except in opposition. He wanted a fallacy to expose, a blunder to pillory. . . . It seemed as if his first instinct upon hearing a proposition was to controvert it, so impatient was he of the limitations of our daily thought.

Such militancy meant that "no equal companion stood in affectionate relations with one so pure and guileless."

Emerson's surviving manuscript of the *Atlantic* essay reflects the confict of emotions Thoreau still aroused in him. His first draft includes many passages from his journals recording Thoreau's truculence or conceit, along with passages praising his vigor, integrity, and purity of heart. The cancellations and revisions Emerson made when he readied the manuscript for the printer softened his criticism but did not wholly remove it. The effect made by the essay is of affection laced with bitterness, admiration mingled with anger, love ending in pain. Thoreau, in Emerson's view, was the one Transcendentalist who had practical skill to match his intelligence and moral power. If he would not have commanded an army, he might at least have built its bridges. Yet instead of "engineering for all America" Thoreau had been content to be "the captain of a huckleberry party."

Emerson's frustration with what he saw as Thoreau's lack of ambition was an old subject, but his sense of disappointment was given a keener edge when he surveyed the state of the Union in 1862. Its armies, unprepared for war and incompetently led, had suffered humiliating defeats on the battlefield; its president, Abraham Lincoln, could not seem to make up his mind to emancipate the slaves. In January 1862 Emerson had traveled to Washington to give a talk concerning American civilization to the Smithsonian Association. He addressed himself to any officials of the Lincoln administration who might be listening. "The evil you contend with has taken alarming proportions, and you still content yourself with parrying the blows it aims, but, as if enchanted, abstain from striking at the cause." Now the person Emerson called his closest friend was dead, and the Union itself seemed to be no closer to the one act that could justify its existence.

Then, a little over a month after Emerson's "Thoreau" appeared in the *Atlantic Monthly,* President Lincoln issued the Preliminary Emancipation Proclamation, declaring that the slaves would be freed by January 1, 1863. Emerson spoke at an abolitionist rally in Boston a few days later. "The Emancipation Proclamation" is full of the imagery of pestilence removed and shame expiated. "With this blot removed from our national honor, this heavy load lifted off the national heart, we shall not fear henceforward to show our faces among mankind. We shall cease to be hypocrites and pretenders, but what we have styled our free institutions shall be such." "Happy are the young, who find the pestilence cleansed out of the earth. . . . Happy the old, who see nature purified before they depart."

At the end of the nineteenth century, the surviving Transcendentalists could look back on the movement they had participated in with a wonder reserved for the fortunate. Born in a period of innocence and hope and grown to maturity in a time of wild experimentation, they were defended from the excesses that plague most Romantic movements by the very rigidities of New England habit they sought to escape. Their minds were free to speculate (as Emerson said) because they were sure of a return. Though they lived through a period of national humiliation, when every year brought new shame, they never lost faith in the ultimate triumph of the moral law; and history, which so often shatters the hopes of idealists, in this case proved them right. The renovation they had first imagined thirty years earlier had not come about as they had imagined it, in peace and joy, but it had come nevertheless, and it proved what they had always believed — that the universe could be trusted. As Emerson had written in the essay "Nature": "Every moment instructs, and every object: for wisdom is infused into every form. It has been poured into us as blood; it convulsed us as pain; it slid into us as pleasure; it enveloped us in dull, melancholy days, or in days of cheerful labor; we did not guess its essence until after a long time."

SELECTED BIBLIOGRAPHY

In attempting to construct a narrative account of Transcendentalist writings I have incurred more intellectual debts than I can hope to acknowledge adequately. The list below is designed chiefly to direct readers to the sources of the many quotations, facts, and interpretations that I have used or been influenced by. Many books, particularly the biographies of individual Transcendentalists, have furnished material for more than one chapter, but they are mentioned only the first time they are cited.

"Unitarian Beginnings" draws upon the work of scholars who have studied the religious and philosophical debates that agitated New England in the early decades of the nineteenth century and the foreign developments in criticism of ancient literary and Biblical texts that were beginning to alter the very notions of textual authority. These include Lewis P. Simpson, *The Federalist Literary Mind: Selections from the "Monthly Anthology and Boston Review," 1803–11* (Baton Rouge: Louisiana State University Press, 1962); James King Morse, *Jedediah Morse: A Champion of New England Orthodoxy* (New York: Columbia University Press, 1939); Conrad Wright, "The Election of Henry Ware: Two Contemporary Accounts, Edited with Commentary," *Harvard Library Bulletin* 17 (1969): 245–78; Andrew Delbanco, *William Ellery Channing: An Essay on the Liberal Spirit in America* (Cambridge, Mass.: Harvard University Press, 1981); Conrad Wright, *The Beginnings of Unitarianism in America* (Boston: Starr King Press, 1955); *Three Prophets of Religious Liberalism: Channing, Parker, Emerson*, introduced by Conrad Wright (Boston: Beacon, 1961); Lilian Handlin, "*Babylon est delenda*—the Young Andrews Norton," in *American Unitarianism 1805–1865*, ed. Conrad Edick Wright (Boston: The Massachusetts Historical Society and Northeastern University Press, 1989); Joseph Henry Allen, *Our Liberal Movement in Theology* (Boston: Roberts Brothers, 1882); John Locke, *Essay Concerning Human Understanding*, ed. Alexander Campbell Fraser (2 vols., 1894; rpt. New York: Dover, 1959); John Locke, *The Reasonableness of Christianity, with A Discourse of Miracles, and Part of A Third Letter Concerning Toleration*, edited, abridged, and introduced by I. T. Ramsey (Stanford, Calif.: Stanford University Press, 1958); Paul Revere Frothingham, *Edward Everett, Orator and Statesman* (Boston: Houghton, Mifflin, 1925);

Daniel Walker Howe, *The Unitarian Conscience: Harvard Moral Philosophy 1805–1861* (2nd ed., rev., with a new intro., Middletown, Conn.: Wesleyan University Press, 1988); Daniel Walker Howe, "The Cambridge Platonists of Old England and the Cambridge Platonists of New England," in Wright, *American Unitarianism*; Merrell Davis, "Emerson's 'Reason' and the Scottish Philosophers," *New England Quarterly* 17 (1944): 209–28; David Fate Norton, *David Hume: Commonsense Moralist, Sceptical Metaphysician* (Princeton, N.J.: Princeton University Press, 1982); Edgely Woodman Todd, "Philosophical Ideas at Harvard College, 1817–1837," *New England Quarterly* 16 (1943): 63–90; Linda Kerber, *Federalists in Dissent: Imagery and Ideology in Jeffersonian America* (Ithaca, N.Y.: Cornell University Press, 1970); Carl Diehl, *Americans and German Scholarship 1770–1870* (New Haven, Conn.: Yale University Press, 1978); F. A. Wolf, *Prolegomena to Homer* (1795), trans., with an introduction and notes by Anthony Grafton, Glenn W. Most, and James E. G. Zetzel (Princeton, N.J.: Princeton University Press, 1985); Lawrence Buell, "Joseph Stevens Buckminster: The Making of a New England Saint," *Canadian Review of American Studies* 10 (1979): 1–29; Jerry Wayne Brown, *The Rise of Biblical Criticism in America 1800–1870* (Middletown, Conn.: Wesleyan University Press, 1969); Elisabeth Hurth, "Sowing the Seeds of 'Subversion': Harvard's Early Göttingen Students," *Studies in the American Renaissance* (1992): 91–105; James Freeman Clarke, *Autobiography, Diary, and Correspondences*, ed. Edward Everett Hale (Boston and New York: Houghton, Mifflin, 1891).

"The Assault on Locke" examines American discontent with the tradition of empirical philosophy and the various routes by which news of Kantian and post-Kantian philosophy began to reach the United States. Sources for this section include Frederick Rudolph, *Curriculum: A History of the American Undergraduate Course of Study since 1636* (San Francisco: Jossey-Bass, 1989); Ronald Vale Wells, *Three Christian Transcendentalists* (New York: Columbia University Press, 1943); J. Christopher Herold, *Mistress to an Age: A Life of Madame de Stael* (New York: Harmony Books, 1979); John J. Duffy, ed., *Coleridge's American Disciples: The Selected Correspondence of James Marsh* (Amherst: University of Massachusetts Press, 1973); Joseph Torrey, ed., *The Remains of the Rev. James Marsh, D.D. . . . with a Memoir of His Life* (Boston: Crocker and Brewster, 1843); John J. Duffy, "Problems in Publishing Coleridge: James Marsh's First American Edition of *Aids to Reflection*," *New England Quarterly* 43 (1970): 193–208; John Clive, *Scotch Reviewers: The "Edinburgh Review," 1802–1815* (Cambridge, Mass.: Harvard University Press, 1957); Joseph Henry Allen, *Sequel to "Our Liberal Movement"* (Boston: Roberts Brothers, 1897); Lawrence Buell, *Literary Transcendentalism: Style and Vision in the American Renaissance* (Ithaca, N.Y.: Cornell University Press, 1973); Conrad Wright, "Rational Religion in 18th Century America," in *The Liberal Christians: Essays on American Unitarian History* (Boston: Beacon,

1970); Ralph L. Rusk, *The Life of Ralph Waldo Emerson* (New York: Columbia University Press, 1949); Gay Wilson Allen, *Waldo Emerson: A Biography* (New York: Viking, 1981).

"Carlyle and the Beginnings of American Transcendentalism" investigates Carlyle's influence upon the young Boston intellectuals who read his anonymous but immediately recognizable articles in British periodicals of the 1820s and early 1830s. Sources for this section include Rene Wellek, "Carlyle and German Romanticism" and "The Minor Transcendentalists and German Philosophy," in *Confrontations: Studies in the Intellectual and Literary Relations between Germany, England, and the United States during the Nineteenth Century* (Princeton, N.J.: Princeton University Press, 1965); William Silas Vance, "Carlyle in America before Sartor Resartus," *American Literature* 7 (1936): 363–75; Joseph Slater, "George Ripley and Thomas Carlyle," *PMLA* 67 (1952): 341–9; James Freeman Clarke, *The Letters of James Freeman Clarke to Margaret Fuller*, ed. John Wesley Thomas (Hamburg: Cram, de Gruyter, 1957); Mary C. Turpie, "A Quaker Source for Emerson's Sermon on the Lord's Supper," *New England Quarterly* 17 (1944): 95–101; Karen Lynn Kalinevitch, "Ralph Waldo Emerson's Older Brother: The Letters and Journal of William Emerson," Ph.D. dissertation, University of Tennessee, 1982; Joseph Slater, ed., *The Correspondence of Emerson and Carlyle* (New York: Columbia University Press, 1964); Arthur S. Bolster, Jr., *James Freeman Clarke: Disciple to Advancing Truth* (Boston: Beacon, 1954).

"*Annus Mirabilis*" surveys the outpouring of books, orations, and pamphlets in the year of Transcendentalism's emergence into public prominence. It draws upon the following sources: Perry Miller, *The Transcendentalists: An Anthology* (Cambridge, Mass.: Harvard University Press, 1950); Octavius Brooks Frothingham, *Boston Unitarianism 1820–1850* (New York: Putnam's, 1890); Joel Myerson, "Convers Francis and Emerson," *American Literature* 50 (1978): 17–36; Joel Myerson, "A History of the Transcendental Club," *Emerson Society Quarterly* 23 (1977): 27–35; Joel Myerson, "A Calendar of Transcendental Club Meetings," *American Literature* 44 (1972): 197–207; Stephen Whicher, *Freedom and Fate: An Inner Life of Ralph Waldo Emerson* (Philadelphia: University of Pennsylvania Press, 1953); Sherman Paul, *Emerson's Angle of Vision* (Cambridge, Mass.: Harvard University Press, 1952); Merton M. Sealts, Jr., "The Composition of *Nature*," in Merton M. Sealts and Alfred R. Ferguson, eds., *Emerson's "Nature": Origin, Growth, Meaning* (2nd ed., enlarged, Carbondale: Southern Illinois University Press, 1979); Frederick C. Dahlstrand, *Amos Bronson Alcott: An Intellectual Biography* (East Brunswick, N.J.: Fairleigh Dickinson University Press, 1982); Arthur M. Schlesinger, Jr., *A Pilgrim's Progress: Orestes A. Brownson* (Boston: Little, Brown, 1966); Charles Crowe, *George Ripley: Transcendentalist and Uto-*

pian Socialist (Athens: University of Georgia Press, 1967); William Hutchison, *The Transcendentalist Ministers: Church Reform in the New England Renaissance* (New Haven, Conn.: Yale University Press, 1959); Nina Baym, "The Ann Sisters: Elizabeth Peabody's Millennial Historicism," *American Literary History* 3 (1991): 27–45; Josephine E. Roberts, "Elizabeth Peabody and the Temple School," *New England Quarterly* 15 (1942): 497–508; *The Letters of Elizabeth Palmer Peabody: American Renaissance Woman*, edited, with an introduction by Bruce A. Ronda (Middletown, Conn.: Wesleyan University Press, 1984).

"The Establishment and the Movement" traces the beginnings of the open war between the conservative forces within Unitarianism and the Transcendentalists, who were increasingly impatient with the slow pace of religious and political reform in a society weakened by economic depression. Sources for the section include William Charvat, "American Romanticism and the Depression of 1837," *Science and Society* 2 (1937): 67–82; Harriet Martineau, *Retrospect of Western Travel* (2 vols., London: Saunders & Otley, 1838); John Jay Chapman, *William Lloyd Garrison* (1913; 2nd ed., rev., Boston: Atlantic Monthly Press, 1921); Edwin Gittleman, *Jones Very: The Effective Years 1833–1840* (New York: Columbia University Press, 1967); Helen R. Deese, "The Peabody Family and the Jones Very 'Insanity': Two Letters of Mary Peabody," *Harvard Library Bulletin* 35 (1987): 218–29; Conrad Wright, "Emerson, Barzillai Frost, and 'The Divinity School Address,'" in Wright, *The Liberal Christians*; Gary Hall, "Emerson and the Bible: Transcendentalism as Scriptural Interpretation and Revision," Ph.D. dissertation, University of California, Los Angeles, 1989; Michael Colacurcio, "The Lucid Strife of Emerson's 'Address,'" *ESQ* 37 (1991): 141–212; Robert Habich, "Emerson's Reluctant Foe: Andrews Norton and the Transcendental Controversy," *New England Quarterly* 65 (1992): 208–37; Henry Steele Commager, "The Blasphemy of Abner Kneeland," *New England Quarterly* 8 (1935): 29–41; Roderick S. French, "Liberation from Man and God in Boston: Abner Kneeland's Free-thought Campaign 1830–1839," *American Quarterly* 32 (1980): 202–21; Robert E. Burkholder, "Emerson, Kneeland, and the Divinity School Address," *American Literature* 58 (1986): 1–14; Clarence L. F. Gohdes, *The Periodicals of American Transcendentalism* (Durham, N.C.: Duke University Press, 1931); Elizabeth R. McKinsey, *The Western Experiment: New England Transcendentalists in the Ohio Valley* (Cambridge, Mass.: Harvard University Press, 1973); Dean David Grodzins, "Theodore Parker and Transcendentalism," Ph.D. dissertation, Harvard University, 1993; John W. Rogerson, *W. M. L. de Wette, Founder of Modern Biblical Criticism: An Intellectual Biography* (Sheffield, U.K.: Journal for the Study of the Old Testament Press, 1992); Siegfied B. Puknat, "De Wette in New England," *Proceedings of the American Philosophical Society* 102 (1958): 376–95; Perry Miller, "Theodore Parker: Apostasy within Liberalism," *Harvard Theologi-*

cal Review 54 (1961): 275–95; Philip F. Gura, "Theodore Parker and the South Boston Ordination: The Textual Tangle of a Discourse on the Transient and Permanent in Christianity," *Studies in the American Renaissance* (1988): 149–78; Dean Grodzins, "The Transient and Permanent in Theodore Parker's Christianity, 1832–1841," *Proceedings of the Unitarian Universalist Historical Society* 22, part 1 (1990–91): 1–18; James Martineau, "Strauss and Parker," *The Westminster and Foreign Quarterly Review* 47 (1847): 136–74.

"Letters and Social Aims" examines the growth of Transcendentalism from a church reform movement into a movement with wider ambitions. Desire to find places to publish without censorship led several of the Transcendentalists to found magazines of their own; these magazines in turn had important effects upon the development of Transcendentalist prose. Sources for the section include Joel Myerson, *The New England Transcendentalists and the "Dial": A History of the Magazine and Its Contributors* (London: Associated University Presses, 1980); Charles Blackburn, "Some New Light on the *Western Messenger*," *American Literature* 26 (1954): 320–36; David Robinson, "The Political Odyssey of William Henry Channing," *American Quarterly* 34 (1982): 165–84; Carl F. Strauch, "Hatred's Swift Repulsions: Emerson, Margaret Fuller, and Others," *Studies in Romanticism* 7 (1968): 65–103; Charles Capper, *Margaret Fuller: An American Romantic Life, Vol. 1: The Private Years* (New York: Oxford University Press, 1992); Julie Ellison, *Delicate Subjects: Romanticism, Gender, and the Ethics of Understanding* (Ithaca, N.Y.: Cornell University Press, 1990); Joel Myerson, "Frederick Henry Hedge and the Failure of Transcendentalism," *Harvard Library Bulletin* 23 (1975): 396–410; Bernard Rosenthal, "*The Dial*, Transcendentalism, and Margaret Fuller," *English Language Notes* 8 (1970): 28–36; Helen Hennessey, "The *Dial*: Its Poetry and Poetic Criticism," *New England Quarterly* 31 (1958): 66–87; Robert Richardson, Jr., *Henry Thoreau: A Life of the Mind* (Berkeley and Los Angeles: University of California Press, 1986); Sherman Paul, *The Shores of America: Thoreau's Inward Exploration* (Urbana: University of Illinois Press, 1958); Richard Lebeaux, *Young Man Thoreau* (Amherst: University of Massachusetts Press, 1977); Walter Harding, *The Days of Henry Thoreau* (New York: Knopf, 1966); Raymond R. Borst, *The Thoreau Log: A Documentary Life of Henry David Thoreau 1817–1862* (New York: G. K. Hall, 1992); Robert Sattelmeyer, *Thoreau's Reading: A Study in Intellectual History with Bibliographical Catalogue* (Princeton, N.J.: Princeton University Press, 1988); James McIntosh, *Thoreau as a Romantic Naturalist: His Shifting Stance toward Nature* (Ithaca, N.Y.: Cornell University Press, 1974); Robert Sattelmeyer, "Thoreau's Projected Work on the English Poets," *Studies in the American Renaissance* (1980): 239–57.

"The Hope of Reform" chronicles the aspirations and defeats of a group of Transcendentalists who were determined to put their theories about the just society into practice by founding associations designed to abolish misery and restore social harmony. Sources for this section include Ellen Tucker Emerson, *The Life of Lidian Jackson Emerson*, ed. Delores Bird Carpenter (Boston: Twayne Publishers, 1980); Carl J. Guarneri, *The Utopian Alternative: Fourierism in Nineteenth-Century America* (Ithaca, N.Y.: Cornell University Press, 1991); Octavius Brooks Frothingham, *George Ripley* (Boston: Houghton, Mifflin, 1882); Henry Sams, *Autobiography of Brook Farm* (Englewood Cliffs, N.J.: Prentice-Hall, 1958); John McAleer, *Ralph Waldo Emerson: Days of Encounter* (Boston: Little, Brown, 1984); Maurice Gonnaud, *An Uneasy Solitude: Individual and Society in the Work of Ralph Waldo Emerson*, trans. Lawrence Rosenwald (Princeton, N.J.: Princeton University Press, 1987); Richard Lee Francis, "Circumstances and Salvation: The Ideology of the Fruitlands Utopia," *American Quarterly* 25 (1975): 202–34; Horace Greeley, *Recollections of a Busy Life* (New York: J. B. Ford, 1868); Marianne Dwight Orvis, *Letters from Brook Farm 1844–1847*, ed. Amy L. Reed (Poughkeepsie, N.Y.: Vassar College, 1928); John Codman, *Brook Farm: Historic and Personal Memoirs* (Boston: Arena Publishing Company, 1894); Linck C. Johnson, "Reforming the Reformers: Emerson, Thoreau, and the Sunday Lectures at Amory Hall, Boston," *ESQ* 37 (1991): 235–89.

"Diaspora" follows the Transcendentalists as they diverge on paths of their own, some to become professional writers and lecturers, others to become social reformers or journalists, some to find new forms of church organization or to embrace new religions, some to become involved in foreign revolutions. Sources for the section include Guy R. Woodall, "Convers Francis, the Transcendentalists, and the Boston Association of Ministers," *Unitarian Universalist Historical Society Proceedings* 21 (1989): 41–8; Joel Myerson, "Convers Francis and Emerson," *American Literature* 50 (1978): 17–36; Guy R. Woodall, "The Record of a Friendship: The Letters of Convers Francis to Frederic Henry Hedge in Bangor and Providence, 1835–1850," *Studies in the American Renaissance* (1991): 1–57; Larry Reynolds, *European Revolutions and the American Literary Renaissance* (New Haven, Conn.: Yale University Press, 1988); Richard Bridgman, *Dark Thoreau* (Lincoln: University of Nebraska Press, 1981); Linck C. Johnson, *Thoreau's Complex Weave: The Writing of "A Week on the Concord and Merrimack Rivers" with the Text of the First Draft* (Charlottesville, Va.: University Press of Virginia, 1986); Carl F. Hovde, "Nature into Art: Thoreau's Use of His Journals in a Week," *American Literature* 30 (May 1958): 165–84; Lewis Perry, *Radical Abolitionism: Anarchy and the Government of God in Antislavery Thought* (Ithaca, N.Y.: Cornell University Press, 1973); James Brewer Stewart, *Wendell Phillips: Liberty's Hero* (Baton Rouge, La.: Louisiana State University Press, 1986); John C. Broderick, "Thoreau, Alcott, and the Poll Tax," *Studies in Philology* 53 (1956): 612–26; Raymond Adams, "Thoreau's Sources for 'Resistance to Civil Government,'" *Studies in Philology* 42 (1945): 640–53; Lawrence Buell, *New England Literary Culture: From Revolution through Renaissance* (New York: Cambridge University Press, 1986); Stephen Fink, *Prophet in the Marketplace: Thoreau's Development as a Professional Writer* (Princeton, N.J.: Princeton University Press, 1992); Robert Sattelmeyer, "'When He Became My Enemy': Emerson and Thoreau, 1848–49," *New England Quarterly* (1984): 187–204; Henry James, *William Wetmore Story and His Friends* (2 vols., Boston: Houghton, Mifflin, 1903); Ednah Dow Cheney, *Reminiscences of Ednah Dow Cheney* (Boston: Lee & Shepard, 1902); Robert Habich, "Margaret Fuller's Journal for October 1842," *Harvard Library Bulletin* 33 (1985): 280–91; Stephen Adams, "That Tidiness We Always Look for in Woman: Fuller's *Summer on the Lakes* and Romantic Aesthetics," *Studies in the American Renaissance* (1987): 247–64; Ann Douglas, "Margaret Fuller and the Search for History: A Biographical Study," *Women's Studies* 4 (1976): 37–86; Albert J. von Frank, "Life as Art in America: The Case of Margaret Fuller," *Studies in the American Renaissance* (1981): 1–26; David Robinson, "Margaret Fuller and the Transcendental Ethos: *Woman in the Nineteenth Century*," *PMLA* 97 (1982): 83–98; Jeffrey Steele, *The Representation of Self in the American Renaissance* (Chapel Hill: University of North Carolina Press, 1987); Paula Kopacs, "Feminist at the Tribune: Margaret Fuller as a Professional Writer," *Studies in the American Renaissance* (1991): 119–39; Bell Gale Chevigny, "To the Edges of Ideology: Margaret Fuller's Centrifugal Evolution," *American Quarterly* 38 (1986): 173–201; Joseph Jay Deiss, *The Roman Years of Margaret Fuller* (New York: Thomas Y. Crowell, 1969); Margaret Fuller, *"These Sad but Glorious Days": Dispatches from Europe, 1846–1850*, ed. Larry J. Reynolds and Susan Belasco Smith (New Haven, Conn.: Yale University Press, 1991); Mary Caroline Crawford, *Romantic Days in Old Boston: The Story of the City and of Its People during the Nineteenth Century* (Boston: Little, Brown, 1910).

"The Antislavery Years" traces the growing involvement of the Transcendentalists in the antislavery movement in the years between the passage of the Fugitive Slave Law of 1850 and President Lincoln's Preliminary Emancipation Proclamation of 1862. Sources for this section include David M. Potter, *The Impending Crisis 1848–1861*, completed and edited by Don Fehrenbacher (New York: Harper and Row, 1976); Len Gougeon, *Virtue's Hero: Emerson, Antislavery, and Reform* (Athens: University of Georgia Press, 1990); Maurice G. Baxter, *One and Inseparable: Daniel Webster and the Union* (Cambridge, Mass.: Harvard University Press, 1984); Allan Nevins, *Ordeal of the Union* (New York: Scribner's, 1947); Robert Perrin, "Power and Probity: Emerson's Perceptions of Daniel Webster," M.A. thesis, University of California, Los Angeles, 1993; Samuel Shapiro, "The Rendi-

tion of Anthony Burns," *The Journal of Negro History* 44 (1959): 34–51; Thomas
Wentworth Higginson, *Cheerful Yesterdays* (Boston: Houghton, Mifflin, 1898);
Barry Kritzberg, "Thoreau, Slavery, and Resistance to Civil Government," *The
Massachusetts Review* 30 (1989): 535–65; David Herbert Donald, *Charles Sumner
and the Coming of the Civil War* (New York: Knopf, 1960); George H. Haynes,
"A Know-Nothing Legislature," *Annual Report of the American Historical Associa-
tion* 1 (1896): 177–97; David Robinson, *Emerson and the Conduct of Life: Prag-
matism and Ethical Purpose in the Later Work* (New York: Cambridge University
Press, 1993); Philip Nicoloff, *Emerson on Race and History: An Examination of
"English Traits"* (New York: Columbia University Press, 1961); Sharon Cameron,
Writing Nature: Henry Thoreau's Journal (New York: Oxford University Press,
1985); J. Lyndon Shanley, *The Making of "Walden," with the Text of the First Version* (Chicago: University of Chicago Press, 1957); Leonard N. Neufeldt, *The
Economist: Henry Thoreau and Enterprise* (New York: Oxford University Press,
1989); James Armstrong, "Thoreau, Chastity, and the Reformers," in *Thoreau's
Psychology: Eight Essays*, ed. Raymond Gozzi (Lanham, Md.: University Press of
America, 1983); Walter Harding, "A Check List of Thoreau's Lectures," *Bulletin
of the New York Public Library* 52 (1948): 78–87; William L. Howarth, "Successor
to *Walden*? Thoreau's 'Moonlight—An Intended Course of Lectures,'" *Proof* 2
(1972): 89–113; Bradley P. Dean, "Reconstruction of Thoreau's Early 'Life without
Principle' Lectures," *Studies in the American Renaissance* (1987): 285–364; Leonard Newfeldt, "The Severity of the Ideal: Emerson's 'Thoreau,'" *Emerson Society
Quarterly* 58 (1970): 77–84; Joel Myerson, "Emerson's 'Thoreau': A New Edition
from the Manuscript," *Studies in the American Renaissance* (1979): 17–92.

2007 ADDENDUM TO THE BIBLIOGRAPHY

Much scholarship has occurred since the original publication of my narrative on
the Transcendentalists in 1995. Among the many new publications are numerous
Transcendentalist texts now available to the general reader. Two important an-
thologies of Transcendentalist writing appearing in the last ten years are Joel Myerson's *Transcendentalism: A Reader* (New York: Oxford University Press, 2000)
and Lawrence Buell's *The American Transcendentalists: Essential Writings* (New
York: Modern Library, 2006). New volumes in scholarly editions of the writings
of the major Transcendentalists continue to come into print, while important
texts by the minor Transcendentalists appear in periodicals or annuals. The tenth
and final volume of Emerson's *Letters* (New York: Columbia University Press),
edited by Eleanor Tilton, appeared in 1995, as did *Emerson's Antislavery Writings*
(New Haven, Conn.: Yale University Press), edited by Len Gougeon and Joel
Myerson. In 1997 Joel Myerson edited a one-volume *Selected Letters of Ralph*

Waldo Emerson (New York: Columbia University Press). A year later Guy Litton edited "Ezra Stiles Gannett's Address at Emerson's Ordination" for *Emerson Society Papers* 9 (1998): 1, 8–9. Ronald A. Bosco and Joel Myerson edited two volumes of Emerson's *Later Lectures* (Athens: University of Georgia Press) in 2001; *The Conduct of Life*, the sixth volume of Emerson's *Collected Works* (Cambridge, Mass.: Harvard University Press), appeared in 2003, edited by Douglas Emory Wilson and others. In 2003 David M. Robinson published the anthology *The Spiritual Emerson: Essential Writings*; he followed it in 2004 with *The Political Emerson: Essential Writings on Politics and Social Reform* (both from Beacon Press, in Boston). In 2005 Bosco published *The Selected Lectures of Ralph Waldo Emerson* (Athens: University of Georgia Press), and in 2005 Bosco and Myerson published *The Emerson Brothers: A Fraternal Biography in Letters* (New York: Oxford University Press), containing letters written between Ralph Waldo and his brothers William, Edward, and Charles. Princeton University Press, in New Jersey, issued new volumes of Thoreau's *Journals*: volume 5, *1852–1853*, edited by Patrick O'Connell (1997); volume 6, *1853*, edited by William Rossi and Heather Kirk (2000); and volume 8, *1854*, edited by Sandra Herbert Petrulionis (2002). Bradley P. Dean edited Thoreau's *Wild Fruits: Thoreau's Rediscovered Last Manuscript* in 2000 (New York: W. W. Norton). In 2001 Elizabeth Hall Witherell edited *Henry David Thoreau: Complete Essays and Poems* for the Library of America (New York). William Rossi published Thoreau's *Wild Apples and Other Natural History Essays* (Athens: University of Georgia Press) in 2002. In 2004 Yale University Press in New Haven, Connecticut, published *Walden: A Fully Annotated Edition*, edited by Jeffrey S. Cramer. Dean Grodzins edited "Theodore Parker's 'Conference with the Boston Association,' January 23, 1843," for *Publications of the Unitarian Universalist Historical Society* 23 (1995): 66–101. Alan Brasher edited "James Freeman Clarke's Journal Accounts of Ralph Waldo Emerson's Lectures," for *Studies in the American Renaissance* (1995): 83–100. Judith Mattson Bean and Joel Myerson edited Margaret Fuller's work for the *New-York Tribune* in an unusual format. Their *Margaret Fuller, Critic: Writings from the* New-York Tribune, *1844–1846* (New York: Columbia University Press, 2000) prints 88 of Fuller's essays, but a CD of all 250 essays is included with the printed book. In 2001 Robert N. Hudspeth, the editor of Fuller's letters, published a selection titled *"My Heart Is a Large Kingdom": Selected Letters of Margaret Fuller* (Ithaca, N.Y.: Cornell University Press).

Scholarly publications about the Transcendentalists have also increased in number almost every year. The length of David Robinson's yearly review of scholarship on "Emerson, Thoreau, Fuller, and Transcendentalism" for *American Literary Scholarship* bears witness to the swelling tide. A survey of individual essays here would be cumbersome because there are so many excellent ones; readers are advised to consult Robinson's review essays (available online since 1998) for a complete list. What follows is a list of books and reference works published since 1995 that students of Transcendentalism will find valuable.

BIOGRAPHIES

Robert D. Richardson, Jr., *Emerson: The Mind on Fire* (Berkeley: University of California Press, 1995); Eve Kornfeld, *Margaret Fuller: A Brief Biography with Documents* (Boston: Bedford Books, 1997); Catherine Mitchell, *Margaret Fuller's New York Journalism: A Biographical Essay and Key Writings* (Knoxville: University of Tennessee Press, 1995); Phyllis Cole, *Mary Moody Emerson and the Origins of Transcendentalism: A Family History* (New York: Oxford University Press, 1998); Joan Goodwin, *The Remarkable Mrs. Ripley: The Life of Sarah Alden Bradford Ripley* (Boston: Northeastern University Press, 1998); Bruce A. Ronda, *Elizabeth Palmer Peabody: A Reformer on Her Own Terms* (Cambridge, Mass.: Harvard University Press, 1999); Dean Grodzins, *American Heretic: Theodore Parker and Transcendentalism* (Chapel Hill: University of North Carolina Press, 2002); Megan Marshall, *The Peabody Sisters: Three Women Who Ignited American Romanticism* (Boston: Houghton, Mifflin, 2005); Patrick W. Carey, *Orestes A. Brownson: American Religious Weathervane* (Grand Rapids, Mich.: W. B. Eerdmans Publishing Co., 2005).

STUDIES OF AUTHORS

EMERSON.   George Kateb, *Emerson and Self-Reliance* (Thousand Oaks, Calif.: Sage Publications, 1995); Susan Roberson, *Emerson in His Sermons: A Man-Made Self* (Columbia: University of Missouri Press, 1995); Richard O'Keefe, *Mythic Archetypes in Ralph Waldo Emerson* (Kent, Ohio: Kent State University Press, 1995); Michael Lopez, *Emerson and Power: Creative Antagonism in the Nineteenth Century* (DeKalb: Northern Illinois University Press, 1996); Carlos Baker, *Emerson among the Eccentrics: A Group Portrait* (New York: Viking, 1996); Christopher Newfield, *The Emerson Effect: Individualism and Submission in America* (Chicago: University of Chicago Press, 1996); Sarah Ann Wider, *The Critical Reception of Emerson: Unsettling All Things* (Rochester, N.Y.: Camden House, 2000). Lee Rust Brown, *The Emerson Museum: Practical Romanticism and the Pursuit of the Whole* (Cambridge, Mass.: Harvard University Press, 1997); Eduardo Cadava, *Emerson and the Climates of History* (Stanford, Calif.: Stanford University Press, 1997); John Carlos Rowe, *At Emerson's Tomb: The Politics of Classical American Literature* (New York: Columbia University Press, 1997); Sallee Fox Engstrom, *The Infinitude of the Private Man: Emerson's Presence in Western New York, 1851–1861* (New York: Peter Lang, 1997); Gustaaf Van Cromphout, *Emerson's Ethics* (Columbia: University of Missouri Press, 1999); Eric Wilson, *Emerson's Sublime*

Science (New York: St. Martin's Press, 1999); Shanta Acharya, *The Influence of Indian Thought on Ralph Waldo Emerson* (Lewiston, N.Y.: Edwin Mellen Press, 2001); Richard Geldard, *The Spiritual Teachings of Ralph Waldo Emerson* (Great Barrington, Mass.: Lindisfarne Books, 2001); Sam McGuire Worley, *Emerson, Thoreau, and the Role of the Cultural Critic* (Albany: State University of New York Press, 2001); Peter S. Field, *Ralph Waldo Emerson: The Making of a Democratic Intellectual* (Lanham, Md.: Rowman and Littlefield, 2002); Stanley Cavell, *Emerson's Transcendental Etudes*, ed. David Justin Hodge (Stanford, Calif.: Stanford University Press, 2003); Kenneth S. Sacks, *Understanding Emerson: "The American Scholar" and His Struggle for Self-Reliance* (Princeton, N.J.: Princeton University Press, 2003); Lawrence Buell, *Emerson* (Cambridge, Mass.: Harvard University Press, 2003); Laura Dassow Walls, *Emerson's Life in Science* (Ithaca, N.Y.: Cornell University Press, 2003); Kris Fresonke, *West of Emerson: The Design of Manifest Destiny* (Berkeley: University of California Press, 2003); Joel Porte, *Consciousness and Culture: Emerson and Thoreau Reviewed* (New Haven, Conn.: Yale University Press, 2004); Patrick J. Keane, *Emerson, Romanticism, and Intuitive Reason: The Transatlantic "Light of All Our Day"* (Columbia: University of Missouri Press, 2005).

THOREAU.   Jane Bennett, *Thoreau's Nature: Ethics, Politics, and the Wild* (Thousand Oaks, Calif.: Sage Publications, 1994); Robert Milder, *Reimagining Thoreau* (New York: Cambridge University Press, 1995); Laura Dassow Walls, *Seeing New Worlds: Henry David Thoreau and Nineteenth-Century Natural Science* (Madison: University of Wisconsin Press, 1995); Robert Kuhn McGregor, *A Wider View of the Universe: Henry Thoreau's Study of Nature* (Urbana: University of Illinois Press, 1997); Harmon Smith, *My Friend, My Friend: The Story of Thoreau's Relationship with Emerson* (Amherst: University of Massachusetts Press, 1999); Michael Benjamin Berger, *Thoreau's Late Career and the Dispersion of Seeds: The Saunterer's Synoptic Vision* (Rochester, N.Y.: Camden House, 2000); Stephen Hahn, *On Thoreau* (Belmont, Calif.: Wadsworth, 2000); Alan D. Hodder, *Thoreau's Ecstatic Witness* (New Haven, Conn.: Yale University Press, 2001); Alfred I. Tauber, *Henry David Thoreau and the Moral Agency of Knowing* (Berkeley: University of California Press, 2001); David Robinson, *Natural Life: Thoreau's Worldly Transcendentalism* (Ithaca, N.Y.: Cornell University Press, 2004); Philip Cafaro, *Thoreau's Living Ethics: Walden and the Pursuit of Virtue* (Athens: University of Georgia Press, 2004); Lance Newman, *Our Common Dwelling: Henry Thoreau, Transcendentalism, and the Class Politics of Nature* (London: Palgrave MacMillan, 2005); Donald W. Linebaugh, *The Man Who Found Thoreau: Roland W. Robbins and the Rise of Historical Archaeology in America* (Durham: New Hampshire University Press, 2005).

FULLER. Christina Zwarg, *Feminist Conversations: Fuller, Emerson, and the Play of Reading* (Ithaca, N.Y.: Cornell University Press, 1995); Jeffrey Steele, *Transfiguring America: Myth, Ideology, and Mourning in Margaret Fuller's Writing* (Columbia: University of Missouri Press, 2001).

RELIGIOUS, INTELLECTUAL, AND SOCIAL HISTORY

Lawrence Buell, *The Environmental Imagination: Thoreau, Nature Writing, and the Formation of American Culture* (Cambridge, Mass.: Harvard University Press, 1995); Richard F. Teichgraber III, *Sublime Thoughts / Penny Wisdom: Situating Emerson and Thoreau in the American Market* (Baltimore: John Hopkins University Press, 1995); Terence Martin, *Parables of Possibility: The American Need for Beginnings* (New York: Columbia University Press, 1995); Nina Baym, *American Women Writers and the Work of History* (New Brunswick, N.J.: Rutgers University Press, 1995); Stanley Cavell, *Philosophical Passages: Wittgenstein, Emerson, Austin, Derrida* (Cambridge, Mass.: Blackwell, 1995); Philip F. Gura, *The Crossroads of American History and Literature* (University Park: Pennsylvania State University Press, 1996); Robin Grey, *The Complicity of Imagination: The American Renaissance, Contests of Authority, and Seventeenth-Century English Culture* (New York: Cambridge University Press, 1997); Daniel Walker Howe, *Making the American Self: Jonathan Edwards to Abraham Lincoln* (Cambridge, Mass.: Harvard University Press, 1997); Anita Haya Patterson, *From Emerson to King: Democracy, Race, and the Politics of Protest* (New York: Oxford University Press, 1997); Albert J. von Frank, *The Trials of Anthony Burns: Freedom and Slavery in Emerson's Boston* (Cambridge, Mass.: Harvard University Press, 1998); Randall Roorda, *Dramas of Solitude: Narratives of Retreat in American Nature Writing* (Albany: State University of New York Press, 1998); Michael West, *Transcendental Wordplay: America's Romantic Punsters and the Search for the Language of Nature* (Athens: Ohio University Press, 2000); Caleb Crain, *American Sympathy: Men, Friendship, and Literature in the New Nation* (New Haven, Conn.: Yale University Press, 2001); Louis Menand, *The Metaphysical Club* (New York: Farrar, Straus, and Giroux, 2001); John Stauffer, *The Black Hearts of Men: Radical Abolitionists and the Transformation of Race* (Cambridge, Mass.: Harvard University Press, 2001); Jeffrey Sklansky, *The Soul's Economy: Market Economy and Selfhood in American Thought, 1829–1920* (Chapel Hill: University of North Carolina Press, 2002); Mark G. Vásquez, *Authority and Reform: Religious and Educational Discourses in Nineteenth-Century New England Literature* (Knoxville: University of Tennessee Press, 2003); Peter Tufts Richardson, *The Boston Religion: Unitarianism in Its Capital City* (Rockland, Maine: Red Barn, 2003); W. Barksdale Maynard, *Walden Pond: A History* (New York: Oxford University Press, 2004); Sterling F. Delano, *Brook Farm: The Dark Side of Utopia* (Cambridge, Mass.: Harvard

University Press, 2004); Barry Hankins, *The Second Great Awakening and the Transcendentalists* (Westport, Conn.: Greenwood Press, 2004); Maurice S. Lee, *Slavery, Philosophy, and American Literature, 1830–1860* (New York: Cambridge University Press, 2005); Helen R. Deese, *Daughter of Boston: The Extraordinary Diary of a Nineteenth-Century Woman* (Boston: Beacon Press, 2005); Tiffany K. Wayne, *Woman Thinking: Feminism and Transcendentalism in Nineteenth-Century America* (Lexington, Mass.: Lexington Press, 2005).

BIBLIOGRAPHIES AND REFERENCE WORKS

Joel Myerson, "Supplement to *Margaret Fuller: A Descriptive Bibliography*," *Studies in the American Renaissance* (1996): 187–240; Joel Myerson, *Margaret Fuller: An Annotated Bibliography of Criticism, 1983–1995* (Westport, Conn.: Greenwood Press, 1998); David A. Wells, "Thoreau's Reputation in the Major Magazines, 1862–1900: A Summary and Index," *American Periodicals* 4 (1994): 12–23; Bradley P. Dean and Ronald Wesley Hoag, "Thoreau's Lectures before *Walden*: An Annotated Calendar," *Studies in the American Renaissance* (1995): 127–228; Bradley P. Dean and Ronald Wesley Hoag, "Thoreau's Lectures after *Walden*: An Annotated Calendar," *Studies in the American Renaissance* (1996): 241–362; Wesley T. Mott, *Encyclopedia of Transcendentalism* (Westport, Conn.: Greenwood Press, 1996); Wesley T. Mott, *Biographical Dictionary of Transcendentalism* (Westport, Conn.: Greenwood Press, 1996); Wesley T. Mott, *The American Renaissance in New England*, 2nd ser., Dictionary of Literary Biography (Detroit: Gale Group, 2000); Wesley T. Mott, *The American Renaissance in New England*, 3rd ser., Dictionary of Literary Biography (Detroit: Gale Group, 2001); Wesley T. Mott, *The American Renaissance in New England*, 4th ser., Dictionary of Literary Biography (Detroit: Gale Group, 2001); Conrad Wright, "American Unitarian and Universalist Scholarship: A Bibliography of Items Published 1946–1995," *Journal of Unitarian Universalist History* 28 (2001).

INDEX

abolition, 116, 130, 189, 190, 221, 233

Abraham, 24, 191

Adams, John, 222

"Address on Education" (R. W. Emerson), 66

"Address to the Citizens of Concord on the Fugitive Slave Law" (R. W. Emerson), 222–4, 239

Aesthetic Papers, 189

Aids to Reflection (Coleridge), 11, 23–5, 31, 43, 45

Aitteon, Joe, 263–5

Alcott, Abigail May (Abba; A. B. Alcott's wife), 43, 145, 148–9, 150

Alcott, Amos Bronson: education theories developed by, 42–4; R. W. Emerson's *Nature* influenced by, 50–1; Fruitlands founded by, 148–50; Fuller advised on holding "Conversations" by, 114; refuses to pay poll tax, 187–90; and rescue of Burns, 226; at H. D. Thoreau's lectures and funeral, 270–2; travels to England, 147–8; mentioned, 47, 66, 67, 73, 77, 112, 117, 123, 128, 165, 208, 256, 260, 263

Alcott, Amos Bronson, works of: *The Doctrine and Discipline of Human Culture,* 58; "Orphic Sayings," 114–6, 120; "Psyche," 51, 115. See also *Conversations with Children on the Gospels*

Alcott, Louisa May (A. B. Alcott's daughter), 42, 115, 272; *Transcendental Wild Oats,* 148–9

Alcott, William (A. B. Alcott's cousin), 103, 255

Allen, Joseph Henry, 6–7

Alton Observer, 68

American Revolution, 53

"American Scholar, The" (R. W. Emerson), 66, 77, 106, 121

"American Slavery" (R. W. Emerson), 229, 231–2

American Unitarian Association, 46, 97, 165–6, 168, 170

Amory Hall, 154, 163, 170

Amory Hall Society, 154

Andover Theological Seminary, 5, 16–7, 23–4, 79

Annunciation, the, 57, 89

annus mirabilis, 46

Antinomian crisis, 9

antislavery movement: A. B. Alcott supports, 226; attracts many Transcendentalists, 165; and R. W. Emerson, 172, 188, 222, 231; H. D. Thoreau supports, 243; Webster attacked by, 220, 222

Apocalypse, the, 91

Apostles, the, 91

Ascension, the, 7, 86

"Assault upon Mr. Sumner, The" (R. W. Emerson), 232

association, doctrine of, 157, 160, 162, 165

Association of the Alumni of the Divinity School, 82

Astruc, Jean, 85

atheism, 33, 98, 167, 221

Atlantic Monthly, 239, 249, 263, 272–3

Atonement, the, 24, 82

"Aulus Persius Flaccus" (H. D. Thoreau), 122–3

Austen, Jane, 94

Austria, 215

"Autumnal Tints" (H. D. Thoreau), 268–72

Babylon, 5

Babylon est delenda, 6

"Babylon is falling" (Brownson), 65

Ballou, Adin, 154

Bancroft, George, 15

Batchelder, James, 226

Bentham, Jeremy, 214

Berkeley, George, 51

Beyle, Marie-Henri (Stendhal), 141

Biblical Repertory, 45

Biographia Literaria (Coleridge), 23, 29–31

Blair, Hugh, 21

Blake, Harrison Gray Otis, 83

blasphemy, 75, 85, 98, 153, 166, 174

Blithedale Romance, The (Hawthorne), 136, 162

"Blodgett, Levi," 88

Bonaparte, Louis-Napoleon, 213

Bonaparte, Napoleon, 21, 28, 177; Napoleonic
    wars, 238

Boston Association of Ministers, 2, 12, 92–3,
    120, 207

Boston Daily Advertiser, 54, 77, 98

Boston Investigator, 74, 75, 78

Boston Melodeon, 169

Boston Music Hall, 169, 235

Boston Quarterly Review: attacks *The Dial,* 116;
    begun by Brownson, 68–9; on Bowen, 105;
    contents of, written mostly by Brownson,
    103; on Emerson, 106; on Harvard's
    aristocratic attitudes, 105; on miracles, 81–2;
    style of, 103–12; mentioned, 111, 117–8, 128,
    170. *See also* Brownson, Orestes

—reviews in: of T. Carlyle's *Chartism* ("The
    Laboring Classes"), 100, 102, 108–11; of R.
    W. Emerson's Divinity School Address,
    107–8, 177; of R. W. Emerson's *Essays* (1841),
    139; of Norton's *Evidences of the Genuineness
    of the Gospels,* 78, 81–2

Boston Reformer, 51

Boston Vigilance Committee, 221, 225

Bowdoin Prize, 70

Bowen, Francis, 62–3, 67, 94, 105–6

Bradford, George, 116

Brisbane, Albert, 132–4, 155; *The Social Destiny
    of Man,* 133

Brook Farm: burning of Phalanstery at, 161;
    discussed at Transcendental Club, 133–4;
    early years of, 134–8; economic hardship
    at, 160–1; memoirs concerning, 162–3,
    172; planned, 119; reorganized as Fourierist
    phalanx, 155–8; women's experience at,
    158–60; mentioned, 65, 172, 201, 245

Brook Farmers, 134–7, 155, 157–8, 161–4

Brooks, Preston, 232

Brown, Charles Brockden, 206

Brown, John, 68–9, 226, 233–7, 239, 251

Browne, Sir Thomas, 21, 95

Brownson, Orestes: conversion of, to
    Roman Catholicism, 171; conversion of,
    to Unitarianism, 52; disillusionment of,
    with laboring classes, 170–1; early life and
    religious experience of, 51–2, 75, 104; praise
    of, for Brook Farm, 137–8; preaching of,
    against capitalism, 65–6. *See also Boston
    Quarterly Review*

Brownson, Orestes, works of: "Babylon is
    falling" sermon, 65; *Brownson's Quarterly
    Review,* 171, 177, 230; "The Laboring
    Classes," 102, 108–12, 118, 137; *New Views of
    Christianity, Society, and the Church,* 53–4,
    97; "The Wants of the Times," 52

Brownson's Quarterly Review, 171, 177, 230

Buckminster, Joseph Stevens, 16

Bulwer Lytton, Edward George, 103, 108

Burleigh, Charles Augustus, 154

Burns, Anthony, 225–6, 229, 231, 234, 250–1

Butler, Andrew P., 232

Byron, George Gordon, Lord, 26, 53, 70, 94,
    119

Calhoun, John, 217

California, 216, 218–9, 271; admission of, to
    Union, 219, 220; Gold Rush, 219, 261

Calvinism, 2, 4, 6, 7, 28, 33, 51, 70, 82, 96

Cambridge, Mass., 27, 44, 47, 105

Cambridge Anti-Slavery Society, 167

Cambridge Platonists, 11–2

Cana, wedding at, 59, 131

Cape Cod (H. D. Thoreau): complete text
    of, published after Thoreau's death, 243;
    Concord Lyceum lectures from, 236; serial
    publication of, halted, 241; and Thoreau's
    first visit to Cape Cod, 194–5

Carlyle, Jane, 40

Carlyle, Thomas: American admirers of, 40–2;
    Fuller meets, 207; Norton ridicules, 77,
    107–9; H. D. Thoreau writes essay about,
    187; transcendental philosophy of, 37;
    mentioned, 50, 96, 132, 179, 194

—R. W. Emerson and: R. W. Emerson

imitates Carlyle, 47; meeting of, in London, 181; and publication of American edition of Carlyle's essays, 139; in Scotland, 39–40, 240; Stonehenge visit of, 241

Carlyle, Thomas, works of: "Characteristics," 32, 34, 40; *Chartism,* 102–3, 108–9, 214; essays on German literature, 32–5; "Goethe's Helena," 32; "Jean Paul Friedrich Richter," 32; "Novalis," 50; *Oliver Cromwell's Letters and Speeches* (ed.), 186, 207; *Sartor Resartus,* 40, 121; "Signs of the Times," 34–5; "State of German Literature," 32

Cass, Lewis, 218

Catholicism, Roman, 52, 162, 171–2, 244

Chadwick, John White, 82

Chambers, Robert, 179

Champollion, Jean-François, 28

Channing, Edward Tyrell, 127

Channing, William Ellery: assists A. B. Alcott in founding Boston school, 44; defends miracles against Hume, 10–1; hopes Brownson's preaching attracts working class, 104; preaches doctrines of liberal Christianity, 4–7; reviewed by Hazlitt, 28–9; urges pardon for Kneeland, 75; mentioned, 25, 52, 55, 74, 90, 96, 103–4, 110, 117, 196, 208

Channing, William Ellery, works of: "The Evidences of Revealed Religion," 11, 55; "Likeness to God," 52, 104; "The Moral Argument against Calvinism," 5; "Remarks on the Genius and Character of John Milton," 6, 11; "Unitarian Christianity: Discourse at the Ordination of the Rev. Jared Sparks," 5–6, 90; "Unitarian Christianity Most Favorable to Piety," 5

Channing, William Ellery, the younger, 121, 194, 208, 272; *Poems,* 183

Channing, William Henry, 101, 106

Chapman, John Jay, 68, 222

"Characteristics" (T. Carlyle), 32, 34, 40

"Chardon Street Convention, The" (R. W. Emerson), 120, 264

Chartism, 179, 180, 262

Chartism (T. Carlyle), 102–3, 108–9, 214

"Chartism" (Vaughn), 101

Chaucer, Geoffrey, 100

Cheney, Ednah Dow, 114, 196

"Chief Sins of the People, The" (Parker), 224

Choate, Rufus, 229

Chopin, Frederic, 211

Christ: Clarke associates with religious liberty, 170; compared with Reason, 26; R. W. Emerson rejects Lord's Supper of, 39; ennobles through example, 2; Fourier seen as Second Coming of, 158; F. H. Hedge remains faithful to idea of, 167; Kneeland deems fictional, 75; as manifestation of invisible, 25; Parker celebrates Word of, 90; Parker defends existence of, 87; Princeton scholars attack R. W. Emerson's view of, 88; H. D. Thoreau rejects conventional views of, 272; Very identifies self with, 79. *See also* Jesus

Christian Examiner: article of, on Lord's Supper, 37; Parker's "Discourse on the Transient and Permanent in Christianity" condemned by, 92; mentioned, 54, 81, 95
—reviews and articles in: by Bowen, 62–3; by Brownson, 87, 103–4; by Francis, 46; by F. H. Hedge, 29–30, 32; by Parker, 86–7; by Elizabeth Peabody, 45

Christianity: effect of, on epic poetry, 70; evidences of, 55–6, 60, 72–3, 85; historical, 73, 78, 83, 107; and individual judgment, 39; institutional, 238, 272; interiority of, 46, 85; liberal, 3–6; and miracles, 55, 76, 82, 107; rational, 2; Unitarian, 90; mentioned, 4, 14, 24, 29, 48, 74, 76–7, 89

Christianity as a Purely Internal Principle (Francis), 46, 85

Christian Register, 55, 87, 89, 92, 104

Church of the Disciples, Boston, 170, 207, 235. *See also* Clarke, James Freeman

"Circles" (R. W. Emerson), 104, 139

Clarke, James Freeman: comments on Brownson's conversion to Catholicism, 171; edits *Western Messenger,* 81, 94–9; exchanges pulpits with Parker, 168–70, 172, 207–8; founds Church of the Disciples, Boston, 101, 170, 207; friendship of, with Fuller, 33, 41–2, 44, 113, 198; preaches at J. Brown's funeral, 235; reads Coleridge, 25; unhappiness of, at Harvard, 20–1; mentioned, 119, 128, 132, 171, 177

Clarke, James Freeman, works of: "Letter on the State of Unitarianism at the East," 98; "R. W. Emerson and the New School," 98–9; *Theodore* (De Wette; trans.), 86, 99, 166

Clay, Henry, 219, 220

Clough, Arthur High, 179

Codman, John, 159, 160, 163, 249

"Coleridge" (F. H. Hedge), 29–31, 32, 166

Coleridge, Samuel Taylor: compared to T. Carlyle, 35; and distinction between Reason and Understanding, 24–6; F. H. Hedge reviews career of, 29–31, 166; Marsh publishes, in Vermont, 23–4, 27, 29; writings of, spark Transcendentalist movement, 11, 20–1, 43; mentioned, 20, 33, 37, 39, 240

Coleridge, Samuel Taylor, works of: *Aids to Reflection*, 11, 23–5, 31, 43, 45; *Biographia Literaria*, 23, 29–31; "Essays on Method," 49; *The Friend*, 27, 29, 45, 49; *Poetical Works*, 29

Common Sense philosophy, Scottish, 18, 21, 23

Compromise of 1850, 219, 250

Concord Lyceum, as site of lectures: by R. W. Emerson ("Human Life" series), 95; by Phillips ("Slavery"), 189; by Very ("Epic Poetry"), 71

—by H. D. Thoreau: "Autumnal Tints," 268–70; "History of Myself," 192; "Moosehunting," 262–3; "Society," 122; "The Succession of Forest Trees," 268–70; two lectures about Cape Cod, 195; "Wendell Phillips before Concord Lyceum," 189; "What Shall It Profit?" 262–3; "Wild Apples," 268–70; "Writings and Style of Thomas Carlyle," 186

Conduct of Life, The (R. W. Emerson), 236, 237–9, 262

Confessions (Rousseau), 181

Congregationalism, New England, 2, 5, 51, 74, 133

Congress, United States. *See* United States Congress

Conjectures (Astruc; trans. Parker), 85

Constant, Benjamin, 104

Constitution, United States, 219, 220–1

"Constitution and Union" (Webster), 219

"Conversations": conducted by A. B. Alcott, 56, 60, 101; conducted by Fuller, 114, 196–8, 201; conducted by Elizabeth Peabody, 44

Conversations with Children on the Gospels (A. B. Alcott), 55–62; "Editor's Preface," 58; reviewed by Clarke, 97; mentioned, 93, 101, 103, 194, 208

Conversations with Goethe in the Last Years of His Life (Eckermann; trans. and ed. Fuller), 95, 112, 206

Cooper, James Fenimore, 28

"correspondence," doctrine of, 48–9, 125, 176

"Courage" (R. W. Emerson), 235–6, 239

Court House Square, Boston, 225–6

Cousin, Victor, 53, 70, 77, 95, 133

Craft, Ellen, 221

Craft, William, 221

Craigenputtock, Scotland, 40, 240

Cranch, Christopher Pearse, 119

creation, Mosaic account of, 14

"Crime against Kansas, The" (Sumner), 232

"Crime against Mr. Sumner, The" (R. W. Emerson), 232

Critique of Pure Reason (Kant), 25, 29

Cromwell, Oliver, 186, 207, 236

Cudworth, Ralph, 11

Dana, Richard Henry, Sr., 94

Dartmouth College, 76

Declaration of Independence, 4

Defence of Christianity, A (Everett), 17

Deists, 16, 24, 92

De l'Allemagne (de Staël), 21, 23, 48

Democratic Party, 3, 68–9, 105, 111, 171, 229

Democratic State Convention, Worcester, Mass., 105

Dennie, Joseph, 26

De Quincey, Thomas, 179

de Staël, Baroness (Anne-Louise-Germaine Necker), 21–4, 27, 37, 48; *De l'Allemagne*, 21, 23, 48

"Destinies of Ecclesiastical Religion, The," (F. H. Hedge), 166

De Wette, Wilhelm Martin Leberecht: *Introduction to the Old Testament* (trans. Parker), 85, 86, 93; *Theodore* (trans. Clarke), 86, 99

Dial, The: R. W. Emerson edits (1842–4), 119–21, 124–8; "Ethical Scriptures," 120; Fuller edits (1840–2), 112, 115–9, 123, 167; journal planned, 112–3; mentioned, 89, 148, 150, 182, 197–8, 206

"Dialogue, A" (Fuller), 118

Discourse of Matters Pertaining to Religion, A (Parker), 92, 168, 183

Discourse of Miracles, A (Locke), 7–8

"Discourse on the Latest Form of Infidelity, A" (Norton), 82

"Discourse on the Transient and Permanent in Christianity, A" (Parker), 90–2, 168

Discourses on the Philosophy of Religion Addressed to Doubters Who Wish to Believe (G. Ripley), 55, 97

"Dispersion of Seeds, The" (H. D. Thoreau), 267, 270–1

Divinity School Address (R. W. Emerson), 73–9; attitude toward Jesus in, 92; mentioned, 59, 111, 238

—attacked: by Brownson, 78, 107–8; by Norton, 77, 98; by *Princeton Review,* 88–9

—defended: by Brownson, 108; by Clarke, 81, 98–9; by Francis, 166; by Parker, 87–9

Doctrine and Discipline of Human Culture, The (A. B. Alcott), 58

Douglas, Stephen A., 220, 227

Douglass, Frederic, 130, 235; *The Narrative of the Life of Frederick Douglass,* 130

Dudevant, Aurore (George Sand), 213

Dwight, John Sullivan, 157–8, 160

Dwight, Marianne (Orvis), 158–63, 249

Eckermann, Johann Peter, 95, 112, 206

Edinburgh Review, 27–9, 32, 40, 103, 178

Edwards, Jonathan, 28, 35, 171

Eichhorn, Johann Gottfried, 15; *Einleitung in das Alte Testament,* 16

Einleitung in das Alte Testament (Eichhorn), 16

Elements (Euclid), 13

Elements of Criticism (Home), 41

Elements of the Philosophy of the Human Mind (Stewart), 13

Eliot, George (Marian Evans), 181

Ellsler, Fanny, 197

emancipation, in the British West Indies, 167, 223

Emancipation Proclamation, 226; preliminary, 273

"Emancipation Proclamation, The" (R. W. Emerson), 273–4

Emerson, Charles Chauncy (R. W. Emerson's brother), 115, 124

Emerson, Edward Bliss (R. W. Emerson's brother), 25–6

Emerson, Ellen (R. W. Emerson's daughter), 131, 227, 269; *The Life of Lidian Jackson Emerson,* 131, 227

Emerson, Ellen Tucker (R. W. Emerson's first wife), 39

Emerson, Lydia Jackson (Lidian; R. W. Emerson's second wife), 73, 78, 131, 178, 227

Emerson, Mary Moody (R. W. Emerson's aunt), 35–6

Emerson, Ralph Waldo: Alcott family rescued by, after Fruitlands collapse, 149–50; and Brook Farm, 133–4, 163; J. Brown supported by, 234–6; and death of brother Charles, 124; and death of son Waldo, 147; defended by friends, 81–9, 98–9, 166; as *Dial* editor, 119–128; and *Dial* editorship of Fuller, 115–8, 139; early career of, as lecturer, 49, 63–6; early life and education of, 10–3, 15, 35; Fuller publishes *Summer on the Lakes* with help of, 198–9; and Fuller's death, 217; and Hedge's Club founding, 46–7; ministerial career of, 35–9; reads de Staël and Coleridge, 23–6; resigns pastorate, 39; Sims rendition protested by, 220–5; speech of, to the Concord Kansas Aid Society, 233–34; H. D. Thoreau invited to live with, 146; H. D. Thoreau relationship with, becomes strained, 181–3, 189, 192–4; travels of, in Europe, 39–40, 180–1; Very assisted by, 71–2, 79–81; mentioned, 1, 2, 41–2, 44, 46, 55, 59, 62, 73–8, 92–3, 95–6, 100–11 passim, 131, 164–5, 167–8, 172, 196, 203, 205, 211, 227, 243, 252, 258, 262–4

Emerson, Ralph Waldo, works of: "Address on Education," 66; "Address to the Citizens of Concord on the Fugitive Slave Law," 222–4, 239; "The American Scholar," 66, 77, 106, 121; "American Slavery," 229, 231–2; "The Assault upon Mr. Sumner," 232; "The Chardon Street Convention," 120, 264;

Emerson, Ralph Waldo, works of (*continued*)
"Circles," 104, 139; *The Conduct of Life,*
236, 237–9, 262; "Courage," 235–6, 239;
"The Crime against Mr. Sumner," 232;
"The Emancipation Proclamation,"
273–4; *English Traits,* 236–7, 239–41,
262; *Essays* (later *Essays: First Series*), 40,
112–3, 139–45; *Essays: Second Series,* 150–5,
168, 204; "Ethics," 63; "Experience," 173,
205; "Fate," 239; "Heroism" (lecture in
"Human Culture" series), 68, 235; "Human
Life" lecture series, 95; "Illusions," 239;
"John Brown," 235; "Lectures on the
Times" series, 130, 146; "Literary Ethics,"
76, 106; "Literature," 129; "The Lord's
Supper," 38–9; "Man the Reformer," 130;
"Montaigne," 163, 173, 221; "Nature"
(*Essays: Second Series*), 274; *Nature, Addresses
and Lectures,* 194; "Ode: Inscribed to W.
H. Channing," 173; "The Philosophy of
History" lecture series, 63–4; *Poems* (1846),
173; "Politics" (lecture), 66; "The Present
Age" (lecture), 1, 129; "The Present State
of Ethical Philosophy," 13; "Prospects,"
146; "Reforms," 131; *Representative
Men,* 174–8, 194, 258; "Representative
Men" lecture series, 174; "The Sphinx,"
120; "Thoreau," 272–3; "The Times,"
119–20; "Transcendentalism," 120; "The
Transcendentalist," 1, 129, 146; "Walter
Savage Landor," 120. *See also* Divinity
School Address; *Nature*
Emerson, Ruth Haskins (R. W. Emerson's
mother), 35
Emerson, Waldo (R. W. Emerson's son), 72
Emerson, William (R. W. Emerson's brother),
36, 38, 146, 150
Emerson, Rev. William (R. W. Emerson's
father), 35
England, Church of, 28
English Traits (R. W. Emerson), 236–7, 239–41,
262
Enlightenment, 22, 76
Enquiry Concerning Human Understanding, An
(Hume), 10
"Epic Poetry" (Very), 71
Essay Concerning Human Understanding, An
(Locke), 7–9, 20

Essays: First Series (R. W. Emerson), 40, 112–3,
139–45
"Essays on Method" (Coleridge), 49
Essays on Rhetoric and Belles Lettres (Blair),
21
Essays: Second Series (R. W. Emerson), 150–5,
168, 204
"Ethics" (R. W. Emerson), 63
Euclid, 13, 18, 91; *Elements,* 13
Evans, Marian (George Eliot), 181
Everett, Edward: *A Defence of Christianity,* 17;
German scholarship brought to Harvard
by, 15–16, 41; Locke memorized by, 9, 20;
as pastor of Brattle Square Church, 18; as
professor of Greek at Harvard, 17; Stuart
friendship with, 16–7; studies in Germany,
14, 17–8; mentioned, 35–6, 45, 224
"Evidences of Revealed Religion, The" (W. E.
Channing), 11, 55
Evidences of the Genuineness of the Gospels, The
(Norton), 78
"Excellence of True Goodness, The" (Parker),
207
"Experience" (R. W. Emerson), 173, 205

Fable of the Bees, The (Mandeville), 12
Faneuil Hall, 221, 225
"Fate" (R. W. Emerson), 239
Faust (Goethe), 42
Federalists, 3, 34
Felton, Cornelius, 66
Fenelon, 28
Ferdinand II (king of the Two Sicilies),
215
Fichte, Johann Gottlieb, 22, 33, 50–1, 70;
Wissenschaftlehre, 33
Field, John, 254
Fillmore, Millard, 220, 224
Follen, Charles, 41
Fort Sumter, 226
Fourier, Charles, 133, 137, 155–8, 163, 172, 215
Fox, George, 38
France, 21
Francis, Convers: *Christianity as a Purely
Internal Principle,* 46, 85; defends
Unitarians to Transcendentalists, 165–6;
R. W. Emerson's lectures admired by,
165–6, 178; as Harvard Divinity School

professor, 85, 165; lends books to Parker, 84; mentioned, 92, 117

Fraser's, 32, 40

Free Enquirers, Boston, 74

Free Soil Party, 224, 228

French Revolution, 34, 53

Friend, The (Coleridge), 27, 29, 45; "Essays on Method," 49

Frost, Barzillai, 72, 95

Frothingham, Octavius Brooks, 32–5, 46

Fruitlands, 148–50, 164

Fugitive Slave Law, 167, 219–24, 228, 237, 249, 261

Fuller, Sarah Margaret: as A. B. Alcott's Temple School assistant, 60; Clarke corresponds with, 96–8; "Conversations" held by, 114, 197–8; death of, 217; as *Dial* editor, 112–3, 115–9, 123, 167; educated by father, 41; invited by Greeley to write for *New-York Tribune,* 130, 201; love of, for Nathan, 208–10; love of, for A. B. Ward, 196–7; G. Ossoli relationship with, 212–3; and Rome's defense, 213; and Rome's siege, 215–6; studies German literature with Clarke, 33; travels of, in Europe, 210–2, 214–6; visits women's Sing Sing prison, 201–2; mentioned, 44, 68, 83, 94–5, 122, 128, 133, 166, 177, 183, 195, 197, 261
—reviews by: of C. B. Brown, 206; of T. Carlyle's edition of Cromwell's letters, 207; of R. W. Emerson, 204–5; of Longfellow, 206–7; of Parker, 207–8

Fuller, Sarah Margaret, works of: *Conversations with Goethe in the Last Years of His Life* (Eckermann; trans. and ed.), 95, 112, 206; "A Dialogue," 118; "The Great Lawsuit," 119–20, 198, 201; "The Magnolia of Lake Ponchartrain," 118; "Meta," 118; *New-York Tribune* dispatches, 210, 212, 213–6; "A Short Essay on Critics," 118; *Summer on the Lakes,* 183, 199, 200, 204, 216; *Woman in the Nineteenth Century,* 196, 201–4, 205

Furness, William, 55, 97, 171, 231; *Remarks on the Four Gospels,* 55, 97, 171

Garibaldi, Giuseppe, 216

Garrison, William Lloyd: criticized by R. W. Emerson, 173, 188; criticized by Fuller, 130; as *Liberator* editor, 189, 227; as Parker's Twenty-Eighth Congregational Society member, 169; reprints H. D. Thoreau's "Slavery in Massachusetts," 227; speaks at Amory Hall, Boston, 154; speaks at Framingham antislavery rally, 227; and H. D. Thoreau's political strategy, 191

"Gastric Sayings" *(New York Knickerbocker),* 116

Germany, 14, 21, 23, 29, 38, 56

Goethe, Johann Wolfgang von, 20, 32–3, 36, 42, 137; *Faust,* 42

"Goethe's Helena" (T. Carlyle), 32

Gospel Advocate and Universal Investigator, 52

Göttingen, 14, 36

Graham, George R., 186–7

Graham, Sylvester, 255

Graham's Magazine, 187

Great Awakening, 9

"Great Lawsuit, The" (Fuller), 119–20, 198, 201

Greece, 44

Greeley, Horace: comments on Fuller, 203; helps H. D. Thoreau find publishers, 186–7, 192, 250; mentioned, 245, 263. See also *New-York Tribune*

Green, Ashbel, 2

Griesbach, Johann Jakob, 16, 41

Growth of the Mind, The (Reed), 27

Guadalupe Hidalgo, Treaty of, 218. *See also* Mexico

Harbinger, The, 161

Harper's Ferry, Va., 234–5, 239

Hartley, David, 25

Harvard, Mass., 148

Harvard Board of Overseers, 3, 5

Harvard College: R. W. Emerson delivers "The American Scholar" at, 66; Everett introduces German philological methods to, 14–8; Fuller allowed to use library of, 198; liberals win control of Hollis Professorship at, 3–5; students detest recitation system at, 20–1, 168; study of German language begins at, 32, 41; Very dismissed from tutorship at, 79–80; mentioned, 35, 63, 84, 105, 114, 269
—alumni of: Clarke, 20–1; R. W. Emerson, 15,

Harvard College (*continued*)
  36; Everett, 9, 20; F. H. Hedge, 29; Parker,
  84; H. D. Thoreau, 121, 127, 190
Harvard Corporation, 3
Harvard Divinity School: Association of the
  Alumni of, 82; Francis becomes professor
  at, 165; F. H. Hedge becomes professor
  at, 167–8; Parker reports on German
  theology to Philanthropic Society of, 85;
  Very's apocalyptic prophecies disrupt, 79;
  mentioned, 6, 29, 36, 41, 54, 70, 72, 83–4,
  190, 223–4. *See also* Divinity School Address
Hawthorne, Nathaniel, 71, 136, 181–2; *The
  Blithedale Romance,* 136, 162
Hazlitt, William, 28–9, 103
Hedge, Frederic Henry: as Cambridge Anti-
  Slavery Society member, 167; declines
  to contribute to *The Dial,* 113, 115, 167;
  emancipation in British West Indies
  address of, 167; free speech for Unitarian
  ministry defended by, 89; and Hedge's
  Club, 46–7, 53, 62 (*see also* Transcendental
  Club); "journal of spiritual philosophy"
  wished for by, 95–6; as professor at Harvard
  Divinity School, 168; studies in Germany
  and at Harvard, 29–30; Unitarian church
  structures supported by, 165–6, 170;
  women's suffrage advocated by, 167; worries
  dissent will undermine belief, 92, 165–6;
  mentioned, 172, 177–8
Hedge, Frederic Henry, works of: "Coleridge,"
  29–31, 32, 166; "The Destinies of
  Ecclesiastical Religion," 166; *Reason in
  Religion,* 168
Hedge, Levi Frederic Henry (father of F. H.
  Hedge), 29
Hedge's Club. *See* Transcendental Club
Herder, Johann Gottfried von, 16–7, 27, 44–5;
  The Spirit of Hebrew Poetry (trans. Marsh),
  44–5; *Vom geist der ebräischen poesie,* 16
"Heroism" (R. W. Emerson), 68, 235
Heyne, Christian Gottlob, 32–3
Hicks, Thomas, 211
Higginson, Thomas Wentworth, 208, 225–6,
  234
higher law, 220–1, 265
Hindu scriptures, 53, 120
History of Britain (Milton), 95

Hoar, Elizabeth, 181
Hoar, Judge Samuel, 188
Hobbes, Thomas, 12, 22
Hollis Professor of Divinity, 3
"Hollis Street Council, The" (Parker), 120
Home, Henry (Lord Kames), 41
Homer, 21, 126–7, 247; *Iliad,* 21; *Odyssey,* 198
"Homer. Ossian. Chaucer" (H. D. Thoreau),
  127–8
House of Representatives, United States, 41,
  218
Huidekoper, Harm Jan, 101–2; "The Right and
  Duty of Accumulation" 102
"Human Life" lecture series (R. W. Emerson),
  95
Hume, David: skeptical arguments of, affect
  Brownson, 52; skeptical arguments of, affect
  R. W. Emerson, 13, 36–7
Hume, David, works of: *An Enquiry
  Concerning Human Understanding,* 10; "Of
  Miracles," 10
Hutcheson, Francis, 12

Idealism, 49, 51
Iliad (Homer), 21
"Illusions" (R. W. Emerson), 239
Indians, 199, 245, 264–6; women, 200
innate ideas, 13
*Inquiry into the Original of Our Ideas of Beauty
  and Virtue, An* (Hutcheson), 12
Introduction to the Old Testament (De Wette;
  trans. Parker), 85, 86, 93
I Promessi Sposi (Manzoni), 211
Italian revolution, 216–7

Jackson, Andrew, 35, 64–5
James, Henry, 195
Jardin des Plantes, Paris, 48–9
"Jean Paul Friedrich Richter" (T. Carlyle),
  32
Jefferson, Thomas, 3–4
Jeffrey, Francis, 103, 178
Jesus: as extraordinary man, 10–1; as historical
  figure, 8, 18, 39, 108; as miracle worker,
  53–5, 88; at Passover supper, 38–9; as perfect
  man, 173–4. *See also* Christ
—discussed: by A. B. Alcott with Temple
  School children, 56–60; by R. W. Emerson

in Divinity School Address, 73–4, 76;
by Noyes in *Christian Examiner,* 85; by
Parker in "Discourse on the Transient and
Permanent in Christianity," 89–92; by
Strauss in *Das Leben Jesu,* 86
"John Brown" (R. W. Emerson), 235
Jonson, Ben, 21

Kames, Lord (Henry Home), 41
Kansas, war in, 232–3, 237
Kansas-Nebraska Bill, 227–9, 231
Kant, Immanuel: *Critique of Pure Reason,* 25,
29; discussed by T. Carlyle, 33; discussed
by Clarke, 25; discussed by Coleridge, 23;
discussed by de Staël, 22–3; discussed by
De Wette, 86; discussed by R. W. Emerson,
25–6; discussed by F. H. Hedge, 29;
discussed by Marsh, 23; mentioned, 20, 27,
43, 133, 157
Keats, George, 96
Keats, John, 96
Kneeland, Abner, 74–5, 77–8, 85, 104
Know-Nothing Party, 229
"Ktaadn" (H. D. Thoreau), 184, 191–3, 263–4.
See also *Maine Woods, The*

"Laboring Classes, The" (Brownson), 102,
108–12, 118, 137
Lafayette, Marquis de (Marie-Joseph-Paul-
Yves-Roch-Gilbert du Motier), 41
Lamartine, Alphonse-Marie-Louis de Prat de,
179
Lamb, Charles, 21
Landor, Walter Savage, 120, 240
Lane, Charles, 148–50, 154, 164
"Last Days of Captain John Brown, The" (H.
D. Thoreau), 235
Leaves of Grass (Whitman), 263
Leben Jesu, Das (Strauss), 86
"Lectures on the Times" series (R. W.
Emerson), 130, 146; "Prospects," 146; "The
Transcendentalist," 146
Lee, Robert E., 235
Leibniz, Gottfried Wilhelm, 22
Lessing, Gotthold Ephraim, 18
"Letter on the State of Unitarianism at the
East" (Clarke), 98
Lexington and Concord, Battle of, 222, 236

Liberator, 189, 227. *See also* Garrison, William
Lloyd
Life of Lidian Jackson Emerson, The (Ellen
Emerson), 131, 227
"Life without Principle" ("Life Misspent,"
"What Shall It Profit?"; H. D. Thoreau),
243, 261–2, 272
"Likeness to God" (W. E. Channing), 52,
104
Lincoln, Abraham, 273
Linnaeus, Carl, 125, 265
"Literary Ethics" (R. W. Emerson), 76, 106
"Literature" (R. W. Emerson), 129
Locke, John, 43, 94, 108; contempt of, for
"enthusiasm," 8–9; de Staël blames,
as source of later skepticism, 22; and
distinction between intuition and
experience, 7; versus Hume, 9–10; influence
of, on Unitarian theology and Harvard
curriculum, 2, 12, 20, 25, 105; Marsh
blames, as source of theological difficulties,
23–4; Parker dismisses, as philosophy's past,
88; versus Reed, 27; views of, on revelation
and miracles, 7–9, 11
Locke, John, works of: *A Discourse of
Miracles,* 7–8; *An Essay Concerning Human
Understanding,* 7–9, 20; *A Paraphrase
and Notes on the Epistles of St. Paul to the
Galatians, First and Second Corinthians,
Romans and Ephesians,* 38
Locofocos, 69
Longfellow, Henry Wadsworth, 206–7; *Poems,*
207
Lord's Supper, 37, 38, 39, 134
"Lord's Supper, The" (R. W. Emerson), 38–9
Louis-Napoleon, 213
Louis-Philippe (king of France), 179, 212
Lovejoy, Elijah, 68–9, 235
Lowell, James Russell, 138, 263–4
Lowell *Advertiser,* 75
Luke, Gospel of, 57
lyceums, 49, 228, 242. *See also* Concord
Lyceum
Lyell, Charles, 179
Lytton, Edward George Bulwer, 103, 108

"Magnolia of Lake Ponchartrain, The"
(Fuller), 118

Maine Woods, The (H. D. Thoreau), 236, 243, 258, 263–7

Malta, 39

Mandeville, Bernard de, 12

"Man the Reformer" (R. W. Emerson), 130

Manzoni, Alessandro, 211

Mark, Gospel of, 57

Marsh, James, 17, 23–4, 27, 33, 42–3; publishes Coleridge's *Aids to Reflection,* 23, 43; publishes Coleridge's *The Friend,* 27, 29

Marsh, James, works of: "Preliminary Essay" to Coleridge's *Aids to Reflection,* 23; *The Spirit of Hebrew Poetry* (Herder; trans. and ed.), 45

Martineau, Harriet, 60, 66

Martineau, James, 54, 60, 221; *Rationale of Religious Inquiry,* 54

Masonic Temple, Boston, 44, 63–4, 92, 138, 170

Matthew, Gospel of, 57, 79, 88, 91

May, Samuel, 60

Mazzini, Giuseppe, 210, 213, 215

McLean Hospital for the Insane, 80

Melville, Herman, 222

"Meta" (Fuller), 118

Mexico, 173, 191, 215, 218; Mexican Cession, 218; Mexican War, 219, 253

Michaelis, 44

Mickiewicz, Adam, 211–2

Middlesex Anti-Slavery Society, 222

Middlesex Association of Unitarian Ministers, 36

Miller, Perry, 46, 209

Milton, John, 6, 25, 28, 71, 118, 123, 169; *History of Britain,* 95; "On the Morning of Christ's Nativity," 167; *Paradise Lost,* 191, 204

miracles, biblical, discussed: by A. B. Alcott and students, 56, 58–60; by Boston Association of Ministers, 89; by Brownson, 82; by W. E. Channing, 7; by R. W. Emerson, 76, 107; by Everett, 18; by Furness, 55; by Hume, 10, 37; by Kneeland, 75; by Locke, 7–9; by Norton, 54–5, 82; by Parker, 87–9; by G. Ripley, 54–5; by Strauss, 87

miracles controversy, 87–9, 121, 221, 230

Mishnah, 17

Missouri Compromise, 225, 227

"Montaigne" (R. W. Emerson), 163, 173, 221

Monthly Anthology, 2, 16, 27, 35

Monthly Miscellany, 92

Moon, The (H. D. Thoreau), 259

"Moonlight" (H. D. Thoreau), 259–60

Moore, Tom, 26

"Moosehunting" (H. D. Thoreau), 258, 263. See also *Maine Woods, The*

"Moral Argument against Calvinism, The" (W. E. Channing), 5

moral law, 12, 76, 220–1, 237, 274

moral sense, 12, 238

Mosaic account of creation, 14

Mozart, Wolfgang Amadeus, 1, 136

myth, 45, 86, 87, 90, 114, 193

Mythi, 87

Mythus, 73

Napoleon. *See* Bonaparte, Napoleon

Narrative of the Life of Frederick Douglass, The (Douglass), 130

Nathan, James, 208–10

National Anti-Slavery Standard, 227

natural history, 49, 267, 269–70, 272

"Natural History of Massachusetts, The" (H. D. Thoreau), 124–6, 183, 267

natural law, 223, 238–9

natural theology, 42

"Nature" (*Essays: Second Series;* R. W. Emerson), 274

Nature (R. W. Emerson), 47–51; closing vision of redemption in, 51, 124, 132, 146; structure of, 4

—admired: by A. B. Alcott, 51; by T. Carlyle, 51; by H. D. Thoreau, 121; by Very, 71–2

—influenced by writings: of T. Carlyle, 47; of Coleridge, 49; de Staël, 23; of Fichte, 50; of the Neoplatonists, 50; of Novalis, 50; of Swedenborg, 48–9

—reviewed: by Bowen, 94, 105; by Brownson, 51; by Clarke, 97

Nature: portrayed as luxuriant in Fuller, 200

—in R. W. Emerson: as comprehensible through theory, 49; as corresponding to mind, 47–8; as emanation from divinity, 50–1; as expression of human traits, 48–9; as saturated with law, 238–9; as savage, 239

—in H. D. Thoreau: as fascinating in all details, 125–6, 243; as primitive and sensual, 259–60; as savage, 247–8; as self-propagating, 269–70; as source of health and innocence, 251–3; as source of hope and freedom, 164; as sublime if terrifying, 191–2; as vast and strange, 253; as wounded by human beings, 264–5

Nature, Addresses and Lectures (R. W. Emerson), 194

Neoplatonism, 43, 50

New England Non-Resistance Society, 154

New Jerusalem Magazine, 48

"New School": as Clarke's admiring term for Transcendentalists, 81, 95, 97–9; as Norton's contemptuous term for Transcendentalists, 77, 88

"New School in Literature and Religion, The" (Norton), 77, 81, 98

New Testament, 16, 17, 41, 76, 86, 87, 158

Newton, Sir Isaac, 7, 76, 156

New Views of Christianity, Society, and the Church (Brownson), 53–4, 97

New York Free Enquirer, 110

New York Knickerbocker, 116

New-York Tribune: Brisbane's columns on "association" in, 155; Fuller's dispatches from Europe in, 210, 212, 213–6; Fuller's reviews and articles in, 130, 200–1, 204–8, 210; H. D. Thoreau's "Slavery in Massachusetts" reprinted in, 243

"Night and Moonlight" (H. D. Thoreau), 259

North American Review, 94, 264

Norton, Andrews: A. B. Alcott's *Conversations with Children on the Gospels* attacked by, 57; antidemocratic sentiments of, 4; and Biblical miracle stories, 10; W. E. Channing's "Unitarian Christianity" admired by, 6; R. W. Emerson attacked by, after Divinity School Address, 77; Herder's *Christian Examiner* articles withdrawn from publication by, 45; Matthew chapters declared spurious by, 88, 91; Parker attacks, 88–9; Princeton scholars attacked by, on Transcendentalists, 88; G. Ripley attacked by, 54–5, 83; storms out of sermon advocating religious liberty, 167; mentioned, 15, 78, 80–1

Norton, Andrews, works of: "A Discourse on the Latest Form of Infidelity," 82; *The Evidences of the Genuineness of the Gospels,* 78; "The New School in Literature and Religion," 77, 81, 98

Notions of the Americans (Cooper), 28

Novalis (Friedrich von Hardenberg), 32–3, 42

"Novalis" (T. Carlyle), 50

Noyes, George, 85

"Ode: Inscribed to W. H. Channing" (R. W. Emerson), 173

Odyssey (Homer), 198

"Of Miracles" (Hume), 10

Oliver Cromwell's Letters and Speeches (ed. T. Carlyle), 186, 207

"On the Morning of Christ's Nativity" (Milton), 167

Origen, 86

Ormond (C. B. Brown), 206

"Orphic Sayings" (A. B. Alcott), 114–6, 120

Orvis, John, 162

Orvis, Marianne Dwight, 158–63, 249

Ossoli, Angelino, 212–3, 216–7

Ossoli, Giovanni Angelo, 211–7

Oudinot, Nicholas Charles Victor, 213, 216

Owen, Robert, 52, 74, 104, 110, 137, 154

Page, Ann, 148

Paine, Tom, 153, 167, 174

Paley, William, 52, 190

Palfrey, John Gorham, 223, 224

Palmer, Edward, 116

Paradise Lost (Milton), 191, 204

Paraphrase and Notes on the Epistles of St. Paul to the Galatians, First and Second Corinthians, Romans and Ephesians, A (Locke), 38

Parker, Theodore: asserts all religions are essentially alike, 89; J. Brown supported by, 234; Divinity School training of, 85; early life and education of, 84; Francis and F. H. Hedge dispute with, on Unitarian church establishment, 166–7; friends who exchange pulpits with, suffer, 168, 170, 207–8; Fugitive Slave Law preached against by, 221, 224; German theology and Biblical criticism studied by, 85; health of, forces

Parker, Theodore (*continued*)
departure for Europe, 235; lectures on religion at Masonic Temple, 92; Norton and Unitarian reliance attacked by, 88; refuses to withdraw from Boston Association of Ministers, 92–3; *Scriptural Interpreter* edited by, 85; Twenty-Eighth Congregational Society of Boston founded by, 169; mentioned, 82, 98, 117, 128, 165, 230

Parker, Theodore, works of: "The Chief Sins of the People," 224; *Christian Examiner* review of Strauss's *Das Leben Jesu*, 86–7; *Conjectures* (Astruc; trans.), 85; *A Discourse of Matters Pertaining to Religion*, 92, 168, 183; "A Discourse on the Transient and Permanent in Christianity," 90–2, 168; "The Excellence of True Goodness," 207; "The Hollis Street Council," 120; *Introduction to the Old Testament* (De Wette; trans.), 85, 86, 93

Passover, 38

Peabody, Elizabeth: as A. B. Alcott's Temple School assistant, 44, 55–60, 93; as W. E. Channing's secretary, 44; "conversations" for women held by, 44; early life and education of, 44; and Fuller's "Conversations," 114; Temple School resignation of, 56; H. D. Thoreau's "Resistance to Civil Government" published by, 189; as Very's friend, 71, 79–80; writes articles on Herder's *Spirit of Hebrew Poetry*, 45

Peabody, Elizabeth, works of: "Recorder's Preface" to *Conversations with Children on the Gospels*, 55, 58; *Record of a School*, 56

Peabody, Ephraim, 96

Pearson, Eliphalet, 3–4

Pentateuch, 85

Persius, 123

"Personality of the Deity, The" (Ware), 77–8

Pestalozzi, Johann Heinrich, 43

Phalanstery, 156, 161

phalanx, 156–8, 164, 172

Phi Beta Kappa Society, 66, 77

Philadelphia Port Folio, 44

Phillips, Wendell, 189, 191, 221

Philosophische Vorlesungen (Schlegel), 32

"Philosophy of History, The," lecture series (R. W. Emerson), 63–4

Pilgrim's Progress, 56

Pius IX (pope), 212–3

Plato, 44, 151, 175, 226, 250

"Plea for Captain John Brown, A" (H. D. Thoreau), 235–6, 268

Plotinus, 47

Poems (W. E. Channing, the younger), 183

Poems (1846; R. W. Emerson), 173

Poems (Longfellow), 207

Poetical Chronology of Ancient and English History (Valpy), 41

Poetical Works (Coleridge), 29

Polis, Joe, 266–7

"Politics" (R. W. Emerson), 66

Polk, James K., 173

post-Kantian Idealists, 22, 33

Prelude, The (Wordsworth), 27, 242

Presbyterianism, 2, 51

"Present Age, The" (R. W. Emerson), 1, 129

"Present State of Ethical Philosophy, The" (R. W. Emerson), 13

Priestley, Joseph, 28

primitive poetry, 45

Princeton, 24

Princeton Review, 88

Prolegomena ad Homerum (Wolf), 14

"Prometheus Bound" (trans. H. D. Thoreau), 126

"Prospects" (R. W. Emerson), 146

Protestantism, 1, 37–8, 53–4, 208

"Psyche" (A. B. Alcott), 51, 115

pulpit exchanges, 89, 92, 168–70, 172

Puritans, 38, 236; doctrine of, 133; past, 72; piety of, 35; theology of, 209; toughness of, 255

Putnam, George, 47

Putnam's Magazine, 245, 263

Pyrrho, 33

Quakers, 38–9

Quarterly Review, 27

Quincy, Josiah (Harvard president), 79

Quincy, Josiah (Temple School student), 57

Rationale of Religious Inquiry (J. Martineau), 54

Reason, Transcendentalist: identified with J. Brown, 236; identified with God, 37, 55

Reason and Understanding: harmony between, 64; Kant's distinction between, in Coleridge's *Aids to Reflection,* 24–6; strife between, 25–6, 37, 113, 129–30; used in theological interpretation, 74

Reason in Religion (F. H. Hedge), 168

Record of a School (Elizabeth Peabody), 56

Red and the Black, The (Stendhal), 141

Reed, Sampson, 27

Reform, 117

"Reforms" (R. W. Emerson), 131

Reid, Thomas, 18

Remarks on the Four Gospels (Furness), 55, 97, 171

"Remarks on the Genius and Character of John Milton" (W. E. Channing), 6, 11

rendition of fugitive slaves, 222, 225–7

Representative Men (R. W. Emerson), 174–8, 194, 258

"Representative Men" lecture series (R. W. Emerson), 174

"Resistance to Civil Government" (H. D. Thoreau), 183–9, 190–2, 228, 237, 251

Richter, Jean Paul Friedrich, 32–3, 42

"Right and Duty of Accumulation, The" (Huidekoper), 102

Ripley, Ezra, 72

Ripley, George: biblical miracles dispute of, with Norton, 54–5, 83, 113; Brook Farm closed by, 162; Brook Farm founded by, 119, 132–6; as Brownson friend, 52–3, 75, 104; T. Carlyle admired by, 40; as Hedge's Club member, 47; resigns from pastorate, 84, 132; reviews Brownson's *Boston Quarterly Review* for *The Dial,* 111; reviews Hawthorne's *Blithedale Romance* for Greeley's *Tribune,* 162; sufferings of urban poor distress, 65; mentioned, 64, 69, 86, 89, 112–3, 117, 137, 155, 177, 230. *See also* Brook Farm

Ripley, George, works of: *Discourses on the Philosophy of Religion Addressed to Doubters Who Wish to Believe,* 55, 97; "Schleiermacher as a Theologian," 54; *Specimens of Foreign Standard Literature* (series editor), 64, 86, 95, 112–3

Ripley, Sophia Dana (wife of G. Ripley), 162, 171–2

Robbins, Chandler, 92

Romanticism, 27

Rose, Ernestine, 154

Rosetta stone, 28

Rousseau, Jean-Jacques, 181

Russell, Anna, 157, 161

"R. W. Emerson and the New School" (Clarke), 98–9

Saint Simon, 52

Salem *Observer,* 81

Sand, George (Aurore Dudevant), 213

Sargent, John, 168, 208

Sartor Resartus (T. Carlyle), 40, 121

Saxon, 47, 128

Schelling, Friedrich Wilhelm Joseph, 86

Schiller, Friedrich, 32, 42, 70, 95

Schlegel, Friedrich von, 33, 44, 53, 70; *Philosophische Vorlesungen,* 32

Schleiermacher, Friedrich, 27, 45, 54, 86

"Schleiermacher as a Theologian" (G. Ripley), 54

Scott, Sir Walter, 21, 214, 234–5

Scott, Winfield, 224

Second Church, Boston, 36–8, 76, 99

Senate, United States, 218, 228–9, 232–4

"Service, The" (H. D. Thoreau), 123

Seventh of March speech (D. Webster), 219, 224

Sewall, William, 39

Seward, William Henry, 220, 221

Shackford, Charles C., 90

"Shadrach" (Fred Wilkins), 221, 225

Shakespeare, William, 71, 79, 123, 176

Shaw, Lemuel, 221–2

Shelley, Percy Bysshe, 209

"Short Essay on Critics, A" (Fuller), 118

"Signs of the Times" (T. Carlyle), 34–5

Sims, Thomas, 221–2, 225–7, 231, 250

Sing Sing Prison, 201, 202–3

"Slavery in Massachusetts" (H. D. Thoreau), 221, 227–8, 251, 257

Smith, Sydney, 28

Social Destiny of Man, The (Brisbane), 133

Society for Christian Union and Progress, 53

Society in America (H. Martineau), 60, 66

Socrates, 44

Sparks, Jared, 5, 90

Specimens of Foreign Standard Literature, 64, 86, 95, 112–3

Spenser, Edmund, 56

"Sphinx, The" (R. W. Emerson), 120

Spinoza, Benedict, 202

Spirit of Hebrew Poetry, The (Herder; trans. Marsh), 44–5

Spring, Marcus, 210

Spring, Rebecca, 210

Staples, Sam, 188, 272

"State of German Literature" (T. Carlyle), 32

State Street, Boston, 66–7

Stendhal (Marie-Henri Beyle), 141

Stewart, Dugald, 18; *Elements of the Philosophy of the Human Mind,* 13

Stowell, Martin, 225–6

Strauss, David Friedrich, 27, 235; *Das Leben Jesu,* 86; "Über Vergängliches un Bleibendes in Christenthum," 90; *Zwei friedliche Blätter,* 90

Stuart, Moses, 16, 23, 45

Sturgis, Caroline, 119, 129, 153

"Succession of Forest Trees, The" (H. D. Thoreau), 270

Summer on the Lakes (Fuller), 183, 199, 200, 204, 216

Sumner, Charles, 227–9, 232; "The Crime against Kansas," 232

Supreme Court, United States, 76

Swedenborg, Emmanuel, 27, 48, 175–6

Symposium, the, 46–47. *See also* Transcendental Club

Tappan, David, 7

Taylor, Thomas, 50

Taylor, Zachary, 218–20

Temple in Jerusalem, 58, 60

Temple School, Boston, 50, 55, 93

Tennyson, Alfred Lord, 198

Theism, 89

Theodore (De Wette; trans. Clarke), 86, 99, 166

"Thomas Carlyle and His Works" (H. D. Thoreau), 187

"Thoreau" (R. W. Emerson), 272–3

Thoreau, Helen (sister of H. D. Thoreau), 193

Thoreau, Henry David: boating trip of, with brother John, 182; J. Brown meets, 234; Brownson boards, 121; Canada excursions of, 243–5; Cape Cod excursions of, 241–2, 245–6; as Concord Lyceum curator, 122; death of, 272; death of brother of, 124, 147; *Dial* essays and poems of, 119, 122–7; early life and education of, 121; R. W. Emerson boards, 124, 146, 181–2; R. W. Emerson friendship with, begins, 121; R. W. Emerson friendship with, deteriorates, 193–4; lectures on "Reformers and Conservatives" at Amory Hall, 154, 163; Maine woods excursions of, 194–5, 243, 258, 263–7; Sudbury woods fire set by, 182; Walden Pond cabin built by, 183

Thoreau, Henry David, works of: "Aulus Persius Flaccus," 122–3; "Autumnal Tints," 268–72; "The Dispersion of Seeds," 267, 270–1; "Homer. Ossian. Chaucer," 127–8; "Ktaadn," 184, 191–3, 263–4 (see also *Maine Woods, The*); "The Last Days of Captain John Brown," 235; "Life without Principle" ("Life Misspent," "What Shall It Profit?"), 243, 261–2, 272; *The Maine Woods,* 236, 243, 258, 263–7; *The Moon,* 259; "Moonlight," 259–60; "Moosehunting," 258, 263 (see also *Maine Woods, The*); "The Natural History of Massachusetts," 124–6, 183, 267; "Night and Moonlight," 259; "A Plea for Captain John Brown," 235–6, 268; "Prometheus Bound" (trans.), 126; "Resistance to Civil Government," 183–9, 190–2, 228, 237, 251; "The Service," 123; "Slavery in Massachusetts," 221, 227–8, 251, 257; "The Succession of Forest Trees," 270; "Thomas Carlyle and His Works," 187; "T. Pomponius Atticus," 122; "Walking, or the Wild," 243, 248–9, 258, 272; "A Walk to Wachusett," 126, 182; "Wendell Phillips before Concord Lyceum," 189; "What Shall It Profit?" ("Life without Principle"), 243, 261–2, 272; "Wild Apples," 269–70, 272; "Wild Fruits," 267, 269; "A Winter Walk," 126, 182; *A Yankee in Canada,* 236, 241, 243–5, 258. See also *Cape Cod; Walden; Week on the Concord and Merrimack Rivers, A*

Thoreau, John (brother of H. D. Thoreau), 121, 124, 127, 182–4

Thoreau, Sophia (sister of H. D. Thoreau), 259, 271

Ticknor, George, 14, 41, 127

"Times, The" (R. W. Emerson), 119–20

Tocqueville, Alexis Charles Henri Clerel de, 11, 105

"T. Pomponius Atticus" (H. D. Thoreau), 122

Tractatus Politicus (Spinoza), 202

Transcendental Club (Hedge's Club; the Symposium): formed, 46; guests of, 72, 113; idea for Brook Farm at meeting of, 133–4; idea for *The Dial* at meeting of, 112–3; last meetings of, 165–6; members of, 46–8, 84–6, 96–7

Transcendentalism, 1, 20, 61, 94, 120–1, 166, 168, 191, 249

"Transcendentalism" (R. W. Emerson), 120

"Transcendentalist, The" (R. W. Emerson), 1, 129, 146

Transcendentalists: as antislavery movement participants, 230, 235–7, 274; as church reformers, 21, 83, 171; as controversialists, 87–9; as editors, 97, 113, 115, 128, 171; as educators, 42; as recipients of wealth, 4, 99, 100, 102; as reformers, 48, 55, 62, 110, 195, 273; as Unitarian ministers, 42, 165–6; as utopian community founders, 134; as writers and translators, 94–5, 101, 116, 127, 196, 214; mentioned, 68, 70, 80, 111

—criticized: for arrogance, 63, 70, 105; for lack of logic, 106; for spiritual sloth, 129

Transcendental Wild Oats (L. M. Alcott), 148–9

Treaty of Guadalupe Hidalgo, 218. *See also* Mexico

Trinitarian, 25, 89

Trinity, the, 24

Twenty-Eighth Congregational Society, Boston, 169

"Über Vergängliches un Bleibendes in Christenthum" (Strauss), 90

Union, the, 218, 219, 220; army, 22

Union Magazine of Literature and Art, 192, 250, 263

"Unitarian Christianity: Discourse at the Ordination of the Rev. Jared Sparks" (W. E. Channing), 5–6, 90

"Unitarian Christianity Most Favorable to Piety" (W. E. Channing), 5

Unitarianism: A. B. Alcott's use of, 54, 59; versus Calvinism, 2, 12; dissatisfaction with, 20, 72, 74, 97, 170; and future church, 54; versus Hume, 10, 12; ideology of tolerance in, 2; miracles controversy of, 10; and nature, 48; and Parker's *Discourse of Matters Pertaining to Religion*, 90, 168; popularity of, 6; and social movements, 101–3, 230; and *Western Messenger*, 101–3. *See also* Divinity School Address

Unitarian Ministers, Middlesex Association of, 36

Unitarians: versus Calvinists, 3–6; and decline of religious feeling, 74, 83, 98; intolerance of dissent among, 132, 169, 208; and poverty, 109, 132, 171; mentioned, 20, 24–5, 39, 41, 47, 54, 56, 75, 81, 91, 96–7, 104–5, 109, 114–5, 118, 120, 128, 165, 168–9, 171, 202, 240

—beliefs of: fidelity to inner conviction, 37; freedom of speech, 89; human perfectibility, 59; moral sense, 14–5; progressive enlightenment, 14; self-culture, 35, 202

—controversies among, 84; over Biblical miracles, 55, 76, 87–9; over Lord's Supper, 37; over New Testament interpretation, 73–4, 90–2

—ordination of Transcendentalist clergy among: Brownson, 52; Clarke, 25; R. W. Emerson, 36; Francis, 46; Furness, 55; F. H. Hedge, 29; Parker, 84; G. Ripley, 40

United States: capital stronger than labor in, 52; economic boom ends in, 64; as fortunate in nativity, 215; Fourier's doctrines in, 156; lyceum movement in, 49; Transcendentalists deplore political situation in, 173, 232; mentioned, 169

United States Congress, 218–20, 222, 224, 227

United States House of Representatives, 41, 218

United States Senate, 218, 228–9, 232–4

United States Supreme Court, 76

Universalists, 51, 74

University of Vermont, 23, 42

Valpy, Richard, 41

Van Buren, Martin, 65

Vaughn, John, 101

Vermont, University of, 23, 42

Very, Jones, 70–2, 79–80; "Epic Poetry,"
    71; "What Reasons Are There for Not
    Expecting Another Great Epic Poem?"
    70

Vestiges of the Natural History of Creation
    (Chambers), 179

Visconti, Constanza Arconti, 211

Voltaire, 22

Vom geist der ebräischen poesie (Herder), 16

Walden (H. D. Thoreau): and R. W. Emerson,
    241; stages of composition of, 183, 192–3,
    249, 251, 257; mentioned, 123, 236, 243
—chapters from: "Baker Farm," 254; "The
    Bean-Field," 253; "Brute Neighbors," 255;
    "Conclusion," 164, 257; "Economy," 251;
    "Former Inhabitants and Winter Visitors,"
    255–6; "Higher Laws," 254–5; "The Pond in
    Winter," 256; "The Ponds," 254; "Reading,"
    94, 252; "Solitude," 252; "Spring," 256; "The
    Village," 253–4; "Visitors," 252–3; "Where I
    Lived and What I Lived For," 251; "Winter
    Animals," 256

Walden Pond: as described in *Walden*, 254,
    256; as site of H. D. Thoreau's cabin, 48,
    77, 164, 178, 183, 231, 252, 254–7

"Walking, or the Wild" (H. D. Thoreau), 243,
    248–9, 258, 272

"Walk to Wachusett, A" (H. D. Thoreau),
    126, 182

Walpole, Horace, 95

"Walter Savage Landor" (R. W. Emerson), 120

"Wants of the Times, The" (Brownson), 52

Ward, Anna Barker, 197, 209

Ward, Samuel Gray, 197, 205

Ware, Henry, Jr., 3, 5, 38, 76–9, 81; "The
    Personality of the Deity," 77–8

War of 1812, 35

Washington, D.C., 44

Webster, Daniel, 219, 220–4, 228–9, 266;
    "Constitution and Union," 219; Seventh of
    March speech, 219, 224

*Week on the Concord and Merrimack Rivers,
    A* (H. D. Thoreau): commercial failure
    of, 194; difficulty in finding publisher for,
    192, 250; "Excursion on the Concord and
    Merrimack Rivers" (early draft), 184–6;

stages of composition of, 183, 192, 193; style
    of, 183; mentioned, 122, 236, 272

Weimar, 36

"Wendell Phillips before Concord Lyceum"
    (H. D. Thoreau), 189

Western Messenger: Clarke edits, 96; Ephraim
    Peabody edits, 96, 101–3; publishes material
    inspired by T. Carlyle's *Chartism* and
    Brownson's "Laboring Classes," 101–3;
    publishes Transcendentalist writings, 81, 86,
    98–9; and Transcendentalist prose style, 128.
    See also Clarke, James Freeman

"What Reasons Are There for Not Expecting
    Another Great Epic Poem?" (Very), 70

"What Shall It Profit?" ("Life without
    Principle"; H. D. Thoreau), 243, 261–2, 272

Whig Party, 105, 111, 117, 218–9, 224, 228–9

Whitman, Walter, 147, 185, 263; *Leaves of
    Grass,* 263

Whittier, John Greenleaf, 220

Wieland (C. B. Brown), 206

"Wild Apples" (H. D. Thoreau), 269–70, 272

"Wild Fruits" (H. D. Thoreau), 267, 269

Wilkins, Fred ("Shadrach"), 221, 225

Willard, Joseph, 3

Wilmot, David, 218

Wilmot Proviso, 218–9

"Winter Walk, A" (H. D. Thoreau), 126, 182

Wise, Henry A., 235

Wissenschaftlehre (Fichte), 33

Wolf, Friedrich August, 14–6; *Prolegomena ad
    Homerum,* 14

Woman in the Nineteenth Century (Fuller), 196,
    201–4, 205

Wordsworth, William, 71, 94; Clarke reviews,
    in *Western Messenger,* 96; R. W. Emerson
    visits, 39, 179, 240; Fuller visits, 214; *The
    Prelude,* 27, 242; reputation of, among
    Unitarians, 20–1, 26–7; H. D. Thoreau
    reads poetry of, 123, 126, 242; Very reads
    poetry of, 70–1

Workingman's Party, 52, 104

Wright, Frances, 52, 74, 104, 110, 167

Wright, Henry, 148

Yankee in Canada, A (H. D. Thoreau), 236,
    241, 243–5, 258

Zwei friedliche Blätter (Strauss), 90